THE TEXT

OF THE

GREEK BIBLE

BY

F. G. Kenyon

Third Edition
Revised and Augmented by

A. W. Adams, D.D.
Fellow of Magdalen College, Oxford

DUCKWORTH

This revised, augmented edition first published in 1975
Original edition 1936
Second edition 1948
Gerald Duckworth & Company Limited
43 Gloucester Crescent, London NW1

ISBN 0 7156 0641 7

Printed in Great Britain
by Unwin Brothers Limited
The Gresham Press, Old Woking, Surrey, England
A member of the Staples Printing Group

Contents

PREFACE TO THE THIRD EDITION

IT is a difficult task to revise the published work of another writer, and especially so in the case of one who, like Sir Frederick Kenyon, was a master of his subject. I have therefore made no attempt to change the plan and arrangement, since that would have been to write another book, and it is highly doubtful that the outcome would have been a better one.

In writing his book it is clear that Sir Frederick regarded knowledge of documents as a matter of first importance, in relation both to textual theory in general and to the application of it in practice. In adding the new manuscript evidence which has come to light since he wrote, I have followed this rule. If, in consequence, much appears to be left out which appears in other manuals of this kind, it may be remarked that the student who works through the examples of readings and variants set out in this book, with his Greek Testament and critical apparatus by his side, will learn a great deal more than is contained in the chapter headings. He will also learn that this is a subject in which there are many problems as yet unsolved, many manuscripts that still await a collator. It may be that as a result he will be encouraged to make some contribution himself. He will certainly read the Greek Bible with increased understanding of its text. In either case, the purpose with which Sir Frederick Kenyon wrote his book will have been fulfilled.

For this edition the text has been entirely re-set.

1974.   A.W.A.

PREFACE TO THE FIRST EDITION

THE object of the present volume is to place at the disposal of students of the Greek Bible the results of the discoveries and researches which have been so plentiful in recent years. The standard works of Swete, Gregory, Scrivener, Hort, Nestle and others are a quarter of a century or more old, and contain no account of the labours of Burkitt, Lake, Streeter, Clark, Rahlfs, von Soden, Ropes and many others, or of discoveries such as the Freer MSS, the Koridethi Gospels, and especially the Chester Beatty papyri. In the following pages the attempt is made to describe all of these, and to estimate their bearing on the history of the text of the two Testaments, and especially that of the New Testament. I have tried to state the evidence dispassionately, and I hope that the lists of characteristic readings of particular manuscripts and text-families will enable the student to form his own opinion; but I have not tried to disguise my own judgment, for what it may be worth.

Naturally such a work is dependent throughout on the labours of those who have gone before. I have tried to indicate my principal obligations in the brief bibliographies appended to each chapter, and in references and footnotes throughout the text. If I have had to refer to some publications of my own, it is because I have had the good fortune to be intimately concerned with some of the recent discoveries, and no other scholars have yet dealt with them. I am quite aware that much more has yet to be said about them.

The textual criticism of the Greek Bible is a fascinating study; much work is still needed on it, and much new material lies ready to the student's hand. I hope there may never be wanting a due supply of young scholars who will carry on the study, in which English scholars have taken so honourable a part in the past, of a Book which has such a special appeal to the English-speaking nations.

F.G.K.

November 1936.

PREFACE TO THE SECOND EDITION

IN this second edition a few small errors in the text have been corrected, and some larger corrections and additions are appended at the end. But there have been no large additions made to the textual material or criticism of the Greek Bible within the last twelve years, and in the main the book remains as first issued.

F.G.K.

August 1948.

CHAPTER ONE

Books in the First Three Centuries

TEXTUAL criticism is a humble handmaid in the great task of Bible study, but its service is indispensable. Its business is to lay the foundations on which the structure of spiritual investigation must be built. For if we are to study any book to advantage, we must first be satisfied that it is authentic, and that we have it approximately in the form in which its author or authors wrote it. It is necessary, in the case of ancient books, to add the qualification 'approximately', because of the conditions under which ancient books have come down to us, which make absolute certainty impossible. It is with these conditions, which apply to all ancient books, that textual criticism has to deal. There are special conditions applying to the books of the Bible, which will be explained in the following pages; but the fundamentals are the same for all works of Greek and Roman literature.

The basis of textual criticism, and the root of all the problems with which it has to deal, is the simple fact that before the invention of printing every copy of a book had to be written by hand; whence they are called *manuscripts*. Owing to the frailties of the human hand and eye and brain, it is impossible to copy large quantities of matter without making mistakes. These mistakes will be repeated by the next scribe who copies this manuscript, with additions of his own, so that as time goes on the text will tend to vary further and further from the true original. Attempts may be made from time to time to correct them, either by comparison with other copies or by conjecture; but in either case there is no certainty that the corrections will be right or will always be the same. There thus grows up a number of *various readings*, as they are called, with competing claims which a modern editor has to consider. It is the function of textual criticism to supply the principles to guide him in his choice and to enable him to answer the questions with which he may be challenged, such as these: How early is the testimony at our disposal for the text of the book under consideration? What do we know of the manner in which the book has been handed down to us? How can we decide between the various readings which the extant manuscripts present to us? What, on the whole, is the condition of the text as we have it? Can we depend on it as substantially accurate, and go forward with confidence to consider its meaning and the lessons which it has to teach us?

In the following pages the attempt will be made to trace the textual history of the books of the Bible, and especially of the New Testament; to describe the conditions under which they were written and handed down in the earliest centuries; to enumerate the principal manuscripts in which they are contained, and to investigate their character; to set out the chief classes of variations, and to indicate on what lines we can estimate their merits. It is a task essential for the thorough study of the Bible, and for meeting the objections which critics may, and do, bring against it. The questions with which it deals are questions to which any student of the Bible should have an answer. It is the history of the Bible as a book; and if it is in itself a non-spiritual science, it is the basis on which the spiritual study of the Bible stands. As was said by one of the greatest of textual scholars, Dr Hort: 'In respect of the Bible especially, it remains true that whatever helps our understanding helps also in the long run our praying and our working.'

In tracing this history, much will have to be said about 'families of manuscripts' and 'types of text', and it will be as well at the outset to explain what is meant by such terms. In essence it is quite simple, though in working out it may become very complicated. If in a given manuscript of any work some words are wrongly transcribed, or a passage omitted, every manuscript copied from it, or from copies of it, will have the same mistake or the same omission; and if among the extant manuscript we find that several have the same important mistake or omission, it is legitimate to argue that they are all descended from the manuscript in which that mistake or omission was first made. That manuscript itself may no longer exist, but its previous existence may be inferred, and its descendants form a group distinct from those which have not this particular defect. There are certain classical authors, the extant manuscripts of which are divided in this way, according as they have or do not have a particular passage, or a particular corruption. Or again (and this applies particularly to the Bible text) at a certain time some scholar or some person in authority, finding discrepancies among the copies accessible to him, may set himself to edit the text so as to put it in what he believes to be its correct form, or, it may be, to revise it so as to improve it or to make it more intelligible or more edifying; and every copy made from his revision, either directly or at some removes, will bear the traces of this revision, and will form what is called a family.

If the author's original manuscript had survived, it would of course be unnecessary to trouble about later and less accurate copies of it, or the work of revising editors; but since in the case of the Bible books, as also of all works of the classical authors and of nearly all medieval works, the original autographs and all early copies of them have disappeared, we have to do as best we can with such later copies as have survived. Where (as in the case of most classical authors) those copies are few in number and late in date, it is quite possible that in many passages the truth has survived in none of them, and can only be recovered, if at all, by conjecture; and such restorations can at best be regarded as probabilities, not as certainties. Where (as in the case of the Bible) the extant copies are very numerous, and some of them very early, it is permissible to hope that the true reading is to be found somewhere among them. To find it is the task of textual criticism. It is necessary to begin by examining the extant manuscripts, to see (with the aid of palæography) which are the oldest and therefore probably (though not necessarily) nearer to the truth, and to ascertain which, by habitually sharing the same readings, show signs of being descended from a common ancestor earlier than themselves. Then it may be possible to determine which manuscript or group or family of manuscripts is most often right, and then in cases of doubt it will be natural to give the preference to the manuscript or group or family which has shown itself generally superior; though it must be remembered that an authority which is generally right cannot really be expected to be always right. But to follow it may be the best we can do until better evidence comes to light.

We find, therefore, that in the case of all ancient literature the extant manuscripts of any work, if they are sufficiently numerous, do in fact tend to fall into groups, of which some are better and some are worse. Particularly is this the case with the books of the Bible, the extant manuscripts of which are far more numerous than those of any other book. The task of criticism, as will be seen when we come to narrate the history of the text, has been to determine which manuscripts show signs of being related to one another, what groups or families can thus be formed of them, how far back the ancestry of each group can be carried, and which, on the grounds of intrinsic merit, is generally to be regarded as superior. It is, however, a very complicated task, because the lines of descent from the common ancestors seldom or never run clear. Copies made from manuscripts belonging to one family were frequently corrected (or depraved) by comparison with manuscripts belonging to another family, and so the evidence becomes mixed and obscured. It is no light task, therefore, to trace the genealogy of our manuscripts, or to determine the true text of the earliest common ancestor of each group; and behind these group-ancestors we want, if we can, to get back to the common ancestor of them all, the author's original manuscript. The nature of this task will become clearer as the story proceeds.

The first essential for the comprehension of the textual history of the Greek Bible is to realize what Greek books were like at the time when the works comprising the two Testaments were written. This is a subject of which our knowledge has been greatly increased within quite recent times. It has always been known, from references and descriptions in classical literature, that books in Greek and Roman days were written on rolls of papyrus; but until the nineteenth century no actual specimens of such books were known to exist. The reason for the disappearance of old papyrus manuscripts lay simply in the perishable nature of the material. Papyrus becomes brittle with age if dry, and is rotted by damp; consequently in any normal climate papyrus manuscripts could not expect a long life. In one country alone were conditions more favourable to their preservation. In Egypt (south of the Delta) the climate is so dry that manuscripts buried in the soil beyond the limits of the inundation of the Nile may be preserved indefinitely, though becoming very brittle; and from Egypt, within the last few generations, great numbers of papyri have been disinterred, to which we owe most of our knowledge of the form and material character of ancient books. Of late years a few papyri have been found outside Egypt, where conditions were sufficiently similar—viz., at Doura in northern Syria on the Euphrates, and in the desert south of Palestine. Then in 1947 came the epoch-making discovery of the remains of the library of the Jewish religious community at Khirbet Qumran on the shores of the Dead Sea, about eight miles south of Jericho. The great bulk of the material consists of scrolls and fragments of scrolls of leather which contained books of the Bible, commentaries, religious treatises, etc., written in Hebrew before A.D. 70 when, as the archaeological evidence seems to show, the community was dispersed.[1] The decipherment, identification and publication of these texts is as yet far from complete, and indeed has to do primarily with the history of the Hebrew Bible. But in addition fragments of the Greek Old Testament on leather and papyrus, written by Jews for Jews, are also included in this material. And mention may be made here of a fragmentary leather scroll of the Minor Prophets in Greek, found by Bedouin in the Dead Sea area in 1952 (though the exact whereabouts are unknown) and dated between 50 B.C. and A.D. 50. These will be referred to later.

One question which used to be put by sceptical critics of the Bible has therefore already been answered, namely, Why have we no copies of any of the books that come anywhere near the dates of their supposed composition? The answer used to be that all books before the adoption of vellum as the principal writing material early in the fourth century (as will be described later) had disappeared because the material on which they were written was so perishable. The Bible was only in the same case as all books of Greek and Roman literature, of which likewise no copies had survived that were earlier than the fourth century. The only difference was in favour of the Bible; for there were more early vellum manuscripts of the Bible than of any other ancient book, and the interval between the date of composition and the earliest

---

[1] For a more detailed account see J. T. Milik, *Dix ans de découvertes dans le désert de Juda* (Paris, 1957), English translation by J. Strugnell, *Ten Years of Discovery in the Deserts of Judah* (1959).

extant manuscript was less in the case of the books of the New
Testament than in that of any work of classical literature. It is now
possible to add that, thanks to the discoveries in Egypt and the
area of the Dead Sea, we now have many examples of books
earlier than the fourth century; that among them are several
substantial portions of books of the Greek Bible; and that the
interval between the date of composition and the earliest extant
manuscripts has been notably reduced, particularly by discoveries
made within recent years. These will be described presently.

Papyrus is a material made from the fibrous pith of a water-
plant which formerly grew plentifully in the Nile, but is now
extinct within the borders of Egypt itself. This pith, being cut in
thin strips, was laid down in two layers, in one of which the fibres
lay horizontally, and in the other vertically. These layers were
fastened together by Nile water, glue and pressure, and were then
polished to produce a smooth surface. The side primarily intended
for writing was that on which the fibres lay horizontally, technically
known as the *recto*; but it was quite possible to write on the other
side, known as the *verso*. The papyrus was manufactured in sheets
of various sizes, the better qualities being those in which the
fibres were longest; and these sheets were fastened together side
by side to make a long strip which was then rolled up. The roll
might be of any length that was found convenient, and in ancient
Egyptian times some rolls of sacred books, made for ritual
purposes, extended to a length of 100 feet or more (the longest
known is 133 feet long); but for practical purposes such a length
was too cumbrous, and for works of Greek literature it would
appear that a roll rarely exceeded 35 feet. The height also varied.
The greatest height known is 19 inches, but for Greek works
12½ inches is an outside measurement, and 9 or 10 inches may be
taken as a normal height, while pocket volumes might be as little
as 5 inches or even less.

The consideration of length is of some importance. A roll of
32–35 feet would contain, in writing of a medium size, books of
the length of one of the longer Gospels, or a single book of
Thucydides, but no more. Hence it follows that so long as the
papyrus roll was the normal vehicle of literature, each of the
Gospels and the Acts must have circulated separately. It was not
possible to possess in a single volume all the four Gospels or all
the Epistles of St Paul, still less a complete New Testament. In

the earliest days each book had its own separate history, and not every Christian community would have had a complete collection of all that we now know as the canonical books.

The writing on the roll thus formed was arranged in columns, which in the case of prose works were normally about 2½ or 3 inches wide. The margins between columns were normally small (½–¾ inch), allowing little space for annotation; but at the top and bottom they were wider, and here lines accidentally omitted in the text are not infrequently inserted. Wide margins are usually a sign of a sumptuously written MS. At the beginning of the roll a blank space was often left, both to protect the roll and to give the reader something to hold when reading the first column. Titles were usually given at the end of a work, not at the beginning.

The writing was normally on one side of the roll only, that on which the fibres lay horizontally; but occasionally, when matter was plentiful or papyrus scarce, the roll might be written both 'within and without' (Ezek. ii. 10). Among the papyri found in Egypt there are also not a few in which the back (*verso*) has been utilized for a work different from that on the *recto*. Thus, to give a Biblical example, a copy of the Epistle to the Hebrews was about the beginning of the fourth century written on the back of an Epitome of Livy, probably of the third century. Such books are likely to have been copies for private use rather than for the market, but it is quite probable that in early days copies of the New Testament books were often produced in this way.

There were very few aids to the reader in ancient books. Words were not separated, punctuation was either wholly wanting or very incomplete (though not infrequently reading-marks were inserted by a later hand), paragraph divisions are rare, and in the earliest manuscripts capitals are not used. Occasionally a rough breathing is indicated, chiefly in the case of relative pronouns, where ambiguity might be caused (e.g. to distinguish οὐ from οὗ). Accents are almost unknown. It must consequently have been difficult to find a particular passage when required, and authors must have been tempted to quote from memory rather than take the trouble to hunt through a roll for the words required. Inexactness of quotation, therefore, should not surprise us.

Such was, in brief outline, the character of the papyrus roll, the form in which Greek and Latin books were produced from the

B

days of the great classical authors to the time at which the books of the New Testament were written. Until quite recently it has been supposed that it continued in full use up to the early years of the fourth century, when it was replaced by the vellum codex, or books in the modern form of leaves and pages. But discoveries in Egypt, especially some of quite recent date, have shown that not later than the early years of the second century the experiment was tried of utilizing the codex form for papyrus. It seems that this was almost certainly the invention of the Christian community and is closely associated with the Bible itself. For whereas the roll continued to be used for works of pagan literature, as indeed for other kinds of Christian writing, and was only slowly ousted from favour, in Egypt copies of the Scripture made for Christian use are almost without exception found to be in codex form. The earliest examples known can be assigned with some confidence to the first half of the second century, and there are quite a number of the third, so that we are justified in concluding that it was in normal use for Biblical texts.

A papyrus codex was formed by taking a number of sheets of papyrus, twice the size of the page required, and folding them once in the middle, thus producing a *quire* or *gathering*, as it is called. The size of this quire would depend on the number of sheets thus treated at once. It was possible (and instances exist) thus to treat a single sheet, forming a quire of two leaves or four pages, like an ordinary double sheet of writing paper, and the codex would then be formed of a number of such two-leaf quires fastened together (as in a modern book) by threads through their inner margins. Or, to go to the opposite extreme, all the sheets estimated to be required for the work to be copied might be laid in a single pile and folded, thus producing a codex in a single enormous quire. Of this form (cumbrous as it seems) several examples are known, the number of sheets sometimes amounting to more than fifty and thus producing single-quire codices of over 100 leaves. It is likely, however, that these were early experiments in the use of the codex form, and before long it was found more convenient to make up quires of 8 or 10 or 12 leaves, such as are found in medieval vellum manuscripts and in modern paper printed books.

The advantage of the codex form was that it could include much more matter than the roll, without becoming unduly cumbrous, was easier for purposes of reference, and if necessary for concealment. The earliest papyrus codex known contained the books of Numbers and Deuteronomy, which would have required three rolls. Another, of the early third century, contained all four Gospels and the Acts, which would previously have occupied five separate rolls. Another, of the same date, contained all the Epistles of St Paul, except (apparently) the Pastorals. It was therefore possible as early as the second century for the four canonical Gospels to be circulated as a single unit, and thus to be marked off from the other narratives of our Lord's life which we know to have been in existence; and we have an actual example of such a volume, as just stated, from the early part of the third century. Apart from such examples on leather from the Dead Sea area noted above it was in the form of the papyrus roll or the papyrus codex that the books of the Greek Bible were written and circulated from the third century B.C., when the Greek translation of the Old Testament was begun, to the end of the third century after Christ. But at the beginning of the fourth century a great change occurred, which vitally affected the tradition of the sacred books. In the first place, Christianity was first tolerated by the Emperor Constantine, and from 381 was recognized as the religion of the Roman Empire. Persecutions came to an end, and with them the destruction of Christian books, which had been a marked feature of the great persecutions of Decius (249–51) and Diocletian (303–5) and under Galerius in the East (305–11) and probably of the sporadic persecutions which occurred at other times; and a great demand arose for copies of the Scriptures in all parts of the Empire. It was just at this time that a revolution occurred in the world of book-production, by the substitution of vellum for papyrus as the material for the best books.

Vellum is a material produced from the skins of cattle, sheep and goats, and especially from the young of these animals, calves, lambs and kids. The hair is removed by scraping, and the skins washed, smoothed down with pumice, and dressed with chalk. The material thus produced is almost white in colour, very enduring in quality, easy to write on, and forming a good background both for black ink and for decoration in colour. The side from which the hairs have been removed is apt to be slightly the darker in colour, but it retains the ink better. In the Codex Alexandrinus, for instance, the writing has repeatedly faded on the flesh-side, while on the hair-side it remains clear and distinct. This is the material which from the fourth century to the fifteenth (almost to the end of the Middle Ages) was the dominant material for book-production. Papyrus continued in use, certainly in Egypt and probably elsewhere, for non-literary purposes and for inferior copies of books, until the Arab conquest of the country in A.D. 640 closed its export trade and put an end to the production of Greek books,[1] and at the other end of the Middle Ages paper began to come into use from about the twelfth century onwards; but for the majority of books, and for all the best books, vellum was regularly employed until the invention of printing, for which paper was both better adapted and cheaper.

Vellum was by no means a new material at the beginning of the fourth century. Its invention is ascribed by Pliny, on the authority of Varro, to Eumenes of Pergamum (probably Eumenes II, 197–159 B.C.), who was ambitious of founding a library which would rival that of Alexandria. His rival, Ptolemy of Egypt (probably Ptolemy Epiphanes, 205–182 B.C.), attempted to obstruct him by prohibiting the export of papyrus; whereupon Eumenes had recourse to the manufacture of vellum, which from its place of origin received the name of περγαμηνή, whence our word parchment, which in general is merely a synonym for vellum, though some writers have restricted it to the less good qualities, used for other purposes than for books. How long the embargo on papyrus lasted we do not know, and there is no evidence that vellum was used for books elsewhere than at Pergamum at this time. Certainly the supremacy of papyrus was not affected at Rome, where, so far as can be gathered from allusions in the classical writers, vellum was only used for note-books and inferior copies of literary works. Towards the end of the first century after Christ, Martial refers to manuscripts of Homer, Virgil, Cicero, Livy and Ovid *in membranis*, i.e. on vellum, and in 2 Tim. iv. 13 St Paul asks Timothy to bring with him 'the books, especially the parchments' (μεμβράναι). While their exact character is doubtful, it is clear that they are not normal books, and that vellum has not yet superseded papyrus. From about the same period come the

[1] In Egypt itself papyrus naturally continued to be employed, especially for non-literary purposes. A large group of official documents from the first quarter of the eighth century is in the British Museum. Some of the Coptic Biblical papyri fall within the Arab period, but their dating is very uncertain.

earliest extant fragments of vellum codices, a leaf of Demosthenes in the British Museum and one of Euripides at Berlin. But until the end of the third century the supremacy of papyrus remained virtually unchallenged.

In the first quarter of the fourth century, however, the superior advantages of vellum and the perishable nature of papyrus seem suddenly to have been realized. When Constantine ordered fifty copies of the Scriptures for the churches in his new capital, Constantinople, it is expressly stated by Eusebius (*vit. Const.* iv. 36) that they were on vellum (πεντήκοντα σωμάτια ἐν διφθέραις). A little later, but apparently before A.D. 350, Jerome records that the volumes in the celebrated library of Pamphilus at Cæsarea, which had become damaged, were replaced by copies on vellum (Ep. 141: 'quam [bibliothecam] ex parte corruptam Acacius dehinc et Euzoius, eiusdem ecclesiæ sacerdotes, in membranis instaurare conati sunt'). This external evidence is confirmed by the extant manuscripts that remain from this period. The two earliest of the vellum codices of the Greek Bible, the Vaticanus and Sinaiticus, belong to just this time, the first half of the fourth century, while the Washington codex of the Gospels and the Sarravianus of the Pentateuch may belong to the second half. There are also manuscripts of Homer, Virgil, and Cicero which may probably be assigned to this century. All these are beautiful examples of the scribe's art, and as specimens of writing, apart from the adventitious aid of decorative illuminations, are as handsome as any books in the world. On the other hand, the papyrus manuscripts that have survived from the fourth century onwards are inferior examples of book-production, being generally coarse in material and rough in writing. The supremacy of vellum is henceforth unquestionable, and from this time onwards we have an ever-increasing flood of extant copies of the Scriptures, which will be described in the chapters that follow.

BIBLIOGRAPHY

E. M. Thompson, *Introduction to Greek and Latin Palaeography* (Oxford 1912); W. Schubart, *Das Buch bei den Griechen und Römern,* 2nd edition (Berlin, 1921); W. Schubart, *Griechische Paläographie* (Handbuch der Altertumswissenschaft, Vol. I, pt. 4, München, 1925); F. G. Kenyon, *Books and Readers in Ancient Greece and Rome,* 2nd edition (Oxford, 1951); C. H. Roberts, 'The Codex', *Proceedings of the British Academy* xl (1954), pp. 169–204; T. C. Skeat, 'The use of dictation in ancient book-production', *Proceedings of the British Academy*, xlii (1956), pp. 196 ff.; E. C. Colwell, 'Scribal habits in early papyri' in *The Bible in Modern Scholarship* (Tennessee, 1965); L. D. Reynolds and N. G. Wilson, *Scribes and Scholars, A Guide to the Transmission of Greek and Latin Literature* (Oxford, 1968).

CHAPTER TWO

The Greek Old Testament

THE story of the first translation of the Hebrew Scriptures into Greek is told in the work known as the *Letter of Aristeas*,[1] which appears to have been written in the latter half of the second century B.C.,[2] and was known to Josephus, who paraphrases a large part of it. According to the writer (who purports to be a contemporary) Demetrius of Phalerum, director of the Alexandrian Library founded by Ptolemy I, being instructed by his successor, Ptolemy Philadelphus (285–246 B.C.), to collect all the books in the world, mentioned that the Jews possessed some books of their law which deserved to be included, but written in their own language and script, and therefore needing to be translated. The king thereupon instructed him to write to the High Priest at Jerusalem, backing his request by a gift of vessels for the Temple and the return of some thousands of Jews who had been compulsorily brought into Egypt. The High Priest sent in return seventy-two scholars (six from each tribe), who, after lavish entertainment by the king, and an elaborate dialectical display of their wisdom, set to work and completed the translation of the Law in seventy-two

[1] Edited by H. St J. Thackeray as an appendix to Swete's *Introduction to the Old Testament in Greek* (Cambridge, 1914), pp. 533–606; M. Hadas, *Aristeas to Philocrates* (New York and London, 1951—Greek text with English translation); H. G. Meecham, *The Letter of Aristeas* (Manchester, 1935), and (in English) H. T. Andrews in R. H. Charles' *Apocrypha and Pseudepigrapha of the Old Testament*, vol. ii, pp. 83–122; H. St John Thackeray, *The Letter of Aristeas* (London, 1917); H. G. Meecham, *The Oldest Version of the Bible* (London, 1932); A. Pelletier, *Lettre d'Aristée à Philocrate* (Sources Chrétiennes 89) (Paris, 1962).
[2] E. Bickermann (*Zeitschrift für die Neutestamentliche Wissenschaft*, xxix (1930), pp. 280–94) dates the *Letter* in the period 145–27 B.C.; A. Momigliano (*Aegyptus*, xii, pp. 161–73) gives *c.* 100 B.C. as the *terminus ad quem*.

days, to the great delight of the Jewish population of Alexandria.

The story of Aristeas, which is embellished by copious details irrelevant to the actual execution of the translation, is quite evidently a work of fiction, but there is no reason to doubt that it rests on a foundation of fact at least to this extent, that the Pentateuch was translated into Greek in Egypt before the middle of the third century B.C. There is confirmatory evidence of this in the fact that the version of Genesis was used by a writer of the name of Demetrius, who lived in the last quarter of that century.[1] But that the translation was made by Palestinian Jews in response to a royal command can be dismissed. The style is Alexandrian, in the vernacular idiom which is known from the papyri. The evidence shows that it was prompted by the need of Jews in Egypt for a version of the Scripture in the Greek language (then more familiar to them than Hebrew or even Aramaic) either for public use in the synagogue or for private reading and study. On the other hand the legend of the seventy-two translators became generally accepted, and is reflected in the name of *Septuagint*, by which the version is generally known.

Aristeas does not claim that the first translation embraced more than the Law, i.e. the Pentateuch. The exaggerations of later writers, which extended it to the whole Old Testament, and added various miraculous details, may be ignored. When and by whom the other books were added is quite unknown; but since the author of the preface to Ecclesiasticus, who states that he came into Egypt in the thirty-eighth year of Euergetes [II=132 B.C.], refers to the existence of translations of 'the law itself and the prophecies and the rest of the books' (αὐτὸς ὁ νόμος καὶ αἱ προφητεῖαι καί τὰ λοιπὰ τῶν βιβλίων) and 'having continued there [i.e. in Egypt] some time', himself proceeded to translate the work of his grandfather, Jesus, son of Sirach, it may be concluded that by about this time the Greek Old Testament as we know it was complete.

Some light has been thrown on the methods and motives of the translators by investigating the renderings of Hebrew words and phrases and details of style and grammar in the different parts of the Greek Bible. The result has been to show the existence of various 'strata' which point to different translators not only between one group or book and another, but, more important,

---

[1] Swete, *op. cit.*, pp. 17, 18.

within the individual books themselves. The late H. St J. Thackeray,[1] who was a pioneer in this field, investigated in particular the second part of the canon for evidence of multiple translation. Thus in the books of Samuel and Kings (which in the Greek are denominated the four books of βασιλεῖαι, usually translated as 'Kingdoms', though Thackeray would prefer 'Reigns') he finds linguistic evidence of the presence of two translators, the first of whom (whose style is of the Palestinian-Asiatic school) omitted the whole of 2 Sam. xi. 2—1 Kings ii. 11, the last chapter of 1 Kings and the whole of 2 Kings, presumably as being less creditable to the nation, while the other, who appears to be of Western Asia, later on added these portions. In the Prophets the division of labour seems to be merely mechanical. Thus in Jeremiah one hand translated the first half, as far as the latter part of chapter xxix (the point of junction cannot be fixed to a verse), and the other the remainder. This division may well correspond to the division between two rolls, for each half about amounts to the normal contents of a Greek papyrus roll. Similarly in Ezekiel Thackeray finds that the first hand proceeds to about the beginning of chapter xxviii; but the second translator, who took up the task, desisted at the end of chapter xxxix, and the first translator then finished the book. In a more recent study of Ezekiel by N. Turner[2] continuing Thackeray's methods, it is suggested that three translators were involved, the third being responsible for the last section; that either the three collaborated to some extent or the book was subsequently revised by a single hand; and that each of the translators was making use of older, though probably only partial versions. This last point may agree with another observation of Thackeray's—namely, that those parts of the Prophets were translated first into Greek which were read in the synagogue as a 'second lesson' after the reading of the Law. It is possible therefore that there was some organization in the translation of the Prophets which may in turn suggest official control; while the Hagiographa (see next paragraph) seem to be the result of individual initiative, as we know was the case with regard to Ecclesiasticus.

[1] *Journal of Theological Studies*, iv (1902–3), 245–86, 398–411, 578–85, viii (1906–7), 262–78; *Grammar of the Old Testament in Greek* (Cambridge, 1909), pp. 6–16; *The Septuagint and Jewish Worship* (Schweich Lectures of the British Academy, 1920, 2nd ed., London, 1923).

[2] *Journal of Theological Studies*, n.s., vii (1956), pp. 12–24.

The Greek Old Testament differs from the Hebrew canon both in contents and in arrangement. The Hebrew canon recognizes three groups: (i) the Law, i.e. the Pentateuch; (ii) the Prophets, subdivided into (a) the Former Prophets, i.e. Joshua, Judges, Samuel and Kings, and (b) the Latter Prophets, i.e. Isaiah, Jeremiah, Ezekiel and the twelve Minor Prophets; (iii) the Writings or Hagiographa, i.e. Chronicles, Ezra-Nehemiah, Daniel, Esther, Ruth, Job, Psalms, Proverbs, Song of Solomon, Ecclesiastes, Lamentations; in all, twenty-four books (the Minor Prophets being reckoned as one book). The Greek Old Testament includes along with these a number of books which apparently circulated in the Greek-speaking world (led by Alexandria) with equal acceptance, but were never part of the Hebrew canon. These are 1 Esdras (a different version of part of Chronicles and Ezra-Nehemiah, with an additional passage, the Greek 2 Esdras being the canonical Ezra-Nehemiah),[1] Wisdom, Ecclesiasticus, Judith, Tobit, Baruch, Epistle of Jeremy, and four books of Maccabees. These books (apart from 3 and 4 Maccabees) passed also into the first Latin Bible, which was translated from the Greek; and the adverse opinion of Jerome, who accepted the Hebrew canon, did not avail in the end to keep them out of the Vulgate as finally adopted by the Roman Church. Luther, on the other hand, followed the Hebrew canon, and the English translators (headed by Coverdale) followed Luther, so that the English Bible conforms to the Hebrew canon, and relegates these books to the Apocrypha.[2]

[1] The relations of the various books called Ezra or Esdras are as follows: (a) the Greek 1 Esdras ($Ε\sigma\delta\rho\alpha\varsigma$ α') = Vulgate 3 Esdras = 1 Esdras of the English Apocrypha; (b) Greek 2 Esdras ($Ε\sigma\delta\rho\alpha\varsigma$ β') = Vulgate 1–2 Esdras = Canonical Ezra-Nehemiah of the Hebrew and English Bibles; (c) the Vulgate 4 Esdras (an apocalyptic work called in some Latin MSS 2 Esdras—its opening words are 'Liber Esdrae prophetae secundus') = 2 Esdras of the English Apocrypha, but has nothing corresponding to it in the Greek.

[2] The Apocrypha in the English Bible includes the books enumerated above, except 3 and 4 Maccabees, but adds to them 2 Esdras (=Vulgate 4 Esdras), 'the rest of Esther' (which are integral parts of the Greek Esther), the Song of the Three Children (which is an integral part of the Greek Daniel), Susanna and Bel and the Dragon (which form the beginning and end of the Greek Daniel, though in the Chigi MS, the Syro-Hexaplar version and the Vulgate Susanna follows Dan. xii), and the Prayer of Manasses (which occurs among the hymns attached to the Psalter in the Codex Alexandrinus, and also in some other MSS). In the Latin Vulgate also only two books of Maccabees are included and the Prayer of Manasses and 3 and 4 Esdras are appended at the end of the whole Bible, as not having full canonical authority.

Other works hovered on the fringe of the Greek Bible, though they did not ultimately find a permanent home in it. The most notable among these are the Psalms of Solomon, which were originally included at the end of the Codex Alexandrinus (the actual text existing in eight MSS of the tenth to fifteenth centuries), the Book of Enoch, which is quoted by Jude, and of which a copy was included in the library of the Church from which the Chester Beatty papyri (to be described later) came, the interesting apocalyptic work known as 4 Esdras (in our Apocrypha 2 Esdras), and others. But these cannot be regarded as part of the Greek Bible.

The arrangement of the books of the Septuagint shows that the books in it which were not included in the Hebrew canon were by no means regarded as on a different level from the rest, but were an integral part of the Greek Bible, being distributed among the others according to their character. The order of the canonical books is also different from that of the Hebrew Bible, the distinction between the three classes of Law, Prophets and Hagiographa not being observed. There are variations in detail in the early MSS, but normally Chronicles–Ezra–Nehemiah are attached to the four books of Kingdoms, Baruch, Lamentations and Epistle of Jeremy follow Jeremiah, and Daniel (with Susanna and Bel and the Dragon) is associated with the three Major Prophets, these latter being preceded by the Twelve Minor Prophets (Hosea–Malachi). The Hagiographa also (including Wisdom, Ecclesiasticus, Judith, and Tobit) are generally placed before the Prophets, as they are in the Vulgate and in our English Bibles. In the Codex Alexandrinus, however, they follow the Prophets.

Such then are the contents of the Septuagint, which may be regarded as the Bible of Alexandria, which spread to the whole Greek-speaking world and was generally adopted by the Greek Christian Church. Its appropriation by the Church, the probability that the text had in some areas been affected by Christian beliefs (e.g. in Psa. xcv (xcvi) 10 Justin Martyr reads 'tell it out among the heathen that the Lord reigneth *from the tree*', and wrongfully accuses the Jews of having suppressed the last three words), as well as changing methods and ideals of scriptural interpretation by the Rabbis, led to its rejection by the Jews, who in controversy repudiated arguments based on Septuagint texts (such as the rendering παρθένος ('virgin') in Isa. vii. 14), and they therefore ceased to copy it. Josephus follows the Hebrew canon of 24 books (22 according to his reckoning in *Contra Apion* I.8, but he grouped the books differently, and 22 corresponds to the number of letters in the Hebrew alphabet), and it is to be observed that no quotation from any of the books of the Apocrypha is to be found in the New Testament, although there are references (in Luke xi. 49–51, John vii. 38, 1 Cor. ii. 9, Eph. v. 14, James iv. 5) to words as Scriptural which do not occur either in the canonical books or in the Apocrypha, and one in Jude to the book of Enoch.

The differences between the Septuagint and the Hebrew are not, however, confined to the difference in the books contained in them. There are also considerable divergences in the text of the books contained in both. Thus in Job the original Septuagint is shorter than the Hebrew text by about one-sixth,[1] and there are large variations in Joshua, 1 Samuel, 1 Kings, Proverbs, Esther and Jeremiah,[2] and lesser ones in other books. The cause of these divergences is one of the major problems of the Septuagint. It is maintained by some that they point to a different Hebrew text from that eventually adopted by the Jews; and since the extant manuscripts of the Septuagint are (apart from the recently discovered Dead Sea texts) older by several centuries than the oldest Hebrew manuscripts, it has been argued that the Septuagint is our best evidence for the original Hebrew Bible. On the other hand, it is maintained that the Greek translators were not always good Hebrew scholars, that they often made mistakes in translation, and in other respects took liberties with their text. In fact there is truth in both views, though the extent to which these causes operate varies in the different books, and it is not always possible in particular cases to say which is responsible for divergences between the Hebrew and the Greek. The Hebrew canon seems to have been finally fixed about A.D. 100, when the leaders of the Jewish community, having lost their country through the destruction of Jerusalem, and threatened by the growth of Christianity, concentrated on their Scriptures as the

---

[1] The gaps were later filled in by Origen from Theodotion (see below, pp. 20–1).

[2] In 1 Sam. the LXX omits xvii. 12–31, 41, 50, 55–8, xviii. 1–5, 10, 11, 17–19. In Jeremiah chapters xlvi–li follow (in a different order) xxv. 13, and the following passages are omitted: viii. 10b–12; x. 6–8, 10; xvii. 1–5a; xxix (=LXX xxxvi) 16–20; xxxiii (=LXX xl) 14–26; xxxix (=LXX xlvi) 4–13; lii. 28–30.

centre of their national existence, and began that process of fixing
the Hebrew text in its minutest particulars which was completed
by the Massoretes, and to which they adhered thenceforward
with the greatest punctiliousness. It does not follow that they
were always right in the text that they accepted. Even in the
Pentateuch, which was always regarded with peculiar reverence
and in which variation was less likely to occur, there are passages
in which the Samaritan version agrees with the Septuagint against
the Hebrew, and here there is a strong probability that they are
the truer witnesses to the original. The same may be the case in
other books, and throughout the Old Testament the evidence of
the Septuagint should be carefully considered on its merits. On
the other hand, mistakes and liberties by the translators are only
too probable, and in some cases are certain; so that the evidence
of the Septuagint must be accepted with caution. It remains,
however, an important fact that it is the form in which the Old
Testament was known to most of the Greek-speaking world, and
was the basis of the original Latin Bible also. For the earliest
Christian communities 'the Scriptures' meant the Septuagint
Old Testament.

The Septuagint is not, however, the only Greek Old Testament.
The differences between it and the Hebrew text accepted by the
Jewish community about the end of the first century after Christ
(which by an anticipation of its later title we may call the Massoretic Hebrew) led in the second century to the production of three
complete alternative versions and some partial ones. The first of
these (said to have been produced about A.D. 128) was the work
of Aquila, a proselyte from Sinope in Pontus. He was a pupil of
the famous Rabbi Akiba, whose reverence for every particular of
the sacred text and methods of interpretation Aquila applied to
his rendering of the Hebrew. The version was executed in the
interests of the Jewish community, to whom the Septuagint was
unpalatable, not only because of its divergence from the accepted
text, but because it had been adopted by the Christians. It carries
Hebraism to an extreme, turning the Hebrew literally into Greek
in defiance of Greek idiom. Although made in the interests of
Judaism, it was highly regarded by Christian scholars like Origen
and Jerome for its fidelity to the original, as well as by the Jews
themselves. The version as a whole has perished, and has to be
reconstructed almost entirely from notes in the margins of Hexa-

plaric MSS (see below p. 24) and from citations in the writings of the Fathers—material which has been collected together in Field's *Hexapla* (see below, p. 24). There survive, however, a few MS remains: at Cambridge are fragments, rescued from the Geniza (receptacle for imperfect and disused MSS) of the synagogue of Old Cairo, of the books of Kings (III Kingd. xx. 9–17, IV Kingd. xxiii. 12–27) in a sixth-century hand (published by F. C. Burkitt, *Fragments of the Books of Kings According to the Translation of Aquila*, Cambridge, 1897) and parts of Psa. xc–ciii together with a hexaplaric fragment of Psa. xx (C. Taylor, *Hebrew-Greek Cairo Genizah Palimpsests*, Cambridge, 1900); the Aquila column of the Milan palimpsest of the Psalms (see below, pp. 23–4); and a fragment among the Amherst Papyri of the late third or early fourth century which contains the first five verses of Genesis in the versions of the LXX and of Aquila (B. P. Grenfell and A. S. Hunt, *The Amherst Papyri*, Part i, London, 1900, pp. 30–1). The opening words of Genesis, as they appear in the Amherst Papyrus, illustrate the un-Greek character of Aquila's style: εν κεφαλεω εκτισεν Θς συν τον ουρανον και την γην· η δε γη ην κενωμα και ουθεν.

The second version was that of Theodotion of Ephesus (so Irenaeus, *c. Haeres.* III. 24—according to Epiphanius he was a native of Pontus), likewise a proselyte to Judaism (though Jerome says he was an Ebionite Christian), whose work is usually said to have been a revision of the Septuagint from the Hebrew, in a style far more readable than that of Aquila. Of this version we have better knowledge than of Aquila's. Origen made use of it to fill lacunae in the LXX text, notably in the case of Job, where it amounts to about a sixth of the whole. In Daniel Theodotion's version eventually supplanted that of the LXX, and the latter has survived complete only in a single Greek minuscule MS at the Vatican (see no. 88 below), in a Syriac translation, and (in part) in a Chester Beatty papyrus (no. 967 in the list below) of the third century. Origen speaks of both versions of Daniel being in circulation in the Church in his time, but Jerome (Preface to Daniel) says that the LXX text had now gone out of use 'quod multum a veritate discordet et recto iudicio repudiatus sit'. It has also been maintained, with some probability, that the ordinary version of Ezra-Nehemiah is in reality that of Theodotion, the original LXX being that which appears in the Apocrypha as 1 Esdras, which would be consistent with the fact that Josephus, who could not have known Theodotion, certainly used the text of 1 Esdras. It is, however, possible that Theodotion was using some earlier translation of which we have otherwise no knowledge; for 'Theodotionic' readings occur in the New Testament, notably in the quotations from Daniel in Hebrews and the Apocalypse (Heb. xi. 33, Apoc. ix. 20, x. 6, xii. 7, xiii. 7, xix. 6, xx. 4, 11), and in early Christian writers such as Barnabas, Clement and Hermas similar readings are found. This suggests that some other version than the LXX was current in the first Christian century which was well known, and as revised by Theodotion was preferred by the Church in the case of Daniel and perhaps of some other books—Thackeray, e.g. considered that the second translator of the book of Kingdoms used this version. Recently, however, D. Barthélemy in his edition of the Greek scroll of the Minor Prophets from the Dead Sea area (see below, p. 40) identifies Theodotion with a process of revision of the LXX which he locates in Palestine before the time of Aquila, of which the latter is the full and final flower. To this recension Barthélemy attributes, besides the Dead Sea Minor Prophets, the 'Theodotionic' version of Daniel and additions to Job and Jeremiah, Lamentations, the recension of Judges found in B and some minuscules (printed separately in Rahlfs' edition), the Quinta of the Psalms (see below), possibly Canticles and Ruth, and (in the earlier stages of the revision) 2 Chronicles and the central section of Ezekiel (xviii–xxxix—Thackeray's β).

The third translation, made apparently towards the end of the second century, is attributed to Symmachus, who is said by Eusebius and Jerome to have been an Ebionite Christian. His version is, in style, at the opposite extreme to that of Aquila; for he aimed at a free and literary rendering of the meaning of the Hebrew, rather than at a minute word-for-word fidelity. At the same time he appears to have been acquainted with the versions of Theodotion and Aquila, as well as the LXX. His work is known to us, like that of Aquila and much of Theodotion, only in isolated fragments, and it seems to have had a more restricted circulation and influence than the other two; but, as will be seen, it was used together with them by Origen in his great *Hexapla*, or six-fold edition, which will shortly be described, and Jerome made use of him in his Vulgate and (along with Aquila and Theodotion) in his commentaries on Old Testament books.

In addition to these three versions, Origen was acquainted with
three others, to which no names of authors are attached, and are
known simply as *Quinta, Sexta* and *Septima*. They were used by
him in the *Hexapla* for the Psalms, and readings have survived
for a few other books: the *Quinta* in 4 Kingdoms, Job, Canticles
and Minor Prophets, the *Sexta* in Job, Canticles and Minor
Prophets. The *Quinta* occupies the last column in the Milan
hexaplaric palimpsest of the Psalms. According to subscriptions
attributed to Origen (G. Mercati, *Studi e Testi* v (Rome, 1901),
pp. 28–46; E. Schwartz, *Gesammelte Schriften* v (Berlin, 1963),
pp. 183–91; P. Kahle, *The Cairo Geniza*, 2nd ed. (Oxford, 1959),
pp. 240–3—cf. Eusebius *Hist. Eccl.* VI. 16) the *Sexta* was found
along with other Greek and Hebrew books in a jar near Jericho
in the time of Caracalla, while the *Quinta* was found at Nicopolis
near Actium. There can be little doubt that these texts are Jewish
in origin—Jerome says as much for the first two—though whether
they represent independent Greek translations, or are revisions of
the LXX, is a matter of debate.

The existence of these alternative versions, and the patent
divergences between the Hebrew and the Greek Old Testaments,
led, in the early years of the third century, to an enterprise which
had a far-reaching effect on the text of the Greek Old Testament.
This was the work of the great Christian scholar, Origen, known
as the *Hexapla*. Origen (185–254) became in A.D. 203 head of the
catechetical school at Alexandria, and, in his work on a series of
commentaries on the books of the Old Testament, which he
produced between 220 and 250, was impressed by the discrepancies which he found in the text. As a basis for the establishment of
the true text, which would enable Christian scholars to meet the
Jews on equal terms, he set himself to produce an edition in which
the main extant texts were set out in six parallel columns. These
columns contained (1) the Massoretic Hebrew text in Hebrew
characters, (2) the same transliterated in Greek characters, presumably to assist in the vocalization of the unpointed Hebrew
text, (3) Aquila (probably as being closest to the Hebrew),
(4) Symmachus, (5) the Septuagint as Origen knew it—presumably
the text current in Alexandria in his day, (6) Theodotion. In
addition, in the Psalms he added the three anonymous versions
mentioned above, and perhaps one or more of them in some other
books. These were arranged in short κῶλα, or phrases, so as to

show the parallel renderings of each small group of words. The most important of these in its ultimate effects was his edition of the Septuagint; for here he set himself to incorporate the Hebrew evidence with the Greek. Words which were in the Hebrew but not in the Greek were added (generally from Theodotion), but marked by an asterisk (*); words which were in the Greek but not in the Hebrew were marked by an obelus (— or ÷ or ÷); a metobelus (: or ·/. or ⅃) marked the conclusion of the passage to which the asterisk or obelus referred; where the order of the Greek and Hebrew differed, the Hebrew order was preferred. It is often said in addition that minor disagreements between the Hebrew and the Greek were silently corrected, but it is equally possible that where such differences are to be seen between Origen's Hexapla text and the LXX, they are due not to Origen himself, but were found in the text as received by him. Moreover, the evidence points to the conclusion that, in the changes which he made, Origen relied not on direct translation from the Hebrew, but on one or other of the versions—Aquila, Symmachus, Theodotion, in the adjacent columns. (See, e.g. I. Soisalon-Soininen, *Der Charakter der asterisierten Zusätze in der Septuaginta*, Helsinki, 1959.) The general object, then, was to bring the Greek into conformity with the Hebrew, while leaving plain the process by which this result was achieved. But it is important to notice that Origen assumed that the Hebrew text current in his day was identical with that from which the LXX translation was originally made. This we know was by no means always so, and the outcome, in the absence of the critical signs, was a recension of the Greek Old Testament rather than a restoration of the LXX.

The *Hexapla* was completed by about A.D. 245, and was followed by a shortened edition, or Tetrapla, in which the first two columns (Hebrew and its transliteration into Greek characters) were omitted. In either form it was a colossal work, and its bulk was fatal to its survival. The originals were preserved in the library at Cæsarea in Palestine, where they were seen by Jerome in the fourth century, and by other scholars or annotators as late as the seventh; but it is probable that they were never fully copied, and that they perished when Cæsarea was taken by the Arabs in 638. The only extant specimens are the tenth-century palimpsest fragments in the Ambrosian Library at Milan containing about 150 verses of the Psalms (omitting the Hebrew column) which

C

has now been edited with full photographic facsimile (G. Mercati, *Psalterii Hexapli Reliquiae, Pars Prima*, Rome, 1958, *Osservazioni*, Rome, 1965), and an eighth-century fragment at Cambridge from the Cairo Geniza, which originally contained part of Psa. xxii in all six columns (C. Taylor, *Hebrew–Greek Cairo Geniza Fragments*, Cambridge, 1900). Much information about Hexaplaric readings from the various Greek columns can be gleaned (as was said above in the case of Aquila) from the notes in the margins of Hexaplaric MSS and from quotations in the Christian Fathers. The most comprehensive collection of this material, with reference to the sources, is still Frederick Field's *Origensis Hexaplorum Quae Supersunt* (Oxford, 1875, in two volumes).

The fifth column, however, containing Origen's revised text of the LXX, was separately edited by Origen's disciples, Pamphilus and Eusebius, and it is this that has affected the subsequent history of the LXX. If Origen's critical symbols had been punctiliously preserved, no great harm might have been done; for it would have been possible to re-establish from it much of the original LXX text on which he worked. But copyists were apt to ignore these troublesome little marks, and the result was that a text was transmitted in which the original LXX was largely contaminated by admixtures from Aquila and especially Theodotion. A considerable number of MSS exist which give information as to Origen's Hexaplaric text and particular passages in the other columns, as well as Paul of Tella's Syro-Hexaplar version (see p. 58 below), but these do not go far towards enabling us to recover the LXX text as it existed before Origen; and this remains the greatest problem which confronts the textual student of the Septuagint. Until we can do that, we are not in a position fully to utilize the evidence of the Greek for the recovery of the pre-Massoretic Hebrew.

Two other recensions of the LXX text are said to have been produced during the third century, which are known by the names of Hesychius and Lucian. Hesychius is connected by Jerome with Alexandria, and is identified by Swete with the bishop whom Eusebius (*Hist. Eccl.* viii. 13) mentions among the martyrs who suffered in the persecution of Diocletian; but Jerome speaks of him with less respect than one would think he would show to a martyr-bishop. In view of his association with Alexandria, his edition has been identified with the text found in the Egyptian versions and in the works of Cyril of Alexandria; and several MSS have been identified with this type, but as yet not much is known about it, if, indeed, it ever existed. His reputed connection with the Alexandrian text of the New Testament will be dealt with in the following chapters.

Lucian, on the other hand, is associated with Antioch, and according to Jerome his edition was current in the churches of Constantinople, Asia Minor and Antioch. He was born at Samosata, worked at Antioch, and was martyred under Maximin in 312. The characteristics usually attributed to his text are smoothness, lucidity and fullness—i.e. stylistic and grammatical improvements, the substitution of synonyms for words found in the LXX, doublets (giving the LXX and Lucianic reading together), and renderings which appear to rest on a superior Hebrew text. Scholars however differ in accounting for these phenomena. Swete thought that it was a revision of the κοινή; Rahlfs and Ziegler that in addition to making stylistic and grammatical changes he used the hexaplaric recension and the later translations associated with it. On the other hand, Kahle and Manson see behind the recension an older Greek version, probably independent of the LXX, which was current in Syria and revised by Lucian. This view is held to account for the fact that 'Lucianic' readings have been noticed in the quotations of Josephus and Justin Martyr and in the Old Latin Bible, all of which antedate the historical Lucian. To this may be added the opinion of Vaccari that the text of the oldest surviving fragment of the Greek Old Testament, the Rylands papyrus of Deuteronomy of the second century B.C. (no. 957 in the list below), is most closely related to the Lucianic type of text. In 1883 Paul de Lagarde published an attempted reconstruction of the Lucianic text of the Octateuch, but his work was largely nugatory, since it was shown by Rahlfs that the MSS on which he relied, though Lucianic from I Samuel onwards, were not so from Genesis–Ruth iv. 10. The result of these various ancient attempts to revise and restore the Greek Old Testament has been a great confusion in the tradition. The types of text associated with Eusebius (=Origen) which circulated primarily in Palestine, with Hesychius in Egypt, and with Lucian in Constantinople and Antioch, inevitably reacted on one another in the course of time, and it is exceedingly difficult to disentangle them. This is indeed one of the great tasks of those who concern themselves with the textual history of the Septuagint.

Before going on to describe in greater detail the principal MSS of the LXX, a word should be said here on the problem which divides scholars working in this field. This is the question whether it is possible, or indeed proper, to speak of an 'original text' ('Ur-Text') of the LXX, or 'proto-Septuagint'. If it is, then we must assume that the surviving text of the LXX as we know it goes back to a single translation, beginning with the Pentateuch in the third century B.C., and followed by that of the other books, the whole admittedly the work of many different hands over a century and more. Thereafter the text suffered many vicissitudes, especially after it was cast off by the Jews. For, as we have seen, its history is not simply a matter of normal textual degeneration as a result of scribal transmission, nor even of continued sporadic revision on the basis of different forms of the Hebrew text. The recensions of the third century in particular (especially that of Origen's Hexapla), and their subsequent mixture, have immensely complicated the disentanglement of the lines of tradition. Nevertheless, it is claimed that in principle this can be done. The great scholar Paul de Lagarde in the last century proposed to do this by first arriving at the recensions of Origen, Hesychius and Lucian, and then to work back to the original LXX which lay behind them. As a step towards this goal he attempted to recover Lucian's text of the Octateuch, but his pupil Rahlfs, as we have seen above, showed that the MSS he depended on were for the most part not Lucianic at all. Nevertheless, Rahlfs and his followers on the Göttingen Septuagint have continued the work on the principles laid down by Lagarde, though with modifications. Instead of concentrating on the third-century recensions, the MS material for each individual book is treated empirically according to its merits. This is sorted out into groups and subgroups (which in practice turn out to be more numerous than Lagarde supposed) and from a critical comparison of these it is possible to arrive at a very early form of the text.[1]

On the other hand it is maintained that an 'original Septuagint' never existed; we should think not so much of diversity arising out of an original uniformity, but of an original (and indeed

---

[1] For the methods and results of the 'Göttingen School' see the bibliography at the end of this chapter and the several volumes of the Göttingen Septuagint (p. 61).

increasing) diversity in which from time to time attempts have been made to impose uniformity. The chief protagonist of this view is Paul Kahle[1] who lays it down as a rule in dealing with translations that a fixed and authorized version comes not at the beginning but at the end of a long process. The proper analogy for the Greek Old Testament is the Aramaic Targum in its various forms. At the outset we must think of communities of Greek-speaking Jews for whom Greek translations of the Scriptures were necessary in public worship and for private use. These versions would vary in quality and were subject to constant revision. Eventually in a city like Alexandria the need for an authoritative text of the Greek Torah would make itself felt, and it is to just such an authorized version that the Letter of Aristeas refers. The Letter, which is properly to be dated towards the end of the second century B.C., is in fact propaganda for an authorized Greek Pentateuch, which it seeks to commend at the expense of other less satisfactory versions in circulation amongst the Jews. However, these other versions did not entirely disappear, and outside the Pentateuch (to which alone Aristeas refers) the other Old Testament books continued to exist in Greek in a variety of forms and versions. When in due time the Christians succeeded to the Jewish Scriptures, they took over the authorized Jewish Pentateuch, and in the case of the other books adopted one or other of the existing Greek versions, the whole in the course of the second century becoming the canonical text of the Church with the title of 'Septuagint'. But by this time the Jews had cast off the older in favour of the new translations made in accordance with the Hebrew text as it was now read by Jewish scholars.

It is against this background that Kahle invites us to see the Quinta, Sexta and Septima columns of the Hexapla, which on his thesis are independent Jewish versions which had been preserved, probably in Jewish genizas. What Theodotion and Lucian revised was not the LXX, but older Greek versions, and it is in this way that we can account for 'Theodotionic' and 'Lucianic' readings which date from before the times of Theodotion and Lucian. Again, several books (e.g. Tobit and Judges) exist in two very different forms: these are not two recensions of the same basic text but, Kahle would say, two independent translations which, it so happens, have survived in the case of

[1] See especially his *Cairo Geniza* (1st ed. London, 1947, 2nd ed. Oxford, 1959.)

these books. Furthermore, he claims, the oldest evidence for the Greek Bible that has been coming to light in recent times tends to support this view-point. The second-century B.C. fragments of Deuteronomy of the Rylands Papyrus are, according to Vaccari, most nearly related to the Lucianic text; the Greek fragments from Qumran 4 show unique readings which are not found in any form of the LXX as we know it; while the leather scroll of the Minor Prophets of about the end of the first century B.C. shows close affinities in Micah and Zechariah with the quotations of Justin Martyr, which is said to be 'Lucianic' in type, as well as having variants agreeing with Symmachus and the Quinta.

If Kahle has made out his case—and it is a very strong one—then it must be conceded that attempts to reach the 'original' text of the LXX are vain. What we have are the remnants of a plurality of versions, or if it be preferred, different forms of the Greek Old Testament targum. T. W. Manson[1] would add that in Theodotion we have an edition of the Greek targum of the Synagogues of Asia, in Lucian a revision of the targum of Syria. And though it may be allowed that it is possible to arrive at certain fixed points in the transmission of the text or texts, 'the task which the LXX presents to scholars is not the "reconstruction" of an imaginary "Ur-Text", nor the discovery of it, but a careful collation and investigation of all the remains and traces of earlier versions of the Greek Bible which differed from the Christian standard text'.[2]

It would be rash, at the present stage of the debate, to attempt to decide the issue between these two schools of thought. But a few observations may be added. It would be admitted by both sides that the Greek text has been repeatedly subject to revision in the course of its history. At what point does a 'revision' become a 'translation'? Anyone setting out to translate a text will make use of any available renderings—schoolboys are not the only persons to use 'cribs'. Are we to call it a 'revision' instead of a 'translation' because it was not done entirely *de novo*? The question is relevant even in the case of Theodotion and Symmachus, and it now seems that Aquila had his predecessors, and is to be regarded as the end of a process rather than as an innovator. The same consideration may apply to the earlier stages of the Greek Old Testament. Again, it should be remembered that the

---

[1] See his review of Kahle in *Dominican Studies*, ii (1949), pp. 183–94.
[2] Kahle, *The Cairo Geniza* (2nd edition), p. 264.

version had a two-fold use among Greek-speaking Jews from the earliest days. The first had to do with the public readings in the liturgical services of the synagogue: these comprised only a portion of the Old Testament, and might well become subject to official supervision and control from an early date, if not from the beginning. But side by side with this would be the need felt by pious Jews for translations of the non-liturgical portions for private study, and here private enterprise may have produced versions, some of which could have survived after an official or standard translation appeared, and indeed may have formed the basis of the standard version. Moreover, it should not be assumed that Alexandria was the only important centre of hellenistic Judaism. The Greek versions read in Antioch, Ephesus and other cities of the Diaspora would each have a history of their own, and even if they had a common origin (though there is no *a priori* reason to assume that this must have been so) that history could be one of largely independent revision. Most important of all is the conclusion which is reinforced by every branch of textual study: that every book, or group of books, or even portion of a book, must be judged on its own merits. It by no means follows that what is true of one—e.g. that it has a single or multiple textual history—will be true of others; that what holds for Genesis and the Pentateuch is valid for Judges. The same is true of manuscripts: it cannot be assumed that the text-type of any MS is uniform throughout, since it may vary not only from book to book, but even within the individual books—a mistake which, as we have seen, vitiated Lagarde's work on the Lucianic text. It may not therefore matter very greatly whether we speak of 'different translations' or 'different forms' of the Greek Old Testament text. What we have to recognize is that as far back as we can go we shall find a mass of textual variants, and in so far as they are ancient they are important. We may if we please select one class of readings and call it 'the original LXX'. What we may *not* do is to discard the rest as valueless, and on this all scholars would agree.

The manuscripts in which the Greek Old Testament has come down to us are usually classified under three heads: Papyri, Uncial Manuscripts, and Minuscule or Cursive Manuscripts; and to these must be added the early versions in other languages, the evidence of which is very important. The papyri are the remains (often very small) which have been recovered from excavations in Egypt, almost all within the last eighty years, important because of their age and for the light which they throw on the early history of the text and the conditions under which the Scriptures circulated before the recognition of Christianity by the Empire. The uncials are the vellum manuscripts from the fourth to the ninth or tenth century, written in large capital letters (called 'uncial' from a phrase of Jerome's[1] of somewhat doubtful meaning, but apparently referring to their size). In the ninth century the size of the volumes necessitated by this style of writing appears to have been found cumbrous, and a new and smaller type of writing, developed from that in common use for documentary purposes (of which we now have many examples among the latest papyri), was invented and taken into use both for pagan and for Christian literature. It is called 'minuscule' from its size or 'cursive' from the fact that the letters are often linked together by ligatures so as to make a running hand. This continued in use, with variations in successive generations by which it is possible approximately to date them when other evidence is lacking, until the invention of printing.[2]

In the following catalogue only the more important manuscripts are included. The uncials are normally indicated by capital letters of the Latin, Greek, or occasionally Hebrew alphabets; the papyri and minuscules by Arabic numerals. The first list of manuscripts was that of Holmes and Parsons, in their great edition of the Septuagint, which will be described subsequently. This has now been superseded by the catalogue of A. Rahlfs, which uses as far as possible the enumeration of Holmes and Parsons, but is based afresh on modern library catalogues and includes all subsequent discoveries to 1914. It is now the accepted official list of Septuagint manuscripts.[3] All MSS (uncials, minu-

---

[1] Preface to Job, where he complains of the extravagant ostentatiousness of many books in his own time 'uncialibus, ut aiunt, literis', i.e. 'inch-long', an extravagant, but not impossibly extravagant, description.

[2] The dating of minuscule Greek manuscripts on purely palaeographical grounds is a hazardous business, since styles of writing were continued long or revived, so that different styles overlap. A great contribution to it has been made by the publication of a large number of dated specimens by Kirsopp and Silva Lake (*Monumenta Palaeographica Vetera*, 1st series: *Dated Greek Manuscripts to the Year 1200 A.D.*, Boston, 1934–45).

[3] *Verzeichnis der griechischen Handschriften des Alten Testaments* (*Mitteilungen des Septuaginta—Unternehmens der Akademie der Wissenschaften in Göttingen*), Berlin, 1914.

scules, and papyri) are included, capital letters being used for those uncials which are customarily so designated, the rest in a single numerical sequence; gaps, however, occur in it, sometimes intentionally to receive additions, sometimes because of errors in Holmes and Parsons. Although Rahlfs includes all in a single list, it will be best for our purposes to group the three main categories separately, since they represent different dates, the papyri being none of them later than the seventh century and including many of the earliest extant MSS of the Old Testament, the uncials ranging from the fourth to the tenth century, and the minuscules from the ninth to the fifteenth. In the large Cambridge edition, which was begun under the editorship of A. E. Brooke and N. McLean, the readings of a large selection from these MSS is given; but the minuscules have letters assigned to them instead of numbers. These are in the following list appended to the numbers, with the initials B—M.

The papyri are mostly very small fragments, and only the larger ones are described here. By far the most important are the group known as the Chester Beatty papyri, which deserve a separate mention, both because of their textual importance and because it is to them, and to the comparable Bodmer Collection (see below, p. 199) that we owe the greater part of our knowledge of the earliest form of the Biblical books and their circulation in the first Christian centuries. They are a group of twelve (or more correctly, as is now known, eleven) papyrus codices, discovered in 1931 in Egypt (apparently in a cemetery or the ruins of a church in the neighbourhood of Aphroditopolis). The greater portion of the collection was secured by Sir Alfred Chester Beatty, well known as a collector especially of illuminated manuscripts, and is now in the Chester Beatty Museum and Library in Dublin; but a considerable number of leaves were acquired by the University of Michigan, and a few found their way elsewhere. The collection, which presumably represents the Biblical library of a Christian community in the fourth century, comprises portions of two MSS of Genesis, one of Numbers and Deuteronomy, one of Isaiah, one of Jeremiah, one of Ezekiel, Daniel and Esther, and one of Ecclesiasticus; with one of the Gospels and Acts, one of the Pauline Epistles, one of Revelation, and one of the Book of Enoch and a homily by Melito of Sardis. The earliest is of the first half of the second century, the latest not later than the fourth; most are of the third. Descriptions are given below.

The following is a select list of the more important MSS:

I. Papyri

U. British Museum Papyrus 37. Thirty-two leaves of a papyrus codex of the Psalms, acquired in 1836, and said to have been discovered among the rubbish of an ancient convent at Thebes; the first Biblical papyrus to come to light, seventh century. Written in a rather large sloping hand. Contains Psa. x (xi in the Hebrew numbering). 2—xviii (xix). 6, xx (xxi). 14—xxxix (xxxv). 6. The text is assigned by Rahlfs to the Upper Egyptian family, along with the Sahidic version and 2013. Edited by Tischendorf *Monumenta Sacra Inedita*, nov. coll. i, 217.

W. Washington Minor Prophets (Freer Greek MS. V). Portions of 33 leaves (out of a probable total of 48) of a single-quire codex of the Minor Prophets. About third quarter of the third century. Contains, besides a few scraps of Hos. i–viii, Hos. xiv. 7–10, Amos i. 1–5, 10—ix. 15, Micah, Joel, Obadiah, Jonah, Nahum, Habakkuk, Zephaniah, Haggai, Zechariah, Malachi, in that order. Its text shows about 30 accommodations with the Hebrew of its own, but whether these are due to independent revision from the Hebrew, or to Hexaplaric or other influences has not been settled. Barthélemy (*Les Devanciers d'Aquila*, pp. 239–45) aligns them with the recension of the Greek scroll of the Minor Prophets (see below, p. 39f.). Of the greater LXX MSS it agrees most frequently with Q and decidedly least with ℵ, but it has many readings which are not in any of the uncials, but are found in some of the minuscules, notably 407, 198, 233, 534 and 410, in that order. All these are regarded as pre-Hexaplaric MSS. Edited by H. A. Sanders, with 911 (see below). In previous editions of this book and elsewhere designated X.

905. (B—M. U_4.) Oxyrhynchus Pap. 656, now in the Bodleian Library, Oxford. Parts of 4 leaves of a codex, early third or possibly end of second century. Contains Gen. xiv. 21–23, xv. 5–9, xix. 32—xx. 11, xxiv. 28–47, xxvii. 32, 33, 40, 41. In text it does not range itself closely with any other MS, whether papyrus or vellum. Important as providing an early text of Genesis where B is lacking and ℵ defective. Edited by Grenfell and Hunt (*Pap. Ox.* iv. 28–36).

911. Berlin Staatsbibliothek Gr. fol. 66 I, II. A codex originally of 32 leaves, of which the first and last (the latter being blank) are lost, and all the others more or less mutilated. The first 9 leaves were in double columns, the rest in single columns with long lines. Very irregularly written, with abnormal divisions of words at the ends of lines, in a document hand probably of the early part of the fourth century. Contains (but with many mutilations) Gen. i. 16–22, ii. 5–9, 11—iv. 7, 9—v. 13, 15–22, 24—vi. 17, 19— viii. 2, 4—xv. 7, 10—xvi. 2 (xv. 4–8, 11—xvi. 2 repeated), xvi. 3—6, 8—xvii. 10, 12–24, 26—xviii. 18, 22—xix. 4, 15–22, 33— xx. 1, 11–18, xxi. 13–17, 29—xxii. 2, 13–17, xxiii. 6–12, xxiv. 4–8, 20–23, 37—xxxv. 8, ending with the title γενεσις κοσμου, showing that the rest of the book was contained in a second codex. The text shows strong affinities with the other papyri of Genesis, **961** and **962**. Edited by H. A. Sanders and C. Schmidt, *The Minor Prophets in the Freer Collection and the Berlin Fragment of Genesis* (University of Michigan Studies, Humanistic Series, vol. xxi, New York, 1927).

912. (B—M. U$_2$.) Amherst Papyrus III. In the Pierpont Morgan Library, New York. Early fourth century. Contains Gen. i. 1–5 in the LXX version, followed by that of Aquila, written on the back of a letter from an Egyptian Christian in Rome. Edited by Grenfell and Hunt, *Amherst Papyri* i, pp. 28–30 (London, 1900). See also A. Deissmann, *Light from the Ancient East* (London, 1910), pp. 192–201.

919. Heidelberg Septuagint Papyrus 1. Twenty-seven leaves, all more or less mutilated, from 4 quires (two of 8 leaves and two of 10) of a codex of the Minor Prophets. Seventh century. Written in a large and coarse uncial hand. Contains Zech. iv. 6—v. 1, 3— vi. 2, 4–15, vii. 10—x. 7, xi. 5—xiv. 21, Mal. i. 1—iii. 7, 10, 11, 13–16, 18—iv. 1, 3–5. In text belongs to the Alexandrian group headed by A and Q. Edited by A. Deissmann, *Veröffentlichungen aus der Heidelberger Papyrus-Sammlung* 1 (1905).

942. Papyrus Fouad 266 at Cairo, consisting of parts of two columns containing Deut. xxxi. 28—xxxii. 7 (the Song of Moses), written in a fine uncial hand by a Jew in the first or perhaps second century B.C. The Divine Name appears in square Hebrew characters, as in the Milan palimpsest of the Psalms. According to A. Vaccari (*Studia Patristica* I. i. (Berlin, 1957), pp. 339–42) the text shows no Hexaplaric elements, belonging to the uncial group A B F, and is closest to B **509** (a$_2$), but containing old elements which later disappeared from the tradition. Described by W. C. Waddel, *Journal of Theological Studies* xlv (1944), pp. 158–61.

952. British Museum Pap. 2486. Early fourth century. Two conjoint leaves of a codex, one containing the Song of Sol. v. 12— vi. 10, the other the *Apology* of Aristides ch. xv. The latter confirms the Syriac version of the *Apology* as against the shorter Greek text preserved as the *Vita Balaam et Joasaph*.

957. John Rylands Library, Manchester, Pap. Gk. 458. Fragments from 4 columns of a roll of Deuteronomy from the cartonnage of a mummy. Acquired by Dr Rendel Harris in 1917. Written, presumably by a Jew, in a fine book-hand of the second century B.C. Contains Deut. xxiii. 24—xxiv. 3, xxv. 1–3, xxvi. 12, 17–19, xxviii. 31–33. The text agrees markedly with Θ (W) and A rather than with B (agreeing in this respect with **963**). According to A. Vaccari (*Biblica*, xvii (1936), pp. 501–4), it is most closely related to Lucian; J. Hempel (*Z.A.W.*, n.f. 14 (1937), pp. 115–27) denies this. The earliest known fragment of a Biblical MS. Edited by C. H. Roberts, *Two Biblical Papyri in the John Rylands Library, Manchester* (Manchester, 1936).

961. Chester Beatty Papyrus IV. Fifty leaves, all more or less mutilated, from a codex originally of 66 leaves of the book of Genesis. Written in double columns, in a rather large and heavy uncial hand. Fourth century. Contains Gen. ix. 1–5, 10–13, 16–27, x. 2–9, 14–20, 22—xi. 5, 8–11, 13–19, 21–32, xii. 3–20, xiii. 2–7, 9–13, 15—xiv. 18, 20—xv. 14, xvii. 7—xviii. 8, 10–25, 27–33, xix. 1—xxi. 2, 5–30, 32—xxii. 18, 20—xxiii. 3, 6–20, xxiv. 2–20, 22–27, 29–67, xxv. 2–7, 9–26, 28–34, xxvi. 2–16, 18–22, 24–34, xxvii. 1–30, 32—xxix. 13, 15–20, 22–27, 29–33, 35—xxx. 4, 6–12, 14–16, 18–22, 25–38, 40—xxxi. 1, 3–7, 9–18, 20–25, 27–30, 32–39, 41–47, 50–54, xxxii. 1–5, 7–10, 12–23, 25–29, 32—xxxiii. 2, 4–7, 10–18, xxxiv. 1–5, 7–9, 11–14, 16–28, 30—xxxv. 1, 3–5, 7–16, 18–22, 26—xxxvi. 1, 4–6, 9–13, 15–19, 22–28, 31–35, 37–40, 43— xxxvii. 2, 4–7, 9–11, 14–16, 19–21, 24–31, 33–36, xxxviii. 2–7, 9–15, 17–20, 22–29, xxxix. 1–7, 9–15, 18, 19, 22, 23, xl. 2–5, 7–10, 13, 14, 16–18, 20—xli. 1, 3–7, 9–12, 14–17, 19–21, 24–27, 30–33, 35, 36, 39–42, 44–46, 48–50, 52–55, 57—xlii. 2, 11–13, 16–18, 28–30, 33, 34, xliii. 6, 7, 9–11, 21, 22, 25, xliv. 17, 21, 22. In text it has several readings in common with **962**, with little or no other support, and is also akin to **911**. Of the other MSS it has most agreement with G and **135**, the representatives of the Origenian text, and least with A. ℵ and B being almost wholly lacking in Genesis, this group of three early papyri, covering the greater part of the book, is particularly valuable. Edited by F. G. Kenyon, *Chester Beatty Biblical Papyri*, fasc. iv (London, 1934), with full photographic facsimile in a separate volume (1935).

962. Chester Beatty Papyrus V. Twenty-seven leaves (17 nearly perfect) out of an original total of 84, arranged in quires of 10 leaves (except the first, which seems to have had 4 leaves, three pages of which were blank). Written in a document hand of the latter part of the third century, with one column to the page. Contains Gen. viii. 13–16, 21—ix. 1, xxiv. 13—xxv. 21, xxx. 24–26, 29, 30, 33–35, 37–41, xxxi. 5–9, 35–38, 40, 41, 43–45, 47—xxxii. 1, 5–9, 14—xxxiii. 8, 10—xxxv. 16, xxxix. 3—xl. 4, 6–13, xli. 9—xlvi. 33. The text is akin to that of **961**. Edited by F. G. Kenyon with **961**, with full photographic facsimile in a separate volume (1936).

963. Chester Beatty Papyrus VI. Fifty leaves (28 substantially preserved) out of an original total of 108 of a codex containing Numbers and Deuteronomy. Written in a small and good hand, probably of the first half of the second century, with two columns to the page. Contains Num. v. 12—viii. 19, xiii. 4–6, 17, 18, xxv. 5, 6, 10, 11, 18, xxvi. 1, 2, 12, 13, 21–25, 32–35, 40–42, 47–51, 55–59, 63—xxvii. 11, 13—xxviii. 17, 19–24, 26–31, xxix. 1–6, 8–18, 21–24, 27–33, 35–39, xxx. 1–17, xxxi. 1, 2, 6–8, 11–17, 19–22, 25–28, 30–32, 35–45, 48–50, 54, xxxii. 1, 2, 5–8, 11–30, 32, 33, xxxiii. 8, 9, 53–56, xxxiv. 1–8, 12, 13, 20–23, 29, xxxv. 1–3, 5–7, 12, 13–15, 24, 25, 28–32, xxxvi. 1, 4, 7, 8, 11–13; Deut. i. 20–33, 35–46, ii. 1—iii. 21, 23—iv. 49, v. 1—vii. 10, 12, 13, 15–20, ix. 26, 29, x. 1, 2, 5–7, 11, 12, 19–21, xi. 12, 13 [17, 18, 31, 32], xii. 2–4, 15–17, xviii. 22, xix. 1, 4–6, 10, 11, 13, 14, 16, xxvii. 6–8, 13–15, xxviii. 1–4, 7–10, 12, 13, 17–20 [22–25, 27–30, 32–35, 38–41], 43–68, xxix. 1–18, 20, 21, 23–27, xxx. 1, 4–6 [10, 11], 12, 13, 16, 17 [19, 20], xxxi. [3, 4], 8–16, 18, 21–23, 26–29, xxxii. [3–5, 10], 11–13, 17–19, 24, 25 [27–29], xxxiii. 24–27, xxxiv. 11, 12. The verses between brackets are on fragments belonging to the University of Michigan, and there are a large number of very small unplaced fragments. In Numbers the text is most akin to that of B and **509** (a₂), and next to G; but in Deuteronomy to G,

Θ, 54, 75 and **509**, and least to B—Θ, **54** and **75** in this book form a closely connected group. Edited by F. G. Kenyon, *Chester Beatty Biblical Papyri*, fasc. v (London, 1935). A photographic facsimile appeared 1938.

964. Chester Beatty Papyrus XI. One complete leaf and part of a second of a codex of Ecclesiasticus, written in a large rough hand, probably of the fourth century. Contains Ecclus. xxxvi. 28— xxxvii. 22, xlvi. 6–11, 16—xlvii. 2. In text most akin to B, and least to ℵ, A and C coming between. Edited by F. G. Kenyon, *Chester Beatty Biblical Papyri*, fasc. vi (London, 1937), with **965** and **966**.

965. Chester Beatty Papyrus VII. Fragments of 33 leaves (out of an estimated total of 112, with 8 blank leaves in addition at the end) of a codex of Isaiah, arranged in a single large quire. Two of the leaves are the property of Mr W. Merton, and several fragments originally belonged to the University of Michigan, but were transferred by it to Sir A. Chester Beatty. Written in a fine hand, apparently of the first half of the third century. Contains Isa. viii. 18, 19, ix. 2, 3, xi. 5–7, 10–12, 15—xii. 1, 5—xiii. 2, 6–9, 12–14, 18–20, xiv. 2–4, 23–27, 29—xv. 1, 3–5, 8—xvi. 4, 7–10, 12— xvii. 3 [5–7, 9–12], xviii. 1–4, 6—xix. 1, 5, 6, 11–13, xxxviii. 14, xxxix. 7, 8, xl. 22, 23, xli. 25, 28—xlii, 2, 5–7, 10–13, 16–18, 22—xliii, 2, 6–8, 10–13, 17–20, 25—xliv, 1, 5–7, 11, 12, 15–17, 19–21, 23–25, 28, xlv. 5, liv. 1–5, 10, 11 [14—lv. 1, 3–7], 9–12, lvi. 1–3, 6, 7, 11—lvii. 3, 9, 10, 15, 17—20, lviii. 2–4, lix. 1–3, 7–9, 12–14, 17–20, lx. 2–5, 9, 10, 14–16, 19–22. The verses in brackets are those in the Merton leaves. Several short Coptic notes in the old Fayyumic dialect (but in Greek writing, probably of the third century) are added in the margins. According to Kenyon the text agrees most with Q and Γ and less with A, ℵ and B, in that order; Ziegler, in the Göttingen edition, classes it as mixed. Edited by F. G. Kenyon, *Chester Beatty Biblical Papyri*, fasc. vi., with **964** and **966**.

966. Chester Beatty Papyrus VIII. Small portions of two leaves of a codex, containing Jer. iv. 30—v. 1, 9–14, 23, 24. Written in a clear and rather large, but not calligraphic, hand, probably of the late second or early third century. The text shows slightly most agreement with Q, and least with ℵ: there are several singular readings, of no great importance. Edited by F. G. Kenyon, *Chester Beatty Biblical Papyri*, fasc. vi, with **964** and **965**.

967, 968. Chester Beatty Papyri IX, X. Portions of a codex (originally described as two separate codices) containing Ezekiel, Daniel and Esther, the Ezekiel being in a different hand from the other books. Eight leaves of Ezekiel, 13 of Daniel, and 8 of Esther (conjoint with the Ezekiel) belong to Sir A. Chester Beatty, and a further 21 leaves of Ezekiel belonging to the J. H. Scheide collection are now at the University of Princeton. The complete codex may be estimated at 118 leaves, in a single quire. Probably first half of third century. Contains Ezek. xi. 25—xii. 6, 12–18, 23—xiii. 6, 11–17, 20—xiv. 3, 6–10, 15–20, 23—xv. 7, xvi. 5–11, 16–22, 28–34, 39–45, 48–53, 57—xvii. 1, 6–10, 15–21 [xix. 12—xxxix. 29 (with gaps of five leaves), Princeton]; Daniel with the order iii. 72–78, 81–88, 92–94, 96—iv. 9 (omitting iii. 98–100 and iv. 3–6), 11–14^a, 16–19, 22–25, 28–30^c, 34–34^c, vii. 1–6, 8–11, 14–19, 22–25, 28—viii. 4, 7–12, 15–20, 24—v. 5, 7–12, 17–29 (omitting 18–22, 24, 25), vi. 1–8, 12, 13, 16–18; Esther ii. 20–23, iii. 4–9, 13–13^c (=iii. 13—xiii. 3), 13^{e-g} (=xii. 5–7), iii. 14, iv. 3–7, 11–16, 17^{d-h} (=xiii. 12–17), 17^{s-w} (=xiv. 13–17), v. 1^{a-d} (=xv. 5–10), 2^a–4 (=xv. 16–19, v. 3–4), v. 9–14, vi. 3–6, 11–14, vii. 6–9, viii. 2–6. The text of Ezekiel (in the Chester Beatty leaves) agrees markedly with B and next with Q, but not with A. In Daniel the text is the original LXX (not, as in all other Greek MSS but one, that of Theodotion) without the Hexaplar additions. In Esther it agrees with B and ℵ, but markedly not with A. The Scheide leaves have been edited by A. C. Johnson, H. S. Gehman and E. H. Kase in *Princeton Studies in Papyrology* 3 (1938), the rest by F. G. Kenyon, *Chester Beatty Biblical Papyri*, fasc. vii (London, 1938).

2013. Leipzig Papyrus 39. Portions of a papyrus roll, about 13 feet 6 inches long, containing Psa. xxx–lv, written on the back of a document dated A.D. 338. Late fourth century. The first five Psalms are much mutilated. The text is said by Rahlfs to contain the Upper Egyptian text, which is found also in the Sahidic version and the British Museum Papyrus U (see above, p. 32, and A. Rahlfs *Psalmi*, pp. 28 ff.). Edited by C. F. Heinrici, *Beiträge zur Geschichte und Erklärung des A. T.* pt. iv (1903).

2019. British Museum Pap. 230. Fragment of a roll containing Psa. xi. 7—xiv. 4. Late third century. Rahlfs aligns it with B ℵ and the Bohairic version. Edited by Kenyon, *Facsimiles of Biblical MSS in the British Museum* (London, 1900).

2055. Papyrus Società Italiana 980. Two leaves of a codex of the Psalms, containing Psa. cxliii. 14—cxlviii. 3. Late third or fourth century. Its text appears to be mixed; it agrees least with ℵ but about equally with A B R T. In several instances it is found supporting the same readings as ℵ^{c.a} R T. Edited by G. Vitelli, *Papiri Società Italiana*, vol. viii, fasc. 2, 1927.

2077. One of six biblical texts included in the collection of papyrus texts discovered at Sheikh Abaden in Egypt, the site of the ancient Antinoopolis. This (no. 7) contains fragments of Psa. lxxxi. 1–4 and lxxxii. 4–9, 16–17 of the second century. The other Old Testament fragments are: no. 8 (Rahlfs **928**) containing third century fragments of Proverbs in a pre-Origen text with a considerable number of readings either unique or found only in the Hebrew or in Greek translations other than the LXX, but otherwise agreeing markedly with V, with which it shares a common ancestor, and also fragments of Wisdom (in an eccentric text) and of Ecclesiasticus; no. 9 (Rahlfs **987**) also contains third century fragments of Proverbs (ii. 9–15, iii. 13–17)—similar to no. 8, but not so close to V; no. 10 (Rahlfs **988**) is on vellum and contains a fourth century text of Ezekiel xxxiii. 27–31, xxxiv. 1–5, 18–24, 26–30 of a remarkably independent kind, though its support of unique readings in the Chester Beatty–Scheide papyrus (**967, 968** above) suggests a common ancestry. All the above are edited, together with the non-biblical texts, by C. H. Roberts, *The Antinoopolis Papyri*, Part I (London, 1950). On the fragments of Proverbs see G. Zuntz, *Zeitschrift für die Alttestamentliche Wissenschaft*, xlviii (1956), pp. 124–84.

2110. Papyrus Bodmer XXIV. A single quire codex originally of 41 folded leaves (plus one or more guard leaves), 82 folios. Written in a small irregular hand of the end of the third or beginning of the fourth century. Contains Psa. xvii–cxviii with gaps. The text is closely related to that of the Sahidic version, some of whose readings, previously unknown in Greek, are here confirmed. Edited by R. Kasser, Bibliotheca Bodmeriana (Cologny–Genève, 1967).

2113. Papyrus Bodmer IX. Three leaves of a codex containing Psa. xxxiii. 2—xxxiv. 16. Beginning of the fourth century. The text is closest to U, **2013**, and the Coptic version. Edited by Michael Testuz, Bibliotheca Bodmeriana (Cologny–Genève, 1959).

Qumran Fragments from Cave IV: some of these are on leather, but like the Antinoopolis fragments may best be taken together here. The Greek texts consist of:

(a) parts of one column of a text (Rahlfs **801**) containing Lev. xxvi. 2–16 written on leather, which differs from the normal LXX texts in having no less than ten unique readings.

(b) a papyrus fragment (Rahlfs **802**) of Lev. ii–v in a hand closely akin to Pap. Fouad 266 (**942** above), the Divine Name appearing as ιαω;

(c) fragments on leather (**803**) of Num. iii. 30—iv. 14, containing unique readings.

(a) is dated by C. H. Roberts about the end of the second century B.C., (b) and (c) towards the end of the first century B.C. or beginning of the first century A.D. According to P. W. Skehan (*Vetus Testamentum*, Suppl. iv (Leiden, 1957), pp. 148–60) we have here the remains of an early rendering which, long before Origen's time, had been subjected to a considerable degree of revision. See also P. Kahle, *The Cairo Geniza* (2nd ed., Oxford, 1959), pp. 223–6 and F. M. Cross, *The Ancient Library of Qumran* (revised ed., 1961).

Here also may be taken the Greek *Dodekapropheton*, the leather scroll of the Minor Prophets from an unknown location, presumably in the Dead Sea region, and now in the Palestine Museum (=Rahlfs **943**). The extant text consists of the remains of 24 columns, the work of two scribes, and comprises, in a fragmentary state, Jonah i. 14, 16, ii. 1, 4–7, iii. 7–10, iv. 1–2, 5; Mic. i. 1–8, ii. 7–8, iii. 5–6, iv. 3–10, v. 1–6, Nahum ii. 5–10, 13–14, iii. 6–17; Hab. i. 5–11, 14–17, ii. 1–8, 13–20, iii. 9–10, 13–15; Zeph. i. 1–5, 13–17, ii. 9–10, iii. 6–7; Zech. i. 1–4, 13–14, ii. 2, 7, 16–17, iii. 1, 4–7, viii. 19–24, ix. 1–4. The Massoretic order of the books is followed, and the Divine Name is written by both scribes in the old Hebrew script (as also in the fragments of Kingdoms from the Cairo Geniza in Aquila's version (see above, p. 20) and also in some of the Hebrew texts from Qumran). The MS is dated by Schubart just before or after the beginning of the Christian era, by C. H. Roberts within the period 50 B.C.–A.D. 50, and by D. Barthélemy about the middle of the first century A.D. The text has now been edited by Barthélemy (*Les Devanciers d'Aquila*, Leiden, 1963) with a copious introduction, the scope of

D

which is indicated on the title-page: 'une étude sur les traductions et recensions grecques de la Bible réalisées au premier siècle de notre ère sous l'influence du rabbinat Palestinien'.

On the basis of characteristic renderings of Hebrew words and expressions—notably of *gam* by καίγε—Barthélemy sees the *Dodekapropheton* (which he designates R) as a recension of the older Greek text, the work of Palestinian scholars of the first century A.D. whose aim was to bring the LXX into closer conformity with the current form of the Hebrew text. To this school Barthélemy assigns Theodotion (see above, p. 20), whom he also identifies with Jonathan ben 'Uzziel. This process of revision was continued under the influence of the rabbis of Palestine and reached its final form in the work of Aquila, who knew and used R, as also did Symmachus. In the Hexapla of the Minor Prophets Origen has placed R in the Quinta column, the sixth (Theodotion) column having a later eclectic text. Looking beyond the Minor Prophets, Barthélemy finds the καίγε recension in Lamentations (probably Ruth and Canticles), 2 Kingd. xi. 2— 3 Kingd. ii. 11, 3 Kingd. xxii. 1—4 Kingd. end, the B- recension of Judges, Daniel in Theodotion's recension, the Theodotion additions to Job and Jeremiah, the Theodotion column of the Hexapla, the Quinta column of the Psalms.[1]

Whether Barthélemy is justified in assigning the recension to Palestine may be questioned. He himself observes that R is the only Greek text which supports the Hebraisms of the Washington Papyrus of the Minor Prophets (W above) and of the Coptic versions, which would suggest an Egyptian provenance. But Barthélemy has made a persuasive case for the history of the LXX as a continuous recensional process, in which, under rabbinical influence, the Greek was being brought into conformity with the Hebrew text-tradition (itself not free from change). In the process R (and the καίγε recension generally) and Aquila are clearly defined stages. Further, Barthélemy's καίγε—Theodotion, if

---

[1] Cf. H. St John Thackeray, *Grammar of the Old Testament in Greek* (Cambridge, 1901), p. 9: 'At the other extreme [from the Pentateuch] stands a group, consisting mainly of some of the later historical books (Jd. + Ruth [B text], 2 K. xi. 2—3 K. ii. 11, 3 K. xxii. 1—4 K. end, 2 Es.: the Psalter has some affinity with it), in which we see the beginnings of the tendency towards pedantic literalism which ended in the second century A.D. in the barbarous "version" of Aquila'; *ibid.*, p. 10, Thackeray notes that the Kingdoms sections above 'have much in common with Theodotion'.

accepted, provides a solution to the problem of the 'Theodo-tionisms' of the New Testament, Justin Martyr, Hermas, etc.

II. UNCIALS

The four great codices ℵ A B C, which contain both Testaments, are more fully described in the New Testament list.

ℵ or S: *Codex Sinaiticus*, fourth century. See p. 78. The Old Testament portion consists of 43 leaves at Leipzig, fragments of 3 at Leningrad, and 199 in the British Museum. Originally it was a magnificent copy of the entire Greek Bible, written in a beautiful hand on about 720 leaves of fine vellum, measuring 15 by $13\frac{1}{2}$ inches, with four columns to the page (two in the poetical books); but the Old Testament portion had suffered severely during its residence at Sinai, and not much more than one-third of it has survived. The extant portions are Gen. xxiii. 19—xxiv. 14, 17–19, 25–27, 30–33, 36–46 (all with mutilations), Num. v. 26–30, vi. 5, 6, 11, 12, 17, 18, 22, 23, vii. 4, 5, 12, 13, 15–20, 1 Chron. ix. 27—xix. 17, 2 Esdras ix. 9—end, Esther, Tobit, Judith, 1 and 4 Maccabees, Isaiah, Jeremiah, Lamentations i. 1—ii. 20, Joel, Obadiah, Jonah, Nahum, Habakkuk, Zephaniah, Haggai, Zechariah, Malachi, Psalms, Proverbs, Ecclesiastes, Song of Solomon, Wisdom, Ecclesiasticus, Job.

According to both Tischendorf, who discovered and first edited the MS, and Lake, who edited a complete facsimile from his own photographs (*Codex Sinaiticus: the Old Testament in Facsimile*, H. and K. Lake, Oxford, 1922), four scribes were employed on it, but according to H. J. M. Milne and T. C. Skeat (*Scribes and Correctors of the Codex Sinaiticus*, London, 1938, pp. 22 ff.), there were only three. Several correctors have also been at work on it, some contemporary (or identical) with the original scribes (ℵᵃ), and others later. By far the most important of the corrections are those made by a group of scholars (denoted by the symbol ℵ ᶜ·ᵃ or ℵᶜ·ᵇ—the latter representing at least three scribes), and one belonging to the Leipzig section (denominated ℵᶜ·ᴾᵃᵐᵖʰ by Kirsopp Lake), who wrote notes at the end of Esdras and Esther, stating that the MS was collated with an exceedingly early copy corrected by the hand of the martyr Pamphilus, with an autograph note by him saying that he corrected it in prison from Origen's own copy of the Hexapla. This note is probably of the sixth or early seventh century, and makes it extremely probable that the MS was then at Cæsarea, where the library of Pamphilus was, and also that the corrections in these hands were taken from a very early MS which itself was only by one step removed from Origen. This gives exceptional value to this group of corrections. In general ℵ has the same type of text as B, but according to Ropes it is superior in the Prophets and in Chronicles and 2 Esdras. In Tobit it has a different recension.

A. *Codex Alexandrinus*, fifth century. See p. 83. The Old Testament portion occupies 630 leaves, measuring 12⅝ by 10⅜ inches, written with two columns to the page. Ten leaves have been lost, containing 1 Sam. xii. 18—xiv. 9, Psa. xlix (l). 20—lxxix (lxxx). 11. In Gen. xiv. 14–17, xv. 1–5, 16–19, xvi. 6–9 are lost by mutilation. Otherwise the whole Old Testament is present, together with 3 and 4 Maccabees, while a table of contents shows that the Psalms of Solomon were originally appended at the end of the whole MS. Two scribes were employed on it, of whom one wrote the Octateuch, Prophets, Maccabees, and the poetical books Job, Proverbs, Ecclesiastes, Song of Solomon, Wisdom and Ecclesiasticus, while the other wrote the historical books from 1 Kingdoms [=1 Samuel] to the end of Chronicles, Esther, Tobit, Judith, 1 and 2 Esdras, and Psalms. The MS has been extensively corrected, especially in the Pentateuch, often by the original scribes, but oftener by a corrector (Aª) who seems to be about contemporary.

In addition to Psa. cli (based mainly on 1 Kingd. xvi, xvii, and included as part of the Psalter proper in ℵ) *Alexandrinus* contains the liturgical Canticles or Odes (passages from the Old and New Testaments including the *Magnificat, Nunc Dimittis* and *Benedictus,* sung at the monastic offices), which are also found in R, T, and many cursives. The text of this MS, which is far from being homogeneous, presents a number of problems still to be fully accounted for. Frequently it appears to be based on a text of considerable antiquity, pre-hexaplaric and perhaps pre-Christian, of early Alexandrian origin. Thus its text in Deuteronomy has close affinities with that found in the oldest Greek biblical MS, the Rylands fragment of the second century B.C. (**957** above), and with Chester Beatty VI (**963**) of the second century A.D. But in the different parts of the Old Testament it shows varying degrees of admixture from quite diverse sources—e.g. in Joshua, Ruth and

Esther there is unsystematic Hexaplaric intrusion, while in 1–4 Kingdoms the text is, in Burkitt's words, 'little more than a transcript of the fifth column of the Hexapla'. 1–2 Chronicles and 1–2 Esdras, again, have an early pre-Hexaplaric Alexandrian text, while Job and Psalms have varying degrees of Lucianic admixture, as have also to some extent the prophetic books, though in the latter Ziegler places A at the head of the Alexandrian group.

Reduced collotype facsimile published by the British Museum: *The Codex Alexandrinus*, I. Genesis–Ruth (1915); II. 1 Samuel to 2 Chronicles (1930); III. Hosea–Judith (1936); IV. 1 Esdras–Ecclesiasticus (1957).

B. *Codex Vaticanus*, fourth century. See p. 85. The Old Testament portion occupies 617 leaves, measuring 10½ by 10 inches, written with three columns to the page. Thirty-one leaves are lost from the beginning, containing Gen. i. 1—xlvi. 28, and ten leaves from the Psalter, containing Psa. cv (cvi). 27—cxxxvii (cxxxviii). 6; while 2 Kingd. [2 Sam.] ii. 5–7, 10–13 are lost by mutilation. The books of Maccabees were never included in it; otherwise all books are present. The poetical books precede the prophets, as in the list given by Athanasius in his *Festal Letter*, whose order corresponds exactly with B, whereas in א and A they are at the end of the Old Testament. The hand is smaller than in א and A, but is graceful in formation. There are corrections by various hands, those indicated as B² being the best. B is generally regarded as having the best text of any single MS of the LXX, and has therefore been made the basis of the two Cambridge editions. This is perhaps partly due to its pre-eminence in the New Testament, and it must be recognized that in the Old Testament it is often found in opposition to the other earliest uncials, and the question of superiority must be regarded as still uncertain. It also seems clear that its character is not uniform throughout; as is only natural, since it must have descended from a number of different rolls, which might well be of different characters. Burkitt observes that it has a good text in Ezekiel, but a bad one in Isaiah, where it belongs to the Hexaplaric recension; and this is confirmed by the papyri. In Judges it has a text differing substantially from that of A and the majority of authorities,[1] but found in the

---

[1] Both texts are printed in full in Rahlfs' edition of the LXX. In the Cambridge editions B is printed, with the variants of A in the apparatus. According to G. F. Moore (in his edition of Judges) the B text is the later.

Sahidic version and in Cyril of Alexandria. In Job it has the additional 400 half-verses from Theodotion, which are not in the Old Latin and Sahidic versions; i.e. it is post-Hexaplaric. The early papyri support B rather than A in Numbers, Ezekiel, Esther, and Ecclesiasticus, but A rather than B in Deuteronomy and Isaiah. According to Ropes B is distinctly inferior to A also in Chronicles and 1 and 2 Esdras. He considers that in Joshua, Ruth, 1–4 Kingdoms, Chronicles, 1 and 2 Esdras, Psalms, Ezekiel, Esther its text is pre-Hexaplar, but in Isaiah, Jeremiah, the Minor Prophets and Job it is Hexaplar; and Rahlfs agrees in respect of the Psalter, but not in the case of Ruth, which he thinks is pre-Hexaplaric. Ziegler groups B with א, Coptic and Old Latin in Jeremiah and Ezekiel as neither Alexandrian nor Hexaplaric, and in the Minor Prophets with the Washington papyrus W, א and V as a distinct uncial group. In contrast to A, B is almost entirely devoid of Lucianic readings.

C. *Codex Ephraemi*, fifth century. See p. 88. Portions of a fine MS of the whole Bible which in the twelfth century was converted into a palimpsest, the original writing being sponged away and some works of Ephraim Syrus written over it. A large part of the MS has disappeared altogether, and the original writing of what is left cannot always be discerned. Of the Old Testament only 64 leaves remain, containing portions of the poetical books, viz. Prov. i. 2—ii. 8, xv. 29—xvii. 1, xviii. 11—xix. 23, xxii. 17—xxiii. 25, xxiv. 22–56, xxvi. 23—xxviii. 2, xxix. 48—end; Eccles. i. 2–14, ii. 18—end. Cant. i. 3—iii. 9; Job ii. 12—iv. 12, v. 27—vii. 7, x. 9—xii. 2, xiii. 18—xviii. 9, xix. 27—xxii. 14, xxiv. 7—xxx. 1, xxxi. 6—xxxv. 15, xxxvii. 5—xxxviii. 17, xl. 20—end; Wisd. of Sol. viii. 5—xii. 10, xiv. 19—xvii. 18, xviii. 24—end; Ecclus. prol. 1—vii. 14, viii. 15—xi. 17, xii. 16—xvi. 1, xvii. 12—xx. 5, xxi. 12—xxii. 19, xxvii. 19—xxviii. 25, xxx. 8—xxxiv. 22[1], xxx, 25— xxxi. 5, xxxii. 22—xxxiii. 13, xxxvii. 11—xxxviii. 15, xxxix. 7— xliii. 27, xlv. 24—xlvii. 23, xlviii. 11—xlix. 12. It is written with a single column to the page, which is unusual in uncials.

D. *Cotton Genesis*, in the British Museum, fifth century. Written in a fine hand, with 250 illustrations, but hopelessly ruined by fire in 1731. Fortunately it had previously been collated

---

[1] In all Greek MSS xxx. 25—xxxiii 16[a] is transposed to follow xxxiii, 16[b]— xxxvi, 10.

by Grabe, and for most of its readings it is necessary to depend on his evidence.

E. *Bodleian Genesis*, at Oxford, ninth–tenth century. Part of a MS, other parts of which are at Cambridge, the British Museum, and Leningrad. The Oxford portion is written in uncials, as is the first side of the leaf at Cambridge, the rest (British Museum and Leningrad) in minuscules, as apparently was the MS from which the whole was copied. It is therefore best regarded, with Rahlfs, as a minuscule, by whom it is numbered 509 (see below).

F. *Codex Ambrosianus*, at Milan, fifth century. Fragments of the Hexateuch, written (like B) with three columns to the page. Contains Gen. xxxi. 15–37, xlii. 14–21, 28—xlvi. 6, xlvii. 16—xlviii. 3, 21—l. 14; Exod. i. 10—viii. 19, xii. 31—xxx. 29, xxxi. 18—xxxii. 6, 13—xxxvi. 3, xxxvii. 10—end; Lev. i. 1—ix. 18, x. 14—end; Num. complete; Deut. i. 1—xxviii. 63, xxix. 14—end; Joshua i. 1—ii. 9, 15—iv. 5, 10—v. 1, 7—vi. 23, vii. 1—ix. 33, x. 37—xii. 12. Many various readings and notes in the margins.

The MS is unique for its period in having, besides varied punctuations, breathings and accents by the original scribe. In addition the wide margins contain numerous notes and varied readings, many of them Hexaplaric. According to Swete, F is in frequent agreement with A against B, especially in Exodus, but not in Leviticus, where it tends to support B against A.

G. *Codex Sarravianus*, mainly at Leiden (130 leaves), but 22 leaves in Paris and one in Leningrad, fifth century. It contains (in its present state) portions of the Heptateuch, viz. Gen. xxxi. 54—xxxvi. 18; Exod. xxxvi. 35—xxxvii. 21, xxxviii. 24—xxxix. 21, xxxix. 37—end; Lev. i. 1—xiii. 17, 49—xiv. 6, 33-49, xv. 24—xvii. 10, xviii. 28—xix. 36, xxiv. 9—xxvii. 16; Num. i. 1—vii. 85, xi. 18—xviii. 2, 30—xx. 22, xxv. 2—xxvi. 3, xxix. 12—end; Deut. iv. 11-26, vii. 13—xvii. 14, xviii. 8—xix. 4, xxviii. 12—xxxi. 11; Joshua ix. 33—xix. 23; Judges ix. 48—x. 6, xv. 3—xviii. 16, xix. 25—xxi. 12. The special importance of this MS lies in the fact that it is a Hexaplar MS having the critical marks of Origen, but unfortunately not completely. It is thus of much value as a guide to the pre-Hexaplar text on which Origen worked.

H. (Rahlfs 624.) *Codex Petropolitanus*, at Leningrad. A palimpsest of which the underlying sixth century text contains a little more than half of Numbers in 22 portions. Frequently supports A and F against B.

I. (H—P, Rahlfs 13.) *Codex Bodleianus* of the Psalms and Odes, with commentary and a catena. Ninth or tenth century. Valuable because in the margin many readings are given from Aquila, Theodotion and Symmachus, and from the Quinta and Septima versions used by Origen.

K. *Codex Lipsiensis* (*Fragmenta Lipsiensia*), 22 leaves (17 of them Greek-Arabic palimpsest) in the University Library at Leipzig, containing fragments of Numbers, Deuteronomy, Joshua and Judges in a seventh century hand. A further six leaves from the same MS and with fragments of the same books are at Leningrad.

L. *Vienna Genesis*, fifth or sixth century. Written on purple vellum, with illustrations in classical style, like those of D. Twenty-four leaves of Genesis, containing Gen. iii. 4–24, vii. 19— viii. 1, 4, 13–17, 19, 20, ix. 8–10, 12–15, 20–27, xiv. 17–20, xv. 1–5, xix. 12–17, 24, 26, 29–35, xxii. 15–19, xxiv. 1–4, 9–11, 15–20, 22–25, 28, 29, 31, xxv. 27–34, xxvi. 6–11, xxx. 30–37, xxxi. 25–34, xxxii. 6–8, 13–18, 22–32, xxxv. 1–4, 8, 16–20, 28, 29, xxxvii. 1–19, xxxix. 9–18, xl. 14—xli. 2, 21–32, xlii. 21–25, 27—xliii. 22, xlviii. 16—xlix. 3, 28—l. 4.

M. *Codex Coislinianus*, at Paris, seventh century. 227 leaves, containing Gen. i. 1—xxxiv. 2, xxxviii. 24—Num. xxix. 23, xxxi. 4—Joshua x. 6, xxii. 34—Ruth iv. 19, 1 Kingd. i. 1—iv. 19, x. 19—xiv. 26, xxv. 33—3 Kingd. viii. 40. Has Hexaplaric signs in the margin and belongs to the same class as G.

N—V (H—P. XI, 23). *Codex Basiliano Vaticanus*, *Codex Venetus*. The remains, bound in two volumes, of what was originally a single MS of the complete Old Testament, of the eighth or ninth century. The first volume (N) is in the Vatican Library, the second (V) in the St Mark's Library at Venice. Formerly regarded as two distinct MSS and so enumerated separately as N and V (but V was numbered 23 by Holmes and Parsons as though a cursive). Rahlfs designates as V throughout. The Vatican codex (132 leaves) contains Lev. xiii. 59—end of Chronicles (with some *lacunae*), 1 Esdras i. 1—ix. 1, 2 Esdras v. 10—xvii. 3, Esther; the Venice codex (164 leaves) has Job xxx. 8—end, Proverbs, Ecclesiastes, Song of Solomon, Wisdom, Ecclesiasticus, Prophets, Tobit, Judith, 1–4 Maccabees. V most probably supplied the basis for the text of 1–4 Maccabees (lacking in B) for the Sixtine edition of 1587. The text is frequently described as Lucianic, but is far from uniform. In the Göttingen Septuagint N—V is grouped as Lucianic in Ezekiel, and as containing Lucianic and Hexaplaric readings in the Minor Prophets, as Hexaplaric in Isaiah (with B), Susanna, Daniel, Wisdom, Ecclesiasticus, and close to Q in Jeremiah and A in Maccabees.

O. (H—P. VIII, Rahlfs **918**.) *Codex Dublinensis Rescriptus* (*Fragmenta Dublinensia*), at Trinity College, Dublin. Early sixth century in an Egyptian land: eight palimpsest leaves containing Isa. xxx. 2—xxxi. 7, xxxvi. 17—xxxviii. 1. Has been regarded as Hesychian in text, but is grouped by Ziegler with mixed authorities.

Q. (H—P. XII.) *Codex Marchalianus*, in the Vatican Library, sixth century. A very handsome MS of the Prophets, written in Egypt. Ceriani believed that the text is that of Hesychius' edition, but Ziegler regards it as Alexandrian in Isaiah, Daniel (though with some Symmachus readings) and the Minor Prophets, Hexaplaric in Ezekiel, and at the head of a group with V **26** and other minuscules in Jeremiah. An almost contemporary scribe has added both in the text and in the margins a great number of critical signs indicating the modifications made by Origen, together with many readings from Aquila, Symmachus, and Theodotion, as well as from Origen's own text. It is therefore a principal authority for the text of the Hexapla in the Prophets.

R. *Codex Veronensis*, at Verona, sixth century. A Graeco-latin MS of the Psalter and Canticles, the Greek text being written in Roman characters. In Rahlfs' classification it represents the Western text of the Psalter, found also in the Old Latin. R, together with the Graeco-latin uncial **156**, provides the only Greek MS authority for the reading of Psalm xcv (xcvi). 10 attested by Justin Martyr. (Apol. i. 4, *Dialogue with Trypho* c. 73) ὁ κύριος ἐβασίλευσεν ἀπὸ τοῦ ξύλου (R reads *apo xylu*, 156 ἀπὸ τῷ ξύλῳ). The reading *dominus regnauit a ligno* is widespread in the Old Latin (which may well be the source of the addition) and Latin Fathers, and occurs also in the Sahidic.

S. = ℵ, *Codex Sinaiticus*—see above, pp. 41–2.

T. (H—P. 262.) *Codex Turicensis*, at Zurich, seventh century. Contains the Psalter and Canticles, but Psalms i–xxv are lost, as also xxx. 2—xxxvi. 20, xli. 6—xliii. 3, lviii. 14—lix. 5, lix. 9, 10, 13—lx. 1, lxiv. 12—lxxxi. 4, xcii. 3—xciii. 7, xcvi. 12—

xcvii. 8, and the first five Canticles and part of the sixth. The text is in silver letters with gold headings, and with readings of Jerome's Gallican version in red in the margins, and was intended for Western liturgical use. Placed by Rahlfs in the Lucianic group along with ℵ$^{c.a}$, and B^c and R^c.

U. See under Papyri, above p. 32.

V. Codex Venetus. See N—V above.

W. (H—P., Rahlfs **43**.) *Codex Parisiensis*; in the Bibliothèque Nationale, Paris. Ninth or tenth century MS of 40 leaves containing Psa. xci. 14—cxxxvi. 1 with some gaps.

W = The Washington papyrus of the Minor Prophets (see p. 32 above).

W = Washington Codex I of Deuteronomy and Joshua; listed below as Θ.

X. (H—P., Rahlfs **258**.) *Codex Vaticanus Iobi*, in the Vatican Library, containing most of Job in a ninth century hand. Contains Hexaplaric material used by Field.

Y. (Rahlfs **719**.) *Codex Taurinensis*, at Turin. Contains the Minor Prophets in a ninth or tenth century hand. Ziegler placed it in the Lucianic group, and closest to the minuscule **48**. See on **36** in the minuscule list below.

Γ. (Rahlfs **393**.) *Codex Cryptoferratensis*, at Grotta Ferrata, eighth century. Palimpsest fragments of the Prophets, but so much has been obliterated that it is very incomplete. A further four leaves from the same MS, but not palimpsest, containing Zach. iv. 9—viii. 16 are in the Vatican Library. Ziegler places the text among the Alexandrian group in Isaiah, and as a secondary witness to the same group in Minor Prophets.

Δ. (Rahlfs **921**.) *Fragmentum Bodleianum*. Fifth or possibly fourth century text of Bel and the Dragon vv. 20—41 in the version of Theodotion, in the Bodleian Library, Oxford.

Θ. *Codex Washingtonianus I* (Rahlfs, W.) in the Freer Library in Washington, sixth century. A codex of Deuteronomy and Joshua, but originally (as the quire-numeration shows) containing the previous books of the Hexateuch, while Judges and Ruth may have been added at the end. Two double leaves are missing, containing Deut. v. 16—vi. 18, Joshua iii. 3—iv. 10. In Deuteronomy its text agrees more with A than with B, but its closest association seems to be with the minuscules **54** and **75**, and often with G and the Chester Beatty papyrus **963**. It is probable therefore that it is to be assigned to the Origenian group. In Joshua the grouping is different; for though Θ still agrees with A more than with B, it parts company with **54** and **75**.

The text was edited by H. A. Sanders, *The Old Testament MSS in the Freer Collection i: i. The Washington MS of Deuteronomy and Joshua* (New York, 1910).

156. (H—P., Rahlfs.) Psalter at Basle, written in the ninth century probably at the Abbey of St Gall. Contains Psa. i—cxlvi. 2 with an interlinear Vulgate text. Classed as Western. See R above.

188. (H—P., Rahlfs.) In the Bibliothèque Nationale. Seventh century bilingual Greek—Latin Psalter now reduced to 89 leaves containing Psa. xviii. 14—lxxii. 10 with gaps. Belongs to the same text group as **156**.

1219. (Rahlfs.) *Codex Washingtonianus II* in the Freer Gallery at Washington, assigned by its editor to the fifth century, but others date it in the sixth or seventh. A much mutilated MS of the Psalms, of which 107 fragmentary leaves are preserved, extending from Psa. i. 1—cxlii. 8, but very incomplete, especially in the earlier psalms. The final quire must have been lost quite early and has been replaced by a quire from another MS probably of the eighth century, containing cxlii. 5—cli. 6. According to Rahlfs, its text is akin to A, forming with it and minuscule **55** a group which is distinct both from the lower Egyptian group (B ℵ Bohairic) and the Upper Egyptian group (U **2013** Sahidic), and also from groups which he classifies as Western, Origenian, and Lucianic. Edited by H. A. Sanders, *The Old Testament Manuscripts in the Freer Collection*, ii: *the Washington Manuscript of the Psalms* (New York, 1917).

III. MINUSCULES

The first list of minuscule MSS was compiled by Holmes and Parsons (see p. 30), who, after beginning with thirteen roman numerals for uncial MSS, continued with arabic numerals from 14 to 311 (with two numbers duplicated) for the minuscules (of which nine, wholly or in part, were actually uncials). This list has been extended by Rahlfs (*Verzeichnis der Griechischen Handschriften des Alten Testaments*, Berlin, 1914) in which the figures run beyond two thousand, with, however, gaps deliberately left which are being filled as fresh MSS and papyri come to light. Very few MSS contain the whole Old Testament, most having particular divisions of it. Brook and McLean have made selections from these, and used them for the apparatus of their large Cambridge edition, as also have Rahlfs and his followers on the Göttingen Septuagint (see p. 26), by whom they are grouped as Alexandrian, Hexaplaric, Lucianic, etc. It is on their grouping that their value principally depends, for only by clarifying and distinguishing the main lines of tradition can some sort of order be imposed on the enormous mass of evidence and an improved text arrived at. This investigation is by no means complete, and the attributions of the earlier editors should be treated with caution.[1] A type of MS included in the catalogue is known as the Catena, which consists of a biblical text strung together with exegetical extracts from the Fathers. This late type of text is found in other MSS from which the patristic passages have been omitted. In addition there are lectionaries, compiled for liturgical use. Commentaries are perhaps best regarded as belonging to patristic evidence; they may be valuable, but must be used with care, since the text of the *lemmata* at the head of each section may have been assimilated to a different (e.g. later) form of the text than that used by the author, and must be carefully checked with the readings contained in the exegetical comments.

Among the more important minuscules are the following:

13 = I in Uncial list above.

15. (B—M. a.) At Paris, Bibliothèque Nationale. Ninth to tenth century. Contains Octateuch; according to Rahlfs its text in Genesis belongs to Origen's Hexaplaric recension, where it is grouped with G **58, 72, 135** and others. According to A. V. Billen (*Journal of Theological Studies*, xxvi (1925), pp. 262–77) it is Hexaplaric, or mainly so, in the other books.

19. (B—M. b.) In the Vatican Library, Rome, twelfth century. Contains Octateuch, 1–4 Kingdoms, 1–2 Chronicles, 1 and 2 Esdras, Judith, Esther, 1–3 Maccabees. Regarded as Lucianic throughout by Lagarde, but this is only so from Ruth iv. 11

[1] Lagarde, e.g. in editing the Lucianic text, used 19, 82, 93 and 108. E. Hautsch (in *Mitteilungen des Septuaginta—Unternehmens, Göttingen,* 1909) questioned this in the Hexateuch, since the readings in the Antiochian Fathers do not usually agree with those of 19 and 108, and Rahlfs (*Septuagintastudien,* 1911) showed that these were Lucianic only from Ruth iv. 11 onwards.

onwards. Rahlfs places it in Genesis with **108** (to which it is closely akin) as a distinct group.

22. In the British Museum, eleventh to twelfth century. Contains the prophetical books in a Lucianic text. Closely related are **36, 48, 231** (tenth to eleventh century) at the Vatican, and **51** (eleventh century) at Florence.

26. Vatican Library, tenth century. Contains the Prophetic books in an Alexandrian text. Others in the group are **86, 106**.

36. Vatican Library, eleventh century. Contains the prophetic books in a Lucianic text. See above on **22**.

44. (B—M. d.) At Zittau in East Germany. Fifteenth century. Contains Octateuch, 1 Kingdom, 2 Esdras, 1–4 Maccabees, Esther, Judith. The text is classed by Billen as Hesychian in the Hexateuch, by Rahlfs as Lucianic in Genesis.

54. (B—M. g.) Bibliothèque Nationale, Paris. Contains the Octateuch in a Lucianic text, though Rahlfs notes that in Genesis it belongs to the Catena group after xxii. 21.

62. New College, Oxford. Eleventh century. Contains the prophetic books: Isaiah, Jeremiah, and Minor Prophets in a Lucianic type of text, Ezekiel and David are Hexaplaric; 1–4 Maccabees are Lucianic.

72. (B—M. m.) Oxford, Bodleian Library, thirteenth century. Contains Octateuch. Rahlfs classes Genesis as Hexaplaric.

75. (B—M. n.) Oxford, University College. Dated 1125. Contains Octateuch in a Lucianic text, akin to **54** above.

82. (B—M. o.) Paris, Bibliothèque Nationale. Twelfth century. Contains Octateuch, 1–4 Kingdoms. One of Lagarde's mainstays for the Lucianic text—as it is in the historical books. But Rahlfs classes Genesis as Hexaplaric.

85. (B—M. z.) Vatican Library. Tenth century. Contains Octateuch, defective at beginning and end. Has many Hexaplaric readings in the margins.

87. Chigi Library at the Vatican. Tenth century. Contains a Catena text of the Prophets.

88. Chigi Library at the Vatican. Tenth century. Contains Jeremiah, Daniel in the original LXX version (of which this is the only complete Greek MS) followed by Theodotion's version, Ezekiel and Isaiah in that order. The text is Hexaplaric apart from Daniel, which is Lucianic.

91. Vatican Library. Eleventh century. Catena of the Prophets.

With **87, 490, 567** it is among the principal representatives of this type of text.

93. (B—M. e₂.) British Museum. Thirteenth century. Contains Ruth, 1-2 Kingdoms, 1-2 Chronicles, 2 Esdras (=canonical Ezra-Nehemiah), Esther (Lucianic text), 1-3 Maccabees, Esther (normal text), Isaiah; but the quire numeration shows that it formerly contained the whole of the Octateuch, and it may have contained the remaining prophets. It is mostly written with two columns, but four quires have three columns to the page, an old-fashioned arrangement which suggests that it may have been copied from an early uncial archetype. The text is in the main Lucianic.

106. (B—M. p.) Ferrara. Fourteenth century, in two volumes, written on paper, containing the complete Old Testament (a third volume contains the New Testament). The Octateuch is Lucianic, the Prophets have a good Alexandrian text.

108. Vatican Library. Thirteenth century on paper. Contains Octateuch, 1-4 Kingdoms, 1-2 Chronicles, 1-2 Esdras, Judith, Esther (in Lucianic and usual text), Tobit. Has Hexaplaric notes in the margins. This was one of the principal MSS used for the Complutensian Polyglot (see below). Used by Lagarde for his edition of the Lucianic text with **19** (see above).

135. (B-M. c₂.) At Basle. Tenth century (Rahlfs), eleventh century (Brooke—McLean). Contains Genesis, Exodus to xv. 1. One of the principal witnesses to Origen's recension in Rahlfs' edition of Genesis.

198. Bibliothèque Nationale, Paris. Ninth century. Contains Minor Prophets, Isaiah, Jeremiah and Ezekiel, with considerable gaps. The text is Alexandrian, except in Jeremiah where it is placed by Ziegler in a sub-group of the Lucianic recension. This MS also contains the New Testament in a very good text (**33** in N.T. list).

248. (B—M. w.) Vatican Library. Thirteenth century. Contains Proverbs, Ecclesiastes, Song of Solomon, Job, Wisdom, Ecclesiasticus, 1-2 Esdras, Esther, Tobit, Judith. Together with **108** was sent to Cardinal Ximenes and was one of the principal MSS for the Complutensian Polyglot. The text is classed by Ziegler in Wisdom and Ecclesiasticus as Lucianic.

509. (E Swete—see above, B—M. a₂.) Ninth to tenth century. MS divided between the Bodleian Library (29 leaves), Leningrad

(146 leaves), Cambridge (1 leaf), and the British Museum (16 leaves). The Bodleian and British Museum portions were brought to England in 1853 by Tischendorf, who published the Bodleian text in 1857. In 1859, as the fruits of a further visit to the East, the Leningrad portion, along with Codex Sinaiticus and other MSS, was presented by Tischendorf to Czar Alexander II. The Cambridge leaf remained in his possession until his death, when it was bought by the University Library. The Bodleian leaves containing Genesis, and written in a rough, sloping uncial, have been somewhat seriously mutilated, lacking xiv. 7—xviii. 24 and xx. 14—xxiv. 54 and ending at xlii. 18. In 1891 Swete and Redpath recognized that the Cambridge leaf (containing Gen. xlii. 18—xliii. 13) belongs to the same MS. Moreover, of this leaf the first page is written in uncials and the second in minuscules. Then in 1898 Rahlfs showed that the minuscule portion at Leningrad (which carries on the text from Gen. xliii. 13 of the Cambridge leaf to 3 Kingd. xvi. 28, with some gaps), and that in the British Museum (Joshua xxiv. 27—end of Ruth) also originally formed part of the same MS as the Bodleian Genesis and the Cambridge leaf. The evidence suggests that the copyists had a minuscule MS before them. Rahlfs leaves the MS unclassified in his editions of Genesis and Ruth; according to Billen it is close to B in Numbers and Deuteronomy, and to A in Joshua.

719. (Y Swete.) *Codex Taurinensis*, at Turin. Ninth to tenth century. Contains Minor Prophets with many lacunae. Placed by Ziegler in the main Lucianic group.

This list is very imperfect. Many of the minuscules, especially those more recently added to the list, have not been fully examined, and less work has been done on the historical and poetical books than on the Octateuch and the Prophets. But the majority of the minuscules contain mixed texts, and are not of much use in arriving at the original form of the several editions, still less of the primaeval Septuagint.

TRANSLATIONS OF THE SEPTUAGINT

Besides the Greek MSS and quotations in the early Fathers, valuable evidence can be derived from the early translations that were made not from the Hebrew but from the Septuagint. These include the Old Latin, Coptic, and (in part) the Syriac versions.

The importance of a translation is that it (so to say) encapsulates the type of text of which it is a translation; for although it is itself subject to transmissional hazards and degeneration, these will affect it in a different way from that in which the parent text is subsequently affected. It is therefore often possible to recover from early translations an early form of the original text which antedates most existing MSS of it.

The Old Latin Version. Until towards the end of the second century the Church of Rome seems to have been predominantly Greek-speaking, and the earliest evidence for a Latin Bible comes from the Roman provinces of Africa and Gaul. Tertullian (*c.* 160–230) certainly used a Latin translation, but Cyprian, Bishop of Carthage (died 258), who quotes copiously and consistently from all parts of the Bible, provides the firmest basis for the investigation of the pre-Vulgate text. The origins of the Latin version were probably similar to those of the LXX, beginning as an oral translation and then taking written form, and gradually extending to the whole Bible. But whether the version had its original home in Africa and spread from there to the northern shores of the Mediterranean, or whether we have to do with a number of independent translations, is still not decided by scholars. St Augustine, writing in the latter part of the fourth century, seems to take the latter view—there were, he says, 'latina interpretum infinita varietas' (*De Doctrina Christiana* II. 16). But this state of affairs may have been due to a process of constant revision from the Greek in what at first was a 'vulgar' text, in the same way that the LXX was subject to revision from the Hebrew. It is usual to distinguish an African and a European form of the text, but these are not mutually exclusive, as the Spanish Bible has much in common with that of North Africa.

The Old Latin was so entirely superseded by Jerome's Vulgate that it has not come down to us complete, and can only be recovered from imperfect MSS and quotations in the early Latin fathers, especially Cyprian. So far as these go, they give us a pre-Hexaplar text. The apocryphal books have fared better than the canonical, since (except Tobit and Judith) they were not revised or re-translated by Jerome, but were incorporated direct in the later Latin Bible. Of the other books, only Numbers (with most of Leviticus), Deuteronomy, Joshua, Judges, Ruth, 1 Esdras

(=Vulgate 3 Esdras), Esther, Judith, Tobit, 1 and 2 Maccabees, Baruch and the Psalms have come down complete. The largest single MS is the Codex Lugdunensis, of the fifth century, which contains portions of Genesis, Exodus and Leviticus, and the whole of Numbers–Judges.

The extant material, both manuscript and patristic, was assembled by the learned Benedictine Pierre Sabatier in his *Bibliorum sacrorum latinae versiones antiquae* in three folio volumes (Rheims, 1743–9; Paris, 1751). Much additional evidence has become available, as well as better editions of the Fathers, and a new edition has been undertaken by the Benedictine community at Beuron: *Vetus Latina. Die Reste der altlateinischen Bibel nach Petrus Sabatier*, etc. So far vol. I (*Verzeichnis der Sigel*, 1949) and Genesis (completed 1954) have appeared.

The Vulgate. When Jerome was invited in 382 by Pope Damasus, in view of the great diversities of text then in existence, to prepare a revised text of the Latin Bible, he began with the New Testament, which was completed by about 391. Proceeding to the Old Testament, he first made a very slight revision of the Old Latin Psalter, with reference only to the LXX; this version is still in use at St Peter's, and is known as The *Roman* Psalter.[1] Next, after his removal to Bethlehem, he made (between 387 and 390) a more thorough revision, still only from the LXX, but using Origen's Hexaplaric text (and incorporating his critical symbols), which is generally in use in the Roman Church (just as in our English Prayer Book we still use the Psalter from the Great Bible of Coverdale, rather than the improved translation of the Authorized Version). Finally, after producing a version of Job from the Hexaplaric text (and probably also of Proverbs, Ecclesiastes, Song of Songs and Chronicles—the Prefaces to these books survive, but not the text), and having by this time satisfied himself of the superiority of the Massoretic Hebrew over the Greek, he abandoned the idea of revising the Old Latin from the Septuagint, and undertook a fresh translation of the whole (including the Psalter, which in this form is known as the *Hebrew* Psalter) from the Hebrew. With this, as it has no bearing on the text of the LXX, we are not concerned.

---

[1] This, the traditional view, has been challenged by R. de Bruyne (*Revue Bénédictine*, xlii (1930), pp. 447–82), who argues that Jerome's first revision is now lost, and that the *Psalterium Romanum* was later wrongly attributed to him.

E

Coptic. Coptic is the language of the native Egyptians, but is written in characters derived from the Greek alphabet with the addition of six others. The earliest Egyptian version is that produced in the Sahidic dialect of Upper (i.e., southern) Egypt, and if, as some have thought, it was made before the end of the second century A.D. it would be from pre-Hexaplaric Greek MSS. Thus Job in this version is in the shorter text which we know to have been characteristic of the early LXX. But Burkitt took the view that the Sahidic Job was made from Origen's text with the additions marked by an asterisk omitted. A date for the Sahidic version about the middle of the third century is now thought more likely, and the evidence points to its having been made from Origen's Hexaplaric text. Because of the antiquity of some of the MSS, and the fact that the text was very carefully transmitted, the version is of importance for establishing Origen's recension in a very early form, and discoveries of late years have added greatly to the material. It includes a complete MS of Deuteronomy and Jonah (with Acts) of the fourth century, in the British Museum, edited by Budge (1912), with revision by Sir H. Thompson (1913); a palimpsest of the seventh century in the British Museum, containing Joshua, Judges, Ruth, Judith and Esther, nearly complete, edited by Sir H. Thompson (1912); 62 leaves of a MS of the Sapiential Books in the British Museum, of about the seventh century, containing considerable fragments of Proverbs, Ecclesiastes, Song of Solomon, Wisdom and Ecclesiasticus, with a small fragment of Job, edited by Sir H. Thompson (1908); three MSS in the collection of Mr Pierpoint Morgan, one (dated 893) containing 1 and 2 Kingdoms, another (eighth to ninth century) Leviticus, Numbers and Deuteronomy, and the third (ninth century) Isaiah (none of these is yet edited); a complete Psalter, seventh century in the British Museum, edited by Budge (1898); a fragmentary Psalter of the sixth century in the Freer Library, containing (with mutilations) Psa. vi. 5—liii. 3, edited by W. H. Worrell (1916 and 1923); a Psalter divided between the Chester Beatty Collection and the University of Michigan (W. H. Worrell, *Coptic Texts in the University of Michigan Collection,* 1942); a fragmentary Psalter at Berlin, edited by A. Rahlfs (1901) and assigned by him to about 400; a sixth century MS of Proverbs edited by W. H. Worrell (1931); and from the Bodmer collection edited by R. Kasser, are *Pap.*

Bodmer VI (1959), a fourth to fifth century text of Prov. i. 1–xxi. 4 in an archaic form of the dialect, *Pap. Bodmer XVI* (1961), containing Exod. i. 1–xv. 21 of the fourth century, *Pap. Bodmer XVIII* (1962) of the fourth century containing Deut. i. 1–x. 7, *Pap. Bodmer XXI* (1963) containing Joshua vi, vii–xxiv (with some gaps) in a fourth-century hand, and *Pap. Bodmer XXII* (1964) containing Jer. xi. 3–lii. 34, Lamentations, the Epistle of Jeremy, and Baruch i. 1–v. 5 from the fourth or fifth century. There is thus now a considerable amount of material for the Sahidic version. According to Rahlfs in the Psalter it is marked by a number of additions of a Christian character, and the relationship of the Sahidic in particular to the Washington Codex of the Minor Prophets and to the Greek *Dodekapropheton* in regard to Hebraisms has been noted above (p. 40).

The Sahidic version eventually gave way to the Bohairic (or Lower Egyptian) version when that dialect became the official language of Coptic Christianity after the Arab conquest, and consequently it survives in a large number of MSS, mostly of relatively late date. However, *Pap. Bodmer III* (edited by R. Kasser, Louvain, 1958), of the fourth century, which contains, besides the Gospel of John, Gen. i. 1–iv. 2 in a form of Bohairic influenced by Sahidic suggests an earlier date for the version than was at one time admitted. In general the Bohairic belongs (as in the New Testament) to the same group as B ℵ.

There are fragments of Coptic versions in other dialects (Achmimic, Fayyumic, etc.), including an Achmimic version of the Minor Prophets (edited by W. Till, 1927), and of Proverbs at Berlin (edited by A. Böhlig, 1958), but they are not extensive, and their character is yet to be fully determined, though they appear to lean rather to the Sahidic than the Bohairic.

Lists of published Coptic MSS and fragments will be found in A. Vaschalde's 'Ce qui a été publié des versions coptes de la Bible', *Revue Biblique* 28–31, *Muséon* 43, 45, 46; W. Till's 'Coptic Biblical Texts Published after Vaschalde's List', *Bulletin of the John Rylands Library* 42, pp. 220–40. See also W. K. M. Grossouw, *The Coptic Versions of the Minor Prophets* (1938); and P. Barthélemy, *Les Devanciers d'Aquila* (Leiden, 1963), pp. 228–43.

Syriac. Of the Syriac versions the Peshitta (or Peshitto), which became the accepted Bible of the Syriac Church, presents many problems which are far from being solved. The Pentateuch seems to have been originally translated from the Hebrew, probably with the aid of Jewish targums, though whether in the first place by Jews or Christians, or by Jews *for* Christians, is debated. The rest of the Old Testament varies greatly in style and quality, as also in the influence of the LXX, which is greatest in Psalms, Isaiah and the Minor Prophets. It was also originally without the apocryphal books, which (apart from Ecclesiasticus) were supplied from the LXX, and here its value for the study of the Greek text is greater. There is a great number of Peshitta MSS, the largest collection being in the British Museum, amongst which is the oldest dated Biblical MS of A.D. 464. The Peshitta was first printed in the Paris Polyglot (1645) from a late and inferior MS, and later editions have not been much better—Walton's *London Polyglot* merely added further mistakes, and Lee's text (1823) is largely based on these two. Another edition, based to some extent on Lee's, was published at Urmia (Iran) in 1852, and reprinted by the Trinitarian Bible Society (1913). W. E. Barnes published an edition of the Psalter in 1904, and of the Pentateuch in 1914, and other individual books have appeared. The *West Syriac Codex Ambrosianus* of the sixth century was published by Ceriani in 1867. A new edition of the Syriac Bible is being prepared under the direction of Professor P. A. H. de Boer for the International Organization of Old Testament Scholars. Much more important for the LXX is the Syro-Hexaplar version produced by Paul, bishop of Tella, in 616–17, at Alexandria, which was a close translation of Origen's Hexapla text, retaining his critical symbols. A MS containing the poetical and prophetical books is in the Ambrosian Library at Milan and was published by Ceriani in 1874; another, now lost, but used by A. du Maes (died 1573) in his edition of the Greek text of Joshua, contained part of Deuteronomy, Joshua, Judges, 3 and 4 Kingdoms, Chronicles, Ezra, Esther, Judith and part of Tobit: and Genesis, most of Exodus, and Ruth have been edited from other MSS, together with fragments of other books. The translation is fortunately extremely literal, so that we have in it one of the principal authorities for the text of Origen, and through it, by observation of the critical symbols, of the pre-Hexaplar Septuagint. It also contains the original LXX of Daniel, which otherwise exists only in the Chigi

MS (no. **88** above) and partially in the Chester Beatty papyrus (**968**).

Considerable fragments, covering most of the books of the Old Testament, also exist of a Syriac version in the Palestinian dialect, made from the LXX. In the Major Prophets the text appears to be Origenic, and Job contains the additions from Theodotion, which also points to a Hexaplar origin; but the small fragments of 2 and 3 Kingdoms are said to be Lucianic. Other Syriac versions may be ignored here.

The other versions are of comparatively small value. Some use is made by scholars of the Armenian and Ethiopic versions, but whether these depend on the Hexaplaric text, and the extent to which they may have been subjected to revision from the Hebrew or from other versions, scholars are by no means agreed. The fragmentary Gothic version is of some interest, being known to have been made in the fourth century from a Lucianic text; but details of these would be superfluous here.

The Greek Old Testament was first printed in the great *Complutensian Polyglot*, produced at Alcala (Complutum) under the direction of Cardinal Ximenes, completed in 1517, but not published until 1522. The four volumes which include the Old Testament exhibit the text in Hebrew (with the Targum of Onkelos below), the Latin Vulgate, and Greek (with an inter-linear translation of the latter) in parallel columns. The position of the Latin Vulgate in the centre is deliberate—'mediam autem inter has Latinam B. Hieronymi translationem uelut inter Synagogam et orientalem ecclesiam posuimus, tamquam duos hinc et inde latrones, medium autem Iesum, hoc est Romanam siue Latinam ecclesiam collocantes'. The editors (who besides Spanish scholars included a Greek, and three converts from Judaism who handled the Hebrew) used for the LXX mainly the minuscules **108** and **248** sent from the Vatican, perhaps a Venetian MS (H—P. **68**, of which a copy is still to be found in Madrid), and presumably other MSS of Spanish provenance, but none of very early date. But as in the case of the New Testament, Ximenes' great work was anticipated by a publisher's enterprise: in February 1518/19 Aldus produced a complete Greek Bible, edited by his father-in-law Andreas Asolanus. For the Old Testament he seems to have depended on MSS at Venice, and the edition had no lasting importance, being superseded by the edition published at Rome in 1587 under the auspices of Pope Sixtus V, and editorially directed by Cardinal Carafa. This edition was based on the recognition by its editors of the general superiority of the Codex Vaticanus over all other authorities, and to that extent it marks a great step forward. Unfortunately the text as printed is not strictly that of Vaticanus, nor of any other MS where that is wanting. It now appears that the editors, using the Aldine edition as a basis, corrected this from Codex Vaticanus and other authorities, adding also notes of variant readings from both LXX and Hexaplaric sources. This edition rightly won general acceptance, with the result that the Septuagint (more fortunate than the Greek New Testament) has almost from the first been available in a text largely conformed to the MS which is generally regarded as the best extant. The Sixtine text was reprinted with collations of other MSS in Walton's *Polyglot* (1657), and with very few changes in the next great edition, that of Holmes and Parsons (1789–1827), which demands special mention. In this, as mentioned above, a list of MSS is given, 313 in number, and readings from them are quoted in a critical apparatus, which has remained until recently (and for some books still remains) the principal repertory for the text of the LXX. Versions and patristic quotations were also used, so far as available. Unfortunately the collations made for it were not always complete or accurate, so that much of the work requires revision, but it remains a colossal performance, to which scholars will always be deeply indebted. It was begun by Robert Holmes, Canon of Christ Church, Oxford, and afterwards Dean of Winchester, in 1788, but he died in 1805, when only one volume had appeared, and the remaining four volumes were edited by James Parsons.

Constantin Tischendorf produced four editions of the Septuagint in 1850, 1856, 1860, 1869, placing below a revised Sixtine text a select apparatus criticus derived from the four principal uncials (Codex Sinaiticus as it became increasingly available, A, C, and from 1860 Mai's edition of B). But the next great advance was made when Dr H. B. Swete in 1887–94 produced a manual edition in three convenient volumes for the Cambridge University Press, in which the main text is that of B when available, elsewhere ℵ or A, with a select apparatus from ℵ A C, supplemented to some extent from other uncials (principally D E F in the Pentateuch, R T U in the Psalter, Q V in the Prophets). This edition has been and is extremely serviceable for students. More recently its pre-eminence as a handy edition has been challenged by one produced by A. Rahlfs in two larger volumes at Stuttgart (1935, 5th edition 1952), with a revised text based upon ℵ A B, and a short apparatus giving the readings of these MSS and occasionally of others.

Meanwhile an edition with large critical apparatus has been in progress at Cambridge under the editorship of A. E. Brooke (late Provost of King's College), N. McLean (late Master of Christ's College) and H. St John Thackeray. This gives the same text as Swete, with slight modifications, but has a copious textual apparatus, giving the readings, not indeed of all extant MSS (as was aimed at by Holmes and Parsons), but of all uncials and available papyri, a considerable number of selected minuscules, all the principal versions, and patristic quotations. This gives, so far as it has gone, all that the scholar can require in the way of a critical edition (*without* revised text), and its progress to completion is greatly to be desired. At present nine parts have appeared (1906–40), comprising the Octateuch, the Historical Books (1–4 Kingdoms, Chronicles, 1–2 Esdras), and Esther, Judith and Tobit. The deaths of Dr Brooke (1939) and Dr McLean (1947) have brought the work to a standstill, which it is to be hoped is only temporary.

A large critical edition has also been set in hand by the Septuaginta-Unternehmen of Göttingen. The Psalter was published by Rahlfs in 1931, and Genesis in a form intermediate between the large edition and the small in 1926. 1 Maccabees appeared under the editorship of W. Kappler (1936), and 2–3 Maccabees (1959–60) under that of R. Hanhart; Isaiah (1939), Minor Prophets (1943), Ezekiel (1957), Susannah, Daniel, Bel and the Dragon (1954), Jeremiah (1957), Wisdom of Solomon (1962), Ecclesiasticus (1965) are all edited by J. Ziegler. The German committee as a matter of policy is devoting its attention first to the books which were not reached in the Cambridge edition of Brook and McLean. Meanwhile, the smaller critical edition of Rahlfs, which is issued by the Württembergische Bibelanstalt at a very moderate price, will meet the needs of most students.

BIBLIOGRAPHY

H. B. Swete, *Introduction to the Old Testament in Greek*, 2nd ed. revised by R. R. Ottley (Cambridge, 1914), by far the best and fullest repertory of information up to 1914; *Mitteilungen des Septuaginta-Unternehmens der Akademie der Wissenschaften in Göttingen*; A. Rahlfs, *Septuaginta-Studien*, 1904–11; F. C. Burkitt, 'Texts and Versions: Old Testament' in *Encyclopaedia Biblica*, ed. T. K. Cheyne and J. C. Black, 1889–1903, cols. 5011–31; R. R. Ottley, Handbook to the Septuagint (London, 1920); H. St J. Thackeray, *Grammar of the Old Testament in Greek*, vol. i (Cambridge, 1909), *The Septuagint and Jewish Worship* (2nd ed. London, 1923); H. St J. Thackeray, *Some aspects of the Greek Old Testament* (London, 1927); F. G. Kenyon, *Recent Developments in the Textual Criticism of the Greek Bible* (London, 1933); F. G. Kenyon, *Our Bible and the Ancient Manuscripts*, 5th ed. revised by A. W. Adams (London, 1958); H. W. Robinson, editor, *The Bible in its Ancient and English Versions* (Oxford, 1940, 1954); B. J. Roberts, *The Old Testament Text and Versions* (Cardiff, 1951); E. Würthwein, *Der Text des Alten Testaments* (Stuttgart, 1952, 2nd ed. 1963), English translation *The Text of the Old Testament* (Oxford, 1957); P. Katz, 'Septuagintal studies in the mid-century', in *The Background of the New Testament and its Eschatology*, edited by W. D. Davies and D. Daube (Cambridge, 1954, 1964), pp. 176–208; P. Kahle, *The Cairo Geniza* (2nd ed. London, 1959); M. Noth, *Die Welt des Alten testaments* (4th German ed. Berlin, 1962), English translation *The Old Testament World* (London, 1966); various *Introductions* to the Old Testament by Aage Benzen (Copenhagen, 1952); Otto Eissfeldt, English translation of 3rd German ed. (Tübingen, 1964), London, 1965; A. Weiser, English translation of 4th German ed. (Göttingen, 1957) London, 1961; see also G. Bertram 'Zur Septuaginta-Forschung', *Theologische Rundschan*, N.F. iii (1931), pp. 283–96, v (1933), pp. 173–86, x (1938), pp. 69–81, 133–67; (by J. W. Wevers), xxii (1954), pp. 85–138, 171–90; J. Ziegler, 'Bibelübersetzungen', in *Lexikon fur Theologie und Kirche* (2nd ed. 1958), II, 375–80.

CHAPTER THREE

The Manuscripts of the New Testament

In dealing with the New Testament it will be convenient first to describe the extant evidence for its text, and afterwards to narrate its history and the theories which have been formed with regard to it. The evidence falls into three classes, (1) Manuscripts, or copies of the text in the original Greek, (2) Versions, or translations into other languages, (3) Fathers, or quotations found in the writings of the early Christian Fathers. The manuscripts, as in the case of the Old Testament, are classified under three main heads, (1) Papyri, (2) Uncials, (3) Minuscules, to which may be added (4) Lectionaries, which are manuscripts (generally of late date) in which the Bible text is arranged for ritual use in the services of the Church.

The accepted catalogue of New Testament manuscripts goes back to that compiled by J. J. Wetstein, a disciple of Bentley, in 1751-2. It was he who established the system of indicating the uncials by capital letters, and minuscules by Arabic numerals; papyri were then unknown. It was perhaps unfortunate that he made separate lists for the four main groups of books, the Gospels, Acts and Catholic Epistles, Pauline Epistles, and Apocalypse, a method which has only recently been abandoned; for though this method economized letters and numbers, it meant that the same letters and numbers denoted different manuscripts in different books. In the Gospels his catalogue ran from A to O in the uncials, and 1 to 112 in the cursives; in the Acts and Catholic Epistles, A to G, 1 to 58; in the Pauline Epistles, A to H, 1 to 60; in the Apocalypse A to C, 1 to 28; with 24 Lectionaries of the Gospels

and 4 of the Epistles. Nearly a century later J. M. A. Scholz
carried on and greatly extended the list. By this time the uncials
had exhausted the Latin capitals, and recourse was had to the
Greek, to which the Hebrew was subsequently added in a few
cases, mainly because Tischendorf wanted a distinctive designation for his great discovery, the Codex Sinaiticus. Scholz's catalogue, published in 1830–6, includes Gospels A–Δ, 1–469; Acts
A–H, 1–192; Paul A–I, 1–246; Apocalypse A–C, 1–88; Lectionaries, Evl. 1–181, Apost. 1–58. The discoveries of the nineteenth
century, and the industry of scholars in searching libraries, led to
large additions to this list, which were separately numbered by
Scrivener in England and by Gregory in Germany as far as
Evan. 774, Acts 264, Paul 341, Apocalypse 122; after which it was
generally agreed to accept Gregory's numbers, and to allow him
to keep the official catalogue of manuscripts.

By this time, however, the system was beginning to break down
by its own weight. The Latin and Greek alphabets were exhausted,
in spite of the expedient of grouping a number of different fragments under a single letter (e.g. W¹, W², W³, Θ¹, Θ², Θ³, etc.);
and the Hebrew alphabet was unfamiliar. Moreover, it was
inconvenient to have the same symbols denoting different MSS,
and the same MS passing under different symbols in different
books. Thus B in the Apocalypse denoted quite a different MS
from B, the great Codex Vaticanus, in the other books, and one
having much less importance; while one of the most valuable of
the cursives was known as 33 in the Gospels, 13 in Acts, and 17 in
the Pauline Epistles.

It was partly on account of these inconveniences that H. von
Soden, in the great critical edition of the New Testament which
he produced in 1902–13, devised a wholly new method of numeration. In this all MSS, whether uncial or minuscule, are grouped
together and are indicated by numerals, preceded by the letter δ,
ε, or α, according to their contents (διαθήκη, εὐαγγέλιον,
ἀπόστολος). The numbers, however, are not arranged in a continuous succession, but an attempt is made to indicate the date of
each manuscript. Manuscripts of the Gospels earlier than the
tenth century are denoted by the numerals from 1 to 99, and
MSS of the entire New Testament, Acts, or Epistles by numerals
from 1 to 49, preceded by the appropriate distinguishing letter in
each case. If these numbers should not suffice, they are to be

repeated with a o prefixed. Gospels MSS of the tenth century have numbers from 1000 to 1099, those of the other groups from 50 to 99. Those of the eleventh century have the numbers 100–99, followed by 1100–99; those of the twelfth century 200–99 and 1200–99; of the thirteenth century, 300–99 and 1300–99; of the fourteenth century, 400–99 and 1400–99; of the fifteenth century, 500–99 and 1500–99. If these numbers do not suffice (as they do not after the eleventh century), the numeration of the twelfth century continues from 2000, the thirteenth from 3000, and so on. But within these classes there are subdivisions. In each hundred of the δ or α categories, the first half (i.e. 100–49, 200–49, etc.) are assigned to MSS which include the Apocalypse, the second half to those which omit it. Further, MSS containing only the Acts and Catholic Epistles have the numbers 1000–19, 1100–19, etc. MSS containing only the Pauline Epistles 1020–69, 1120–69, etc., and MSS containing only the Apocalypse 1070–99, 1170–99, etc. Manuscripts containing commentaries in addition to the text have a separate numeration with a distinguishing abbreviation.

Von Soden's system, ingenious as it is, is open to serious objections. In the first place, it is intolerably complicated. It is easy to look up a MS in a continuous numeration, but it is bewildering to have to look for ε1011 before ε101, ε1180 before ε200, and so on. Habitual usage would no doubt overcome this difficulty, but it is a serious obstacle to occasional reference. Then the chronological information which it is designed to give is doubtful in itself and of little value. The dating of Greek minuscules is very dubious, and those who know most are apt to be the least confident about it; and when it is known, it is of little value for textual purposes. It is important to know whether a manuscript is of the fourth, fifth, sixth or seventh century; but here von Soden fails one, since all MSS earlier than the tenth century are lumped together. On the other hand, it is of little importance whether they are of the tenth century or later, for here their importance depends on whether they contain the ordinary ecclesiastical text, or have retained some traces of earlier recensions. Their actual date matters little, and it is not worth while to complicate the list in order to given information of doubtful accuracy and negligible value. Finally, it is a very serious drawback to change the designations of important manuscripts. When manuscripts are so well-known, and have been so constantly referred to in textual literature, as $\aleph$, A, B, C, D, it is darkening counsel to substitute for them the symbols δ^2, δ^4, δ^1, δ^3, δ^5.

To avert the danger of the introduction of a new system which had so little to recommend it, C. R. Gregory (the author of the Prolegomena to Tischendorf's New Testament) produced, after prolonged consultation with the principal students of textual criticism in Europe and America, an amended form of the previously-accepted method, which should meet the recognized need for expansion with the minimum of change in the familiar nomenclature. The principles on which his list[1] is formed are as follows: (1) Papyri are denoted by a P (preferably of 'antique' form, $\mathfrak{p}$) followed by a number; (2) Uncials are denoted by numbers in thick ('clarendon') type preceded by o; but for the first forty-five of them their old designations by Latin or Greek capital letters are retained (Hebrew in the case of $\aleph$ only); this involves double designations in the case of eight letters only, D, E, F, G, H, K, L, P, the duplicates being distinguished as D_2 or D^{paul}, etc.; the long series of fragments previously grouped under the letters, O, T, W and Θ are abolished, thus setting free those letters for substantial MSS recently discovered; (3) minuscule MSS are indicated by Arabic numerals, as before, but in a continuous numeration, so that the designations of Gospel MSS are unchanged, while those of the other groups follow on or fill accidental gaps. This system, which is easily intelligible and involves the minimum of change in familiar symbols, has been generally accepted, and is used in the following list, the numbers of von Soden being added for the benefit of those who wish to refer to his edition. Gregory's list was continued after his death by von Dobschütz, and the addition of newly discovered MSS is now in the hands of Dr K. Aland.

For the full description of all MSS reference must be made to the catalogues of Scrivener (*Plain Introduction to the Criticism of the New Testament*, 4th ed. by E. Miller, 1894, vol. I, pp. 90–376), C. R. Gregory (*Prolegomena* to Tischendorf's *Novum Testamentum Graece*, 1894, pp. 345–800, *Textkritik des Neuen Testamentes*, 1900–9, pp. 18–478, 1018–1292, 1363–75), E. von Dobschütz

[1] Printed in *Die Griechischen Handschriften des Neuen Testaments* (Leipzig, 1908). Tables showing the previous uses of all letters and numbers are added, so that it is easy to identify any reference.

(*Zeitschrift fur Neutestamentliche Wissenschaft*, 1922, 1926, 1927, 1933), G. Maldfeld (*Zeitschrift für Neutestamentliche Wissenschaft*, xlii (1949), pp. 228 ff., xliii (1950–1), p. 260 f.), K. Aland (*ibid.* xlv (1954), pp. 179–217, xlviii (1957), pp. 141–91) and *Theologische Literaturzeitung*, lxxv (1950), cols. 58–60, lxxviii (1953), cols. 465–96, and K. Aland, *Kurzgefasste Liste der griechischen Handschriften des Neuen Testaments: 1. Gesamtübersicht* (Berlin, 1963), *Materialen zur Neutestamentlichen Handschriftenkunde* (Berlin, 1969).

In the following list a full selection of the more important MSS is given, which is likely to be sufficient for most students.

I. Papyri

𝔭¹. (Sod. ε 01.) Philadelphia, University of Pennsylvania Museum E.2746. Discovered at Oxyrhynchus by B. P. Grenfell and A. S. Hunt, published by them in *The Oxyrhynchus Papyri* (i. 4–7, no. 2). Contains Matt. i. 1–9, 12, 14–20, 23. Third century. Alexandrian text, closer to B than ℵ.

𝔭⁴. (Sod. ε 34.) Paris, Bibliothèque Nationale Gr. 1120, suppl. 2°. Discovered at Coptos in 1891 by Scheil, and published by him in the *Révue Biblique*, 1892. Text also (with commentary) in M.-J. Lagrange, *Critique textuelle*, II, *La Critique rationelle* (Paris, 1935), pp. 118–23; see also J. Merell, *Revue Biblique*, xlvii (1938), pp. 5–22. Contains Luke i. 74–80, v. 3–8, 30—vi. 4. Third century. Alexandrian text, remarkably close to B, but with an occasional old Western reading.

𝔭⁵. (Sod. ε 02.) British Museum, Pap. 782 and Pap. 2484. Discovered by Grenfell and Hunt and published by them (*Pap. Oxy.* ii. 1–8, no. 208, xv. 8–12, no. 1781). Contains John i. 23–31, 33–41, xvi. 14–30, xx. 11–17, 19–25. Second half of third century. Pap. 208 (containing the fragments of John i and xx) formed the outermost leaf but one of a single quire probably of 25 sheets (50 leaves) containing the whole Gospel. Notable as the first example to be discovered of the single-quire form of papyrus codex (see p. 8 above). Pap. 1781 (containing John xvi. 14–30) was later recognized by Grenfell and Hunt as coming from the same codex. Single column to a page. The text is Alexandrian, without any of the readings characteristic of D, and is described by Lagrange as 'more neutral than B itself', being a good copy of the textual family from which Vaticanus and Sinaiticus were derived, and shows that this type of text was already domiciled in Egypt.

𝔭⁸. (Sod. α 8.) Berlin Staatliche Museen Pap. 8683 (now lost). Contained Acts iv. 31–7, v. 2–9, vi. 1–6, 8–15. Published by C. R. Gregory in *Textkritik des N.T.*, iii. pp. 1086–90. Fourth century. On the whole close to B, but with some admixture of readings of the Cod. Bezae type.

𝔭¹³. (Sod. α 1034.) British Museum Pap. 1532 and Florence, Biblioteca Medicea Laurenziana. Published by Grenfell and Hunt (*Pap. Oxy.* iv. 36–48, no. 657), and the Florence portion in *Pubblicazioni della Società Italiana, Papiri Greci e Latini*, xii (1951), pp. 209–10, no. 1292. Contains Heb. ii. 14—v. 5, x. 8–22, 29—xi. 13, 28—xii. 17. Late third or fourth century. Written on the back of an epitome of Livy of the third century. Important as containing parts of Hebrews which are lacking in B, to which (and also to 𝔭⁴⁶) it is akin in character.

𝔭¹⁵. (Sod. α 1044.) Cairo, Museum of Antiquities no. 47423. Published by Grenfell and Hunt (*Pap. Oxy.* vii. 4–8, no. 1008). Contains 1 Cor. vii. 18—viii. 4. Third or fourth century. Agrees for the most part with ℵ B A, but has some admixture of D readings.

𝔭¹⁶. (Sod. α 1045.) Cairo, Museum of Antiquities no. 47424. Published by Grenfell and Hunt (*Pap. Oxy.* vii. 8–11, no. 1009). Contains Phil. iii. 9–17, iv. 2–8. Similar text and date to 𝔭¹⁵— probably from the same MS.

𝔭¹⁸. (Sod. α 1074.) British Museum Pap. 2053. Published by Grenfell and Hunt (*Pap. Oxy.* viii. 13–14, no. 1079). Contains Rev. i. 4–7. Third or fourth century. Belongs to the A C group, the best for this book.

𝔭²⁰. (Sod. α 1019.) Princeton University Library, Classical Seminary A M 4117 (15). Published by Grenfell and Hunt (*Pap. Oxy.* ix. 9–11, no. 1171). Contains Jas. ii. 19—iii. 9. Third century. Alexandrian type, nearer to B than to ℵ.

𝔭²². Glasgow University Library, MS 2—x. 1. Published by Grenfell and Hunt (*Pap. Oxy.* x. 14–16, no. 1228). Contains John xv. 25–7, xvi. 1–2, 21–32. Third century. Mixed text.

𝔭²³. University of Illinois Museum, Urbana, G.P. 1229. Published by Grenfell and Hunt (*Pap. Oxy.* x. 16–18, no. 1229).

Contains Jas. i. 10–12, 15–18. Early third century, Alexandrian type.

𝔭²⁷. Cambridge University Library, Add. MS 7211. Published by Grenfell and Hunt (*Pap. Oxy.* xi. 9–12, no. 1355). Contains Rom. viii. 12–22, 24–27, 33–39, ix. 1–3, 5–9. Third century. Alexandrian, close to B, but a sprinkling of Western readings.

𝔭³⁰. Ghent University Library, U. Lib. P. 61. Published by Grenfell and Hunt (*Pap. Oxy.* xiii. 12–14, no. 1598). Contains 1 Thess. iv. 13, 16–18, v. 3, 8–10, 12–18, 26–28, 2 Thess. i. 1–2. Third century. Eclectic text.

𝔭³². Manchester, John Rylands Library, P. Ryl. 5. Published by A. S. Hunt, *Catalogue of Greek Papyri in the John Rylands Library*, i. 10–11. Contains Titus i. 11–15, ii. 3–8. Second to third century.

𝔭³⁷. Michigan University Library, Ann Arbor, no. 1570. Published by H. A. Sanders, *Harvard Theological Review*, xix (1926), 215–26, and *Michigan Papyri*, 9–14. Contains Matt. xxvi. 19–52. Cæsarean text, closest to Θ.

𝔭³⁸. Michigan University Library, Ann Arbor, no. 1571. Published by H. A. Sanders, *Harvard Theological Review*, xx (1927), 1–19. Contains Acts xviii. 27—xix. 6, 12–16, with mutilations. Third to fourth century. (Sanders dates it early third, Hunt and Schubart early fourth, Wilcken fourth or fifth.) The text is substantially that of Codex Bezae (D), including the very marked variants quoted below (pp. 92–3) in xviii. 27, xix. 1, 14. Important as showing that a Greek text of this type was extant in Egypt.

𝔭⁴⁵. *Chester Beatty Pap. I.* Chester Beatty Museum, Dublin, and Nationalbibliothek Vienna. Portions of 30 leaves of a codex, which originally contained all four Gospels and Acts, apparently occupying about 110 leaves, written in a small hand in a single broad column on a page of about 10 × 8 inches. Early third century. It is possible that Mark stood last of the Gospels—i.e. that here the papyrus followed the Western order as in the Freer MS (W), Codex Bezae (D) and some Old Latin MSS. The extant remains include portions of 2 leaves of Matthew, 6 of Mark, 7 of Luke, 2 of John, and 13 of Acts, those of Luke and John being the best preserved. Some small fragments of the second Chester Beatty leaf of Matthew are at Vienna (published by H. Gerstinger in *Aegyptus*, xiii (1933), 67–72). The text includes (though often much mutilated) Matt. xx. 24–32, xxi. 13–19, xxv. 41—xxvi. 39 (partly at Vienna), Mark iv. 36–40, v. 15–26, 38—vi. 3, 16–25, 36–50, vii. 3–15, 25—viii. 1, 10–26, 34—ix. 8, 18–31, xi. 27—xii. 1, 5–8, 13–19, 24–28, Luke vi. 31–41, 45—vii. 7, ix. 26–41, 45—x. 1, 6–22, 26—xi. 1, 6–25, 28–46, 50—xii. 12, 18–37, 42—xiii. 1, 6–24, 29—xiv. 10, 17–33, John x. 7–25, 31—xi. 10, 18–36, 42–57, Acts iv. 27–36, v. 10–20, 30–39, vi. 7—vii. 2, 10–21, 32–41, 52—viii. 1, 14–25, 34—ix. 6, 16–27, 35—x. 2, 10–23, 31–41, xi. 2–14, 24—xii. 5, 13–22, xiii. 6–16, 25–36, 46—xiv. 3, 15–23, xv. 2–7, 19–26, 38—xvi. 4, 15–21, 32–40, xvii. 9–17. This MS with $\mathfrak{p}^{46}$ and $\mathfrak{p}^{47}$, forms part of the Chester Beatty find, described on p. 31 above, and until the publication of the Bodmer collection of papyri was the most important Biblical discovery since that of the Codex Sinaiticus. In the Gospels its text may be generally described as standing between B and D, but in Mark it can be more distinctly categorized as belonging to the textual type classed as Cæsarean (see below, pp. 189–91), and within this is closest to W. The Codex proves that this type of text also was circulating in Egypt in the third century. In Acts its relationship is closer to the Alexandrian type (א A B C) and although there are minor agreements with the Western group, it has none of the more striking variants which are so characteristic of that text in this book. At the same time the papyrus has a remarkably high number of singular readings, many of which would appear to be due to scribal freedom in handling the text—e.g. preference for a simple verb over a compound, for the omission of redundant or dispensable words and phrases, and for changes in word-order. Its character is described more fully below (Chapter VI). Edited by F. G. Kenyon, *Chester Beatty Biblical Papyri*, fasc. ii (1933) with complete photographic facsimile in a separate fasciculus.

$\mathfrak{p}^{46}$. *Chester Beatty Pap. II*. Eighty-six leaves (all slightly mutilated) of a single-quire codex of 104 leaves, of which the last 5 were probably blank, written in a good hand in a single column on a page of about 11 × 6½ inches. Thirty of the leaves are in the library of the University of Michigan. Early third century, perhaps *c.* 200 and, according to U. Wilcken, may be late second century. Originally contained all the general Epistles of St Paul, in the order Romans, Hebrews (only one other MS—an eleventh to twelfth century minuscule—is known to have the order Romans–Hebrews), 1 and 2 Corinthians, Ephesians,

Galatians, Philippians, Colossians, 1 and 2 Thessalonians; but the following portions are missing: Rom. i, 1–v. 17, vi. 14—viii. 15, 1 Thess. ii. 3—v. 4, 2 Thess. The Pastoral Epistles were apparently never included in it, since there is not room for them on the leaves missing at the end. Also a few lines (generally not more than 1–4), are lost from the bottom of each page. Ten leaves were included in the original Chester Beatty acquisition, and were edited (with $\mathfrak{p}^{47}$) by F. G. Kenyon in *Chester Beatty Biblical Papyri*, fasc. iii (1934). Subsequently the University of Michigan obtained 30 more leaves, which were edited (with the above-mentioned ten) by H. A. Sanders (*A Third-Century Papyrus Codex of the Epistles of Paul*, University of Michigan Humanistic Series, xxxviii, Ann Arbor, 1935). Finally, Sir A. Chester Beatty obtained the remaining 46, and the whole MS was edited by F. G. Kenyon in *Chester Beatty Biblical Papyri*, fasc. iii supplement (1936). A complete photographic facsimile appeared in 1937. The papyrus is remarkable in respect of the position assigned to Hebrews, which seems to indicate the high position assigned to this Epistle in the Eastern Church, where its Pauline authorship was generally accepted, and in the fact that the doxology to Romans (xvi. 25–27), which in the earlier MSS stands at the end of ch. xvi, is here placed at the end of ch. xv. Although it contains many surface errors, G. Zuntz (*The Text of the Epistles*, 1953) finds the text of $\mathfrak{p}^{46}$ to be 'of supreme quality'. It is found supporting B when it stands alone, proving the antiquity of B's text, and has much in common with other Alexandrian witnesses, and with 1739. As regards the Western readings which have been noticed, $\mathfrak{p}^{46}$ offers no support for those attested by D alone, and thus raises the question whether the 'Western' readings it supports are properly so called, and are not rather very early elements common to both East and West which have disappeared from the Alexandrian and Eastern traditions. In relation to the Byzantine text (see below, chs. VI and VII) $\mathfrak{p}^{46}$ shows that some readings (faulty as well as genuine) go back to a very early period.

$\mathfrak{p}^{47}$. *Chester Beatty Pap. III.* Ten leaves of a codex of Revelation, written in a rather rough hand in a single column on a page of about $9\frac{1}{2} \times 5\frac{1}{2}$ inches. It is either a single quire of 10 leaves, preceded and followed by quires probably of 12 and 10 leaves respectively, or the central portion of a single-quire codex of 32 leaves. Third century. Contains ix. 10—xvii. 2, with the loss

F

of 1–4 lines from the top of each page. In text it is grouped by J. Schmid with ℵ Origen and the Sahidic version, a group inferior to A and C, but superior to almost all other MSS; but it shows a good deal of independence. Edited by F. G. Kenyon in *Chester Beatty Biblical Papyri*, fasc. iii (1934), with photographic facsimile in a separate fasciculus (1936).

𝔭⁴⁸. Florence, Museo Medicea Laurenziana. Text edited by M. G. Vitelli in *Pubblicazioni della Società Italiana, Papiri Greci e Latini*, x (1932), 112–18, no. 1165. Third century. A fragment containing Acts xxiii. 11–16, 24–29, in a text definitely of the Codex Bezae type. It is the more valuable because D is deficient here. For instance, it reads in verse 13 οἱ ἀναθεματίσαντες ἑαυτούς (with the Old Latin MS *h*), 14 inserts τὸ σύνολον after γεύσασθαι (with Old Latin *g*, *h*), 15 νῦν οὖν παρακαλοῦμεν [τοῦτο] ποιήσατε ἡμῖν, 24 adds ἐφοβήθη γὰρ μήποτε ἐξαρπάσαντες αὐτὸν οἱ Ἰουδαῖοι ἀποκτείνωσιν, καὶ αὐτὸς μεταξὺ ἔγκλημα ἔχῃ ὡς εἰληφὼς ἀργύρια (with Old Latin *c g p*, Syr.ʰ, etc.), 25 ἐν ᾗ ἐγέγραπτο, 27 ἐρυσάμην κράζοντα [καὶ λέγοντα] εἶναι Ῥωμαῖον (with Old Latin *g*).

𝔭⁴⁹. Yale University Library, P.415. Edited by W. H. P. Hatch and C. B. Wells, *Harvard Theological Review*, li. (1958), 33–35. Late third century. Contains Eph. iv. 16–29, 31—v. 13. Alexandrian text.

𝔭⁵⁰. Yale University Library, P.1543. Edited by C. H. Kraeling, *Quantulacumque* (London, 1937), 163–72. Fourth to fifth century. Contains Acts viii. 26–32, x. 26–31. Alexandrian, close to B.

𝔭⁵¹. British Museum. Edited by C. H. Roberts (*Pap. Oxy.* xviii. 1–3, no. 2157). About 400. Contains Gal. i. 2–10, 13, 16–20. Mixed text, closest affinity with B.

𝔭⁵². Papyrus Ryl. Gk. 457 in the John Rylands Library at Manchester. Early second century. A small fragment of a codex of St John's Gospel, discovered by Mr C. H. Roberts among some papyri acquired in 1920 by B. P. Grenfell. Contains John xviii. 31–33, 37, 38. The earliest known fragment of any MS of the New Testament and important as a proof of the early circulation of the Fourth Gospel. Published by C. H. Roberts, *An Unpublished Fragment of the Fourth Gospel in the John Rylands Library* (Manchester 1935).

𝔭⁵³. Michigan University Library, Ann Arbor, no. 6652. Edited by H. Kraeling, *Quantulacumque* (London, 1937), 151–61. Third century. Contains Matt. xxvi. 29–40, Acts ix. 33–38, 40—x. 1. Mixed text.

$\mathfrak{p}^{54}$. Princeton University Library, Garret Depos. 7742. Edited by E. H. Kase, *Papyri in the Princeton University Collections*, ii. (Princeton, 1936), 1–3. Fifth century. Contains Jas. ii. 16–18, 21–25, iii. 2–4. Alexandrian text.

$\mathfrak{p}^{64}$. Magdalen College, Oxford, MS Gk. 18. Edited by C. H. Roberts, 'An early Papyrus of the First Gospel', *Harvard Theological Review*, xlvi. (1953), 233–37. Fragments of a codex in a hand described as a precursor of Biblical Uncial, two columns to the page. Late second century. Contains Matt. xxvi. 7, 10, 14–15, 22–23, 31–33, and is the earliest witness to the Gospel. See below on $\mathfrak{p}^{67}$.

$\mathfrak{p}^{65}$. Florence, Biblioteca Medicea Laurenziana. Text in *Pubblicazioni della Società Italiana, Papiri Greci e Latini*, xiv (1957), 5–7. Third century. Contains 1 Thess. i. 2–10, ii. 6–13. Alexandrian text.

$\mathfrak{p}^{66}$. *Papyrus Bodmer II*. In the collection of M. Martin Bodmer. The first biblical text to be published of a number of papyri, Greek and Coptic, comprising classical, Biblical, and non-Biblical Christian texts of various dates from the beginning of the third century, or possibly somewhat earlier, being presumably the remains of an Egyptian Christian Library. The texts are comparable in importance to the Chester Beatty papyri already described. Most of the MSS are in the collection of M. Bodmer at Geneva, but others, apparently from the same source, have been acquired by the University of Mississippi and another (a text of Joshua in Coptic), is in the Chester Beatty collection in Dublin. The exact provenance of the find has not as yet been disclosed, but such evidence as there is—e.g. that the Coptic texts are mostly in the Sahidic dialect—points to Upper (i.e. Southern) Egypt.

The text has been published in three stages: (*a*) *Papyrus Bodmer II: Evangile de Jean chap. 1–14*, Bibliotheca Bodmeriana (Cologny Genève 1956) edited by Victor Martin; (*b*) subsequently fragments of the remaining Chapters appeared as *Supplément: Evangile de Jean chap. 14–21* (*ibid.* 1958), edited by Victor Martin; (*c*) finally a corrected and amplified edition of the above *Supplément* with a photographic reproduction of the whole MS (*ibid.* 1962), edited by Victor Martin and J. W. B. Barns. A valuable Appendix, *Annotated Corrections to the Editio Princeps of* $\mathfrak{p}^{66}$ will be found in G. D. Fee, *Papyrus Bodmer II: Its Textual Relationships and Scribal Characteristics, Studies and Documents,* xxxiv (1968), pp. 85–97.

The MS measures 16·2 × 14·2 cm., and the main portion (John i. 1—xiv. 26) consists of five unequal quires—originally six, but the third, which consisted of a single folded sheet containing vi. 11–35 is missing—of 5, 4, 5, 5 and 8 folded sheets respectively, in a remarkably good state of preservation. The first leaf was left blank. The MS has been repaired at some time with narrow strips of parchment sewn longitudinally down near the fold of the inside middle leaf of the quires. Fragments of the later chapters come from a further much damaged 46 pages, and contain xiv. 29–30, xv. 3–26, xvi. 2–4, 6–7, xvi. 11—xx. 22, xx. 25—xxi. 9 (with some gaps).

The script is a good literary hand of *c.* 200. The Gospel is divided into sections similar to those in the Freer Codex (W) and Codex Bezae (D), but in an earlier stage of development. Although the script is well formed, the copyist was exceedingly careless, especially in the way of small omissions, letters, syllables, words and even phrases being left out with considerable frequency. Most of these have been corrected by the original hand, but there are other corrections from which it would appear that another MS has been used in going over the text. If so, this raises the question of the nature and relationships of the texts which lay before the scribe. Most scholars who have examined $\mathfrak{p}^{66}$ have concluded that its text is to be classed as in general Alexandrian, its closest neighbour being ℵ rather than B, and with an admixture of Western readings of the D-type—i.e. not a pure text, nor a direct ancestor of the later uncial texts as we know them. A detailed analysis has been carried out by G. D. Fee (*The Correctors of Papyrus Bodmer II, Novum Testamentum,* vii (1965), 247–57, *Papyrus Bodmer II: Its Textual Relationships and Scribal Characteristics, Studies and Documents,* xxxiv (1968), who finds that $\mathfrak{p}^{66}$ is basically a text of 'neutral' type, this being particularly so in the first five chapters of John; but in Chapters vi and vii there is a strong swing to Western-type readings, while the remainder of the Gospel is a mixture of Alexandrian and Western, but closer to the former than the latter. Moreover, the alleged close relationship to ℵ is characteristic only of chapters vi and vii, due to the fact that ℵ itself has many Western readings in John i–viii. As to the corrections of substance in 𝔭⁶⁶, they are not all in one direction: while the majority are changes of Western to Alexandrian readings, the reverse also occurs. This would suggest that if a second MS was used in going over the text, this too was a mixed Alexandrian and Western text, though closer to the 'neutral' than that used in the original copying. Yet another characteristic of the corrections is that they tend in many cases towards a smoother and more lucid Greek—an early example of the kind of process which went towards the making of the later Byzantine text—though the apparent Byzantisms are perhaps better regarded as coincidental rather than shewing textual relatedness.

𝔭⁶⁷. Barcelona, Fundación San Lucas Evangelista, P. Barc. 1. Published by R. Roca-Puig, *Un Papiro Griego del Evangelio de San Mateo* (Barcelona, 1956, 2nd ed., with a note by Colin Roberts, 1962). Contains Matt. iii. 9–15, v. 20–22, 25–8, on parts of two leaves identified by C. Roberts as coming from the same codex as the fragments 𝔭⁶⁴. Late second century. Alexandrian, closer to ℵ than B.

𝔭⁷². *Papyrus Bodmer VII–IX*. A codex containing a miscellany of Biblical and other Christian texts as follows: The Nativity of Mary, the apocryphal Correspondence of St Paul with the Corinthians, the eleventh Ode of Solomon, the Epistle of Jude, Melito's Homily on the Passion, a fragment of a hymn, the Apology of Phileas, Psalms xxxiii and xxxiv, 1–2 Peter. The Epistles of Peter and Jude are complete: text edited by Michael Testuz, *Epître de Jude, les deux Epîtres de Pierre, Psaumes 33 et 34,* Bibliotheca Bodmeriana (Cologny/Genève, 1959). The codex is small in size (15·5 × 14·2 cm.) and was probably intended for private use. Four scribes in all are responsible for the different works (Scribe B wrote the Paul-Corinthian correspondence, the Ode of Solomon as well as the New Testament texts), and the orthography suggests that they were Copts. Moreover, scribe B, who apparently wrote somewhat carelessly from dictation, is responsible for numerous errors, mostly in spelling. The MS is dated in the third century. In the Pauline Epistles the text is Alexandrian, but according to F. W. Beare closer to A and Ψ than to B in 1 Peter; in 2 Peter the closest approximation is to B. In Jude, although for the most part the text would be included among the Alexandrian group, there are elements of other ancient forms found in the Philoxenian and Old Latin versions. (See

F. W. Beare, *Journal of Biblical Literature*, lxxx (1961), 253–60, *Studia Evangelica*, iii (Berlin, 1964), 263–5; J. N. Birdsall, *Journal of Theological Studies*, n.s. xiv (1963), 394–99; Sakae Kubo, *Studies and Documents*, xxvii (Salt Lake City, 1965); J. D. Quinn, *Catholic Biblical Quarterly*, xxvii (1965), 241–9.

$\mathfrak{p}^{74}$. *Papyrus Bodmer XVII.* A codex, in a bad state of repair, containing the Acts and Catholic Epistles, and consisting of 16 quires of 8 folios and one of four, 132 pages in all, measuring originally about 32 × 44 cm. The extant text comprises Acts i. 1–11, 13–15, 18–19, 22–5, ii. 2–4, 6—iii. 26, iv. 2–6, 8–27, 29—xxvii. 25, 27—xxviii. 31; Jas. i. 1–6, 8–19, 21–5, 27—ii. 15, 18–22, 25—iii. 1, 5–6, 10–12, 14, 17—iv. 8, 11–14, v. 1–3, 7–9, 12–14, 19–20; 1 Pet. i. 1–2, 7–8, 12–13, 19–20, 25, ii. 7, 11–12, 18, 24, iii. 4–5; 2 Pet. ii. 21, iii. 4, 11, 16; 1 John i. 1, 6, ii. 1–2, 7, 13–14, 18–19, 25–6, iii. 1–2, 8, 14, 19–20, iv. 1, 6–7, 12–13, 16–17, v. 3–4, 10, 17–18; 2 John 1, 6–7, 12–13; 3 John 6, 12; Jude 3, 7, 12, 18, 24. The hand is dated in the seventh century. The text is Alexandrian in Acts, nearer to ℵ A than B, without Western admixture. Edited by R. Kasser, Biblioteca Bodmeriana (Cologny/Genève, 1961).

$\mathfrak{p}^{75}$. *Papyrus Bodmer XIV–XV.* A single-quire codex (cf. the Chester Beatty Papyri II (Pauline Epistles), VII (Isaiah) and IX–X (Ezekiel, Daniel, Esther)) of Luke and John, originally consisting of about 144 pages measuring 26 × 13 cm., single column to the page. Fifty-one leaves (102 pages) remain, some of them very fragmentary, containing Luke iii. 19–22, 33—iv. 2, 34—v. 10, 37—vi. 4, 11—vii. 32, 33–43, 45—xi. 2, 4—xvii. 15, 19—xviii. 18, xxii. 4—xxiv. 53; John i. 1—xi. 45, 49–57, xii. 3—xiii. 1, 8–10, xiv. 8–30, xv. 7–8. Edited by Victor Martin and Rodolphe Kasser, *Papyrus Bodmer XIV–XV*, Bibliotheca Bodmeriana (Cologny/Genève, 1961), including a photographic reproduction of the entire text (apart from some portions glued into the binding). The script is a fine uncial hand, dated by the editors between 175–225, and if the median date is taken the MS is comparable to $\mathfrak{p}^{66}$ for John and is the earliest text of Luke, as well as being prior to Origen. The text is divided into sections, which sometimes agree with those of $\mathfrak{p}^{66}$, but it would appear that no fixed system was as yet in use.

Not only is the text of $\mathfrak{p}^{75}$ Alexandrian, but is closer to B than that of any other MS, while the influence of readings of the

Western type (Cod. D and its allies) is almost non-existent. This goes a long way to showing that the B-type of text was already in existence in Egypt, and in a relatively pure form, before the end of the second century. If so, the view, much canvassed in recent years, that the Alexandrian text-type (of which B and א were the chief representatives) was a third or fourth century recension— i.e. a deliberately revised or 'made' text formed out of the 'popular' texts of the second century—will need considerable revision. Indeed, Hort's theory that the 'neutral' text of B א—and especially B—was an ancient text which had survived in almost pure form, apart from scribal errors, and without serious editorial revision, now returns into the foreground of serious discussion. Amongst the more arresting readings that have been noticed are the following: Luke xvi. 19, where $\mathfrak{p}^{75}$ adds that the rich man was ὀνόματι Νεύης, unique in the Greek evidence, but clearly related to the tradition which appears in the Sahidic version that the rich man was called Nineues; John iv. 11 where $\mathfrak{p}^{75}$ omits ἡ γυνή with B, the Sinaitic Syriac and the sub-Achmimic; John viii. 57 where $\mathfrak{p}^{75}$ reads with א* 0124 the Sinaitic Syriac and the Coptic versions καὶ ᾿Αβραὰμ ἑώρακεν σέ; 'has Abraham seen thee?' instead of the usual 'hast thou seen Abraham?'; John x. 7 where $\mathfrak{p}^{75}$ alone with the Sahidic and Achmimic reads 'I am the shepherd (ὁ ποιμήν) of the sheep' for 'door (ἡ θύρα) of the sheep' in all other witnesses. Apart from their intrinsic interest, these readings, whether right or wrong, support the view that, like $\mathfrak{p}^{66}$, $\mathfrak{p}^{75}$ is the kind of Greek text from which the Coptic versions were made.

All the books of the New Testament appear in the list of papyri so far known except 1–2 Timothy, though not all are early, some being dated as late as the seventh or eighth centuries. It is interesting to notice the preponderence of Matthew and John over the other Gospels, evident in the overall figures and also in those papyri written before the end of the third century: thus out of the 75 listed Matthew appears in 15 papyri (counting $\mathfrak{p}^{64}$ and $\mathfrak{p}^{67}$ as one) of which 7 are before the fourth century, John in 17 (8 pre-fourth century), Luke in 7 (4 pre-fourth century), and Mark in only one (of the third century). Acts is found in 13 papyri (5 pre-fourth century) and Romans and Corinthians in 7 each.

II. Uncials

‏א‎ *Codex Sinaiticus.* (Sod. δ 2.) Now British Museum Additional MS 43725. Early fourth century. Contains (in addition to the Old Testament leaves described above, p. 41) the entire New Testament, with the addition of the Epistle of Barnabas and part (Vis. i. 1—Mand. iv. 6) of the *Shepherd* of Hermas. Written on 148 leaves of fine vellum, measuring 15 × 13½ inches, with four columns to the page (a reminiscence perhaps of the narrow columns of the papyrus rolls from which the MS was copied). No ornamentation and no enlarged initials, but the first letter of a paragraph projects slightly into the left-hand margin.

The Codex Sinaiticus is not only one of the two oldest vellum MSS of the Greek Bible, but is also famous because of the circumstances of its discovery. It was first seen by Constantin Tischendorf in 1844, when, on a visit to the monastery of St Catherine at the foot of Mt Sinai, he noticed a number of leaves of vellum in a basket destined for the furnace, in which, as he was informed, two baskets-full had already been consumed. In all he saw 129 leaves, all of the Old Testament, and 43 of these he was allowed to take away and present to his patron, King Frederick Augustus of Saxony, by whom they were placed in the University Library at Leipzig, where they still are. For the rest he could only secure that they should not be destroyed. In 1853 he revisited the monastery, but could neither hear nor see anything of the manuscript, which he suspected had been disposed of to some other visitor. In 1859 he was there again, and on the last evening of his visit he chanced to show the steward of the monastery a copy of the edition of the Septuagint which he had lately produced; whereupon the steward remarked that he also had a copy of the Septuagint, and produced a quantity of leaves wrapped in a cloth, which Tischendorf recognized at once as belonging to the MS that he so eagerly coveted. Moreover he quickly discovered that the prize was far greater than he had ever dreamed; for not only did it include 199 leaves of the Old Testament in addition to the 43 which he had already acquired, but also the entire New Testament, with the Barnabas and Hermas as above mentioned. The Barnabas was wholly new, and Tischendorf sat up all night copying it, and next morning asked if he might take the whole MS to Cairo (where there was a branch of the monastery) to be copied. One monk objected, so Tischendorf proceeded to Cairo and persuaded the Superior, who was there, to send for the MS, which thereafter was handed out to him, leaf by leaf, to be copied by himself and his assistants. So far is the story, subsequently put about by Tischendorf's enemies, that he stole the MS from being true, that it never was out of the hands of the representatives of the monastery.

An offer to buy the MS having been refused, Tischendorf suggested that it would be an appropriate gift for the monks to offer to the Tsar of Russia, the patron of the Greek Church, with a letter of commendation from whom he was himself travelling. The monks were disposed to accede to this suggestion, since there was a vacancy at the time in the Archbishopric of Sinai, and they desired the assistance of the Tsar to secure the acceptance of their nominee by the Porte, in face of the strong opposition of the Patriarch of Jerusalem. Tischendorf interested himself in supporting their case at Constantinople, and through the intervention of the Russian Ambassador obtained that he should take the MS to St Petersburg to be deposited there for his use until the monastery was in a position (through the election of a new Archbishop as its head) to make the gift officially to the Tsar. Ultimately (the full story is a long one) the Archbishop was appointed, the gift was made, and (after Tischendorf, on the request of the Archbishop, had intervened on their behalf) the return gift which the monks had no doubt always expected was obtained from the Tsar. It consisted of a sum of 9,000 roubles (a substantial price in those days) and a number of decorations. In view of the fact that subsequent generations of monks have considered that they were cheated out of a valuable possession, and have put about stories which European travellers have repeated, it is right to emphasize that Tischendorf's own story, which is confirmed by contemporary documents, shows that he acted with perfect correctness throughout, that everything was done through and with the approval of the official heads of the monastery, and that he remained on friendly terms with them to the end of his life.[1]

A comic episode followed the announcement of Tischendorf's

[1] The fullest and fairest account of the whole affair is to be found in the pamphlet, *The Mount Sinai Manuscript of the Bible*, published by the British Museum in 1934, on the occasion of the purchase of the MS.

great discovery. An ingenious Greek, Constantine Simonides, had about 1855 brought to England a number of manuscripts, among which was one which purported to be a lost history of Egypt by one Uranius. The well-known scholar, W. Dindorf, accepted it as genuine and prepared an edition for the Oxford University Press; but when a few sheets of it had been printed, another German scholar detected that the chronology was obviously taken from a modern history, and after a short controversy the fraud was exposed and the edition suppressed. Tischendorf had taken a hand in denouncing the imposture, and Simonides took his revenge by declaring that, while the Uranius was perfectly genuine, he *had* written another MS, viz. the Codex Sinaiticus, which he had copied from a Moscow Bible in about six months at Mt Athos in 1840. The story was patently absurd; for in 1840 Simonides was only 15 years old, he could not have obtained 350 large leaves of ancient vellum (modern vellum is quite different), he could not have copied it in six months, and no Moscow edition of the Bible with a similar text exists. Moreover the codex is written by at least three different scribes, and has a large number of corrections in various hands. The story is merely one of the comedies of crime, and is only worth mentioning because it has since been revived. The character of Simonides is further illustrated by the fact that he subsequently claimed to have discovered among the Egyptian collections of a Liverpool gentleman a papyrus copy of St Matthew written fifteen years after the Ascension, with fragments of first-century manuscripts of the Epistles of St James and St Jude and other equally surprising documents. These ingenious forgeries may still be seen at Liverpool.

Tischendorf published the Codex in full in facsimile type in 1862, when some sheets of it were exhibited in the Great Exhibition at London, and the manuscript found what might have been expected to be its permanent home in the Imperial Library of St Petersburg. But after the revolution in Russia, the Government of the Union of Soviet Republics, not being interested in the Bible, and being in need of cash, entertained the idea of selling it. Negotiations in America failed in consequence of the financial collapse in that country in 1931, and in 1933, after rather prolonged negotiations, it was purchased by the Trustees of the British Museum for £100,000, of which the British Government guaranteed £50,000, while the Trustees undertook to raise the other half. Ultimately, however, so great was the general interest taken in this great Biblical treasure that over £60,000 was raised, mostly in small contributions from individuals and congregations of all sects. At Christmas, 1933, the MS was received, amid much popular excitement, at the British Museum, and there, having been handsomely bound in two volumes, it may be hoped that it has secured a permanent home, side by side with the only less great Codex Alexandrinus.

The Codex Sinaiticus, therefore, consists in its present state of 393 leaves, of which 43 are at Leipzig, 3 fragments (extracted by Bishop Porphyry in 1845 from bindings) at Leningrad,[1] and 347 in the British Museum. The original total must have been about 720. They are arranged generally in quires of eight leaves. The writing is a rather large and very graceful uncial. According to Tischendorf, who is followed by Lake, four scribes took part in the original writing, but an exhaustive study by H. J. M. Milne and T. C. Skeat (*Scribes and Correctors of the Codex Sinaiticus*, 1938) has shown that there were only three. One of them (scribe A) wrote almost the whole of the New Testament and Barnabas, another (scribe D, whose orthography is quite the best) rewrote six pages in the New Testament where the first scribe, apparently, made serious mistakes, and was also responsible for the opening verses of Revelation (i. 1–5). From the evidence of variations in spelling of the different scribes it appears that the MS was written from dictation. Several correctors' hands are discernible, some of whom are identical or contemporary with the original scribes (אa)—these worked over the MS before it left the *scriptorium*, wherever that was; others belong to the seventh century (אc, see p. 41 above). Tischendorf's assertion that one of the scribes of א is identical with the scribe who wrote the New Testament in B is universally discredited. In the margins of the Gospels the section-numbers compiled by Eusebius (who died in 340) have been added by a corrector who (since they do not appear on two leaves which were re-written by the corrector אa) must be about contemporary with the MS. This would make a date for the original writing of the MS earlier than the second quarter of the fourth century impossible.

---

[1] These show that the mutilation of the MS began at some time considerably earlier than Tischendorf's first visit.

The place of origin of the MS cannot be stated with certainty. Cæsarea, Rome, southern Italy, have all been advocated, but the preponderance of opinion is in favour of Egypt. Every detail in its writing can be paralleled in Egyptian papyri; and though this is not conclusive, since no equally early MSS from other countries exist for comparison, the occurrence of unusual forms, such as the 'Coptic' μ and an ω with a much elongated central upright, which are found also in the papyri, is a strong confirmation of this view. Its kinship in text with the Codex Vaticanus, which also has instances of these peculiar forms, and with the Coptic versions is a further argument for an Egyptian origin; and if Egypt, then Alexandria is the most probable home for so splendid a piece of book-production.[1]

The character of the text of the Codex Sinaiticus and its allies will call for more detailed consideration. Here it will be sufficient to state that it is closely allied to the Vaticanus, and that these two fourth-century MSS form the head and main substance of a group which in the opinion of Westcott and Hort and their followers presents the most authentic text of the New Testament. Substantially it is the text represented in our Revised Version. To quote only a few instances: ℵ agrees with B in omitting the doxology of the Lord's Prayer in Matt. vi. 13; in omitting Matt. xvi. 2, 3 and xvii. 21; in adding οὐδὲ ὁ υἱός in Matt. xxiv. 36, and the piercing of our Lord's side in Matt. xxvii. 49; in omitting Mark ix. 44, 46 and the end of 49; in omitting the last twelve verses of Mark xvi; in having the shortened version of the Lord's Prayer in Luke xi. 2–4; in omitting the moving of the water and the mention of the angel in John v. 3, 4. On the other hand, it differs from B in including the incident of the Bloody Sweat (Luke xxii. 43, 44) and the word from the Cross ('Father, forgive them', etc.) in Luke xxiii. 34, though these passages were bracketed for omission by an early corrector (ℵ^a), and subsequently the brackets were erased by ℵ^c; these are both 'Western' readings (see below, Chapters VI and VII), and other readings of this type are to be found elsewhere in ℵ, most noticeably in John. In Acts and Epistles it is habitually to be found in the same group with A and B, though not without some variations.

---

[1] Lake notices a close similarity between the superscription in Acts (the title πράξεις at the top of many of the pages) in ℵ and B, which suggests that they may have been produced in the same scriptorium.

Besides Tischendorf's editions in facsimile and ordinary type, a complete photographic facsimile, from negatives taken by Professor Kirsopp Lake, has been published by the Oxford University Press (with the financial assistance of the British Academy through the munificence of a private benefactor), the New Testament in 1911 and the Old in 1922, with valuable introductions by Professor Lake.

A. *Codex Alexandrinus* (Sod. δ 4). In the British Museum (Royal MS D. v–viii). Early fifth century. Contains both Testaments, nearly complete. In the New Testament Matt. i. 1—xxv. 6 has been lost by mutilation, also John vi. 50—viii. 52 (where however calculation of the space shows that the *pericope adulterae* could not have been present), and 2 Cor. iv. 13—xii. 6. At the end, the two Epistles of Clement follow the canonical books; but 1 Clem. lvii. 7—lxiii. 4 and 2 Clem. xii. 5 to end are lost, together with the Psalms of Solomon, which a table of contents at the beginning shows to have been appended, though its title is separated by a space from those of the canonical books. It consists of 773 leaves (Old Testament 630, New Testament 143) and 10 leaves have been lost from the Old Testament and probably 37 from the New Testament, making a total of 820 leaves, measuring $12\frac{5}{8} \times 10\frac{3}{8}$ inches, with two columns to the page. The quires (before a modern rebinding) were of eight leaves, as is shown by a quire-numeration in Greek characters. Initials of paragraphs are enlarged, and (except in the poetical books) stand in the margin.

Sir Frederick Kenyon in his Introduction to the reduced facsimile edition of the New Testament portion of the MS states that five scribes were employed on it, three of whom were responsible for the New Testament. But Milne and Skeat (*Scribes and Correctors of the Codex Sinaiticus*, pp. 91–3) are of the opinion that two scribes were responsible for the Old Testament, and that the first of these wrote the whole of the New Testament with the possible exception of Luke i. 1—1 Cor. x. 8, which may be by a third scribe. The Clementine Epistles were written by the second scribe of the Old Testament (see above, p. 42). Several correctors have left their mark on the MS, the most important, apart from corrections made by the original scribes (A[1]), being A[a], who is nearly contemporary with the MS.

The MS not only contains the Eusebian canons and sections,[1]

---

[1] Eusebius made a division of the Gospels into numbered sections (Matt. 355,

but also (prefixed to the Psalter) treatises by Eusebius and
Athanasius. As the latter died in 373, a date before the latter part
of the fourth century is impossible. The writing also is later in
character than that of the Vaticanus and Sinaiticus. It is heavier
and firmer, and less reminiscent of the papyrus type; and the
arrangement in two columns (which thenceforward is habitual in
uncial MSS), points to a later stage than the four columns of the
Sinaiticus or the three of the Vaticanus. On the whole, the first
half of the fifth century is the most probable date.

With regard to the place of origin, everything points to Egypt.
A note by the Patriarch Cyril says that according to tradition it
was written by Thecla, a noble lady of Egypt, shortly after the
Council of Nicaea (A.D. 325), and that her name originally appeared
in a note (since lost by mutilation) at the end of the volume. This
date is too early, but the tradition points to Egypt. The Coptic
forms of a and μ appear in the titles of some of the books, and in
the Old Testament the text appears to be generally of the
Alexandrian type. In the New Testament it is Alexandrian (i.e.,
akin to א B) except in the Gospels, where it shows signs of the
Antiochian revision which eventually produced the received
ecclesiastical text.

An Arabic note, at the foot of the first page of Genesis, signed
by Athanasius 'the Humble' (=Athanasius II, elected Patriarch
of Alexandria in 1276, died c. 1316) states that the MS was given
to the patriarchal cell of Alexandria, though it is probable that
Athanasius himself acquired it in Constantinople, where he spent
many years in the imperial service. Its modern history begins

---

Mark 233, Luke 342, John 232), and then drew up ten tables, called 'Canons',
in which he placed in parallel columns the numbers of those sections which
contained accounts of the same event. Thus Canon I contains the parallel
sections common to all four Gospels: Canon II, those of Matt., Mark and Luke;
Canon III, Matt., Luke and John; Canon IV, Matt., Mark and John; Canons
V–IX, the various combinations of two Gospels (Matt.–Luke, Matt.–Mark,
Matt.–John, Luke–Mark, Luke–John), while Canon X lists the sections in each
Gospel which have no parallel in the others. The canons are prefixed to many
MSS, and the section numbers, with references to the canon in which they
appear, are placed in the margin of the text, often with the numbers of the
corresponding sections in other Gospels. Eusebius based his section-division
on a harmony of the Gospels by Ammonius of Alexandria, whence the sections
are often called the Ammonian sections. This Eusebian material is given in full
in Nestle's edition of the Greek New Testament published by the Würtembergische Bibelanstalt, and in that published by the British and Foreign Bible
Society, London, 1958.

when it was brought back to Constantinople by Cyril Lucar, who was Patriarch of Alexandria before being translated to Constantinople in 1621. Cyril offered it to the British Ambassador, Sir Thomas Roe, as a gift to James I; but by the time it reached England in 1627 Charles I was on the throne, and the binding which it then received bears the initials C.R. In 1757 it passed with the rest of the Royal Library to the newly founded British Museum.

It was the arrival of the Codex Alexandrinus in England (sixteen years after the publication of the Authorized Version) that gave the first stimulus towards the criticism of the text of the Greek New Testament. Patrick Young published the previously unknown Epistles of Clement in 1633, collations of its New Testament text were given by Walton in his Polyglot Bible of 1657, and by Mill in his New Testament in 1707. The complete Old Testament was edited by J. E. Grabe and completed after his death by Francis Lee and William Wigan in four volumes 1707–20, and this edition provided the basis for that prepared for the S.P.C.K. by Frederick Field in 1859. The New Testament, edited by C. G. Woide and printed in uncial type, came out in 1786, and this was reproduced by B. H. Cowper in 1860. The Old Testament was published in facsimile type by Baber in 1816–28, and a complete photographic facsimile was edited by E. Maunde Thompson in 1879–83. A reduced photographic facsimile of the New Testament, with introduction by Sir Frederick Kenyon, was published in 1909, and three parts of the Old Testament have since followed (1915–36), containing respectively the Octateuch, Kingdoms and Chronicles, and the Prophets with Esther, Tobit and Judith. In the Gospels the text of A is Byzantine, of which it is amongst the best examples; in the Acts and Epistles Alexandrian, though with some Western readings. In the Apocalypse (as in some Old Testament books) it has the best text of all MSS. (See J. Schmid, *Studien zur Geschichte des griechischen Apokalypse— Textes:* 2 Teil, *Die alten Stämme,* Munich 1955.)

B. *Codex Vaticanus* (Sod. δ 1). In the Vatican Library at Rome (Vat. gr. 1209). Early fourth century. Contains both Testaments, but in the New Testament all is lost after Heb. ix. 14, including the Pastoral Epistles and Apocalypse, with any non-canonical books that may have followed. It consists of 759 leaves (out of an original total of about 820) of very good quality vellum, measuring

$10\frac{5}{8} \times 10\frac{5}{8}$ inches, arranged in quires of 10 leaves, with three columns to the page—an unusual arrangement which could suggest the papyrus roll, were it not for the fact that there is reason to believe that from the first (or at any rate very soon after the arrival of Christianity in Egypt) the New Testament circulated in codex form (see above, p. 8). Of the New Testament there are 142 leaves out of an original total of about 162. There is no ornamentation and no enlarged initials. Accents and breathings are lacking, and there is practically no punctuation. The writing is small and neat, but its appearance has been spoilt by a later scribe, who found the ink faded and went over every letter except those which he thought incorrect. A few passages therefore remain to show the original appearance of the writing. There appear to have been two scribes in the Old Testament and a different one in the New Testament, and two correctors, one (B²) about contemporary.

The Eusebian sections (see above, p. 83) do not appear, which points to a date before they were generally known; there is however a different numeration of the Gospels (sometimes referred to as the Vatican sections), which is found only in one other uncial MS (Ξ) and one minuscule 579, and divides them as follows: Matthew 170, Mark 62, Luke 152, John 50. In Acts B exhibits two systems of numeration, both apparently based on the work of Euthalius (about whom little of certainty is known), who divided the book into 40 sections and 48 sub-sections. In the older system—possibly added at the time when Vaticanus was written, or very soon after—the text is divided into 36 sections; in the later (in which Euthalius' numeration has undergone a greater degree of modification or corruption) there are 69. In the Pauline epistles the numeration is continuous as though they comprised a single book, and from the fact that the sequence in B is dislocated at one point it is clear that in the system, as originally worked out (or in the MS from which the Vatican numeration was copied) the Epistle to the Hebrews stood between Galatians and Ephesians. It is interesting that this order (with Hebrews after Galatians) agrees with that given in the Sahidic version of the Festal (or Easter) Letter of Athanasius, written in A.D. 367, while the actual order of the Epistles in B (in which Hebrews precedes the Pastoral Epistles) follows that of the Greek text of Athanasius' Letter.

With regard to its date and place of origin, the extreme simplicity of its writing and the arrangement in three columns point to a very early place among vellum uncials, and the first half of the fourth century is generally accepted. With regard to its place, Hort was inclined to assign it to Rome, and others to southern Italy or Cæsarea; but the association of its text with the Coptic versions and with Origen, Athanasius and Cyril, as well as the style of writing (notably the Coptic forms used in some of the titles, and the order of the Pauline Epistles in relation to that in the two versions of Athanasius' Festal Letter (see above)), point rather to Egypt and Alexandria.

The MS was apparently the first of the great uncials to come to Europe, though it was the last to become fully known. It was certainly in the Vatican Library in 1481, since the catalogue of that year mentions a 'Biblia in tribus columnis ex membranis in rubeo'; and this may be the same as the 'Biblia ex membranis in rubeo' which appears among the Greek MSS in the catalogue of 1475.[1] It is enough to say that it was certainly there by 1481. It was fully used by Carafa for Pope Sixtus V's Septuagint in 1587, but in the New Testament it was unfortunate. Collations were made by various scholars in 1669, 1720, and 1780, but none of these collations was published, so that its evidence remained unknown to scholars. Hug called attention to its importance when it was brought to Paris by Napoleon, but on its return to Italy the Vatican authorities undertook to publish it, and therefore refused access to it to foreign scholars, while their own edition failed to appear. In 1843 Tischendorf was kept waiting for several months before he was allowed to see the manuscript for six hours, and two years later Tregelles, though allowed to see it, was forbidden to copy it and had to turn out his pockets in case he had brought in pen and ink. The fact was that Cardinal Mai, to whom it was entrusted, executed his work so poorly that it was held back during his life, and the two editions which appeared after his death, in 1857 and 1859, differed so much from one another as to be quite untrustworthy. In 1866 Tischendorf obtained access to it for forty-two hours, spread over fourteen days, and made a rapid collation, but as he violated his contract by transcribing twenty pages in full, it was withdrawn

---

[1] The description 'in rubeo' is not so distinctive as may appear at first sight, since 19 of the 57 volumes of Biblical texts are so described.

from his use. Nevertheless he was able in 1867 to publish an edition of it which greatly increased the knowledge of the MS, and in 1868 the New Testament was finally published by Vercellone and Cozza, and was followed by the Old Testament in 1881. A full photographic facsimile was published in 1889–90, and another by Hoepli (Milan, 1904) which provide scholars with an accurate knowledge of this most important MS.

The character of its text will be a main subject of consideration in the following chapters. It is the leading representative of the type of text which scholars associate with Alexandria, and of which Westcott and Hort thought so highly that they dubbed it 'neutral', and indeed made the Vaticanus the sheet-anchor of their edition. Powerfully supported by $\mathfrak{p}^{75}$, $\aleph$, by several early uncial fragments and a few minuscules, by the Coptic versions and, in the main, by the quotations in Origen, and by Jerome in his revision of the Latin New Testament, it certainly represents a type of text of great antiquity, and one which commands respect by its character. How it is affected by recent discoveries will appear later.

B_2. *Codex Vaticanus 2066.* The great Codex Vaticanus being deficient in the Apocalypse, Tischendorf unfortunately assigned the letter B in that book to another Vatican MS. Since, however, this MS is of quite different date and character, it is better to avoid confusion. It is described below as **046**.

C. *Codex Ephraemi Rescriptus* (Sod. δ 3). A palimpsest in the Bibliothèque Nationale in Paris, fifth century. Originally contained the whole of both Testaments, but in the twelfth century it was converted into a palimpsest; that is, the original writing was washed out, and some works of Ephraim Syrus in a Greek translation were written over it in double columns. Many leaves also were thrown away, so that what remains is very incomplete, and the readings not always decipherable. It now contains 64 leaves of the Old Testament and 145 (out of an original 238) of the New Testament, measuring $12\frac{1}{4} \times 9$ inches, with writing in a single column. Every book of the New Testament is represented except 2 Thessalonians and 2 John, but none is perfect. Contents: Matt. i. 2—v. 15, vii. 5—xvii. 26, xviii. 28—xxii. 20, xxiii. 17—xxiv. 10, xxiv. 45—xxv. 30, xxvi. 22—xxvii. 11, xxvii. 47—xxviii. 14; Mark i. 17—vi. 31, viii. 5—xii. 29, xiii. 19—xvi. 20; Luke i. 2—ii. 5, ii. 42—iii. 21, iv. 25—vi. 4, vi. 37—vii. 16,

viii. 28—xii. 3, xix. 42—xx. 27, xxi. 21—xxii. 19, xxiii. 25—xxiv. 7, xxiv. 46-53; John i. 1-41, iii. 33—v. 16, vi. 38—vii. 3, viii. 34— ix. 11, xi. 8-46, xiii. 8—xiv. 7, xvi. 21—xviii. 36, xx. 26—xxi. 25; Acts i. 2—iv. 3, v. 35—x. 42, xiii. 1—xvi. 36, xx. 10—xxi. 30, xxii. 21—xxiii. 18, xxiv. 15—xxvi. 19, xxvii. 16—xxviii. 4; Jas. i. 1—iv. 2; 1 Pet. i. 2—iv. 6; 2 Pet. i. 1—1 John iv. 2, 3 John 3-15; Jude 3-25; Rom. i. 1—ii. 5, iii. 21—ix. 6, x. 15— xi. 31, xiii. 10—1 Cor. vii. 18, ix. 6—xiii. 8, xv. 40—2 Cor. x. 8; Gal. i. 20—vi. 18; Eph. ii. 18—iv. 7; Phil. i. 22—iii. 5; Col. i. 1— 1 Thess. ii. 9; Heb. ii. 4—vii. 26, ix. 15—x. 24, xii. 15—xiii. 25, 1 Tim. iii. 9—v. 20, vi. 21—Philem. 25; Apoc. i. 2—iii. 19, v. 14— vii. 14, vii. 17—viii. 4, ix. 17—x. 10, xi. 3—xvi. 13, xviii. 2—xix. 5.

The writing is a rather heavy uncial, not unlike the Alexandrinus, and probably of approximately the same date. Initials are enlarged, and the Eusebian sections are indicated in the margins. Its text is of a mixed character: generally Alexandrian, but with some Western admixture in the Gospels; in Acts the Western element is less marked. In the Apocalypse C takes its place alongside A as the purest form of the text. Hort shows, from some displacements of text in the Apocalypse, that it must have been copied from a MS with pages only about a quarter of its own size—probably a small papyrus codex, intended for private use. It is therefore a witness to the variety of texts which were in circulation in the early centuries, and through its correctors with the later Byzantine text.

The codex belonged in the sixteenth century to the Medici family, and was brought to France by Catherine de Medici. It was collated for Bentley in 1716, but not fully made known until the full publication by Tischendorf of the New Testament in 1843 and the Old Testament in 1845.

D. *Codex Bezae* (Sod. δ 5). In the University Library at Cambridge, to which it was presented by Theodore Beza, the great Reformation scholar and himself an editor of the Greek New Testament, in 1581. Probably fifth century. Contains the Gospels and Acts, with a small fragment of the Catholic Epistles, in Greek and Latin, the two versions facing one another on opposite pages, with the Greek on the left. The Gospels are arranged in the order common in the Western Church, Matthew, John, Luke, Mark. The text is not written continuously, but arranged in short sense-clauses, or κῶλα, so as to facilitate comparison of phrases in the two languages. The following passages from the Greek text are lost by mutilation: Matt. i. 1–20, vi. 20—ix. 2, xxvii. 2–12, John i. 16—iii. 26, Acts viii. 29—x. 14, xxi. 2–10, 15–18 (but these verses can be restored from collations), xxii. 10–20, xxii. 29 to end, and the following are also lost from the original text, but supplied by a later scribe: Matt. iii. 7–16; Mark xvi. 15–20; John xviii. 14—xx. 13. On the Latin side Matt. i. 1–11, vi. 8—viii. 27, xxvi. 65—xxvii. 1; John i. 1—iii. 16; Acts viii. 20—x. 4, xx. 31—xxi. 2, 7–10, xxii. 2–10, 20—xxviii. 31, are entirely lost, and Matt. ii. 21—iii. 7; Mark xvi. 6–20; John xviii. 2—xx. 1 are supplied by the scribe. The Catholic Epistles preceded Acts, but all are lost except the Latin version of 3 John 11–15, the subscription to which shows that this Epistle, and not Jude, stood last in this group. The hand is a difficult one to date, being unlike those of the vellum uncials in general. This is probably due to the MS having been written in the West (as the presence of a Latin version would suggest) at some place where trained Greek scribes were not available. It was formerly assigned to the sixth century; but MSS in untrained hands generally look later than they are, and a fifth-century date (which Burkitt would prefer on textual grounds) is certainly not impossible and may be regarded as probable. The place of origin is even more doubtful. Clark advocated Egypt; but it is not likely that a bilingual Græco-Latin MS would be required there, and the Greek script is not like that of any MS written in Egypt. It must almost certainly have been written somewhere where, though the Scriptures might be read in Greek (as appears from the fact that the liturgical directions are all on the Greek side), Latin was the language in normal use, so that a Latin interpretation was needed (just as, in our own country, Anglo-Saxon translations were added to the Latin Vulgate). In Rome itself, more skilled Greek scribes would probably have been available; and the same is probably true of southern Italy, which has been suggested on the ground that certain lection-marks which have been added in the MS are in accordance with the Byzantine use. Sicily is advocated by Ropes. Northern Africa is possible, and it is to be observed that the text of D finds its closest ally in the African form of the Old Latin version; Sardinia also has been suggested, on the ground that another Græco-Latin MS (E_2) probably originated there. On the other hand, agreements with the quotations of Irenaeus, Bishop of Lyons (died *c.* 203), and in the ninth century with those of Ado, who probably worked in Lyons, suggest the south of France. But there is in fact no sufficient evidence to decide the question.

In its text Codex Bezae is the most peculiar manuscript of the New Testament, showing the widest divergences both from the Alexandrian type headed by ℵ B and from the Byzantine or Ecclesiastical type which eventually prevailed in the Greek Church and which appears in our Received Text and Authorized Version. These divergences are most marked in Luke and Acts, so much so as to have suggested that they represent a different edition of these books. A few of the most notable may be mentioned, in order to indicate the character of the MS, which will be much in question later. In Matt. xx. 28 it adds (with Φ, the Old Latin, a few MSS of the Vulgate, and the Curetonian MS of the Old Syriac) ὑμεῖς δὲ ζητεῖτε ἐκ μικροῦ αὐξῆσαι καὶ ἐκ μείζονος ἔλαττον εἶναι, εἰσερχόμενοι δὲ καὶ παρακληθέντες δειπνῆσαι μὴ ἀνακλίνεσθε εἰς τοὺς ἐξέχοντας τόπους, μήποτε ἐνδοξότερός σου ἐπέλθῃ, καὶ προσελθὼν ὁ δειπνοκλήτωρ εἴπῃ σοι, ἔτι κάτω χώρει, καὶ καταισχυνθήσῃ. ἐὰν δὲ ἀναπέσῃς εἰς τὸν ἥττονα τόπον καὶ ἐπέλθῃ σου ἥττων, καὶ ἐρεῖ σοι ὁ δειπνοκλήτωρ, σύναγε ἔτι ἄνω, καὶ ἔσται σοι τοῦτο χρήσιμον. In Luke v. 10, 11 the call of James and John is quite differently worded: ἦσαν δὲ κοινωνοὶ αὐτοῦ Ἰάκωβος καὶ Ἰωάνης, υἱοὶ Ζεβεδαίου· ὁ δὲ εἶπεν αὐτοῖς, δεῦτε καὶ μὴ γείνεσθε ἁλιεῖς ἰχθύων, ποιήσω γὰρ ὑμᾶς ἁλιεῖς ἀνθρώπων· οἱ δὲ ἀκούσαντες πάντα κατέλειψαν ἐπὶ τῆς γῆς καὶ ἠκολούθησαν αὐτῷ. After verse 14 it inserts Mark i. 45; and it omits verse 39. After Luke vi. 4, it inserts a new incident: τῇ αὐτῇ ἡμέρᾳ θεασάμενός τινα ἐργαζόμενον τῷ σαββάτῳ εἶπεν αὐτῷ, ἄνθρωπε εἰ μὲν οἶδας τί ποιεῖς, μακάριος εἶ· εἰ δὲ μὴ οἶδας, ἐπικατάρατος καὶ παραβάτης εἶ τοῦ νόμου, and transfers verse 5 to follow verse 10. In Luke ix. 55 it has the words καὶ εἶπεν, οὐκ οἴδατε ποίου πνεύματός ἐστε with Old Latin and Old Syriac support, which are omitted by ℵ A B C and several other Greek MSS; but it omits (with ℵ A B C, etc.) the following words, ὁ γὰρ υἱὸς τοῦ ἀνθρώπου οὐκ ἦλθεν ψυχὰς ἀνθρώπων ἀπολέσαι ἀλλὰ σῶσαι. In Luke xi. 2–4 it has the fuller form of the Lord's Prayer, and prefixes the words (after ὅταν προσεύχησθε) μὴ βαττολογεῖτε ὡς οἱ λοιποί· δοκοῦσιν γάρ τινες ὅτι ἐν τῇ πολυλογίᾳ αὐτῶν εἰσακουσθήσονται· ἀλλὰ προσευχόμενοι λέγετε, which are taken from Matt. vi. 7. In the narrative of the institution of the Lord's Supper

(Luke xxii. 15 ff.) it omits the latter part of verse 19 and the whole of 20 (τὸ ὑπὲρ ὑμῶν διδόμενον . . . ἐκχυννόμενον), thus removing the second mention of the Cup, and leaving the order of institution inverted. In Luke xxii. 43 it includes the incident of the angel and the Bloody Sweat, with ℵ and the Old Latin, but against ℵ^a A B, etc. In Luke xxiii. 34 the Word from the Cross, πάτερ, ἄφες αὐτοῖς· οὐ γὰρ οἴδασι τί ποιοῦσι, is omitted by the first hand (with ℵ^a B W) but added by a corrector (with ℵ C, etc.); the Old Latin and Old Syriac evidence is divided. In xxiii. 53 it has an extraordinary and obviously non-authentic addition, καὶ θέντος αὐτοῦ ἐπέθηκεν τῷ μνημείῳ λίθον ὃν μόγις εἴκοσι ἐκύλιον. In the narrative of the Resurrection it omits xxiv. 6, οὐκ ἔστιν ὧδε ἀλλ᾽ ἠγέρθη, the whole of 12, the end of 36, καὶ λέγει αὐτοῖς, εἰρήνη ὑμῖν, and the whole of 40; and all mention of the Ascension disappears by the omission of the words καὶ ἀνεφέρετο εἰς τὸν οὐρανὸν in 51.

In Acts the variations are so numerous that it is necessary to recognize drastic editorial action, either by the editor of the D–text in additions and variations, as generally held, or by the editor of the ℵ B-text in excisions, as maintained by A. C. Clark in his edition of the book. A few examples are given here[1]: v. 15, it adds ἀπηλλάσσοντο γὰρ ἀπὸ πάσης ἀσθενείας ὡς εἶχεν ἕκαστος αὐτῶν; v. 39 (οὐ δυνήσεσθε καταλῦσαι αὐτους), οὔτε ὑμεῖς οὔτε βασιλεῖς οὔτε τύραννοι· ἀπέχεσθε οὖν ἀπὸ τῶν ἀνθρώπων τούτων; vi. 10, it adds διὰ τὸ ἐλέγχεσθαι αὐτοὺς ἐπ᾽ [? ὑπ᾽] αὐτοῦ μετὰ πάσης παρρησίας· μὴ δυνάμενοι οὖν ἀντοφθαλμεῖν τῇ ἀληθείᾳ; viii. 24 it adds ὃς πολλὰ κλαίων οὐ διελίμπανεν; x. 25, προσεγγίζοντος δὲ τοῦ Πέτρου εἰς τὴν Καισάρειαν προδραμὼν εἷς τῶν δούλων διεσάφησεν παραγεγονέναι αὐτόν, ὁ δὲ Κορνήλιος ἐκπηδήσας κ.τ.λ.; xi. 2 ὁ μὲν οὖν Πέτρος διὰ ἱκανοῦ χρόνου ἠθέλησεν πορευθῆναι εἰς Ἱεροσόλυμα· καὶ προσφωνήσας τοὺς ἀδελφοὺς καὶ ἐπιστηρίξας αὐτούς πολὺν λόγον ποιούμενος διὰ τῶν χωρῶν διδάσκων αὐτούς· ὃς καὶ κατήντησεν αὐτοῖς καὶ ἀπήγγειλεν αὐτοῖς τὴν χάριν τοῦ Θεοῦ, omitting ὅτε δὲ ἀνέβη Πέτρος εἰς Ἱεροσόλυμα; xii. 10 καὶ ἐξελθόντες κατέβησαν τοὺς ἑπτὰ βαθμούς; xii. 23; καὶ καταβὰς ἀπὸ τοῦ βήματος γενόμενος σκωληκόβρωτος ἔτι ζῶν καὶ οὕτως ἐξέψυξεν; xiii. 29 ἠτοῦντο τὸν Πιλᾶτον τοῦτον μὲν σταυρῶσαι καὶ ἐπιτυχόντες πάλιν; xiii. 33 it adds αἴτησαι παρ᾽ ἐμοῦ καὶ δώσω σοι ἔθνη τὴν κληρονομίαν σου καὶ

---

[1] Other examples of the readings of D and its allies are given below, pp. 229–237.

τὴν κατάσχεσίν σου τὰ πέρατα τῆς γῆς; xiv. 2 οἱ δὲ ἀρχισυνάγωγοι τῶν Ἰουδαίων καὶ οἱ ἄρχοντες τῆς συναγωγῆς ἐπήγαγον αὐτοῖς διωγμὸν κατὰ τῶν δικαίων . . . ὁ δὲ Κύριος ἔδωκεν ταχὺ εἰρήνην; xiv. 7 καὶ ἐκινήθη ὅλον τὸ πλῆθος ἐπὶ τῇ διδαχῇ· ὁ δὲ Παῦλος καὶ Βαρνάβας διέτριβον ἐν Λύστροις; xv. 2 (after Βαρνάβᾳ) σὺν αὐτοῖς· ἔλεγεν γὰρ ὁ Παῦλος μένειν οὕτως καθὼς ἐπίστευσαν διϊσχυριζόμενος· οἱ δὲ ἐληλυθότες ἀπὸ Ἱερουσαλὴμ παρήγγειλαν αὐτοῖς τῷ Παύλῳ καὶ Βαρνάβᾳ καί τισιν ἄλλοις ἀναβαίνειν . . . ὅπως κριθῶσιν ἐπ' αὐτοῖς; xv. 20 (after αἵματος) καὶ ὅσα μὴ θέλουσιν ἑαυτοῖς γίνεσθαι ἑτέροις μὴ ποιεῖτε (so also in 29); xvi. 35, ἡμέρας δὲ γενομένης συνῆλθον οἱ στρατηγοὶ ἐπὶ τὸ αὐτὸ εἰς τὴν ἀγορὰν καὶ ἀναμνησθέντες τὸν σεισμὸν τὸν γεγονότα ἐφοβήθησαν; xvi. 39, καὶ παραγενόμενοι μετὰ φίλων πολλῶν εἰς τὴν φυλακὴν παρεκάλεσαν αὐτοὺς ἐξελθεῖν εἰπόντες· ἠγνοήσαμεν τὰ καθ' ὑμᾶς ὅτι ἐστὲ ἄνδρες δίκαιοι, καὶ ἐξαγαγόντες παρεκάλεσαν αὐτοὺς λέγοντες· ἐκ τῆς πόλεως ταύτης ἐξέλθατε, μήποτε πάλιν συστραφῶσιν ἡμῖν ἐπικράζοντες καθ' ὑμῶν; xvii. 15 (after Ἀθηνῶν) παρῆλθεν δὲ τὴν Θεσσαλίαν· ἐκωλύθη γὰρ εἰς αὐτοὺς κηρύξαι τὸν λόγον; xviii. 27 ἐν δὲ τῇ Ἐφέσῳ ἐπιδημοῦντές τινες Κορίνθιοι καὶ ἀκούσαντες αὐτοῦ παρεκάλουν διελθεῖν σὺν αὐτοῖς εἰς τὴν πατρίδα αὐτῶν· συγκατανεύσαντος δὲ αὐτοῦ οἱ Ἐφέσιοι ἔγραψαν τοῖς ἐν Κορίνθῳ μαθηταῖς ὅπως ἀποδέξωνται τὸν ἄνδρα· ὃς ἐπιδημήσας εἰς τὴν Ἀχαίαν πολὺ συνεβάλλετο ἐν ταῖς ἐκκλησίαις; xix. 1 θέλοντος δὲ τοῦ Παύλου κατὰ τὴν ἰδίαν βουλὴν πορεύεσθαι εἰς Ἱεροσόλυμα εἶπεν αὐτῷ τὸ Πνεῦμα ὑποστρέφειν εἰς τὴν Ἀσίαν; xix. 9 (after Τυράννου τινός) ἀπὸ ὥρας πέμπτης ἕως δεκάτης; xix. 14 ἐν οἷς καὶ υἱοὶ Σκευᾶ τινος ἱερέως ἠθέλησαν τὸ αὐτὸ ποιῆσαι· ἔθος εἶχαν τοὺς τοιούτους ἐξορκίζειν· καὶ εἰσελθόντες πρὸς τὸν δαιμονιζόμενον ἤρξαντο ἐπικαλεῖσθαι τὸ ὄνομα λέγοντες· παραγγέλλομέν σοι ἐν Ἰησοῦ ὃν Παῦλος κηρύσσει ἐξελθεῖν; xxi. 16 (after ξενισθῶμεν) καὶ παραγενόμενοι εἴς τινα κώμην ἐγενόμεθα παρὰ Μνάσωνι. For the rest of Acts D is wanting, but the other authorities for this type of text (principally the Old Latin) continue to show variants of the same character (see description of 𝔭[48] above).

The MS is corrected by many hands; Scrivener in his edition distinguishes nine, but his descriptions and datings are untrustworthy. The most active is D[g], whom Burkitt and Lowe consider to be contemporary with the MS and who is certainly not much later; he deals chiefly with the Latin side.

There has been much dispute as to whether the Greek text of D really represents a current recension of the Greek Gospels and Acts, or is the result of retroactive influences from versions in other tongues. One group of critics, including Griesbach, Scrivener and Hort, have held that the Greek is the main text, and that the Latin has been influenced by it. Others, including Mill, Wetstein, Rendel Harris, von Soden, Ropes and Vogels, have held the opposite view, that the Greek has been influenced by the Latin, so much so that it has even been questioned whether this type of text should be regarded as properly Greek at all, and not rather an Old Latin (and to some extent Old Syriac) form. Against this extreme view has now to be put the evidence of the Michigan and Florence papyrus fragments ($\mathfrak{p}^{38}$ and $\mathfrak{p}^{48}$), which show that Greek texts of Acts of this type were extant in Egypt in the third and fourth centuries; while A. C. Clark came to the conclusion that the Latin is in basis a servile translation of the Greek of D with some alterations due to a Latin text resembling that of **g**. He regards it as of little value except as evidence for the Greek of D where that is mutilated. Burkitt suggested that its ancestry included a Greek MS of which a Latin translation was made by someone who was familiar with one of the current Latin versions. This would explain the agreements and disagreements of the Latin side both with the Greek of D and with other Old Latin MSS; and the probability (to put it no higher) of the Greek having been now and again touched up to agree with the Latin should not be excluded. It may well be, then, that there is truth in both views—i.e. that in varying degrees each side has been influenced by the other. The conflict of authority between eminent scholars who have studied the MS minutely shows how difficult a decision is.

There is also a question as to Syriac influence. Bishop Chase (*The Old Syriac Element in the Text of Codex Bezae*, 1893, and *The Syro-Latin Text of the Gospels*, 1895) held that D is descended from a bilingual Græco-Syriac MS, probably produced at Antioch, and that many of its variations, especially the apparently pointless substitution of synonyms for words in the normal Greek text, are due to re-translations from the Syriac. Plooij agrees as to this Syriac influence, and argues that this is a proof that this type of text is not due to Luke himself; but most scholars have not accepted it. It is of course possible that the D text, in the course of its ancestry, has been subject to influences of all these various kinds, Greek, Latin and Syriac; and this possibility, while it hardly affects the problem of the larger variants, throws some doubt on the value of the MS in respect of verbal variations.[1]

As to the history of the MS, wherever it was written, it was in France (probably at Lyons) by the ninth century, when a note was added in a French charter hand, and nine leaves supplied in a Caroline script. It was at Lyons that Beza found it in 1562, in the monastery of St Irenaeus; but it had previously been collated by someone for Robert Stephanus, who inserts readings from it in the margin of his edition of 1550. Beza used it little, and gave it to Cambridge in 1581. It was used by Walton and Mill in their critical apparatus, and fully edited by Kipling in 1793, and again by Scrivener in 1864. In 1899 a complete photographic facsimile was published by the Cambridge University Press. It has been elaborately studied by Scrivener, Rendel Harris, Chase, Weiss, Ropes and Clark, and has held a foremost place in textual discussion since the time of Westcott and Hort. More will be said about it when the Western text comes to be considered as a whole.

D₂ or D^paul. *Codex Claromontanus* (Sod. α 1026). In the Bibliothèque Nationale in Paris. Sixth century. Contains the Pauline Epistles, with Hebrews (which did not belong to the Latin canon in the early centuries) as a kind of appendix, in Greek and Latin, colometrically arranged in sense-lines, with the Greek on the left-hand pages. The text is almost complete, except for both Greek and Latin of Rom. i. 1–7, 27–30 and the Latin of 1 Cor. xiv. 8–18, while the Greek of 1 Cor. xiv. 13–22 and the Latin of Rom. i. 24–7 are supplied by a somewhat later hand. The Greek is very well written, which points to a country of origin where good Greek scribes were available, though a Latin translation was required. This would suggest Italy; but Professor Souter has argued for Sardinia, on the ground that Lucifer, bishop of Cagliari in that island in the fourth century, used a Latin text practically identical with that in this MS. The difference in date

---

[1] On the whole of this bewildering question see especially J. Rendel Harris, *A Study of the Codex Bezae* (1891); J. H. Ropes, *The Text of Acts* in Jackson and Lake's *Beginnings of Christianity*, vol. iii (1926); A. C. Clark, *Acts of the Apostles* (Oxford, 1933); A. F. J. Klijn, *A Survey of Researches into the Western Text of the Gospels and Acts* (Utrecht, 1949); *ibid.* in *Nouun Testamentum*, iii, 1959, pp. 1–27, 169–73; J. D. Yoder, *Concordance to the Distinctive Greek Text of Codex Bezae* (Leiden, 1961); E. J. Epp, *The Theological Tendency of Codex Bezae Cantabrigiensis in Acts* (Society for N.T. Studies Monographs, Cambridge, 1966).

somewhat weakens this argument. The Latin text is independent of the Greek, and (though somewhat corrected from the Vulgate in the longer Epistles) is generally a good example of the Old Latin version. Before Hebrews a list of New Testament books (including Barnabas, Hermas, the Acts of Paul, and the Apocalypse of Peter, but omitting, probably by accident, Philippians, Thessalonians and Hebrews) is inserted, with the number of στίχοι in each.[1]

In text D_2 forms a group with E_3 (which was directly copied from it) F_2 G_3, representing the Latin or Western type of text, as opposed to the Alexandrian (‎ℵ A B).

Like D_1, D_2 once belonged to Beza, who acquired it from the monastery of Clermont, near Beauvais, and used it in his edition of 1582. After his death it passed through private hands till it was bought by Louis XIV for the Bibliothèque du Roi. It was edited by Tischendorf in 1852.

E or E^{ev}. *Codex Basiliensis* of the Gospels (Sod. ϵ 55). In the Library of the University of Basle. Eighth century. A good example of the Byzantine text, von Soden's K^1.

E_2 or E^{act}. *Codex Laudianus* (Sod. a 1001). In the Bodleian. Probably end of sixth century. Contains Acts (except xxvi. 29—xxviii. 25) in Greek and Latin, arranged in very short κῶλα, with the Latin in the left-hand column. The hand is large and coarse. It is the earliest MS that contains the eunuch's confession of faith (viii. 37). It was formerly held that the Latin has been accommodated to the Greek, but Ropes and Clark maintain that the Western additions in the Greek side (which is basically non-Western) are due to retranslation from the Old Latin. The Greek of E_2 should not therefore be classed as a Greek Western text along with D, with which it has little in common, but with the Byzantine type. The Latin side is based on a text similar to **gig**, and also has resemblances to the Vulgate. On a fly-leaf is a copy of an edict of Fl. Pancratius, Dux of Sardinia, and it may probably have been written in this island. It must have come to England by about the beginning of the eighth century, since it was certainly used by Bede in his *Expositio* and *Liber Retractationis*. It may have been brought over by Theodore of Tarsus in 669, as was probably

---

[1] The στίχος was the unit of measurement for the purpose of payment of copyists, and was normally taken as equivalent to 36 letters. In $\mathfrak{p}^{46}$ the number of στίχοι is given at the end of each Epistle. The numbers are not identical with those in D_2, but are not greatly different.

the original from which the Lindisfarne Gospels (see p. 164) was copied. Afterwards it found its way to Germany in the wake of Boniface, or one of the other English missionaries, and was part of the spoil taken from Würzburg when that town was sacked by the Swedes in 1631. It was presented by Archbishop Laud to the Bodleian Library in 1636, but whence he acquired it is unknown. It was edited by Hearne in 1715, by Hansell in 1864, and by Tischendorf in 1870.

E_3 or E^{paul}. *Codex Sangermanensis* (Sod. α 1027). At Leningrad. Ninth or tenth century. A copy of D_2, made later than the fifth corrector of that MS.

F or F^{ev}. *Codex Boreelianus* (Sod. ε 86). In the University Library at Utrecht, ninth century. Formerly belonged to Johannes Boreel, Dutch Ambassador in England in the reign of James II. Byzantine text of good quality, but with many passages missing.

F_2 or F^{paul}. *Codex Augiensis* (Sod. α 1029). Ninth century. In the library of Trinity College, Cambridge. Contains the Pauline Epistles (lacking Rom. i. 1—iii. 19), in double columns of Greek and Latin, the former always on the inside. Hebrews is given in Latin only. Belongs to the same group as D_2, but the Latin is closer to the Vulgate. It came from the abbey of Reichenau (Augia Dives or Major), where it may have been written, and was presented to Trinity College by Bentley, who collated it. Published in full by Scrivener in 1859.

G or G^{ev}. *Codex Seidelianus* (or *Wolfii* or *Harleianus*) (Sod. ε 87). In the British Museum. The various names indicate successive owners. Ninth to tenth century. Contains the four Gospels with many gaps. Belongs to von Soden's K^1, and included in Family E (see above and p. 212) of which it is claimed to be the best representative in Matthew.

G_3 or G^{paul}. *Codex Boernerianus* (Sod. α 1028). In the National Library at Dresden, ninth century. Contains the Pauline Epistles (but not Hebrews) in Greek, with a Latin version between the lines. Closely akin to F_2, both probably being copies of the same original. It was originally part of the same MS as Δ of the Gospels, and may have been written at St Gall, where Δ now is.

H or H^{ev}. *Codex Seidelianus II* (or *Wolfii II*) (Sod. ε 88). Hamburg City Library, ninth to tenth century. Contains about five-sixths of the four Gospels in a Byzantine text of the same type as G^{ev}.

H₂ or H^{act}. *Codex Mutinensis* (Sod. α 6). In the Grand Ducal Library at Modena, ninth century. Text of Acts (about seven chapters missing) of Byzantine type.

H₃ or H^{paul}. *Codex Coislinianus* 202 (Sod. α 1022). Sixth century. Forty-one leaves of a MS of the Pauline Epistles, of which 8 are in the monastery of the Laura on Mt Athos (where the whole MS once was), 22 at Paris, 3 at Leningrad, 3 at Moscow, 3 at Kieff, and 2 at Turin. Written in a very large hand. It contains scattered portions of the Epistles, ending with Titus, to which is appended a note saying that it was corrected from the copy in the library of Cæsarea, written by the holy Pamphilus. It has the colometric arrangement of the text in sense-lines and some of the additional material—prologues, chapter divisions and headings and tables of Old Testament quotations, which exist also for Acts and the Catholic Epistles—associated with Euthalius, a seventh-century bishop of Sulki in Sardinia, or with Evagrius, another shadowy figure of earlier date, but the identification of these names and the extent of their work is still far from clear. This 'Euthalian' material recurs also in some Greek minuscules, and in part in the Armenian, Georgian and Philoxenian Syriac versions, and is probably the basis of the later section-numeration found in B (see p. 86). The text is therefore of some importance. Edited by Omont; photographic facsimile of the Athos leaves by Kirsopp Lake (1905), who also recovered the text of five more pages from the offsets from them on the opposite pages.

I. *Codex Washingtonianus II* (Sod. α 1041). In the Freer Gallery at Washington, fifth or sixth century. A much mutilated manuscript of the Pauline Epistles (including Hebrews, which follows Thessalonians), with fragments of all except Romans. The quire numeration shows that it originally included Acts and the Catholic Epistles. The text is strongly Alexandrian in character, and agrees with ℵ and A more than with B. Edited by H. A. Sanders (1918).

K or K^{ev}. *Codex Cyprius* (Sod. ε 71). In the Bibliothèque Nationale in Paris. Previously dated ninth century, but according to Lake hardly earlier than 1000, and perhaps as late as the mid-eleventh century. A complete copy of the Gospels, and a typical representative of the normal ecclesiastical or Byzantine text.

K₂ or K$^{cath\ paul}$. *Codex Mosquensis* (Sod. A^{πρ1}, I^i). At Moscow. Ninth century. Contains Catholic and Pauline Epistles (Rom. x. 18

—1 Cor. vi. 13, 1 Cor. viii. 7–11 missing) with Hebrews. Von Soden classes it with the I-text.

L or L^{ev}. *Codex Regius* (Sod. ϵ 56). In the Bibliothèque Nationale in Paris, eighth century. Contains the Gospels (lacking Matt. iv. 22—v. 14, xxviii. 17–20; Mark x. 16–30, xv. 2–20; John xxi. 15-end) in a text which (apart from Matt. i–xvii) has largely escaped the Byzantine revision, so that it often agrees with B, and forms part of the Alexandrian group. There are, however, many mistakes in copying, as well as omissions and harmonizing readings, which suggest an ignorant scribe. It is remarkable as containing both the shorter ending of Mark referred to in the margin of the R.V. and then the ordinary last twelve verses, with a note prefixed to each saying that it is found in some copies. Both endings are also found in Ψ, 579, two uncial fragments, and some MSS of the Sahidic, Syriac and Ethiopic versions. Published by Tischendorf (1846).

L$_2$ or L$^{act\ cath\ paul}$. *Codex Angelicus* (Sod. α 5). At Rome, Bibliotheca Angelica, ninth century. Contains Acts (from viii. 10), Catholic and Pauline Epistles, and Hebrews to xiii. 10, the beginning and end of the MS being mutilated. Byzantine text, collated by Tischendorf and Tregelles.

M. *Codex Campianus* (Sod. ϵ 72). In the Bibliothèque Nationale, Paris, ninth century. Contains the four Gospels in a Byzantine text with some Cæsarean admixture.

N or N^{ev}. *Codex Purpureus Petropolitanus* (Sod. ϵ 19). Mainly (182 leaves) at Leningrad, but with 33 leaves at Patmos, 6 in the Vatican, 4 in the British Museum, 2 at Vienna, 1 in private hands in Italy, and recently 2 further single leaves have come to light, one now in the Byzantine Museum at Athens and another in the Pierpont Morgan Library in New York; in all, 230 leaves out of a probable total of 462. Sixth century. Contains portions of all four Gospels, written in silver, the *nomina sacra* in gold, on purple vellum. Closely connected with Σ (probably copied from the same original), and less so with two other purple MSS, O and Φ. Probably produced at Constantinople, and dismembered in the twelfth century, perhaps by Crusaders. The main surviving portion was acquired from Sarumsahly (Cæsarea in Cappadocia) by the Russian Government in 1896. The text is of Byzantine type, in a rather early stage of its evolution. Streeter classes it as a tertiary witness to the Cæsarean text. Edited by H. S. Cronin,

Texts and Studies V, 4 (Cambridge, 1899), the Athens and New York portion by S. Rypins, *Journal of Biblical Literature*, lxxv (1956), 27–39.

O. *Codex Sinopensis* (Sod. ϵ 21). In the Bibliothèque Nationale in Paris, sixth century. Forty-three leaves of Matthew (mainly xii–xxiv) written in letters of gold on purple vellum, with five illustrations. Akin both in form and text to N and Σ. Edited by Omont (1900).

P or P^{ev}. *Codex Guelpherbytanus* (Sod. ϵ 33). At Wölfenbüttel, sixth century. A palimpsest containing fragments of the Gospels. Byzantine text with some early readings.

P$_2$. *Codex Porphyrianus* (Sod. α 3). At Leningrad, ninth century. A palimpsest, containing (with some small gaps) Acts, Epistles and Apocalypse, and valuable as one of the few uncial MSS of the latter book. In Acts and 1 Peter the text is Byzantine; elsewhere it is classed by Gregory and von Soden as Alexandrian and close to $\aleph$ A C. Bousset and J. Schmid relate its text of Revelation to that used by Andreas, Bishop of Cæsarea in his commentary, which in turn closely resembles the corrector of Sinaiticus $\aleph^a$. Edited by Tischendorf (1865, 1869).

R or R^{ev}. *Codex Nitriensis* (Sod. ϵ 22). In the British Museum, sixth century. One of a collection of 550 MSS including the Curetonian Syriac MS of the Gospels (see below, p. 118) brought to England in 1847 from the monastery of St Mary Deipara in the Nitrian Desert. A palimpsest copy of Luke, imperfect, only about half being preserved in separate portions. Akin in character to the $\aleph$ B family; in von Soden's grouping belongs to the I text. Edited by Tischendorf in 1857.

S or S^{ev}. *Codex Vaticanus II* (Sod. ϵ 1027). In the Vatican Library. The MS is dated by the scribe Michael A.D. 949. Contains the Gospels in a Byzantine text, in its early form, von Soden's K. The passages Luke xxii. 43–44 (the Strengthening Angel) and John vii. 53—viii. 11 (the *pericope adulterae*) are marked with an obelus, as in some other MSS.

S$_2$ or S$^{act\ cath\ paul}$. (Sod. α 2). In the library of the Laura on Mount Athos, eighth or ninth century. Contains Acts and Catholic Epistles with Romans and part of 1 and 2 Corinthians and Ephesians. The text is Byzantine in its early form, to which H$_2$, L$_2$, P$_2$ also belong.

T. *Codex Borgianus* (Sod. ϵ 5). In the library of the Propaganda at Rome, fifth century. Fragments of a bilingual Greek-Sahidic Codex (Greek on the right) of Luke xxii—xxiii and John vi—viii, with a text remarkably close to ℵ and B, especially the latter. Edited by Tischendorf.

V. *Codex Mosquensis* (Sod. ε 75). In Moscow, formerly on Mount Athos, eighth century. Contains the Gospels to John vii. 39 (the rest in a thirteenth-century hand) in a Byzantine text, classed by von Soden as a leading member of the K¹ group.

W. *Codex Washingtonianus I* (Sod. ε 014). In the Freer Gallery at Washington. Late fourth or early fifth century. Contains Gospels (except Mark xv. 13–38, John xiv. 25—xvi. 7) in the Western order (Matthew, John, Luke, Mark), with a text of very varied character. Matthew, John i. 1—v. 12 (a quire added about the seventh century, presumably to replace one which was damaged) and Luke viii. 13 to end are of the common Byzantine type, John v. 12 to end and Luke i. 1—viii. 12 are Alexandrian, Mark i. 1—v. 30 is Western, akin to the Old Latin version, while the rest of Mark is of a different family which is described below as Cæsarean. This mixture of text-types in one MS is remarkable in itself, besides providing further evidence for the Western text in Egypt, and also as the earliest witness to the Byzantine text. Inserted in the ending of Mark after verse 14 is a remarkable addition: κἀκεῖνοι ἀπελογοῦντο λέγοντες ὅτι ὁ αἰὼν οὗτος τῆς ἀνομίας καὶ τῆς ἀπιστίας ὑπὸ τὸν Σατανᾶν ἐστίν, ὁ μὴ ἐῶν τὰ ὑπὸ τῶν πνευμάτων ἀκάθαρτα τὴν ἀλήθειαν τοῦ Θεοῦ καταλαβέσθαι δύναμιν· διὰ τοῦτο ἀποκάλυψόν σου τὴν δικαιοσύνην ἤδη. ἐκεῖνοι ἔλεγον τῷ Χριστῷ, καὶ ὁ Χριστὸς ἐκείνοις προσέλεγεν ὅτι πεπλήρωται ὁ ὅρος τῶν ἐτῶν τῆς ἐξουσίας τοῦ Σατανᾶ, ἀλλὰ ἐγγίζει ἄλλα δεινὰ καὶ ὑπὲρ ὧν ἐγὼ ἁμαρτησάντων παρεδόθην εἰς θάνατον, ἵνα ὑποστρέψωσιν εἰς τὴν ἀλήθειαν καὶ μηκέτι ἁμαρτήσωσιν· ἵνα τὴν ἐν τῷ οὐρανῷ πνευματικὴν καὶ ἄφθαρτον τῆς δικαιοσύνης δόξαν κληρονομήσωσιν. The first part of this obviously apocryphal addition (κἀκεῖνοι . . . δικαιοσύνην) is quoted by Jerome (*Contra Pelag.* ii. 15) who says that it was found in some copies, chiefly Greek ones. The rest is new.

This interesting MS was acquired by Mr C. L. Freer (with I and two Old Testament MSS, described above, pp. 48, 49) in Egypt in 1906, and was edited by H. A. Sanders, with a separate complete facsimile, in 1912.

X. *Codex Monacensis* (Sod. A³). In the University Library at

Munich, ninth to tenth century. A Gospel MS, with considerable gaps, in which the original order (later changed in binding) was Matthew, John, Luke, Mark. The script is approaching the minuscule form; the accompanying commentary (lacking for Mark) is in minuscules. The text is Byzantine, but with many readings of earlier type.

Z. *Codex Dublinensis* (Sod. ε 26). At Trinity College, Dublin, fifth or sixth century. A palimpsest containing 295 verses of Matthew, written in large uncials of a strongly Egyptian type, and Egyptian also in text, with many agreements with ℵ. Edited by Barrett in 1801, and more fully by T. K. Abbott in 1880.

Γ. *Codex Tischendorfianus IV* (Sod. ε 70). Partly in the Bodleian Library, Oxford (158 leaves), partly at Leningrad (99 leaves), ninth or tenth century. Contains Luke and John complete and most of Matthew and Mark. Von Soden classes it with his I text.

Δ. *Codex Sangallensis* (Sod. ε 76). At St Gall. Probably ninth century. A Græco-Latin copy of the Gospels (lacking only John xix. 17–35), originally forming one volume with G_3, the Latin being written between the lines of the Greek. In Matthew, Luke, John, the text is ordinary Byzantine, but Mark is of the Alexandrian type, akin to C and L. The Latin is a mixture of Old Latin and Vulgate, somewhat modified from the Greek, so that it is of little value. The text was published by H. C. M. Rettig (1836). See also *The Codex Sangallensis*, J. Rendel Harris (1891).

Θ. *Codex Koridethianus* (Sod. ε 050). At Tiflis, seventh to ninth century. Contains the Gospels, very roughly written by a scribe poorly acquainted with Greek, but with a very interesting text. Lake first showed that in Mark at any rate it was akin to the groups of minuscules described below under the numbers 1 and 13, and subsequent study has given this family the name of the Cæsarean text, of which more will be said in later chapters. Attention was first called to this MS, which formerly belonged to the monastery of Koridethi, in the neighbourhood of the Caspian, by von Soden in 1906, and it was fully published by Beerman and Gregory in 1913. For a study of its origin and text, see K. Lake and R. P. Blake, *Harvard Theological Review*, xvi (1923), pp. 267 ff., xxi (1928), pp. 207 ff. In the Gospels other than Mark its text has been revised into closer conformity with the Received Text.

Λ. *Codex Tischendorfianus III* (Sod. ε 77). In the Bodleian Library, Oxford, ninth century. Contains Luke and John complete, in small Slavonic uncials. The size, text-type and marginal notes show that it was originally part of the same MS as **566** at Leningrad containing Matthew and Mark, although the latter is in minuscules (cf. E and **509** of the LXX), while the Oxford portion has the subscription to Mark which belongs to **566**. The subscription or colophon to Matthew reads: ευαγγελιον κατα ματθαιον. εγραφη και αντεβληθη εκ των ιεροσολυμοις παλαιων αντιγραφων· των εν τω αγιω ορει αποκειμενων, and similarly for the other Gospels. Subscriptions of the same kind appear in a group of minuscules (see on **157** below). The text is for the most part Byzantine, placed by von Soden in the K^r grouping.

Ξ. Codex Zacynthius (Sod. A^1). In the library of the British and Foreign Bible Society, eighth century. A palimpsest containing most of Luke i. 1—xi. 33, with a commentary in the form of a Catena drawn from Origen, Chrysostom and other Fathers surrounding the text, also in uncials—the only one of its kind. Its text is akin to that of B, and it has the same section-division, which is peculiar to these two MSS and the minuscule **579**. Published by Tregelles (1861). W. H. P. Hatch (in Casey and Lake *Quantulacumque*, 1937) assigns the MS to the sixth century, but the argument is not conclusive.

Π. Codex Petropolitanus (Sod. ε 73). Leningrad, ninth century. Contains the four Gospels complete, except for some 77 verses in Matthew and John. See S. Lake, *Family Π and the Codex Alexandrinus* (Studies and Documents, v, 1936) and below, p. 212.

Σ. Codex Rossanensis (Sod. ε 18). In the library of the Archbishop of Rossano in Calabria, sixth century. Contains Matthew and Mark to xiv. 14, written on purple vellum with silver letters, the first three lines of each gospel in gold, with illustrations. A sister MS of N (q.v.).

Φ. Codex Beratinus (Sod. ε 17). At Berat in Albania, sixth century. Contains most of Matthew and Mark, written in silver letters on purple vellum. Forms part of the same group as N, O and *Σ*, having the Byzantine text in an early stage; but it is remarkable for having the long insertion at Matt. xx. 28, which is also found in D. Edited by Batiffol in 1886.

Ψ. Codex Laurensis or *Athusiensis* or *Athous Laurae* (Sod. δ 6). In the monastery of the Laura on Mount Athos, eighth or ninth century. Contains the Gospels (from Mark ix. 5 onwards), Acts and Epistles. In Heb. viii. 12–end is missing, and in the Catholic

H

Epistles 1–2 Peter come before James. It agrees with L in inserting
the short ending to Mark before the longer one; and Lake has
shown that in Mark it has a non-Byzantine type of text, with
readings characteristic of the CL 33 type and some of the D type
(K. Lake, *Studia Biblica* v (1902), pp. 92–131).

Ω. *Codex Dionysiacus* or *Athusiensis* or *Athous Dionysiou* (Sod. ε 61).
At Mount Athos, in the monastery of Dionysius. Variously dated
eighth to tenth century. Contains the four Gospels (complete apart
from Luke i. 15–28) in the early Byzantine text-form, von Soden's
K¹. Luke xxii. 43–4 and John vii. 53—viii. 11 are marked with an
obelus, as in E, S and Π. Published by M. W. Wainslow in
K. and S. Lake, *Six Collations of N.T. Manuscripts*, Cambridge,
Massachusetts, 1932.

046. *Codex Vaticanus 2066* (Sod. α 1070). In the Vatican
Library, eighth century. Contains the Apocalypse, where it heads
a group of about forty minuscules, with a recension of the text
different both from the early uncials and the later ecclesiastical
text. Edited by Tischendorf (1869).

0171. Fragments of a page of parchment found at Achmen
(Hermopolis Magna, near Antinoopolis) containing Luke xxii.
44–56, 61–3, fourth century. Lagrange (who prints the text with
commentary in *Critique Textuelle*, II, pp. 71–6) points out its
strongly Western character, adding to the witness for the circulation of this type of text in Egypt. It retains xxii. 44 (the Bloody
Sweat) with ℵ* D, and omits xxii. 62 with the Old Latin against
ℵ B D; it also omits xxii. 51 alone.

III. Minuscules

The latest catalogue of minuscule manuscripts reaches a total of
2768. Only a small minority of these contain the complete New
Testament. Manuscripts of the four Gospels are by far the most
numerous; others contain either the Acts and Catholic Epistles,
or the Pauline Epistles, or the Apocalypse, or some combination
of these. Only a small minority, however, need be mentioned in a
handbook of the present description. An overwhelming majority
contain the common ecclesiastical text, which, originating in a
revision which seems to have begun in Syria at the end of the
fourth century, was generally adopted throughout the Church,

and is known as the Byzantine or Received Text.[1] The chief object of textual criticism is to get behind this revision, and to ascertain the text of the earliest centuries. It is therefore interested mainly in those MSS which, of whatever date, appear to have in some degree escaped this revision and to preserve some evidences of earlier texts. It is with these, or with some of these, that the following brief list is concerned.

1. (Sod. δ 254.) The manuscript which heads the list is a twelfth-century MS at Basle, which was one of those used by Erasmus in preparing the first printed Greek Testament. If he had made it his chief authority for the Gospels, the text of our ordinary Bibles would have been very different from what it is; but in fact he based his text for the printer on another Basle MS **2,** which contains the ordinary Byzantine text. MS **1** in fact belongs to an important group with characteristics of its own and a common archetype. Its allies are **118, 131,** and **209,** and the four MSS are collectively known as Family **1**; but **1** is the best of the group. They were first thoroughly studied by Lake (*Texts and Studies,* vii. 3, Cambridge, 1902). **1582** is now included in this group—according to Streeter (*The Four Gospels,* p. 80) the only member comparable in importance to **1,** and others associated with it are **22, 872** (Mark), **1278, 2193.** They are now recognized as forming part of what is known as the Cæsarean text (see below, pp. 189–91, 220–3).

2. (Sod. ε 1214.) At Basle, twelfth century. Only notable as having provided Erasmus' printer's copy in the Gospels (with corrections by him from **1** and other sources)—see C. C. Tarelli, 'Erasmus's Manuscripts of the Gospels', *Journal of Theological Studies,* xliv (1943), pp. 155–62. In the Acts and Paul he used another Basle MS, **2**[ap]. (Sod. α 253) and in the Apocalypse one at Maihingen in Bavaria (**1**[r], Sod. *Av.*[20]).

13. (Sod. ε 368.) At Paris, twelfth century. This MS is one of a group originally recognized and studied by W. H. Ferrar and T. K. Abbott (1877), and hence known as the Ferrar group or Family **13.** It consists primarily of the MSS **13, 69, 124, 346,** which may all be descended from a single MS now lost; but other MSS (**230, 543, 713, 788, 826, 828, 983, 1689, 1709**) have been

---

[1] Von Soden devoted much labour to the division of this great mass of MSS into groups (see p. 191).

shown to have traces of the same type of text. Three of them
(**13, 124, 346**) were written in Calabria, where the archetype (from
which **69** also descends) must have been in the twelfth century.
The group contains many peculiar readings, especially the transference of the *pericope adulterae* to follow Luke xxi. 38. It is now
associated with Family 1 as forming part of the Cæsarean group.
See K. and S. Lake *Family 13 . . . with a Collation of Codex 28 of
the Gospels* (*Studies and Documents*, xi, 1941), J. Geerlings
Family 13, The Text According to Matthew (*ibid.* xix, 1961), . . .
The Text According to Luke (*ibid.* xx, 1961), . . . *The Text According
to John* (*ibid.* xxi, 1962).

28. (Sod. ε 168.) At Paris, eleventh century. Gospels: Mark is
complete, with some gaps in others. Contains many non-Byzantine
readings in Mark akin to W and the Cæsarean group. See K. and
S. Lake, *Family 13* as above.

33. (Sod. δ 48.) At Paris, ninth century. Considered by Eichhorn
(who called it 'the Queen of the Cursives') and Hort to be the best
of all the minuscules of the Gospels, its text being of the same
type as that of B, though with some Byzantine influence. Formerly
known as 13 in Acts and 17 in Paul, and referred to under these
symbols in earlier works.

61. (Sod. ε 603.) At Dublin, fifteenth or sixteenth century.
Historically of importance because it was the first Greek MS to
be discovered which contained the passage relating to the Three
Heavenly Witnesses (1 John v. 7, 8). This passage occurs in the
Vulgate, and when Erasmus, not finding it in his Greek authorities,
omitted it in his first New Testament, he was sharply criticised,
and promised to insert it if any Greek MS could be produced that
contained it. Accordingly, when this very late MS (in which the
passage had been intruded by translation from the Latin) was
brought to his notice he inserted the words in his third edition
of 1522. One other MS (**629**) also has it.

69. (Sod. δ 505.) At Leicester in the City Museum, fifteenth
century. Belongs to Family 13, and in spite of its late date is one
of the best of the group. Written by a Greek, Emmanuel, from
Constantinople, for Archbishop Neville of York. In the Gospels
Matt. i. 1—xviii. 15 is wanting.

81. (Sod. α 162.) In the British Museum, written A.D. 1044.
Contains Acts only (except iv. 8—vii. 17, xvii. 28—xxiii. 9), for
which it is the best of the minuscules, being singularly free from

'Western' influence and ranking with the leading uncials ℵ B in quality. Formerly known as Act. 61.

118. (Sod. ε 346.) At Oxford, thirteenth century. Belongs to Family **1**.

124. (Sod. ε 1211.) At Vienna, twelfth century. Belongs to Family **13**.

131. (Sod. δ 467.) In the Vatican, thirteenth century (having a note dated 1303). Belongs to Family **1**.

157. (Sod. ε 207.) In the Vatican, twelfth century. Specially mentioned by Hort as in the same class as **33**, having an Alexandrian text, but also showing some links with Marcion and the Palestinian Syriac. Like *Λ* and **565**, **157** has a colophon at the end of each of the Gospels stating that the text has been 'copied and corrected from the ancient copies in Jerusalem'. The colophon is also found in **20, 164, 215, 262, 300, 376, 428, 686, 718, 1071**. See H. C. Hoskier (*Journal of Theological Studies*, xiv (1913), pp. 78–116, 242–93, 359–84).

209. (Sod. δ 457.) At Venice, variously dated; palaeographic opinion points to the fourteenth century, but Lake gives reasons for believing it to be the parent of **118**, which is assigned to the thirteenth century. If not, they have a close common ancestor. Belongs to Family **1**. A fifteenth-century MS of Revelation is bound with it.

274. (Sod. ε 1024.) At Paris, tenth century. Contains in the margin the shorter ending to Mark.

346. (Sod. ε 226.) At Milan, twelfth century. Belongs to Family **13**. In Matt. i. 16, along with *Θ* and other members of the Ferrar group **543, 826, 828**, and many Old Latin witnesses, it has the same reading as the Curetonian MS of the Old Syriac: Ἰωσήφ, ᾧ μνηστευθεῖσα παρθένος Μαριὰμ ἐγέννησεν Ἰησοῦν τὸν λεγόμενον Χριστόν.

383. (Sod. α 353.) At Oxford, thirteenth century. Contains many readings of the Codex Bezae type in Acts xiii–xxii.

424. (Sod. O¹².) Vienna, eleventh century. Contains Acts, Epistles, Apocalypse. Includes valuable marginal notes which, according to Hort, include a relatively large number of very ancient readings, some of them distinctively Western, which otherwise have no cursive attestation. Specially valuable for the Pauline Epistles. **424**⋆⋆ indicates the readings of the marginal notes.

565. (Sod. ε 93.) At Leningrad, ninth to tenth century. Written in gold letters on purple vellum with the same colophon as Λ stating that it was copied and corrected from MSS from Jerusalem. Has a good text with ancient readings, and in Mark is akin to the Cæsarean type. See **700** below.

566. (Sod. ε 77.) At Leningrad, ninth century. The minuscule portion of Λ, q.v.

579. (Sod. ε 376.) At Paris, thirteenth century. Has the double ending to Mark, as in L. John xx. 15—xxi. 25 is lacking. According to Schmidtke in Mark, Luke and John **579** is a copy of an old uncial, and has a very good text akin to א B, with some Byzantine infiltration. Matthew is Byzantine.

614. (Sod. α 364.) At Milan, variously dated eleventh and thirteenth century. A MS of Acts and Paul, with a number of striking readings of the Codex Bezae type, and useful for the end of Acts, where D is deficient. Formerly numbered 137.

700. (Sod. ε 133.) In the British Museum, eleventh or twelfth century. Has a text akin to Θ and **565**, and is like them nearer to the Old Georgian version than other members of the Cæsarean Group. It also has some remarkable readings (e.g. in Luke xi. 2, it reads with Marcion ἐλθέτω τὸ πνεῦμά σου τὸ ἅγιον ἐφ᾿ ἡμᾶς καὶ καθαρισάτω ἡμᾶς in place of ἐλθέτω ἡ βασιλεία σου). Specially studied by H. C. Hoskier, *A Full Account and Collation of the Greek Cursive Codex* 604 (1890), also K. Lake and S. New, *Six Collations* (*Harvard Theological Studies*, xvii, 1932).

826, 828 (Sod. ε 218, 219.) At Grotta Ferrata, eleventh to twelfth century. Written in Calabria, and belong to Family **13**.

892. (Sod. ε 1016.) British Museum, ninth or tenth century. Preserves the line and page divisions of its uncial ancestor, as well as many early readings of the Alexandrian type. Collated by J. Rendall Harris in *Journal of Biblical Literature*, ix (1890).

1071. (Sod. ε 1279.) In the monastery of the Laura on Mount Athos, but written in South Italy, with the same subscriptions as Λ **157**, etc. The first hand alone among minuscules omits Luke xxii. 43–4 (fam. **13** transposes to Matt. xxvi. 39), though the verses are supplied in the margin; and the *pericope adulterae* (John vii. 53—viii. 11) is in a text almost identical with D.

1241. (Sod. δ 371.) Mount Sinai, twelfth or thirteenth century. Gospels, Acts and Epistles. According to Lake the text of the Gospels (especially remarkable in Luke and John) is basically

Western, which has been successively revised to the Neutral standard, and later to the Byzantine, more particularly in Matthew and Mark.

1424. (Sod. δ 30.) Ninth to tenth century. The oldest of a group of minuscule MSS, called fam. **1424** by Streeter, which corresponds largely to von Soden's I$^\phi$ group. Related to fams. **1** and **13**, Streeter claims it as a tertiary witness to the Cæsarean text, though with occasional readings that have fallen out of the better witnesses.

1739. (Sod. α 78.) Mount Athos, mid-tenth century. Contains Acts, Catholic and Pauline Epistles, with marginal notes derived from Irenaeus, Clement, Origen, Eusebius and Basil. The text of the Paulines (including Hebrews) is different from the rest. Collated by E. von der Golz (*Texte und Untersuchungan*, xvii, 1899) and by K. Lake and S. New, *Six Collations of N.T. Manuscripts* (*Harvard Theological Studies*, xvii, 1932). See also G. Zuntz (*The Text of the Epistles*, 1953). The prescript to the Pauline Epistles shows that its archetype was copied (probably *c.* 400 at Cæsarea) from a very ancient MS, but the marginal notes indicate that the writer of the archetype also had access to Origen's commentaries on Romans and other Epistles. For most of Romans the text is that of Origen's *Tomoi*, in the epistles that of the ancient MS, with marginal notes indicating agreements and disagreements with Origen. Zuntz finds close links between the archetype of **1739** and 𝔭^{46} and B. It also stands at the head of a group which includes **6, 424**, 1908**, and the British Museum uncial fragments **0121**.

1908 (Sod. Oπ^{103}.) At Oxford, eleventh century. A good text of the Pauline Epistles, with the commentary of Oecumenius.

2040. (Sod. Aρ^{11}.) In the British Museum, twelfth century. A good text of the Apocalypse, with the commentary of Andreas (not Arethas, as stated by von Soden).

2344. (Sod. —.) In the Bibliothèque Nationale, Paris, eleventh century. Contains Acts, Epistles and Apocalypse. In the latter book, according to J. Schmid (*Studien zur Geschichte des Griechischen Apokalypse—Textes*, 2. Teil, Munich, 1955) it has a very good text, belonging to the same type as A and C, found also in a thirteenth century Messina MS **2053**.

The most important of these are the two groups, **1–118–131–209** and **13–69–124–346**, and their satellites. These will be referred to later in dealing with the text-families into which the general mass of authorities has been divided. In addition, **33, 81, 424**** and **1739** deserve special mention, as containing texts of a very early type.

There remain only the Lectionaries, of which the latest catalogue enumerates 2146. These have an importance of their own in connection with liturgical history and also with the history of the text during the Middle Ages. In general, they give only the ordinary ecclesiastical type of text, but a pioneer study by E. C. Colwell and D. W. Riddle[1] has shown that the lections from Mark include a high proportion of readings of the א B, and not a few of the Codex Bezae type. According to the statistics compiled by the American scholars there are 347 variants from the Received Text in the week-day lections from Mark (which include about three-fourths of the text of the Gospel); and of these variants 200 have the support of א, 185 of B, 163 of C, 191 of L, and 202 find a place in the text of Westcott and Hort. On the other hand, only 27 have the support of D and its allies; but by a curious and unexplained contrast the lection-introductions, or *incipits*, show a considerable number of readings supported by D W Θ, family **13**, the Old Latin and the Sinaitic Syriac. These figures show that the lectionaries would repay fuller study than they have yet received, though more from the point of view of the history of the text than for the recovery of its original form. It seems clear that there was a definite lectionary text, since a comparison of lectionaries shows a high level of uniformity; but it is also clear that different parts of it were compiled at different times or from different sources. Thus the lections from Mark for Saturday and Sunday do not show anything like the same high proportion of א B readings as the lections for the other days of the week; and the lections from the other Gospels are generally of the Received Text type. This is in accordance with a phenomenon observed elsewhere, and to which reference will be made again, that the text

---

[1] *Prolegomena to the Study of the Lectionary Text of the Gospels* (University of Chicago Press, 1933), which includes a survey of the use hitherto made of lectionaries by textual students; see also E. C. Colwell, 'Is there a Lectionary Text of the Gospels?', *Harvard Theological Review*, xxv (1932), pp. 73–84, reprinted in E. C. Colwell, *Studies in Methodology in Textual Criticism of the New Testament* (Leiden, 1969), pp. 84–95; A. P. Wikgren, 'Chicago Studies in the Greek Lectionary of the New Testament' in *Biblical and Patristic Studies in Memory of Robert Pierce Casey*, edited by J. N. Birdsall and R. W. Thompson (Freilburg, 1963), pp. 96–121.

of Mark has much more often escaped the Byzantine revision than that of the other Gospels, which were more popular and in more general use.

Another point of view from which it is profitable to observe the evidence of lectionaries is that of the influence which they may have exerted on ordinary MSS. This is most apparent in the introduction into an ordinary text of the opening phrases characteristic of lections, such as τῷ καιρῷ ἐκείνῳ or εἶπεν ὁ Κύριος. It must, however, suffice here to call attention to the interest of the lectionaries, as a branch of textual study which deserves cultivation. In an elementary handbook such as this it is not possible, in the present state of knowledge on the subject, to make effective use of them.

BIBLIOGRAPHY

C. R. Gregory, *Prolegomena* to Tischendorf's *Novum Testamentum Graece* (1894), *Textkritik des Neuen Testamentes* (1900–9), *Die griechischen Handschriften des Neuen Testaments* (1908); F. H. A. Scrivener, *Plain Introduction to the Criticism of the New Testament* (4th ed. by E. Miller, 1894); H. von Soden, *Die Schriften des Neuen Testaments*, vol. i, pt. 1 (1902); F. G. Kenyon, *Handbook to the Textual Criticism of the New Testament* (2nd ed., 1912), *Our Bible and the Ancient Manuscripts* (5th ed. revised by A. W. Adams, 1958); E. Nestle, *Einführung in das Griechische Neue Testament* (4te Auflage E. von Dobschütz, 1923); K. Lake, *The Text of the New Testament* (6th ed. revised by Silva New, 1928); M. J. Lagrange, *Introduction à l'étude du Nouveau Testament*, II *La critique rationelle* (1935); A. Vaganay, *Initiation à la critique textuelle néotestamentaire* (1934), English translation by B. V. Miller, *An Introduction to the Textual Criticism of the New Testament* (1937); A. Souter, *The Text and Canon of the New Testament* (2nd ed. by C. S. C. Williams, 1954); M. M. Parvis and A. P. Wikgren (editors), *New Testament Manuscript Studies* (1950); V. Taylor, *The Text of the New Testament* (1961); B. M. Metzger, *The Text of the New Testament* (2nd ed., 1968).

CHAPTER FOUR

The Versions and Fathers

HARDLY less important than the actual manuscripts of the Greek New Testament is the evidence of the early translations of it into other languages. Their value depends, first on the earliness of their date, and next on the certainty with which we can ascertain the Greek text from which the translation was made. In the case of the New Testament there are two translations which we know to have been made before the end of the second century, and others somewhat later. If we can determine their text with certainty, we shall have evidence earlier than almost all extant MSS in the original Greek. More than that, we shall have evidence showing what sort of text was current at that date in a particular part of the Christian world.

As Christianity spread outwards from Palestine on its world mission, it addressed itself primarily to the Greek-speaking communities of the eastern part of the Roman Empire, as far as Rome itself, where Greek was almost as much a language in common use among the mixed population of the capital as Latin. But also it was passing into and through countries where a considerable part of the population did not speak Greek, and before long a demand grew up for versions of the Christian books in their vernaculars. Of these, three were earliest in urgency and of chief importance: Syriac, for the countries spreading from Antioch to the Euphrates valley; Coptic, for Egypt, which bordered Palestine on the south-west, and where a strong Hellenistic colony was surrounded by a native Egyptian population; and Latin, not only or even primarily for Italy, where much of the population spoke Greek, but certainly for the flourishing provinces of Roman Africa and Roman Gaul. We will take the Eastern versions first.

I. Syriac

Syriac is an Aramaic dialect, akin to, but not identical with, that which was in common use in Palestine in the time of our Lord. Aramaic was the language of the mass of the population of Mesopotamia, whence it spread, with dialectical varieties, over northern Syria and Palestine, where for all except scholars it entirely superseded Hebrew. Palestinian Aramaic was no doubt the language habitually spoken by our Lord; and this gives a special interest to the Syriac Gospels, as coming nearest to the form in which His teaching was originally delivered. There is, however, no *direct* connection between that original teaching and the Syriac Gospels. The headquarters of Syriac literature and Syriac Christianity was Edessa, an independent principality east of the Euphrates in the great bend of that river; and to this province Christianity must have come (presumably by way of Antioch) in Greek, and there is no doubt that the Syrian Scriptures were translated from Greek. What is doubtful is the exact form in which they first circulated.

(a) *The Diatessaron.* The most certain fact that we know about the early dissemination of the Christian Scriptures in Syria is that about A.D. 170–180 Tatian, himself a native of the Euphrates valley, but a disciple of Justin Martyr at Rome about the middle of the century, made a harmony of the Gospels which circulated extensively in a Syriac form among the churches of Syria. Tatian, having travelled much and having finally been converted to Christianity, appears to have spent many years at Rome as a disciple of Justin; but after the latter's martyrdom (*c.* A.D. 165) his extremely austere and ascetic views brought him into suspicion of heresy (of the Encratite type), and about 172 he left Rome and returned to his native land, where he died about 180. Whether he had prepared his Harmony of the Gospels before leaving Rome, or did so after his return to Syria, is unknown. In the former case it would no doubt have been made in Greek, in the latter probably in Syriac; and this is one of the questions in dispute among scholars. In favour of the former is its Greek title and the fact that Latin and eventually other translations were made of it; also the fact that it never fell under the suspicion of heresy, and shows no signs of Encratite prepossessions; and that its text, so far as ascertainable, shows strong affinities with D and the Old Latin; of the latter, that its main circulation was unquestionably in Syriac.

On the other hand F. C. Burkitt[1] suggested that the original language of the *Diatessaron* was Latin, and indeed that this was the earliest form in which the Latin Gospels were read in Rome. This would account for its textual characteristics, and also for its anonymity in the West. On his return to the East (according to Burkitt) Tatian used or compiled, and at the same time revised, and rearranged, a Greek version of the Roman harmony, which he then translated into Syriac, and this in the East (but only there) was associated with his name as *Diatessaron*.

The history of the *Diatessaron* is curious. Until the fifth century, it seems to have been the form in which the Gospel narrative was principally known in Syria. Theodoret, bishop of Cyrrhus on the Euphrates, writing in 453, says that he found more than two hundred copies of it in reverential use in his district, which he removed, substituting for them copies of the four Gospels, no doubt in the then established Peshitta version. Thereafter it fell into complete oblivion. Victor of Capua, in the early sixth century, found an anonymous Latin Harmony (the existence of which in the West is an argument in favour of a Greek original) which he thought must be that recorded by Eusebius (*Hist. Eccl.* IV. 29) to have been made by Tatian, and edited, substituting a Vulgate text for that which he found; and this is still extant in the Codex Fuldensis (see below, p. 163), written in 541–6. There is also a Dutch Harmony of the Middle Ages, discovered at Liège by Dr D. Plooij in 1923, which has been shown to have been made from a Latin Harmony closely akin to that in the Fuldensis, but with Old Latin readings instead of Vulgate, and therefore much nearer to the original *Diatessaron*.[2] There were also other Gospel Harmonies in use in medieval times, which may or may not be descended from Tatian. But in the middle of the nineteenth century all knowledge of the work was so completely lost that the anonymous author of *Supernatural Religion* (1876), in his attack on the authenticity and early date of the Gospels, could maintain that there was no proof that the *Diatessaron* was a harmony of the

[1] *Journal of Theological Studies*, xxv (1924), pp. 113–30, xxxvi (1935), pp. 255–8.
[2] Edited by D. Plooij and C. A. Phillips, *The Liège Diatessaron* (Amsterdam, 1929, etc.).

four canonical Gospels, and could even question its existence; while so learned a scholar as Bishop Lightfoot could only answer him with indirect arguments. Yet so long before as 1836 the Mechitarist Fathers at Venice had actually published a commentary on the *Diatessaron* originally written in Syriac by St Ephraim (d. 373), which conclusively established both the existence and character of the work; but since it was in Armenian, it remained completely unknown, and even when a Latin translation of it was published by Moesinger in 1876, this also remained unnoticed until Dr Ezra Abbot called attention to it in 1880. This stimulated research, which led to the discovery of two MSS of the twelfth and fourteenth centuries (one in the Vatican and one in Egypt, whence it was removed to Rome) containing Arabic texts of the *Diatessaron* itself, which was accordingly edited from them by Ciasca in 1888. A more recent edition with additional material and French translation is by A. S. Marmadji (Beyrouth, 1935). An English translation of the Arabic text was published by H. W. Hogg, *The Diatessaron of Tatian*, Edinburgh, 1897.

Meanwhile further evidence has been accumulating on the Commentary of Ephraim. The Armenian version has been re-edited from the two Venice MSS, dated 1195, by Louis Leloir (*Corpus Scriptorum Christianorum Orientalium* 137, 142, Louvain, 1953-4). Then in 1957 a Syriac MS of the fifth or sixth century was discovered—it is now in the Chester Beatty collection—containing rather more than half the commentary in the original Syriac and published by Leloir (*Saint Éphrem, Commentaire de l'Évangile concordant, Syriaque (manuscrit Chester Beatty, 709*), Dublin, 1963), and the same editor has since published a French translation of the whole Commentary based on the Syriac and supplemented, where that is not available, from the Armenian (*Éphrem de Nisibe: Commentaire de l'Évangile concordant ou Diatessaron*, Paris, 1966).

There is therefore now complete evidence of the existence and general character of the *Diatessaron*; but since we possess it only in late copies of secondary and tertiary forms, Latin, Armenian, Arabic, Persian, Dutch, French and Italian, which have been subject to the universal tendency towards conforming strange texts to that generally received, and in Ephraim's commentary and quotations in other Syriac Fathers, we are far from certainty as to its original wording, and there is often divergent testimony as to its arrangement. One small additional piece of evidence has come to light. In 1920 some English officers discovered the remains of a Roman fort at Dura on the Euphrates, once the eastern frontier of the Roman Empire, wherein were some remarkable wall-paintings of the first century and later. Subsequently, when the site had fallen into the French mandated area, excavations were carried out by French and American investigators; and among the debris of houses (including a Christian church and a Jewish synagogue) which had been destroyed by the Romans to strengthen the fortifications just before the final capture of the place by the Persians in 256 a number of vellum and papyrus fragments were found which had been sealed up by these operations. Among these, when they were examined at Yale in 1933, was found a small vellum fragment of the *Diatessaron* itself, in *Greek*, in a hand of the first half of the third century (and necessarily before 256). It consists only of fourteen imperfect lines, and contains the narrative of the petition of Joseph of Arimathaea for the body of our Lord, in a mosaic made up of phrases from all four Gospels, with some editorial adjustments.[1] The text as reconstructed by Kraeling is as follows:

ζεβεδαιου και σαλωμη και αι γυναικες των συνακολουθησαντων
αυτω απο της γαλιλαιας ορωσαι τον σ̅τ̅α̅ (=σταυρωθεντα). ην δε η
ημερα παρασκευη σαββατον επεφωσκεν οψιας δε γενομενης επι τη
παρασκευη ο εστιν προσαββατον προσηλθεν ανθρωπος βουλευτης
υπαρχων απο ερινμαθαιας πολεως της ιουδαιας ονομα ιωσηφ
αγαθος δικαιος ων μαθητης του Ι̅Η̅ κατακεκρυμμενος δε δια τον
φοβον των ιουδαιων και αυτος προσεδεχετο την βασιλειαν του Θ̅Υ̅,
ουτος ουκ ην συνκατατιθεμενος τη βουλη

Thus in the first eight words of the fragment, Ζεβεδαίου is taken from Matthew, καὶ Σαλώμη from Mark, καὶ γυναῖκες and αὐτῷ from Luke. Also noteworthy is the strange reading αἱ γυναῖκες τῶν συνακολουθησάντων αὐτῷ in place of (αἱ) γυναῖκες αἱ συνακολουθοῦσαι (—θήσασαι) of all Greek MSS of Luke xxiii. 49: Kraeling points out that as an Encratite Tatian might be expected to look unfavourably on marriage but the alteration to 'wives' of those who had followed Jesus may reflect an even

[1] Published by C. H. Kraeling (*A Greek Fragment of Tatians's Diatessaron from Dura*, in *Studies and Documents*, edited by K. and S. Lake, no. iii, London, 1935).

stronger distaste for the idea that unmarried women were to be found in his entourage. It may be that the Old Latin MS **c**, which reads *stabant autem omnes noti eius de longinquo et mulieres eorum* reflects the same tradition. Further down the fragment has ὄνομα ᾽Ιωσήφ (Matthew), ἄγαθος δίκαιος (Luke), ὢν μαθητὴς τοῦ ᾽Ιησοῦ (John). These examples are sufficient to show that Tatian handled his materials with freedom, and that even if we had the original *Diatessaron* intact, great caution would have to be used to determine the Gospel texts on which he worked.

The Dura fragment has been claimed as a proof that Greek was the original language of the *Diatessaron*. It is certainly remarkable to find a Greek copy of it in the farthest corner of Syria; but it is not decisive, since Dura was a military and commercial post, where there must have been many dwellers who were not Syrians by nationality or language. The manuscripts with which the fragment was found are military documents in Latin or business documents in Greek (with one Syriac). The proof of its Greek origin must still rest on the other considerations indicated above.

The *Diatessaron* therefore still presents several unsolved problems; its original language, its text, its relation to the medieval Latin and other harmonies that have come down to us, still more its influence on the text tradition as a whole. Von Soden and H. J. Vogels are disposed to attribute to it much of the confusion of the earliest texts, not only in Syriac but in Greek. This view has not generally been accepted. If we may assume that Tatian made his harmony first in Greek, which was then translated into Syriac, then it is likely that his Greek gospel text was brought from Rome, and was of the type current there in the second century. This appears to be borne out by the textual characteristics of the *Diatessaron*, which is Western in the geographical sense, being closer to Codex Bezae and the Old Latin than to the Old Syriac (which however also has some Western characteristics —see below), besides having close resemblances to the Gospel quotations of Justin Martyr, whose disciple Tatian had been in Rome. Some such link seems to be needed to account for the readings common to the Old Latin, but whether this is in fact due to a second century Western text having been brought to the East by Tatian and disseminated there by the *Diatessaron*, or whether some of these 'Western' readings were originally common to both East and West, is as yet far from being settled. Again, although it may be allowed that harmonizing readings might be derived from the *Diatessaron* in one or other of its forms, it by no means follows that every reading of this kind implies a harmony: harmonization is a common scribal failing.[1]

(*b*) *Old Syriac*. It is clear therefore that from the last quarter of the second century a Gospel narrative, made up of interwoven selections from the four canonical Gospels, was in circulation in Syria. The questions remain, Were the four Gospels also known by that time, as separate entities, and were the other books of the New Testament extant in Syriac? Until about the middle of the last century, no Syriac translation of the New Testament was known earlier than the Peshitta, which was then variously assigned to the fourth, third, or second century. But in 1842, among a large number of Syriac MSS brought by Archdeacon Tattam and others from the monastery of St Mary Deipara in the Nitrian desert in Egypt, and acquired by the British Museum, W. Cureton found some eighty leaves of a version evidently different from, and in his view older than, the Peshitta. This MS was printed and privately circulated in 1848, and definitely published in 1858. Then in 1892 two Cambridge ladies, Mrs Lewis and Mrs Gibson, brought back photographs of a palimpsest in the monastery of St Catherine at Mount Sinai, which proved to contain the same version as the Cureton MS, though with important variants and apparently of earlier date.[2] These two MSS constitute for us the Old Syriac version.

---

[1] In addition to the works mentioned in the text see also Th. Zahn, *Tatians Diatessaron* (Erlangen, 1881); J. Rendel Harris, *The Diatessaron of Tatian* (1890); J. H. Hill, *The Earliest Life of Christ* (Edinburgh, 1893); F. C. Burkitt, *Evangelion da—Mepharreshe* (Cambridge, 1904); H. Vogels, *Die altsyrischen Evangelien in ihrem Verhältnis zu Tatians Diatessaron* (Freiburg-im-B., 1911); P. Essabalian, *Le Diatessaron de Tatian et la première traduction des évangiles arméniennes* (1937); C. Peters, *Das Diatessaron Tatians*, Orientalia Christiana Analecta, 123 (Rome, 1939); S. Lyonnet, *Les origines de la version arménienne et le Diatessaron* (Rome, 1950); A. Vööbus, *Studies in the History of the Gospel Text in Syriac* (Louvain, 1951), *Early Versions of the New Testament* (Stockholm, 1954); H. Vogels, 'Der Einfluss Marcions und Tatians auf Text und kanon des N.T.', *Synoptische Studien* (Munich, 1953), pp. 278–89; P. Kahle, *The Cairo Geniza* (2nd ed. Oxford, 1959).

[2] Published by R. L. Bensly, J. Rendel Harris and F. C. Burkitt, *The Four Gospels in Syriac transcribed from the Sinaitic Palimpsest* (Cambridge, 1894). The standard edition of the O.S. version, giving the readings of both Cur. and Sin., is F. C. Burkitt's *Evangelion da—Mepharresche* (Cambridge, 1904), with a very valuable introduction.

The Sinaitic MS is a palimpsest, made up of portions of five older MSS, and consists of 182 leaves, 142 of which contain the text of the Syriac Gospels. The original Gospel MS comprised 164 leaves. The upper text consists of lives of female saints and was written in the year 778 at Ma'arrath Mesrên between Antioch and Aleppo. The quires have Georgian as well as Syriac signatures. The underlying script of the Gospels is dated in the fourth century, and it is reasonable to suppose it was written at some place in the Antioch–Edessa region. How and when the MS reached Sinai is unknown, but it was probably part of a considerable collection of MSS in Georgian or containing Georgian writing to be found there. The Gospels are in the usual order, and the text which has been recovered consists of Matt. i. 1— vi. 10, viii. 3—xvi. 15, xvii. 11—xx. 24, xxi. 20—xxviii. 7; Mark i. 12-44, ii. 21—iv. 17, iv. 41—v. 26, vi. 5—xvi. 8 (omitting the last 12 verses); Luke i. 1-16, i. 38—v. 28, vi. 12—xxiv. 53; John i. 25-47, ii. 16—iv. 37, v. 6-25, v. 46—xviii. 31, xix. 40— xxi. 25.

The Curetonian MS, which originally contained 150 leaves, now consists of 82½ leaves in the British Museum and 3 at Berlin. It was given to the monastery of St Mary Deipara, in the Natron Valley west of Cairo, by the monk Habib in the tenth century. Since there were large numbers of Syrian monks in Egypt it is possible that the MS was written there, probably in the first half of the fifth century. The Gospels are in the unusual order of Matthew, Mark, John, Luke, and the following portions are extent: Matt. i. 1—viii. 22, x. 32—xxiii. 25; Mark xvi. 17-20; John i. 1-42, iii. 5—viii. 19, xiv. 10-12, 15-19, 21-24, 26-29; Luke ii. 48—iii. 16, vii. 33—xvi. 12, xvii. 1—xxiv. 44.

The MSS are written in good idiomatic Syriac, in contrast to the more literal translation of the Peshitta and even more servile rendering of the Harkleian version.

Although most scholars are of the opinion that the Sinaitic MS is the older, some, including J. M. Lagrange and H. J. Vogels, maintain the priority of the Curetonian.

The problems raised by the Old Syriac version—its relation to the *Diatessaron*, and also to the main groupings of Western and Alexandrian authorities—in other words its origins and history— are formidable and have been much discussed. It is not unfair to say that a complete and satisfactory solution of them is not as yet

I

forthcoming; and in the present state of the subject seems unlikely to be so. For this reason a more detailed presentation of the evidence is attempted below.

With regard to the character of the text of the version, it will be convenient first to quote some of the more noteworthy readings. In Matt. i. 16, Sin. has the remarkable reading Ἰωσὴφ ᾧ ἐμνηστεύθη παρθένος Μαριάμ, ἐγέννησεν Ἰησοῦν τὸν λεγόμενον χριστόν, which in the Curetonian appears as (τὸν Ἰωσήφ), ᾧ ἐμνευστεύθη παρθένον Μαριὰμ ᾗ ἔτεκεν Ἰησοῦν Χριστόν. Both MSS have the shorter version of v. 44 (with ℵ B fam. 1 OL k and the Coptic, but against D). Cur. gives the doxology to the Lord's Prayer (except ἡ δύναμις καὶ) in vi. 13—Sin. is defective here. Both omit xii. 47 (with ℵ* B OL. ff.¹ k against D and the rest of the Old Latin). They omit xvi. 2, 3 with ℵ B fam. 13 against D OL., and similarly xvii. 21 with ℵ* B Θ OL. e ff¹ against D and the remaining OL. In xviii. 11 their testimony is divided, Sin. omitting the verse with ℵ B Θ, famm. 1 and 13 OL e ff¹ and Cur. retaining. In xix. 17 they agree with ℵ B D Θ fam. 1 in reading τί με ἐρωτᾷς περὶ του ἀγαθοῦ; εἷς ἐστιν ὁ ἀγαθός but Cur. adds ὁ Θεός with OL. In xx. 28 Cur. has the additional passage found also in D and Φ (see p. 91); Sin. is defective here. Sin. agrees with D, part of the OL. and apparently the *Diatessaron* in omitting xxi. 44, and with ℵ B D Θ fam. 1 in omitting xxiii. 14, but Cur. has both. In xxvii. 16 Sin. has the reading Ἰησοῦν βαραββᾶν, found also in Θ fam. 1—Cur. is defective. In Mark Cur. is wholly lacking, except a fragment containing xvi. 17–20, just long enough to show that it had the disputed longer ending, while Sin. agrees with ℵ B OL. k. in omitting. Elsewhere in this Gospel Sin. omits ix. 44, 46 with ℵ B W fam. 1 OL. k against D Θ fam. 13, and has the shorter version of ix. 49, with ℵ B, but in x. 24 adds τοὺς πεποιθότας χρήμασιν ἐπὶ with D and the majority against ℵ B OL. k, and in xiii. 33 adds καὶ προσεύχεσθε with ℵ and the majority against B D. In xiv. 24 it has καινῆς with the majority against ℵ B D OL. k. In Luke ii. 14 Sin. has εὐδοκία against all the principal uncials except Θ. It is deficient in vi. 4 where D has the remarkable addition (see p. 91 above). It omits the last words of vi. 48 with 𝔭⁴⁵ 700. In ix. 35 Sin. supports 𝔭⁴⁵, ⁷⁵ ℵ B in reading ἐκλελεγμένος, while Cur. follows A D and the bulk of the MSS with the *Diatessaron* and Marcion in reading ἀγαπητός as in the parallel passages in

Matthew and Mark. Similarly in ix. 55-6 Sin. agrees with $\mathfrak{p}^{45,75}$ ℵ B in omitting the words καὶ εἶπεν . . . σῶσαι while Cur agrees with Θ famm. 1, 13, the OL., Marcion, the *Diatessaron* and the majority of later witnesses in retaining them. In x. 42 Sin. omits ἑνὸς δέ ἐστιν Χρεία with D OL., while Cur. has them with $\mathfrak{p}^{45,75}$ A W Θ and most MSS. In the Lord's Prayer (xi. 2-4) Sin. gives the shorter version throughout with $\mathfrak{p}^{45,75}$ (ℵ) B, while Cur. omits only 'thy will be done, as in heaven, so in earth'. In xiv. 5, where $\mathfrak{p}^{45,75}$ B W have υἱὸς ἢ βοῦς, ℵ famm. 1, 13 have ὄνος ἢ βοῦς and D πρόβατον ἢ βοῦς, Sin. has βοῦς ἢ ὄνος, and Cur. υἱὸς ἢ βοῦς ἢ ὄνος. In the institution of the Lord's Supper (xxii. 17-20) Sin. gives the verses in the order 19, 20ᵃ, 17, 20ᵇ, 18, while Cur. has them in the order 19, 17, 18, omitting 20; which seem to be attempts to avoid the double mention of the Cup found in ℵ B and most other MSS. In xxii. 43, 44 Sin. with $\mathfrak{p}^{75}$ B omits, while Cur. retains, the Vision of the Angel and the Bloody Sweat. Similarly in xxiii. 34 Sin. omits while Cur. retains, the Word from the Cross 'Father, forgive them'; but in 38 both agree with $\mathfrak{p}^{75}$ B and omit 'in letters of Greek and Roman and Hebrew'. In xxiv, however, both side with D and Old Latin in their omission of 40; in 42 Sin. omits with ℵ B D, but Cur. retains, and in 51, 52 Sin. has the shorter reading with D and OL., Cur. being absent; while in 6 and 12 both have the longer form with $\mathfrak{p}^{75}$ ℵ B. In John i. 18 Cur. reads ὁ μονογενὴς υἱός against the μονογενὴς Θεός of $\mathfrak{p}^{75}$ ℵ B. In iv. 9 both have the reading οὐ γὰρ συγχρῶνται Ἰουδαῖοι Σαμαρείταις with $\mathfrak{p}^{66,75}$ B and the majority, which ℵ* D and some OL. omit. In iv. 42 Cur. omits ὁ Χριστός at the end of the verse with $\mathfrak{p}^{66,75}$ ℵ B against D Θ and the majority. In v. 3, 4 Cur. omits with $\mathfrak{p}^{66,75}$ ℵ B the stirring of the water (ἐκδεχομένων . . . νοσήματι,)—Sin. is defective here. Both omit the *pericope adulterae* (with $\mathfrak{p}^{66,75}$ ℵ B, but against D). In ix. 35 Sin. supports $\mathfrak{p}^{66,75}$ ℵ B D in reading ἀνθρώπου, not θεοῦ with the majority—Cur. is defective. In xi. 39 Sin. (Cur. is defective) has a quite singular addition after κύριε, 'Why are they taking away the stone?'. In xviii by an alteration in the order of the verses in Sin. (13, 24, 14, 15, 19-23, 16-18, 25-27) Caiaphas is made to appear as the questioner instead of Annas, and the three denials by Peter are brought together.

The above list of more noteworthy variants is enough to show

that, apart from singular readings, the Old Syriac Gospels are to
be classed as a whole neither with the Alexandrian ($\aleph$ B type)
nor with the Western (D Old Latin) texts. Thus, as Burkitt
pointed out, Sin. has none of the greater Western interpolations
(by contrast Cur. has about half of these), and both are free
from the conflate Byzantine readings. At the same time, in minor
variants there are frequent agreements with the Western D—
Old Latin group either as a whole, or with parts of it, and this
is particularly striking in two respects, namely in minor omissions,
and in a number of agreements with the African Old Latin (k, e
Cyprian) against the other Old Latin witnesses. The extent of
this Western element in the Old Syriac may be gathered from
the following examples:

(a) *Matthew*

   (i) *Old Syriac varies with D Old Latin:*
   iv. 24 (καὶ πάντας ἐθεράπευσεν), x. 35 (υἱόν), xiii. 52 (λέγει),
   xiv. 34 (Γεννῆσαρ), xv. 26 (ἔξεστιν), xvii. 2 (χιών—Sin.
   defective), xvii. 23 (μετὰ τρεῖς ἡμέρας Sin.; Cur. with $\aleph$ B
   etc.), xxii. 7 (τὸ στράτευμα Cur.; Sin. with $\aleph$ B etc.),
   xxii. 34 (ἐπ᾽ αὐτόν), xxii. 46 (ὥρας), xxiii. 9 (ὑμῖν); and Sin.
   (Cur. defective), xxiii. 37 (πρός σε), xxvi. 73 (ὁμοιάζει).

   (ii) *Old Syriac adds with D Old Latin:*
   i. 20 (Ησαΐου), iii. 17 (πρὸς αὐτόν), v. 41 (ἔτι ἀλλά), xviii. 10
   (τῶν πιστευοντων εἰς ἐμέ Cur.; Sin. with $\aleph$ B etc.), xxvi. 42
   (τὸ ποτηριον).

   (iii) *Old Syriac omits with D Old Latin:*
   iii. 1 (δέ Sin. *om.*, Cur. reads with $\aleph$ B etc.), v. 11, (ψευδόμενοι
   Sin. *om.*, Cur. with $\aleph$ B etc.), xiii. 1 (τῆς οἰκίας Sin. *om.*,
   Cur. with $\aleph$ B etc.), xiii. 30 (εἰς *pr.*), xiii. 46 (ἕνα Cur.
   om., Sin. with $\aleph$ B etc.), xxi. 25 (οὖν); and Cur. defective,
   xxiv. 2 (οὐ *pr.*), xxviii. 7 (ἀπὸ τῶν νεκρῶν).

   (iv) *Old Syriac omits with Old Latin without D:*
   vi. 27 (μεριμνῶν Cur., Sin. and D defective), xviii. 10
   (ἐν οὐρανοῖς Sin., Cur. with $\aleph$ etc.), xxi. 23 (διδάσκοντι).

(b) *Mark* (Sin. only; Cur. defective)

   (i) *Sin. varies with D Old Latin:*
   iii. 5 (νέκρωσει, $\aleph$ B etc. πωρώσει), vii. 9 (στήσητε), xii. 20
   (ἀπέθανε καί), xiv. 72 (ἤρξατο κλαίειν).

(ii) *Sin. omits with D Old Latin:*

ii. 26 (ἐπὶ Ἀβίαθαρ ἀρχιερέως), iii. 7 (ἠκολούθησεν), iv. 16 (ὁμοίως, εὐθύς), v. 21 (ἐν τῷ πλοίῳ), vi. 25 (μετὰ σπουδῆς), x. 2 (προσελθόντες φαρισαῖοι), x. 6 (κτίσεως).

(c) Luke

(i) *Old Syriac varies with D Old Latin:*

vi. 37 (ἵνα bis, Cur. defective), vii. 6 (ἐπορεύετο δὲ μετ' αὐτῶν ὁ Ἰησοῦς, Cur. defective), ix. 37 (διὰ τῆς ἡμέρας), xi. 52 (ἐκρύψατε), xvii. 15 (ἐκαθαρίσθη), xxii. 7 (τοῦ πάσχα), xxii. 26 (μικρότερος).

(ii) *Old Syriac varies with Old Latin against D:*

xvii. 31 (ὥρᾳ).

(iii) *Old Syriac omits with D Old Latin:*

iv. 34 ("Εα, Cur. defective), vii. 7 (διὸ . . . ἐλθεῖν, Cur. defective), viii. 5 (τοῦ οὐρανοῦ), ix. 26 (λόγους Cur., Sin. = ℵ B etc.), x. 22 (μου, Cur. defective), x. 23 (κατ' ἰδίαν), xi. 44 (ὡς τά), xii. 14 (ἢ μεριστήν), xiv. 3 (λέγων), xiv. 10 (πάντων Sin., Cur. with ℵ B etc.), xiv. 25 (πολλοί Cur., Sin. with ℵ B etc.), xv. 3 (λέγων), xv. 8 (δραχμήν), xviii. 39 (πολλῷ), xviii. 40 (πρὸς αὐτόν), xix. 7 (λέγοντες Cur., Sin. with ℵ B etc.), xix. 12 (ἑαυτῷ), xx. 36 (καὶ υἱοί εἰσιν Sin., Cur. with ℵ B etc.), xxi. 15 (ἢ ἀντειπεῖν), xxii. 52 (Ἰησοῦς), xxiii. 29 (ἰδού), xxiv. 1 (ἀρώματα), xxiv. 39 (με).

(iv) *Old Syriac omits with Old Latin against D:*

ii. 17 (ἰδόντες δέ, Cur. defective), iii. 8 (ἐν ἑαυτοῖς), xiii. 5 (πάντες), xvii. 24 (λάμπει), xx. 3 (λόγον Cur., Sin. reads with ℵ B D etc.), xx. 32 (ὕστερον), xxiii. 27 (πολύ).

(d) John

(i) *Old Syriac varies with D Old Latin:*

x. 25 (λάλω Sin., ℵ B etc. εἶπον), xi. 28 (σιωπῇ Sin., ℵ B etc. λάθρα), xvi. 21 (ἡμέρα Sin., ℵ B etc. ὥρα)—Cur. defective for all these.

(ii) *Old Syriac adds with D Old Latin:*

vi. 38 (Πατρός), xii. 19 (ὅλος—Cur. defective), xiii. 14 (πόσῳ μᾶλλον—Cur. defective).

(iii) *Old Syriac omits with D Old Latin*

vi. 23 (εὐχαριστήσαντος τοῦ κυρίου), vi. 37 (ἔξω), viii. 34 (τῆς ἁμαρτίας), viii. 52 (εἰς τὸν αἰῶνα), viii. 53 (πατρὸς ἡμῶν), ix. 2 (λέγοντες), x. 38 (καὶ γινώσκετε/πιστεύετε), xi. 54 (ἐκεῖθεν), xvi. 18 (ἔλεγεν οὖν), xvi. 28 (ἐξῆλθον ἐκ τοῦ πατρός), xviii. 5 (ὁ Ἰησοῦς)—Cur. defective for all except vi. 23.

(iv) *Old Syriac omits with Old Latin against D:*
   xi. 25 (καὶ ἡ ζωή), xi. 39 (ἡ ἀδελφὴ τοῦ τετελευτηκότος)— Cur. defective.

Besides these agreements of the Old Syriac with the Western text in general there are others where it is found supporting the African Old Latin (*k, e,* Cyprian) against the rest of the Old Latin witnesses. The following examples may be cited:

(i) *Old Syriac reads with k alone:*
   Matt. i. 25 (*om.* οὐκ ἐγίνωσκεν αὐτὴν ἕως οὗ Sin.), iv. 17 (*om.* μετανοεῖτε, γάρ Sin., Cur.), v. 47 (*om.* verse Sin.), xi. 5 (*om.* καὶ πτωχοὶ εὐαγγελίζονται Sin.)—except for iv. 17 Cur. reads with the majority.
(ii) *Old Syriac reads with e alone:*
   Luke vi. 21 (γελάσονται Sin.—Cur. defective).
(iii) *Old Syriac reads with D k alone:*
   Matt. xiii. 33 (*om.* ἐλάλησεν αὐτοῖς), Mark xv. 43 (πτῶμα Sin., *rell.* σῶμα—Cur. defective).
(iv) *Old Syriac reads with D e alone:*
   Luke i. 63 (*om.* λέγων—Cur. defective), iv. 2 (σατανᾶ Sin., *rell.* διαβόλου—Cur. defective), x. 2 (*om.* οὖν Sin., Cur. with אB etc.), xii. 51 (ποιῆσαι Cur., βαλεῖν Sin. and some Old Latin, *rell.* δοῦναι), xx. 20 (τῷ ἡγεμόνι Cur., Sin. with *rell.* τῇ ἀρχῇ καὶ τῇ ἐξουσίᾳ τοῦ ἡγεμόνος), xxi. 27 (καὶ δύναμει πολλῇ καὶ δόξῃ Sin., Cur., *rell.* μετὰ δυνάμεως καὶ δόξης πολλῆς), xxiv. 30 (*om.* μετ' αὐτῶν Sin., Cur.), John xiv. 23 (ἐλεύσομαι . . . ποιήσομαι Cur., Sin. with *rell.* ἐλευσόμεθα . . . ποιησόμεθα).

This list of minor agreements with the Western text, by no means exhaustive, can be verified in the ordinary manual editions. It clearly shows that the textual history of the Old Syriac and the Western text must have crossed—perhaps twice if we are to explain the agreement with the African Latin against the other Western witnesses. But also it is evident that the Old Syriac is a short text, particularly so in the case of Sin., which, as has been noted, omits all the greater Western interpolations and with Cur. is on the side of omission for nearly half the 'Western non-interpolations', as well as having other omissions peculiar to itself—e.g.,

Matt. xvii. 26 (εἰπόντος δέ), Mark i. 32 (ὀψίας δὲ γενομένης), vii. 4 (καὶ χαλκίων καὶ κλινῶν), vii. 8 (whole verse), Luke xxiii. 10–12, John v. 12 (perhaps by homoioteleuton), xiv. 10ᵇ–11.

Indeed Sin. is the shortest of all New Testament texts, and Lagrange has argued that at some stage it has undergone a radical excision of repetitions and redundancies. On the other hand, many of the omissions are found in both Sin. and Cur. and have support from Alexandrian or Western authorities, though whether these represent the old text of Antioch is a difficult question. At any rate it would be hazardous to assume that the shorter readings of the Old Syriac are to be accepted as pointing to the original text on their own merits.

Another characteristic pointed out by Burkitt in his edition (*Evangelion da—Mepharreshe*, II, pp. 245–51) is the agreements of the Old Syriac with what he called secondary Greek authorities, namely the MSS of families 1 and 13, 28, 565 and 700. These have now been recognized as part of the Cæsarean family (see below pp. 187–91), which has since been extended by the more recently discovered uncials Θ and W and the Chester Beatty papyrus (𝔭⁴⁵) as well as the Armenian and Georgian versions. One example of this type is the reading 'Jesus Barabbas' in Matt. xxvii. 16, 17 already mentioned, which is supported by Θ fam. 1. 700* and the Armenian and Georgian versions. Among others cited by Burkitt (to take only Mark, where this grouping has been most extensively studied) are

i. 13 (ἐκεῖ fam. 1. 28*), ii. 27 (ἐκτίσθη W. fam. 1. 700), v. 1 (Γεργεσηνῶν Θ fam. 1. 28. 565. 700 arm. geo.), vii. 33 (καὶ πτύσας before εἰς τὰ ὦτα 𝔭⁴⁵ fam. 13. 28), x. 14 (add ἐπιτιμήσας W Θ famm. 1. 13. 28. 565).

But an inspection of an ordinary apparatus will easily bring others to light—e.g.

Mark vii. 37 (*om.* [τοὺς] ἀλάλους W 28), ix. 25 (*om.* τῷ ἀκαθάρτῳ 𝔭⁴⁵ W fam. 1), ix. 43 (*om.* εἰς τὴν γέενναν W famm. 1. 13. 28 geo.),

xi. 10 (Εἰρήνη for Ὡσαννά W 28. 700), xii. 41 (ἑστώς W Θ
famm. 1. 13. 28. 565 arm. geo.), xv. 39 (ὅτι κράξας W Θ 565,
arm. geo.):

the presence of these typical Cæsarean readings, quite distinct
from those of the Alexandrian, Western and Byzantine families
(and it should be noted that five of these last seven are omissions)
does not make the history of the Old Syriac easier of solution.

Relation of the Old Syriac to the Diatessaron

The relation of the *Diatessaron* to the Old Syriac gospels is not
easy to determine. It seems that the translators of the Old Syriac
not infrequently adopted the renderings of Tatian, and it would
be reasonable to suppose that some of the harmonizations (of
which there are more in Cur. than Sin.) are due to the influence
of the *Diatessaron*—though, as has been previously remarked,
aberrations of this kind are common enough scribal failings without
having recourse to a harmony. On the one hand, the absence of
such distinctive Tatianic passages as the interpolation at Matt. iii.
15 (the light at the Baptism, read also by the Old Latin *a* and
g[1], and apparently known to Justin Martyr), and Matt. xvii. 26
(after οἱ υἱοί the addition of ἔφη Σίμων, Ναί. λέγει ὁ Ἰησοῦς,
Δός οὖν καί σύ ὡς ἀλλότριος αὐτῶν, found in Greek only in the
minuscule 713), as well as the Western additions at Matt. xvi. 2–3
(the face of the sky), Luke xxii, 43–44 (the sweat of blood), John v. 4
(the angel at the pool—Sin. is lacking here), all of which are
found in the *Diatessaron* but not in the Old Syriac, argues for
an independent translation for the separated Gospels. On the
other hand, the influence of the *Diatessaron* may be seen in such
passages as Mark viii. 31–2 where Sin. reads (Cur. defective) with
k and Tatian 'and the third day he will rise and openly speak
the word' (though this might be derived ultimately from the old
Western text), Mark x. 21, 'then Jesus looked on him lovingly
and said to him' (Cur. defective), Luke ii. 36 ἡμερᾶς for ἔτη
(Cur. defective)—perhaps an Encratite touch, xviii. 13 rendering
οὐκ ἤθελεν as 'not daring' (Cur. only), the addition in both Sin.
and Cur. to Luke xxiii. 48 'Saying: "Woe to us! What has befallen
us? Woe to us for our sins"', found in a slightly different form
in the Old Latin *g*[1] (which is remarkable for a number of apparently *Diatessaron* readings—see above on Matt. iii. 15) and the

Apocryphal Gospel of Peter,[1] and the rendering of σάρξ by 'a body' in John i. 14 (Sin. defective).

Textual comparison of Sin. and Cur.

Where Sin. and Cur. diverge, the tendency to adopt the shorter reading comes out more strongly on the side of Sin. This can clearly be seen on any page of Burkitt's edition where the two are extant, but a careful reading of the apparatus to the Greek text will show the same phenomenon.

A more generalized idea of the textual relationships of the Old Syriac may be gathered from the following analytical tables of agreements and disagreements with the main representatives of the Alexandrian and Western groups.[2]

Sinaitic Syriac

	ℵ with	ℵ against	B with	B against	D with	D against	Old Latin with	Old Latin against
Matthew	54	97	53	98	76	55	78	73
Mark	53	78	49	83	45	85	55	71
Luke	66	89	67	88	70	83	68	85
John	48	70	34	84	53	55	60	52
Totals	221	334	203	353	244	278	261	281

Curetonian Syriac

	ℵ with	ℵ against	B with	B against	D with	D against	Old Latin with	Old Latin against
Mark	56	80	50	85	68	48	73	61
Luke	48	64	39	73	57	54	54	56
John	28	31	12	47	26	26	31	27
Totals	132	175	101	205	151	128	158	144

[1] The quotations in Ephraim's commentary and elsewhere show that this, or something like it, appeared in the *Diatessaron*. Tatian's use of the Gospel of Peter here, and the fact that Victor of Capua, in the prefatory matter to the Cod. Fuldensis, says that Tatian 'unum ex quattuor, compaginauerit euangelium cui titulum diapente composuit' has given rise to the suggestion that he made use of an extra-canonical gospel. But it seems unlikely that the 'diapente' can bear this interpretation—see F. Bolgiani *Vittore di Capua e il Diatessaron* (*Memorie dell'Academia della Scienze di Torino*), 1962.

[2] In previous editions of this book the tables were based on the list of passages in W. Sanday's *Appendices ad N.T. Stephanicum* (Oxford, 1889), which ranged over 158 passages in the Gospels where there are specially notable variations of

These figures, for what they are worth, show that Cur. is closer to the Western text than Sin.; the apparent discrepancy between the figures for ℵ and B in John, more noticeable in the text of Cur., is due to the fact that in the first eight chapters of this Gospel ℵ is Western in character.

In conclusion, it will be apparent that the problems presented by the Old Syriac Gospels are still far from solution. How far the text as we have it represents that form of the Greek current at Edessa when the version was made is one of these, and another, which is related to it, is its date. If, as some scholars have maintained, the separated Syriac Gospels were already in existence before Tatian returned to the East c. 170, then it could be argued that their Western character shows that this type of text was prevalent in both East and West at an early date. But if, as most scholars think, the version was made about 200, and therefore after the Diatessaron, the Western characteristics could be due to the influence of the latter, which in turn may have been based on the type of Greek text which Tatian found in Rome during his sojourn there and brought back with him. What is further to the point, perhaps, is the gap of two centuries or more between the making of the version and our two MSS, a period during which, as the evidence would seem to suggest, the ancestors of the Sinaitic and Curetonian have been subject to revision and influence from various sources, and ancient though its origin may be, it would be hazardous to suppose that the version represents in its entirety an independent line of tradition.

No MS of an Old Syriac version of any other part of the New Testament is extant, but there is good reason to suppose that the other books were also translated; for Armenian translations of Syriac commentaries by St Ephraim (died 373) on the Acts (reconstructed by F. C. Conybeare in *The Beginnings of Christianity*, *III, The Text of Acts*, ed. J. H. Ropes, London, 1929, pp. 373–453) and Pauline Epistles (reconstructed by J. Molitor, *Der Paulustext des heiligen Ephräm, Monumenta Biblica et Ecclesiastica*, iv, Rome, 1938) are extant. Although allowance has to be made for the Armenian translator having accommodated the text to that of the

text. The above tables are based on the much larger selection of variants (over 600) in the United Bible Societies' edition, edited by K. Aland, M. Black, B. M. Metzger and A. Wikgren (Stuttgart, 1966). The figures for the Old Latin version must be taken with some reserve, since the MSS for this version often differ.

Armenian Vulgate, it is now clear that in both Acts and the Epistles Ephraim's Syriac text was of the Western type. This in turn may have some bearing on the problem of the Old Syriac text of the Gospels; for unless one is to suppose that Tatian brought from Rome to Edessa a Western text of the Acts and Epistles as well as of the Gospels, the inference would be that the so-called 'Western text' belongs equally to the East.

(c) *The Peshitta.* This was the version which eventually became the official Bible of the Syriac Church, just as the Vulgate did of the Roman. Before the discovery of the Old Syriac, it was generally assigned to the third, or even to the second, century. But it was shown by Burkitt that the belief that it was used by St Ephraim was unfounded, and that in fact there is no evidence of its existence before the fifth century. Moreover, he pointed out that Rabbula, bishop of Edessa from 411–35, is recorded by his biographer to have translated the New Testament from Greek into Syriac, and that it was consequently not only legitimate but inevitable to identify his translation with the Peshitta, when once the latter was shown to belong to this period. Materially later the Peshitta could not be, since there are extant MSS of it which are assigned to the latter part of the fifth century; and it would be sheer perversity to maintain that Rabbula's version has perished without trace, while an anonymous production of the same date had captured the Church of Edessa. As the work of this great bishop, on the other hand, its immediate success would be quite intelligible. The *Diatessaron* and Old Syriac dropped out of existence, and the Peshitta became the accepted Syriac Bible. Since, moreover, it was used by both the Monophysite and the Nestorian Churches, it must have been generally accepted before 431, when the Nestorian secession took place. Burkitt's view, which rests on probabilities, may however require modification. Professor M. Black (*Bulletin of the Rylands Library* xxxiii (1951), pp. 203–10), on the basis of an examination of the gospel quotations in Rabbula's translation of the *De recta fide* of Cyril of Alexandria, concludes that Rabbula's text still contained a not inconsiderable Old Syriac element, and was something in the nature of a half-way stage between Old Syriac and the form of the Peshitta text found in the MSS. A. Vööbus (*Studies in the History of the Gospel Text in Syriac*, Louvain, 1951) finds that towards the end of his life only the shortest of Rabbula's New Testament quotations resemble the

Peshitta, many of them agreeing with the *Diatessaron* or the Old Syriac, and he rejects Burkitt's hypothesis.

Something like 180 copies of the Peshitta Gospels are known, and 150 of the rest of the New Testament, of which more than 100 are in the British Museum. Two of these are assigned to the fifth century, and four bear actual dates in the sixth. In character, it shows the influence of the revision which, beginning perhaps at Antioch, ultimately developed into the received Byzantine text. Since a form of this appears in the writings of Chrysostom, who was born and worked at Antioch until 398, it was easily available at the beginning of the fifth century, and the Peshitta shows many readings of this type. On the other hand, it retains considerable elements of the earlier types which are found in the Old Syriac and Alexandrian uncial MSS. In the readings analysed above, the Peshitta is found agreeing with Sin. in 293 instances (52.5%) and disagreeing in 265, while the figures for Cur. are 174 (57%) in agreement and 130 against. The higher ratio of agreements between the Peshitta and Cur. may be used as an argument that the Curetonian, as compared with the Sinaitic, has been somewhat revised in the direction of the later types of text. There are also not infrequent examples of the Peshitta and the *Diatessaron* agreeing together against the two Old Syriac authorities, or, when these are divided, with one against the other.

The Peshitta in its original form did not include the Apocalypse or the four minor Catholic Epistles (2 Pet., 2 and 3 John, Jude), which were not accepted as canonical by the Syriac Church. It was first edited at Vienna in 1555 by C. Widmanstadt. The standard edition is that of G. H. Gwilliam (completing the work begun by Philip Pusey), which was published in 1902. Gwilliam used some forty MSS, but he states that they differ little. Syriac scribes, like Hebrew, were very careful copyists.

(d) *The Philoxenian and Harkleian Syriac.* About a century later than the Peshitta, in 508, a fresh translation was made to the order of Philoxenus, Jacobite bishop of Hierapolis in eastern Syria, by Polycarp, a χωρεπίσκοπος. It was from this version that the four minor Catholic Epistles were added to the Syriac Bible; and a copy of the Apocalypse in this version was discovered by Dr Gwynn of Dublin in a twelfth-century MS now in the John Rylands Library at Manchester, and published by him in

1897. From these books it is clear that the Philoxenian version was written in good idiomatic Syriac, and that its text was of the early Byzantine type. For the rest of the New Testament its character is obscured by the inability of scholars to agree as to the nature of the revision at the hands of Thomas of Harkel in 616. According to some, Harkel merely added marginal notes from a few Greek MSS, while others take the view that the Philoxenian text was drastically revised besides being given the marginal apparatus. His method too is said to have been the reverse of that of Philoxenus in that he was literal without respect for idiom. The Harkleian marginal readings in Acts are a most important witness to the Western text in this book. A new edition of this version is in preparation which should clear up the questions connected with it.

About fifty MSS of this version have come down to us, all representing it under the form of the Harkleian revision. The oldest (at Rome) is assigned to the seventh century. The Harkleian Apocalypse was edited by de Dieu in 1627, and the four Philoxenian Epistles by Pococke in 1630, but otherwise the version was unknown until the whole was edited by J. White in 1778–1803, and this remains the only available text.

(e) *The Palestinian Syriac*. Finally, considerable portions remain of another version in the Palestinian dialect, which was thought by Burkitt to have originated at Antioch in the sixth century, probably as a result of the efforts of Justinian and Heraclius to eradicate Judaism in Palestine, and to have become popular on the occasion of a revival of Palestinian Christianity in the eleventh century. Nearly all the surviving MSS are in the form of lectionaries, the two most important being a pair of Gospel lectionaries, dated 1104 and 1118, which were edited by Mrs Lewis and Mrs Gibson in 1899. Some portions of Acts and Epistles have survived in other fragmentary copies. Its text is mixed in character, but contains early elements, both of the ℵ B and D type, such as are found in the Cæsarean group.

Two other Oriental versions deserve brief mention on account of their connection with the Syriac.

II. ARMENIAN

Armenia was evangelized by Syrian Christians during the third century, and the natural inference would be that its Scriptures were translated from Syriac, as indeed a fifth-century Armenian writer, Moses of Khorene, states, naming St Sahak (=Isaac) as the translator. But there are also native Armenian traditions that the version was made from the Greek of St Mesrop, the successor of Sahak and inventor of the Armenian and Georgian alphabets. Modern scholars are to be found ranged on either side. The presence of Syriacisms in the text, and the fact that the Armenian New Testament apparently included the apocryphal 3rd Epistle to the Corinthians and omitted Philemon (as did the Old Syriac Canon) supports a Syriac origin. But there are also strong affinities with the Greek which make the other view equally tenable. In the latter case the Syriacisms are explained as a result of the use of the Syriac version (or an early version made from the Syriac) as a 'crib' in translating the more difficult Greek passages, and also to unconscious assimilation. But F. C. Conybeare suggested (and this has been taken up by some recent writers) that behind the surviving text was an Armenian version of Tatian's *Diatessaron* which has left its mark. These differing views may to some extent be reconciled by postulating an original version (Arm.[1]) made from the Syriac (whether the Diatessaron or the Old Syriac) by Sahek at the beginning of the fifth century; this would correspond to quotations in Armenian Fathers which, according to Lyonnet, have much in common with the Syriac writer St Ephraim. Then, after the Council of Ephesus in 431, the text was revised on the basis of Greek MSS by St Mesrop (Arm.[2]). On this theory Arm.[1] has disappeared, while Arm.[2], with its Cæsarean characteristics, is represented by the extant MSS of the version.

There are dated MSS of the Armenian version of 887, 902, 960, 986, and 989. Three early MSS examined by Conybeare at Edschmiadzin (the principal library of Armenian literature) omit the last twelve verses of Mark, and a fourth, which has them, adds a note saying that they are 'of the elder Ariston'. This has been taken to mean that, the original ending of the Gospel having been lost at a very early date, these verses (which are in quite a different style from the rest of the Gospel) were added by the elder Aristion, who is named by Papias as one of the disciples of our Lord from whom he derived information. It may be so (the difference in the spelling of the name may be ignored), but there is no confirmation of it. Three of Conybeare's MSS also omit Luke xxii. 43, 44, but the passage is in the oldest of them, and according to Theodore it was also in the ancient Armenian version but was subsequently omitted (by Mesrop and Sahak). The early Armenian MSS also omit the *pericope adulterae*, and the earliest that has it (that of 989) gives it in a different form from the Greek, with the curious addition that what our Lord wrote on the ground was the sins of the several self-constituted judges.

Of more importance is the fact that the version is an important witness to the type of text, partly Alexandrian, partly Western, which is called Cæsarean in the Gospels, though some writers assert that the Cæsarean element has been reduced through later revision.

A similar mixture is found in the Acts and Pauline Epistles, while the Catholic Epistles are Alexandrian in type. In the Apocalypse F. C. Conybeare showed that the Armenian version was made in the fifth century—i.e. before the first Syriac translation, from which therefore it cannot be derived. In view of some surprising affinities it appears to have been influenced by, if not actually to have been translated from (as Conybeare thought) the Old Latin. Thereafter it went through a number of revisions, but nevertheless preserves a remarkably good text in this book.

The version was first printed at Amsterdam in 1666 and again in 1805 in a critical edition by J. Zohrab of the Mechitarist fathers at Venice. See also F. C. Conybeare in the 4th edition of Scrivener's *Introduction* (1894), Hastings' *Dictionary of the Bible*, I, 883–912, *Journal of Theological Studies*, xxv (1924), 232–45; Armitage Robinson, *Euthaliana* (1895); F. Macler, *Le texte arménien de l'évangile d'après Matthieu et Marc*, Paris, 1919; A. Merk in *Biblica*, vii (1926), 40–70; R. P. Blake, *The Caesarean Text of Mark*, in *Harvard Theological Review*, xxi (1928), 307–10; A. Baumstark, *Oriens Christianus*, 3te Serie, iii–iv (1930), 117–24; C. S. C. Williams, *Journal of Theological Studies*, xliii (1942), 161–7, xlviii (1947), 196–200; S. Lyonnet in Lagrange, *Critique textuelle*, pp. 342 ff. and *Les Origines de la version arménienne et la Diatessaron* (*Biblica et Orientalia*, xiii, 1950); E. C. Colwell, *Anglican Theological Review*, xvi (1934), pp. 113–32, *Journal of Religion*, xvii (1937), pp. 48–61; E. F. Rhodes, *An Annotated List of Armenian New Testament Manuscripts* (Tokio, 1959).

III. Georgian

The Georgian version has only more recently come under notice, and has been studied by few scholars. So far as England and America are concerned, the main guides are Conybeare (in Scrivener, *Academy* of Feb. 1, 1896, *American Journal of Theology* i, 1897, 883–912, *Zeitschrift für die neutestamentliche Wissenschaft*, xi, (1910), pp. 232–49) and R. P. Blake, *Harvard Theological Review*, xxi (1928), pp. 286–307, 358–75, *Quantulacumque* (1937), pp. 355–63, E. C. Colwell, *Anglican Theological Review*, xvi (1934), 113–37; cf. also A. Baumstark (*op. cit.*), G. Peradse (*Oriens Christianus*, 3te Serie, ii (1927), pp. 205–22, *Zeitschrift für die neutestamentliche Wissenschaft*, xxix (1930), pp. 304–9; also G. Garitte, *L'ancienne version georgienne des Actes des Apôtres* (Louvain), 1955. According to Blake, the Gospels and Pauline Epistles were always in separate MSS until modern times, and have distinct textual traditions. The version appears to have been made before the middle of the fifth century, but the Apocalypse, first translated about 978, was never fully accepted. The earliest and best Georgian Gospels is the Adysh MS, written in 897, which stands by itself. A second group is headed by the Opiza MS (913) and the Tbet' MS (995). Others represent a revision in the eleventh century from Greek MSS of the Byzantine type, which became the accepted version of the Georgian Church, and is of little importance. The language from which the original version was made has been variously assigned, and at one time Greek and Syrian had each their proponents. But the close relationship of the Georgian to the Armenian, either as a sister version or as child to parent, has now been clearly established, and according to Blake, Lyonnet and others the Georgian depends directly on the Armenian. Again, according to Blake, the original version was made from an Armenian text older than, or better preserved than, any now extant Armenian MS; and its special interest is that it goes back to a Greek text of the type described below as Cæsarean, of which the leading Greek representatives are $\mathfrak{p}^{45}$, W (in part of Mark), Θ, fam. 1 and fam. 13. Blake's conclusion is that 'the Old Georgian version, represented at present by the Adysh manuscript and by Codices A and B' [Opiza and Tbet'] 'was one of the best witnesses to the Cæsarean text. It has been corrected by Ecclesiastical' [Byzantine] 'copies in the Adysh MS and somewhat more extensively, but quite independently, in A and B. Further, this Georgian was made from the Armenian. But the Armenian from which it was made has been greatly revised in the MSS which are the basis of the printed text and in all of the oldest Armenian MSS which have been the object of special study', as is shown by the fact that one or both of the Georgian recensions contain a number of Cæsarean readings which are not in the Armenian as now extant. E. C. Colwell, however, maintains that the Armenian version is a better representative of the Cæsarean tradition than the Georgian, and that the Opiza and Tbet' MSS have a closer affinity to the Armenian than the Adysh MS.

It may be observed that the Adysh and Opiza MSS omit the last twelve verses of Mark, while the Tbet' MS contains them.

A critical edition of Matthew and Mark based upon the Opiza and Tbet' MSS was published by V. N. Benesevic at St Petersburg in 1909–11 but this is now superseded by an edition based on the Adysh MS (with Latin translation) published in *Patrologia Orientalis* as follows: Mark (ed. R. P. Blake), xx. 3 (1929); Matt. (ed. R. P. Blake), xxiv. 1 (1933); John (ed. R. P. Blake and M. Brière), xxvi. 4 (1950); and Luke (ed M. Brière), xxvii. 3 (1955). The Acts has been edited by G. Garitte, *L'ancienne version Géorgienne des Actes des Apôtres d'après deux manuscrits de Sinaï*, Louvain, 1955. The later Vulgate text, published at Moscow as long ago as 1743, is available from the Bible Society.

IV. Coptic

Coptic is the ancient language of the people of Egypt. Its native script was hieroglyphic, later distinguished into hieratic and demotic forms. But in the early centuries of the Christian era, as a result of the presence of Greek-speaking settlers, the language, as well as having acquired a good many loan-words from Greek, began to be written in Greek uncial characters, with the addition of six native letters to represent sounds not heard in Greek. In a rather primitive form the script appears in a papyrus in the British Museum, written on the back of a horoscope, the date of which is either 95 or 155, but more probably the former. The Chester Beatty papyrus of Isaiah (see above, p. 36) has in its margins, in a hand of the early third century, a number of notes

K

in the Old Fayyumic dialect of Coptic, but written in Greek
without any additional letters, which seems to show that the
script was in an early stage. From all the evidence available it
would appear that round about the end of the second century
this form of writing was available to receive the Christian
scriptures.

The early history of Christianity in Egypt is far from clear.
From the first, however, its headquarters were at Alexandria, and
Greek was for long the principal language of the Church and
was used for all official purposes. The Rylands fragment of John
(see p. 72) which in all probability comes from the Fayyum,
points to the existence of Greek-speaking communities outside
Alexandria early in the second century, but it is not until the
third century that evidence begins to accumulate for the spread
of Christianity amongst the native population. Thus, Origen
refers to Αἰγύπτιοι as Christians, and many appear to have
suffered in the Decian persecution in 250 (cf. Eusebius, *Hist.
Eccles.* VI. 40–2). St Anthony, the first of the hermits, who was
born about 250, is recorded to have been greatly affected at the
age of twenty by hearing the Scriptures read in Church. He did
not know Greek, and what he heard may have been an oral paraphrase from the Greek, similar to the Aramaic paraphrases used
in Jewish synagogues. Indeed, it may well be that the rapidly-
growing number of hermits and monks who followed the example
of St Anthony, and were often drawn from the lower classes and,
like him, knew no Greek, provided the strongest impetus to the
translation of the Bible into the native tongue. By the beginning
of the fourth century Pachomius, the great organizer of monachism
in Egypt (who is said to have learnt Greek only late in life)
required his monks to be diligent in the study of the Scriptures
and to know the Psalter and the New Testament by heart, which
implies their existence already in the vernacular.

The Coptic language of the native Egyptians existed in a
number of dialects, and the accepted view has been that of these
Sahidic was spoken in Upper or Southern Egypt in and around
Thebes, and Bohairic in Lower or Northern Egypt (i.e. the Delta)
while, intermediate between these, both geographically and
linguistically, were various other dialects, Fayyumic, Memphitic
or Middle Egyptian, and Achmimic. It now seems, however, that
originally Sahidic came from the North; spreading from the Delta

to the South and becoming assimilated to the dialects spoken there, it was well established in Upper Egypt by the fourth century. Sahidic was the language of the educated native classes before the advent of Christianity, and continued as the official dialect under the Arabs, until in the tenth or eleventh centuries it was superseded in the Delta and later in the rest of Egypt by Bohairic. (See further P. E. Kahle, *Bala'izah*, London, 1954.)

(*a*) *Sahidic.* Until the discoveries of papyri in Egypt the Sahidic version was known in relatively few and scattered fragments, some of which were edited by Woide in 1799 and by Zoega in 1810. By the turn of the last century, however, enough material was available for G. Horner to produce an edition of the Coptic New Testament in both the main dialects: the Bohairic in four volumes (Oxford, 1898–1905) and the Sahidic in seven (Oxford, 1911–24). For the Sahidic version Horner had to rely for the most part on incomplete and fragmentary MSS, and valuable though his work was in its time, on the grounds of accuracy and completeness, especially in the light of more recent discoveries, a new edition is needed.

Of the larger MSS, the most notable are: a text of Acts, almost complete (together with Deuteronomy and Jonah) in the British Museum (Or. 7594) edited by E. A. W. Budge in 1912 and by H. Thompson in 1913, used by Horner and dated by Kenyon and H. Thompson in the mid-fourth century; three seventh-century MSS in the Chester Beatty collection at Dublin containing (*a*) the Pauline Epistles and John, (*b*) Acts and the Gospel of John, (*c*) Pss. i–l with Matt. i. 1–ii. 1—(*a*) and (*b*) were published by H. Thompson together with a collation of John against Horner's edition in *The Coptic Versions of the Acts and Pauline Epistles in the Sahidic Dialect* (Cambridge, 1932); from the Pierpont Morgan collection of Coptic MSS in New York (the whole of which is published by H. Hyvernat in photographic facsimile in *Bybliothecae Pierpont Morgan Codices Coptici* (Rome, 1922)) is a MS of the four Gospels, eighth–ninth century, complete except for Luke iv. 33–ix. 31, ix. 62–xiii. 18; and from the Bodmer collection a fourth–fifth century text of Matt. xiv. 28–xxviii. 20 and Romans i. 2–ii. 3, edited by R. Kasser, *Papyrus Bodmer XIX* (Cologny—Genève, 1962).

In text the Sahidic used formerly to be classed as, to some extent at least, an ally of D and the Old Latin, but increasing knowledge has greatly modified this view and shows that it is predominantly associated with the Alexandrian א B group. Thus in the selected readings in the Gospels referred to above (p. 127) the Sahidic agrees with א B against D in 195 instances, and with D against א B in 69; to these may be added: agreements with א against B D 41, with B against א D 80, with א D against B 44, and with B D against א 45. The overall figures are:

	With Sahidic	*Against Sahidic*
א	360	252
B	401	212
D	225	347
O.L.	282	317

It is clear from the above that the Sahidic is in the main Alexandrian, and closer to B than to א. The proportions, however, vary in the different Gospels, the influence of D being greatest in John and least in Luke. Moreover, the Alexandrian preponderance would lead us to expect a close agreement with the two Bodmer papyri 𝔭⁶⁶ and 𝔭⁷⁵, and indeed this is the case; and as has been pointed out by G. D. Kilpatrick (*Greek, Roman and Byzantine Studies*, iv (1963), pp. 33–47) if the Coptic versions, or some of them, were made in the third century, it is not unreasonable to suppose that they would be based on such early Egyptian Greek texts as these. Thus the Sahidic, together with the Sub-Achmimic (see below) and one MS of the Bohairic reads at John viii. 57 ἑώρακεν σέ with 𝔭⁷⁵ א* and the Sinaitic Syriac against the rest of the Greek witness, and at x. 7 the Sahidic and Achmimic read ἐγώ εἰμι ὁ ποιμὴν τῶν προβάτων with 𝔭⁷⁵ against all other Greek MSS. In addition the following agreements in Luke between 𝔭⁴⁵, 𝔭⁷⁵ and the Sahidic (but not the Bohairic) may be noted: vi. 26 *om.* πατέρες αὐτῶν with 𝔭⁷⁵ B 700 Sin. Syriac, x. 38 *om.* εἰς τὴν οἰκίαν (εἰς τὸν οἶκον) αὐτῆς with 𝔭⁴⁵,⁷⁵ B, xi. 11 *om.* ἄρτον μὴ λίθον ἐπιδώσει αὐτῷ; ἢ καί before ἰχθύν with 𝔭⁴⁵,⁷⁵ B OL. *ff*² *i l* Sin. Syriac, xi. 11 καὶ ἀντὶ ἰχθύος ἐπιδώσει with 𝔭⁴⁵,⁷⁵ B against μὴ ἀντὶ ἰχθύος, μὴ ἐπιδώσει and also xi. 33 *om.* οὐδὲ ὑπὸ τὸν μόδιον with 𝔭⁴⁵,⁷⁵ L fam. I Sin. Syriac.

Although there is a proportion of D-type readings to be found in the Sahidic Gospels, there is a notable absence of the longer additions characteristic of Cod. Bezae (in contrast to the Bohairic—

see below) and the Sahidic almost always sides with the Alexandrian against the longer omissions of D. Thus in the following passages Sah. omits with the main Alexandrian authorities:

Matt. xii. 47 (the Mother and brethren of Jesus) with ℵ* B L OL. *ff*¹ *k* OS.

Matt. xvi. 2–3 (Signs in the Sky) with ℵ B fam. 13 OS.

Matt. xvii. 21 (prayer and fasting) with ℵ B Θ 33 OS.

Matt. xviii. 11 (the Son of Man . . . lost) with ℵ B L* Θ famm. 1, 13 OS.ˢⁱⁿ

Mark ix. 44, 46 (worm and fire) with ℵ B W fam. 1 OS.ˢⁱⁿ

Mark xi. 26 (on forgiveness) with ℵ B W OL *k* OS.ˢⁱⁿ

Luke ix. 54ᵇ (as Elijah did) with 𝔭⁴⁵,⁷⁵ ℵ B OS.

Luke ix. 55ᵇ (ye know . . . spirit ye are) with 𝔭⁴⁵, ⁷⁵ ℵ B etc. OL *e l* OS.ˢⁱⁿ

Luke xvii. 36 (two in the field) with 𝔭⁷⁵ ℵ B fam. 1. etc.

Luke xxii. 43–4 (angel and Sweat) with 𝔭⁷⁵ B W OS.ˢⁱⁿ

John vii. 53–viii. 11 (*pericope adulterae*) with 𝔭⁶⁶,⁷⁵ ℵ B etc. OL OS.

On the other hand, in the case of the major omissions of D the Sahidic is always for inclusion with the Alexandrian and other authorities: Matt. ix. 34 (exorcism), xxi. 44 (the stone that crushes), Luke v. 39 (old and new wine), xii. 21 (treasure with God), xix. 25 (they said, Lord he hath ten pounds), xxii. 19ᵇ–20 (Last Supper—second cup), xxiv. 6ᵃ, 12, 36ᵇ, 40 (the Resurrection), John xii. 8 (the poor always with you).

Other notable omissions in the Sahidic are: Matt. xxiii. 14 (widows' houses) against the Byzantine MSS and part of the Bohairic, in xxiv. 36 it omits οὐδὲ ὁ υἱός with the Byzantines and OS.ˢⁱⁿ against ℵ B D Θ fam. 13 OL. and the Fayyumic, in xxvii. 49 it omits the piercing of the side with D W Θ famm. 1, 13 and almost all the versions against ℵ B C L. In Luke xxiii. 17 (release of a prisoner) it omits with 𝔭⁷⁵ B and part of the Bohairic against ℵ W famm. 1, 13 and the Byzantine MSS (D places the verse after xxiii. 19), in xxiii. 34 it omits the Word from the Cross (Father, forgive . . .) with 𝔭⁷⁵ B D* W Θ OS.ˢⁱⁿ against ℵ* A C and the great majority, the Bohairic being divided. In John it omits v. 4 (the angel and the stirring of the water) with 𝔭⁶⁶,⁷⁵ ℵ B C* D W OL. (part) OS.ᶜᵘʳ the Achmimic and part

of the Bohairic, and in viii. 59 the Byzantine addition with
$\mathfrak{p}^{66,75}$ ℵ B D W Θ* OL. OS.^{sin} the sub-Achmimic and part of
the Bohairic.

The Sahidic is, then, on the whole a short text, though it has
some additions of the Byzantine type: e.g. it includes Mark vii. 16
(ears to hear) with part of the Bohairic; it has the 'longer ending'
after Mark xvi. 8 together with the Bohairic and Fayyumic, and
some MSS, together with part of the Bohairic, have the 'shorter
ending' also; while, somewhat curiously, it has with the Fayyumic
the doxology to the Lord's Prayer in Matt. vi. 13 in the same
form as the Didache (some Bohairic MSS have the ordinary
Byzantine form, the majority omit altogether with ℵ B D OL.);
and at the end of Luke xxiii. 53 the Sahidic adds the curious
description of the rolling of the stone to the Sepulchre as in D,
while the Bohairic adds the more pedestrian version found in
fam. 13.

In Acts, on the same basis of selected readings as in the Gospels
above, the Sahidic agrees with ℵ B against D 57 times, with D
against ℵ B 31 times; the overall figures are:

	With Sahidic	*Against Sahidic*
ℵ	101	83
B	101	83
D	56	91
O.L.	79	73

It is clear that, although Alexandrian readings predominate,
there is a strong Western element, as can easily be seen by inspection of an *apparatus criticus*. On the other hand, of the major
additions and variants characteristic of D and its allies it has very
few. Thus of the twenty-two listed on pp. 92–3 as specially characteristic of D the Sahidic has only part of D's addition at v. 39
(οὔτε οἱ τύραννοι ὑμῶν) and the addition of the negative form
of the Golden Rule at xv. 20, 29; while of the thirty-five listed on
pp. 232–7, the Sahidic is in support of the Western text only
at i. 2 (in part), i. 5, xxi. 25, and xxviii. 16. (To these may be
added the addition in xx. 15 of $\mathfrak{p}^{41}$ D καὶ μείναντες ἐν Τρωγυλλίῳ,
which has also found its way into the Byzantine text as well
as the Sahidic, but not into the Bohairic, and which Ropes thinks
is probably the original reading.) This remarkable absence of
almost all the major Western readings, coupled with the presence

of a large number of minor Western variants points, in Ropes's opinion, to the likelihood that the Greek text of Acts on which the Sahidic version was based was in origin a Western text which had been corrected in accordance with another of the Alexandrian type: the reverse would require us to suppose that a corrector inserted into an Alexandrian type of text the smaller and unimportant Western variants while ignoring the more attractive and important ones.

In the Pauline and Catholic Epistles the Sahidic is Alexandrian in text and closest to B, and in the Apocalypse is associated with $\mathfrak{p}^{47}$ ℵ.

(b) *Bohairic*. The Bohairic version has been much longer and more fully known. Readings from it were contributed by T. Marshall to the critical editions of the New Testament by Fell (1675) and Mill (1707) and a complete text was published by David Wilkins at Oxford in 1716. At present the standard edition is that of G. Horner (Oxford, 1898–1905): in this forty-six MSS were used for the Gospels and thirty-four for the other books. In Horner's view the best Gospel MS is Huntingdon MS 17 in the Bodleian dated 1174 and the oldest known complete MS of the Bohairic Gospels, though the Curzon Catena, in which text and commentary are intermingled, is older (889). For the Acts and Epistles British Museum Or. 424 (1307) is considered the best, and for the Apocalypse Curzon MS 128 (1320). It will be seen that these MSS, though among the oldest, are relatively late, and come mostly from the time when Bohairic was the official dialect of Egypt (as it still is of the Coptic Church), but the variations among them are slight, and the text shows very little sign of having been seriously altered by revision. However, among the Bodmer collection of MSS is a Bohairic text of the Fourth Gospel (*Papyrus Bodmer III* (Louvain, 1958), ed. R. Kasser) containing fragments of John i. 1–iv. 15 and the whole of iv. 20–end. It is dated by its editor in the fourth century, and this, together with the probability that the Fayyumic St John (see below), also of the fourth century, is based on the Bohairic, makes a late third century date not impossible for the version itself.

The character of the Bohairic version is generally reckoned as being more literal in style than the Sahidic, and closer to the Alexandrian ℵ B type—i.e. freer from the influence of the Western text. But as far as the Gospels are concerned the agreements and disagreements in selected readings are very similar to those given above for the Sahidic:

	With Bohairic	Against Bohairic
א	390	223
B	388	227
D	218	354
OL.	282	317

If anything these figures indicate that, whereas the Sahidic is somewhat closer to B than to א, in the Bohairic the balance is slightly the other way; in fact this leaning towards א is more marked in the Synoptic Gospels, particularly in Luke, whereas in the fourth Gospel where א has a not inconsiderable Western element, both Boharic and Sahidic are closer to B.

In the case of the more notable Alexandrian omissions (or Western additions) as set out above (p. 139), whereas the Sahidic sides always with the shorter Alexandrian text, the Bohairic has the D addition in Matt. xii. 47, and its witness is divided between Alexandrian and Western readings at Matt. xvi. 2–3, xvii. 21, Luke ix. 54^b, 55^b, xxii. 43, John vii. 53—viii. 11. A similar division of the Bohairic witness between omission and exclusion occurs in the following passages, all of them omitted by the Sahidic: Matt. xxiii. 14, Luke xxiii. 17, 34, John v. 4, viii. 59. On the other hand, so far as the major Western omissions are concerned, the Bohairic agrees with the Sahidic in having the longer Alexandrian reading except in one instance, Luke xix. 25, where its witness is divided between inclusion with א B etc. and omission with D. In regard to this divided witness of the Bohairic two facts are to be noted: first, that the fourth century Bodmer papyrus of John, in each of the three instances of a longer Western reading (v. 4, vii. 53—viii. 11, viii. 59) is on the side of the shorter Alexandrian text; and second, that in each of the cases cited above where the Bohairic is divided between an Alexandrian and Western reading, the Western reading has been assimilated into the Byzantine text. The inference to be drawn from this is that the earlier forms of the Bohairic Gospels were closely associated with the א B type, but that they had, as we see in the later forms, undergone revision not on the basis of Western Greek MSS but on those of Byzantine type. This would seem to be proved by instances where the Western text is on the side of the Alexandrian

witnesses against the Byzantine and the Bohairic moves from one
to the other: e.g. John ix. 35 the Bodmer MS renders εἰς τὸν
υἱὸν τοῦ ἀνθρώπου with $\mathfrak{p}^{66,75}$ ℵ B D W and the Sahidic, sub-
Achmimic and Fayyumic, but the rest of the Bohairic MSS read
εἰς τὸν υἱὸν τοῦ θεοῦ with the great mass of Greek MSS;
similarly at John xiv. 11 the Bodmer MS, like the Sahidic and
sub-Achmimic, renders πιστεύετε with $\mathfrak{p}^{66,75}$ ℵ D W OL.
(part) OS.^{cur}, the rest of the Bohairic πιστεύετε μοι with the
Greek majority. Indeed, it is sometimes possible to see more than
one stage in the process of revision—e.g. at John vi. 69 the
Bodmer MS with one Sahidic MS renders ὁ ἅγιος τοῦ Θεοῦ
with $\mathfrak{p}^{75}$ ℵ B D, though the majority of both Sahidic and Bohairic
together with the sub-Achmimic support $\mathfrak{p}^{66}$ ὁ Χριστὸς ὁ ἅγιος
τοῦ Θεοῦ, while some Boharic MSS have the Byzantine form
ὁ Χριστὸς ὁ υἱὸς τοῦ Θεοῦ τοῦ ζῶντος; at John vi. 14 the Bodmer
MS with the Sahidic and sub-Achmimic has what was presumably
the original Coptic rendering with ℵ D W OL. OS. ὃ ἐποίησεν
σημεῖον, but the rest of the Bohairic reads (apparently alone)
ἃ ἐποίησεν σημεῖα ὁ Ἰησοῦς, which suggests a revision to $\mathfrak{p}^{75}$
B's ἃ ἐποίησεν σημεῖα before receiving the Byzantine addition
ὁ Ἰησοῦς. Examples in the other Gospels of division in the
Bohairic between early (Alexandrian–Western) and Byzantine
readings may be found at Matt. xix. 16 διδάσκαλε (add ἀγαθέ),
xxvii. 24 τουτου (τοῦ δικαιοῦ τούτου), Mark iv. 24 προστεθήσεται
ὑμῖν (add τοῖς ἀκούουσιν), xv. 28 (add verse), Luke xi. 48
οἰκοδομεῖτε (add αὐτῶν τὰ μνημεῖα), xxiv. 42 μέρος (add καὶ
ἀπὸ μελισσίου κηρίου). Indeed it might seem from some of the
above examples (e.g. Matt. xxvii. 24) that a similar process,
though in a lesser degree, had been going on in the Sahidic, as
appears also at Mark vii. 31 ἦλθεν διὰ Σιδῶνος (καὶ Σιδῶνος
ἦλθεν), but in fact the attestation shows that these are ancient
readings which have been taken up into the Byzantine tradition.

In Acts the table of comparison based as above is:

	With Bohairic	Against Bohairic
ℵ	127	57
B	132	50
D	36	107
OL.	73	76

These figures show that the Bohairic is very close to the ℵ B
text, containing far fewer readings of the D type than the Sahidic.

(c) *Other Egyptian Dialects.* For the most part these are fragmentary, but an almost complete Gospel of John in the sub-Achmimic dialect, in the library of the British and Foreign Bible Society, was published by H. Thompson in 1924, and dated by him in the latter part of the fourth century. There is also an early fourth-century papyrus codex of St John's Gospel consisting of 29 folios (none complete) in the University of Michigan collection, edited by E. M. Husselman (*The Gospel of John in Fayyumic Coptic*, Ann Arbor, 1962) with a text closer to the Sahidic than the Bohairic. It is possible, therefore, that the New Testament was rendered into the various native dialects of Middle and Southern Egypt during the course of the third century or early in the fourth. The indications also are that, in origin at any rate, these dialect versions were based on the Sahidic rather than being independent translations from the Greek. Thus, at John iv. 25 Sahidic, sub-Achmimic and Fayyumic, as well as the Bohairic read with the slightly-attested οἴδαμεν (𝔭⁶⁶ᶜ ℵᶜ L fam. 13, 33) against the great majority; at viii. 57 the Sahidic, sub-Achmimic together with the Bodmer Bohairic papyrus have ἑώρακέν σε read by 𝔭⁷⁵ ℵ* 0124 alone among the Greeks; at x. 7 the Sahidic and Achmimic support ὁ ποιμήν, read by 𝔭⁷⁵ only against all the Greek witnesses; and at xiv. 22 the Sahidic, sub-Achmimic and Fayyumic alone read Ἰούδας ὁ κανανίτης.

The remaining Eastern versions—Ethiopic, Arabic, Persian—can be passed over in a handbook of this scope, as having no importance for the main textual problems of the New Testament. The Ethiopic has one special interest in that it has preserved the Book of Enoch, which at one time hovered on the verge of the Canon, as having been quoted in the Epistle of Jude. It was supposed to be wholly lost, until the traveller James Bruce brought back three MSS of it from Abyssinia in 1773, from one of which (presented by Bruce to the Bodleian) it was edited by Dr Laurence, Archbishop of Cashel, in 1821. The original Greek remained unknown (except for some considerable extracts in Syncellus) until 1886, when a small vellum book was found at Akhmim in Egypt, containing the first thirty-two chapters, with extracts from the Gospel and Apocalypse of Peter, in hands which can probably be assigned to the sixth century. More recently, the Chester Beatty papyri discovered in 1931 include several leaves of a codex (of the fourth or fifth century) containing Enoch (here entitled the Epistle of Enoch) and a homily by Melito of Sardis.[1] The portion of Enoch preserved is the end of the book, chapters 97–107. It is interesting to find that this book was kept along with the canonical Scriptures in a Christian community as late as the fourth century.

V. LATIN

The Latin versions have a double importance and a special interest. In their earlier forms they throw valuable (though somewhat puzzling) light on the original text of the New Testament and its fortunes in the early centuries. In its later form, the Vulgate of St Jerome, it became the accepted Bible of the Western world for over a thousand years, and is the Bible of the Church of Rome today. It was also the text from which all translations of the Scriptures into English were made before the sixteenth century. As an element in the history of religion and of civilization, it is of unique importance.

(a) The Old Latin. Much obscurity involves the history of the translation of the New Testament into Latin. It seems certain that it did not first take place in Rome. Rome was a cosmopolitan town where Greek was almost as well known as Latin, and it was among the Greek-speaking population that Christianity first took root. St Paul writes to them in Greek, St Clement at the end of the first century writes in Greek, so do Justin Martyr and Hermas in the middle of the second century, and Hippolytus at the beginning of the third; and nearly all the bishops of Rome until the end of the second century have Greek names. Indeed, Victor, Bishop of Rome in the last decade of the second century, is said by Jerome to have been the first to write theological works in Latin. It was not there that a Latin translation was first needed, but rather in such provinces of the Empire as Gaul or Africa. For both of these districts we have some evidence from the last

---

[1] These have been edited by Prof. Campbell Bonner, of the University of Michigan, in *Studies and Documents*, edited by K. and S. Lake: vii, *The Last Chapters of Enoch in Greek*, 1937; xii, *The Homily on the Passion by Melito Bishop of Sardis and Some Fragments of the Apocryphal Ezekiel*, 1940.

quarter of the second century. The Scillitan martyrs at Carthage in 180 possessed a copy of the Pauline Epistles, and apparently of the Gospels, and there is no sign that they were acquainted with Greek; and the letter which describes the persecution of the Churches of Lyons and Vienne in 177 shows familiarity with a Latin New Testament. Tertullian (*c.* 150–220) writing in Africa in Latin, quotes the Scriptures freely, but he is by no means an accurate writer, and he seems often to have made his own translations from the Greek, so that his quotations have to be used with caution.

Firmer ground is reached with Cyprian (*c.* 200–58), bishop of Carthage, who quotes extensively and accurately, and who certainly used a Latin Bible which, judging from the internal evidence, was not in its earliest stages. Moreover of this Bible we have acutal MSS; for a Bobbio MS (known as **k**), of the fourth or at latest fifth century, contains Mark viii–xvi (ending at verse 8) and Matt. i–xv, in a text almost identical with that of Cyprian, and a Codex Palatinus (**e**) at Vienna has all the Gospels (though considerably mutilated) in a similar text, while the commentary of Primasius in the sixth century gives an almost complete text of the Apocalypse of this African type. These collectively represent a considerable part of the New Testament as it circulated in Africa in the first half of the third century, and it is to Africa that we must assign the beginnings of the Latin Bible as we know it, though it is possible that a version was simultaneously in existence on the northern side of the Mediterranean.

The African is not the only form of the Old Latin. A greater number of other manuscripts with pre-Vulgate texts are known which have their home in Europe, and though they have much in common with the African text, they have also many differences, which raises the much disputed question of whether the African and European forms represent originally a common version or independent translations. The common ground is the close relationship to the text found in Codex Bezae, and the combination D and Old Latin (both in its African form and that found elsewhere) constitutes a definite textual family to which the designation 'Western' may properly be given. At the same time the relationship of the Old Latin authorities to D is by no means uniform. In the Gospels, for example, the European MSS are found supporting D in the latter's longer additions in Matthew and Mark, but the African text, although it sides with D and the European Latin at Matt. xvi. 2–3 and xx. 28, omits along with the Alexandrian authorities at Matt. xii. 47, xvii. 21, xviii, 11, Mark ix. 44, 46, xi. 26. In Luke the African text sides with the shorter Alexandrian at ix. 54, but reads with D and the European OL. in the longer readings at ix. 55, xvii. 36, xxii. 43–4, as it also does at John vii. 53–viii. 11. On the other hand, except at Luke xii. 21, and at John xii. 8 (where D and the Sinaitic Syriac stand alone), the African text, with varying European support, agrees with D in its characteristic longer omissions (Matt. ix. 34, xxi. 44, Luke v. 39, xix. 25, xxii. 19^b–20, xxiv. 6^a, 12, 36^b, 40). Moreover, the remarkable fact noted above (p. 124) of the African Latin agreeing with the Old Syriac alone, or with D and the Old Syriac in small omissions against the rest of the Old Latin, helps to characterize the African Latin as a short text.

It is also possible to distinguish considerable linguistic differences in the development of the version. The Latin is essentially that of popular speech—'vulgar' in the sense not so much that it is corrupt by classical standards, but in showing greater freedom in vocabulary and syntax. One characteristic is the number of words which were simply transliterated or formed on the Greek instead of being rendered by Latin equivalents—e.g. in the African text of the Gospels we find (besides the titles of books cata Matheum, cata Lucanum) agape, anastasis, apotheca, baptizator, cataclysmus, daemonizare, daemoniacus, discolum, eremus, which did not survive into the Vulgate, as well as the following which did: angelus, angariare, azuma, baptisma, cetus, clibanus, cophinus, eleemosyna, grabbatus, hypocrita, moechari, parapsis, pera, pisticus, probaticus, propheta, proselytus, satum, scandalizare, sinapi, teloneum, thesaurizare, thesaurus, zizania. But there are also instances where the African text translates by a Latin word, while the European (or part of it) and the Vulgate prefer a transliteration of the Greek: e.g. benenuntiare or adnuntiare (euangelizare), palla (sindon), retia or retiaculum (sagena), sacramentum (mysterium), similitudo (parabola), sessio (cathedra). Other renderings found in the African Gospels are: cauerna (eur., vg. foramen), coruscatio, coruscare (fulgur, fulgurare), claritas, clarificare (gloria, glorificare, magnificare), colligere (congregare), discens (discipulus), legis doctor (legis peritus, gr.

νομικός), uolatilia (uolucres). But it would be a mistake to suppose that there is anything like uniformity. Thus, e.g. ἀρχιερεύς in Mark is rendered by the African **k** almost always (16/20) as *pontifex*, while the European Old Latin prefers *princeps sacerdos* and the Vulgate *summus sacerdos*; in Luke, however, the European **a** renders by *pontifex* (as it does also at Mark xi. 18, xv. 3, and by *pontifex sacerdotum* at x. 33 and xi. 27), but the African **e** has *pontifex* in only four instances, generally reading *princeps sacerdotum* with the rest of the European MSS and also the Vulgate; in Matthew the European OL. and the Vulgate invariably read *princeps sacerdotum*, the African dividing between this and *sacerdos*. Again, the rendering of λόγος by *sermo* or *uerbum* is far from consistent. In Mark **k** has *sermo* except at xiii. 31, but the overall distribution for **k** in Mark and Matthew is *sermo* ten times, *uerbum* thirteen. Otherwise in the Synoptic Gospels the two renderings fluctuate in all the Latin versions, Vulgate included: in Matthew *uerbum* preponderates, in Luke the African Latin (**e**) has *sermo* fifteen times against *uerbum* thirteen, whereas in the European OL. and the Vulgate *uerbum* is somewhat more usual, while in John *sermo* prevails in all sources. It can scarcely be maintained, as it is sometimes said, that *sermo* is a characteristically African word. The same is true of *lumen*, *lux* for φῶς. In the Synoptic Gospels the European OL. and Vulgate read *lumen* eight times out of twelve against the African (**k**, **e**) ten times, yet *lumen* is said to be 'African'. One of the more striking examples in this respect is the rendering of γεωργός in the Synoptic parable of the Wicked Husbandman. The African rendering is *rusticus* in Mark (**k**), *colonus* in Matthew (**e**), *agricola* in Luke (**e**), while at the other end the Vulgate reads *agricola* in Mark and Matthew, *colonus* three times and *cultor* once in Luke, the European MSS varying between *colonus* (most frequently), *agricolus*, *cultor* (**d** in Matthew, **i** in Mark, **r**[1] in Luke), and *uinitorius* (**a** in Mark).

These textual and linguistic differences, as is to be expected, have divided scholars on the question of whether the Old Latin is to be regarded as a single version in a plurality of local and temporal forms, or as a plurality of versions which have come into existence on both sides of the Mediterranean. Before going further into this question two points should be made. First, it is scarcely to be expected that the whole of the Latin New Testament was made at one time. It may reasonably be assumed that those books would be translated first which were of the greatest interest and usefulness to the Christian communities, the rest being added as time went on. This would allow for different translators at different times and in different localities, perhaps for more than one translation of particular books, while continuously copies would be made and compared and gain ever wider circulation. The second point is the ambiguity, in this context, of the term 'revision' and 'translation', as will be seen when we deal with Jerome's New Testament. Anyone acquainted with both languages, dissatisfied with the form or forms of the Latin version known to him, might decide to compare it afresh with the Greek. But in doing so he is hardly likely to have ignored the work of his predecessors, and whether we call the result of his labours a revision or a fresh translation is, in the absence of clear evidence, perhaps best left undecided. One thing is clear: each book, or group of books, must be judged on its own evidence both as to text and latinity, and much more needs to be done on these lines. That revision was a continuous process is evident, and this can be seen in the way in which, as time goes on, the Latin is brought into more exact conformity with the Greek. Thus the opening verse of **e** in Mark (i. 21) reads *et ingredientes Capharnaum continuo intrauit sabbatis in sinagoga et docebit eos*, while the European Vercelli MS (**a**) has *et ingressi sunt in Capharnaum et statim sabbatis intrauit in synagoga et docebat illos*, which is a closer word-for-word rendering of the Greek western text καὶ εἰσεπορεύοντο εἰς Καφαρναούμ, καὶ εὐθὺς τοῖς σάββασιν εἰσελθὼν εἰς τὴν συναγωγὴν ἐδίδασκεν αὐτούς, while the rest of the European MSS replace **e** and **a**'s *intrauit* with *ingressus* for εἰσελθών. It is also possible to see from time to time corrections towards the Alexandrian text in European MSS—in the above example **d ff**[2] **q r**[1] **t** have *ingrediuntur*, with ℵ B εἰσπορεύονται, and **t** omits the final αὐτός with the majority of Greek MSS.

In Acts Ropes, following Jülicher, finds evidence for a revision of the Latin text, made presumably in Europe before 450 and found in Codex Gigas (**g**) and the quotations of Lucifer, Ambrosiaster and Niceta of Remesiona. Based on a non-Western Greek text, it avoids the peculiarities of the African version and the Latin is clear and idiomatic.

In the Pauline Epistles most of the Old Latin material is

consistent with a continuous development out of the early form of the text found in Cyprian. But in the Freising Fragments (**r**) there is evidence of a deliberate and thorough-going revision based on an Alexandrian Greek text. Augustine began to use this text about 390 and continued to use it (with some modifications) for the rest of his life, and the same version was used by his successor at Hippo, Capreolus, and such later African writers as Vigilius and Fulgentius of Ruspe. For the Catholic Epistles we have the same type of revised text from the same Freising source (but in a later hand) which was also adopted by Augustine and used by his African successors, and this text appears also in the Fleury fragments (**h**), in the Wolfenbüttel Lectionary (a palimpsest of the sixth century written in France), and for 1 John i. 1–iii. 15 in Codex Harleianus (Z—a Vulgate MS listed below). This revised text apparently passed over from Africa to Spain, where its influence can be seen in **m** (the pseudo-Augustinian *Speculum*) and the Vulgate MSS C and T.

In the Apocalypse H. J. Vogels (*Untersuchungen zur Geschichte der lateinischen Apokalypse—Übersetzung*, Dusseldorf, 1920) claimed to distinguish no less than three distinct translations of the book made from the Greek, but it is doubtful whether this can be sustained, or even that the African and European texts are independent of each other.

The most convenient way of stating the case and of indicating the available materials will be a short catalogue of the principal MSS. Most of them are fragments, but most are of early date. The following are the MSS of the Gospels.

a. *Codex Vercellensis*, at Vercelli, fourth century. Traditionally written by Eusebius, Bishop of Vercelli (martyred 371)—as such it *ante*-dates the Vulgate. Contains the Gospels, somewhat mutilated, in the Western order (Matthew, John, Luke, Mark). In Matthew **a** is close to **b** and **ff²**, in Luke Jerome quotes a very similar text, and Novatian and Lucifer of Cagliari frequently agree in John.

a². see **n** below.

aur. *Codex Aureus*, at Stockholm, seventh century. Vulgate Gospels, but with considerable OL. elements.

b. *Codex Veronensis*, at Verona, fifth century. Contains the Gospels in the Western order written in silver letters on purple vellum. Matt. i. 1–11, xv. 12–23, xxiii. 18–27, Mark xiii. 9–19,

24—xvi. 20, Luke xix. 26—xxi. 29, John vii. 44—viii. 12 are lacking. Burkitt believed that this type of text was used by Jerome in his revision of the Vulgate. **b** stands in a central position in the European group. In Luke Lucifer quotes a similar text, while in John **r**[1] is nearest.

c. *Codex Colbertinus*, at Paris, twelfth century. Written in Languedoc, where the Vulgate seems to have been very slow in superseding the Old Latin. Contains the four Gospels, complete, in a mixed OL.-Vulgate text; the rest of the New Testament (except Acts—also mixed) is Vulgate. Matthew and John are much less Old Latin than Mark and Luke. Has a sprinkling of African readings, which are to be found in Spanish texts also.

d. The Latin text of *Codex Bezae*. The text is not a translation of the Greek side, but has been influenced by it. Basically it is of great antiquity, and on occasion is to be found agreeing with both **a** and **k** against other authorities.

e. *Codex Palatinus*, at Vienna, with one leaf in Dublin and one in the British Museum. Fifth century. Contains Matt. xii. 49—xiii. 58, xiv. 3-4, 6-7, 9—xxiv. 49, xxviii. 2-20, John i. 1—xviii. 12, 25—xxi. 25, Luke i. 1—viii. 30, 48—xi. 4, 24—xxiv. 53, Mark i. 21—iv. 8, 19—vi. 9, xii. 37-40, xiii. 2-3, 24-7, 33-6 in that order in silver letters on purple vellum. Akin in text to **k**, though somewhat modified by revision, and its agreement with African Fathers suggests that it was written in Africa.

f. *Codex Brixianus*, at Brescia, sixth century. Gospels, complete (except for Mark xii. 5—xiii. 32, xiv. 70—xvi. 20), in silver on purple. Regarded by Wordsworth and White as representing the type of Old Latin on which Jerome based his revision. This, however, is doubted by Burkitt, who regards it as a corrupted Vulgate text.[1] It is now thought that its ancestor was a bilingual codex in which the one side was occupied by a Gothic text, to which the mixed Old Latin and Vulgate opposite has been accommodated.

ff[1]. *Codex Corbeiensis I*, at Leningrad, tenth century. Contains Matthew only in a mixed OL.-Vulgate text.

ff[2]. *Codex Corbeiensis II*, at Paris, fifth or sixth century. Gospels in a text akin to **a** and **b**. Matt. i. 1—xi. 16, John xvii. 15—xviii. 9, xx. 23—xxi. 8, Luke ix. 48—x. 20, xi. 45—xii. 16 are lacking.

---

[1] Prof. Souter has argued that in Luke at any rate Jerome used a text practically identical with **a**.

L

g¹. *Codex Sangermanensis I,* at Paris, eighth or ninth century. Contains all Gospels, but only Matthew is Old Latin, and that is of a mixed type.

g². *Codex Sangermanensis II,* at Paris, tenth century. Gospels, in an Irish hand, with a mixed OL.-Vulgate text.

h. *Codex Claromontanus,* in the Vatican, fifth or sixth century. Contains the Gospels, but only Matthew, which is in a different hand from the others, is OL., and is of a mixed type like **g¹.**

i. *Codex Vindobonensis,* at Naples, formerly at Vienna, fifth or sixth century. Contains Luke x. 6—xxiii. 10, Mark ii. 17—iii. 29, iv. 4—x. 1, 33—xiv. 36, xv. 33–40 in silver on purple vellum.

j. *Codex Sarzanensis or Saretianus,* fifth–sixth century, at Sarezzano in Piedmont. Contains Luke xxiv. 41–53, John i. 1— x. 34 in silver on purple. Said to be akin to **a b.** With it is bound up John xviii. 36—xx. 14 in a different fifth–sixth century hand, much of which is illegible.

k. *Codex Bobiensis,* at Turin, fourth or fifth century. See above, p. 148, and on **e.** Contains Mark viii. 8–11, 14–16, 19— xvi. 8, Matt. i. 1—iii. 10, iv. 1—xiv. 17, xv. 20–36. It has the shorter ending to Mark. Probably written in Africa.

l. *Codex Rehdigeranus,* at Breslau, seventh–eighth century. Gospels, lacking last five chapters of John. The OL. text of the first hand has been revised by a corrector who has inserted Vulgate readings.

m. Not strictly an OL. manuscript, but the pseudo-Augustinian *Speculum,* which contains copious extracts arranged under subject-headings from nearly all books of the Bible (but noticeably omits Hebrews which was not accepted as Pauline in the West, Philemon and 3 John). The text is usually classed as Spanish or African, but further investigations will probably show that it is not as uniform in character as has been supposed. In the Catholic Epistles the text is remarkably close to Priscillian, the Spanish heretic.

n. *Fragmenta Sangallensia,* at St Gall, fifth century, containing fragments of the Gospels, mainly Matthew and Luke. A further leaf of the same MS containing Luke xi. 11–29 is at Coire (in the canton Grisons, Switzerland)—in some lists designated **a²,** this siglum being applied also to **n** by Gregory and Vogels. The text is very close to **a** in the Synoptics.

o. A single leaf at St Gall in a seventh century hand, containing Mark xvi. 14–20, written to supply a lost leaf in **n.**

p. *Fragmentum Sangallense,* at St Gall; two leaves of a Mass-book in a seventh- or eighth-century Irish hand containing John xi. 14–44. The text resembles **r¹.**

q. *Codex Monacensis.* At Munich, sixth or seventh century, formerly belonged to Freising, contains the Gospels, lacking Matt. iii. 15—iv. 23, v. 25—vi. 4, 28—vii. 8, John x. 11—xii. 39, Luke xxiii. 22–35, xxiv. 11–39, Mark i. 7–21, xv. 5–36. A mixed text, close to **b,** but with elements resembling **f.**

r¹. *Codex Usserianus I,* sixth–seventh-century Irish MS of the Gospels, at Trinity College, Dublin, with the order Matthew, John, Luke, Mark. The synoptics have a text closely related to the gospel quotations of Hilary of Poitiers, that of the Fourth Gospel is akin to **b.**

r². *Codex Usserianus II,* also at Dublin, is an eighth–ninth-century Gospel text of mixed OL. and Vulgate type: the OL. element is strongest in Matthew.

s, t, v are fragments of Luke (xvii–xxi), Mark (i–iii) and John (xix. 27—xx. 11) respectively at Milan, Berne and Vienna.

β, π, ρ are also fragments, and dated seventh century. β at St Paul in Kärnten (Luke i. 64—ii. 51), π at Stuttgart (Matt. xiii. 6–15, 31–8, Luke xiv. 8–13, John iii. 34–6, vi. 39–41, vii. 24–38, ix. 22–32, xi. 19–48, xx. 25–30), ρ in the Ambrosiana, Milan (John xiii. 3–17).

For Acts there are the following:

d = **d** of Gospels. Acts viii. 20—x. 3, xx. 31—xxi. 2, 7–10, xxii. 2–10, xxii. 2–10, 20—end of book lost by mutilation.

dem. *Codex Demidovianus,* now lost, formerly at Lyons, thirteenth century. Published by C. F. Matthaei, 1782. Contains Acts, Pauline and Catholic Epistles, Apocalypse in a mixed Old-Latin and Vulgate text of the same type as Codex Colbertianus (**c**).

e. The Latin text of Codex Laudianus (E₂)—see above, p. 96.

g. (gig). *Codex Gigas* at Stockholm, thirteenth century. A huge MS of the whole Bible, but only Acts and Apocalypse are OL. The close agreement in Acts with the quotations of Lucifer, as well as with those of 'Ambrosiaster' and Niceta of Remesiana indicates that its text in this book had a wide circulation. Written in Bohemia, which perhaps explains the appearance of an OL. text in so late a MS.

h. *Palimpsestus Floriacensis*, at Paris, fifth or sixth century. Contains fragments of Acts (iii. 2—iv. 18, v. 23—vii. 2, 42—viii. 2, ix. 4-23, xiv. 5-23, xvii. 34—xviii. 19, xxiii. 8-24, xxvi. 20—xxvii. 13), Catholic Epistles (1 Pet. iv. 17—2 Pet. ii. 7, 1 John i. 8—iii. 20) and Apocalypse (i. 1—ii. 1, viii. 7—ix. 12, xi. 16—xii. 14, xiv. 15—xvi. 5) in an African type of text which has much in common with the quotations of Cyprian in Acts, of Augustine in the Catholic Epistles, and of Tyconius and Primasius in the Apocalypse. Much used by Clark in his edition of Acts.

l. *Codex Legionensis*, in the Cathedral Library at Leon in northern Spain. A palimpsest MS of the later translation of Eusebius by Rufinus in a tenth-century hand, below which are a sixth-century text of the *Lex Romana Visigothorum*, and early seventh-century fragments of Acts: viii. 27—xi. 13, xv. 6-12, 26-38 in a Spanish type of OL. text resembling that of **t**, while other fragments of xiv. 21—xvii. 25 are Vulgate. The text is edited by B. Fischer in *Biblical and Patristic Studies in memory of R. V. Casey*, ed. J. N. Birdsall and R. W. Thomson (Freiburg-in-B., 1963).

p. (perp). *Codex Perpinianus*, a thirteenth-century MS from Perpignan, on the borders of France and Spain, of the complete New Testament, now at Paris. Only Acts i. 1—xiii. 6 and xxviii. 16-31 are Old Latin, but pre-Vulgate readings are found scattered over the rest, which is related to the Spanish Vulgate type of text. In the OL. sections various African characteristics support the view that Spain originally derived its Latin bible from Africa.

s. *Codex Bobiensis*, palimpsest at Naples, from 1717-1919 at Vienna. Sixth-century Italian MS, reused at Bobbio in the eighth century. Contains fragments of Acts xxiii—xxviii, James and 1 Peter. The text in Acts resembles **g** with Vulgate admixture.

t. *Liber Comicus*, an eleventh-century Spanish lectionary MS according to the seventh-century use of Toledo. Half the passages from Acts are Old Latin in a text similar to **g** but with influence from the Vulgate.

For the Catholic Epistles, besides **h, m, r** (see below) and **s**, only one MS need be mentioned:

ff. *Codex Corbeiensis*, at Leningrad, tenth century. Contains

James and the unique Latin text of the Epistle of Barnabas. Predominantly Old Latin, but with Vulgate admixture.

For the Pauline Epistles there are:

d-g. The Latin texts of Codex Claromontanus (D₂), *Sangermanensis* (E₃) *Augiensis* (F₂), *Boernerianus* (G₃) (see above, pp. 95, 97).

gue. *Codex Guelpherbytanus,* at Wolfenbüttel, sixth century. Bi-lingual (Gothic-Latin) fragments of Romans xi–xv in the palimpsest MS which also contains P and Q of the Greek Gospels.

mon. At Monza, tenth century. The remains (55 leaves) of the second volume of a Bible, apparently a copy of a much older MS. Contains Tobit ix. 10 to end, Esther, and Judith to viii. 31 in a Vulgate text, and Rom. i. 1—x. 2, small fragments of xii–xiv, xv. 11–end, 1 Cor. i. 1–5, Eph. iv. 1–end, Col. 1–2, Thess., 1 Tim., 2 Tim. i. 1—iv. 1 (with some gaps) in a fourth-century type of Milanese text very similar to that used by Ambrose. In Romans the doxology (xvi. 20–25) is inserted after xiv. 23, as in the later Greek Byzantine MSS, which is rare in Latin authorities. Edited by H. J. Frede, *Altlateinische Paulus-Handschriften,* Freiburg, 1964.

r (r², r³). *Fragmenta Freisingensia* or *Monacensia.* The remains (35 leaves—33 at Munich, 2 at Gottweig) of a MS of the Pauline and Catholic Epistles, originating from Freising Cathedral. The Paulines are in a hand of the second half of the sixth century, containing Rom. xiv. 10—xv. 13, 1 Cor. i–iii. 5, v. 13—vii. 12, 19–26, xiii. 13—xiv. 5, 11–18, 25–27, xv. 14–43, xvi. 12–24, 2 Cor. i. 1—ii. 10, iii. 17—vi. 3, vii. 10—viii. 12, ix. 10—xi. 21, xii. 4—xiii. 10, Gal. ii. 5—vi. 8; Eph. i. 1—ii. 16, vi. 24, Phil. i. 1–20, 1 Tim. i. 12—ii. 15, v. 18—vi. 13; Heb. vi. 6–16, vii. 7–18, 20—viii. 1. Written in Spain or possibly Africa. The Catholic Epistles are in an early seventh-century Spanish hand comprising 1 Pet. i. 7–9, ii. 20—iii. 7, iv. 10—v. 14, 2 Pet. i. 1–4, 1 John iii. 8—v. 21, and the same hand is responsible for supplying two leaves of the Pauline's containing Rom. v. 16—vi. 19 and Phil. iv. 11–23, 1 Thess. i. 1–10. The text is African, and is very close to St Augustine's quotations of St Paul after *c.* 390, and de Bruyne, in his edition of the Fragments (Rome, 1921) suggested that **r** represents the Pauline text revised from the Greek by Augustine himself—a hypothesis which has not found favour with most scholars. The text of the Catholic Epistles is similar to that of **h**

and very close to that used by St Augustine in his *Tractatus in Epistulam Johannis*—see also p. 150 above.

x². *Codex Bodleianus*, at Oxford, ninth century. Nearly complete, with a text akin to **d**.

For the Apocalypse the principal authority for the African text is the commentary of Primasius, with the extensive quotations by Cyprian and Tyconius. There are also **g** and **h** of the Acts, and the Speculum (**m**).

Of these, **k** and **e** represent the African family in the Gospels, **h** and **m** in Acts, **m** and Priscillian (a Spanish writer of the fourth century) in the Pauline Epistles, **h**, Primasius and Tyconius in the Apocalypse, and Cyprian throughout. For the European family, **a** and **b** are the leading representatives in the Gospels, with the Latin version of Irenaeus; in Acts, **g**, **s** and quotations in Lucifer of Cagliari. The majority of the MSS present mixed texts, with much variety, for it is one of the characteristics of the Old Latin version that in consequence of frequent revision its MSS differ widely among themselves, so that one frequently finds Old Latin evidence on both sides of a doubtful reading. Augustine, the greatest of all the Latin Fathers, uses both Old Latin and Vulgate. This usage was examined by Professor Burkitt,[1] who showed that in short passages from the Gospels, such as an author may easily quote from memory, he often used the Old Latin even to the end of his life; but in longer passages, for which reference to a manuscript would be necessary, he generally in his later years used Jerome's Vulgate, which he calls the *Itala interpretatio*.[2] Outside the Gospels Augustine continued to use an Old Latin (or non-Vulgate) text to the end of his life. In particular Burkitt refers to the *Acta contra Felicem*, a report of a heresy trial in 404, in which a long passage from Luke is quoted and another from Acts; the Luke is Vulgate, and the Acts African Old Latin, which throws some light on the usage of the Church at Hippo at the beginning of the fifth century.

The most copious collection of Old Latin evidence for the New Testament (as for the Old) is to be found in P. Sabatier's monumental edition *Bibliorum Sacrorum Latinae Versiones Anti-*

---

[1] *The Old Latin and the Itala* (Cambridge, *Texts and Studies*, iv. 3, 1896).

[2] Wordsworth and White do not accept this explanation of the phrase, preferring the older interpretation, according to which the *Itala* is a subdivision of the European class of Old Latin texts.

quae seu Vetus Italica (tom. iii, Rheims, 1749, Paris, 1751), but this will eventually be superseded by the new edition prepared by the Benedictines of Beuron, *Vetus Latina, Die Reste der Altlateinischen Bibel*. In the New Testament the following have appeared: Ephesians (five fascicles 1962–64), Catholic Epistles (three fascicles 1956–60). A. Jülicher has edited the Old Latin text of the Gospels (but without patristic evidence) in *Das Neue Testament in Altlateinischer Überleiferung*, I Matthäus (1938), II Markus (1940), III Lucas (1955), IV Johannes (1963).

(*b*) *The Vulgate*. Such was the state of things when Pope Damasus, about 382, invited Jerome, the leading Biblical scholar of the day, to undertake a revision of the Latin Bible with a view to putting an end to the confusion caused by the existence of such a multiplicity of conflicting texts. The first sentence of the preface which Jerome eventually prefixed (in the form of a letter to the Pope) to his edition of the Gospels defines the task which was laid upon him.

> Novum opus facere me cogis ex veteri, ut post exemplaria scripturarum toto orbe dispersa quasi quidam arbiter sedeam, et, quia inter se variant, quae sint illa *quae cum Graeca consentiant veritate decernam*.

Of the disorder then existing in the current Latin Bibles, he makes no doubt:

> Si enim Latinis exemplaribus fides est adhibenda, respondeant quibus: tot sunt paene quot codices.

The remedy is to have recourse to the best available Greek manuscripts, since Greek is the original language of the Gospels, and to revise the Latin so as to bring it into accordance with them. At the same time he wishes to do as little violence as possible to the feelings of those who would resent change in the words familiar to them (as we have found when the Revised Version was produced to supersede the Authorized). Therefore he will only make changes when the sense demands it:

> Quae ne multum a lectionis Latinae consuetudine discrepent, ita calamo temperavimus ut, his tantum quae sensum videbantur mutare correctis, reliqua manere pateremur ut fuerunt.

It was on these principles that he undertook his revision of the New Testament—a revision, not a new translation; and on these lines he produced the Gospels in 384. The remaining books (published, according to Chapman, in 391) in which there was less confusion, since the influence of harmonistic alterations of the synoptic texts was absent, he treated more summarily—or so it would seem. But there is room for considerable doubt as to whether Jerome revised the rest of the New Testament. For in his commentaries on St Paul's Epistles Jerome's text is not the Vulgate as we know it, and the same is true of his innumerable quotations in his other writings. Augustine, too, who used and commended Jerome's revised text of the Gospels and was acquainted with his Vulgate Old Testament (though he preferred the older Latin version based on the Septuagint) says nothing of Jerome's work beyond this and, as we have seen, used a different text of the Epistles and an African text of Acts and the Apocalypse. Again, Lucifer of Cagliari, who died according to Jerome in 371, used a Pauline text very close to our Vulgate, as also did Jerome's contemporary Pelagius. The possibility is, then, that Jerome's revision of the New Testament did not go beyond the Gospels, or that if it did, it has disappeared. On the other hand, it should be said that even in the Gospels his revision shows throughout a gradual diminution in extent, being most in evidence in the early chapters of St Matthew, and least in St John, and it is therefore possible that his interest waned as he went on, until by the time he reached the Apocalypse the text was left virtually untouched. Consequently large elements of the Old Latin remain in the Vulgate.

In the Gospels, which are undoubtedly his, he selected the variants which agreed with the Greek MSS which he regarded as the best, or introduced new readings from such MSS. What these were can only be ascertained by comparison with the MSS that have come down to us, since he rarely gives even the slightest indication of the authorities consulted by him. The conclusion to which Wordsworth and White came with regard to the Gospels, after most careful investigation, is that, while he sometimes followed Greek MSS differing from any that we know, in the main he used MSS of the class represented by ℵ B L, and especially a MS or MSS closely resembling ℵ. In Jerome's hands, then, the Old Latin version, already considerably modified from its African form in the direction of the Greek MSS, took on a distinctly Alexandrian colour. With regard to the type of Old Latin Gospel text Jerome used as the basis for his revision opinions vary. Wordsworth and White were of the opinion that it was best represented by **f** (see above, p. 151), but this is unlikely. Burkitt favoured **b**, Souter (in Luke at any rate) **a**, while Vogels casts his net wider and thinks that Jerome knew and made use of a number of text-types such as are found in **e, ff², b, i,** and **q**.

With the Old Testament, for which, as described above (p. 55), he eventually deserted the Greek of the Septuagint and made a fresh translation from the Hebrew, we have nothing here to do. When Jerome's work was completed about 404, it encountered much hostile criticism, occasioned not so much by the revision of the Old Latin in the New Testament, as by the wholesale changes caused by the abandonment of the Old Latin (and the LXX from which it was translated) in the Old Testament. Not being an officially authorized version, it had to make its way on its own merits, and although these would become obvious to scholars, the traditional conservatism of churchmen for long clung to the Old Latin. Consequently its adoption was gradual, and in the process it suffered much contamination. This could come about in a variety of ways—e.g. copyists whose memories unconsciously reproduced the older text in familiar passages or who consciously preferred it, and by the insertion of the more important Vulgate renderings in Old Latin codices, which would in their turn be copied and so give rise to the mixed texts so often found.

At Rome, as Pope Gregory (*c.* 540–604) tells us, both versions were in use there, as indeed he used both versions himself, and likewise in South Italy Cassiodorus (*c.* 485–580), who edited the Vulgate text, nevertheless used the Old Latin in his *Complexiones in Epistolas, Acta Apostolorum et Apocalypsin*. In Gaul (which was the first province to adopt Jerome's second version of the Psalter—hence its name *Gallican*) the Vulgate seems to have gained ground more rapidly: Prosper of Aquitaine (*c.* 390–463) commended it, though Avitus of Vienne (*c.* 450–523) is still using the Old Latin along with the Vulgate in his writings. But Isidore of Seville (died 636) can say that the Vulgate is in general use throughout the churches. From our description of the Old Latin MSS it will have been seen that, for some obscure reason,

Matthew in several MSS (g^1, **h**, r^2) remains Old Latin, while the other books are Vulgate; also that in such outlying districts as Languedoc and Bohemia the Old Latin was still being copied in the twelfth and thirteenth centuries (**c**, **g**). Furthermore, prefatory and other material from older sources was incorporated into Vulgate MSS—e.g. the Priscillianist Prologues to the Gospels (probably of fourth-century Spanish origin), the Marcionite Prologues and chapter headings to the Pauline Epistles, and the Donatist chapter headings to Acts. It was thus in a much corrupted form that the Vulgate gradually became the Bible of the Western world. From time to time attempts were made to revise it. Alcuin, a Northumbrian educated at York, was charged by Charlemagne with the restoration of the Vulgate, which he carried out towards the end of his life after his retirement to Tours in 796. He sent for MSS from England, and the outcome, presented to Charlemagne in 801, was a text of which the best examples are Codd. Vallicellianus and Karolinus. Only a little later another revision was made by Theodulf, Bishop of Orleans and Abbot of Fleury, who died in 821. Theodulf was of Gothic stock, probably from Septimania in Southern France, and like his friend and near contemporary was taken into the service of Charlemagne. As Alcuin turned to his native England, Theodulf looked to Spain for the source of his rescension, of which the best representative is Codex Theodulfianus, with a text close to the Spanish MSS Cavensis and Toletanus. Later in the ninth century the abbey of St Gall became a prominent centre of sacred learning, and from its scriptorium many biblical MSS, written in the Irish style, were disseminated throughout central Europe, but the text prepared by Hartmut (Abbot 872–83) from Alcuin and the older St Gall text did nothing to restore St Jerome. Much later, in the thirteenth century, came a revision associated with the University of Paris, but this did little more than to establish the late Vulgate text which was to be given wider circulation in the early printed editions. It was consequently in a far from correct form that the Vulgate appeared as the first book produced by the printing-press, the famous Gutenberg or Mazarin Bible of 1456. Other editions were published by Stephanus in 1540 and by Hentenius in 1547, but the first authoritative edition was that which, in pursuance of a decree of the Council of Trent, was produced in 1590 by Pope Sixtus V. This was, however, quickly superseded in 1592 by a new edition prepared under the direction of Clement VIII, which became (and remains) the official Bible of the Church of Rome.

It was not until our own times that a serious attempt was made to recover the true text of Jerome's Vulgate. For the New Testament this was undertaken at Oxford by Bishop John Wordsworth of Salisbury, with the collaboration of H. J. White (afterwards Dean of Christ Church). The Gospels appeared, in a revised text with a large critical apparatus, in 1889–98, and Acts in 1905, and after Wordsworth's death in 1911 and the interruption caused by the First War the work was carried on by White as far as Ephesians before his death in 1934. Since then the rest of the Pauline Epistles have appeared under the editorship of H. F. D. Sparks, completing Vol. II in 1941. The Catholic Epistles edited by Sparks and A. W. Adams came out in 1949, the Apocalypse edited by Sparks in 1951, and these, with Acts, constitute Vol. III (1954).

Meanwhile White produced in 1911 a very handy pocket edition of the whole New Testament, with revised text and a select apparatus of the more important various readings from the nine leading MSS (A, C, D, F, G, H, M, V, Z), and the Sixtine and Clementine editions. The most recent edition of the whole Vulgate, published by the Württembergische Bibelanstalt in two volumes (Stuttgart, 1969) is edited by R. Weber with B. Fischer, J. Gribomont, H. F. D. Sparks and W. Thiele. Under a critical text it gives the readings of all the more important MSS—in the New Testament some twenty in all. The practical needs of students are therefore well provided for.

The extant MSS of the Vulgate greatly exceed in number those of the Greek New Testament. Gregory in 1909 (appendix to his *Textkritik*) enumerated 2472, but White estimated the total as at least 8000. For the Gospels Wordsworth and White used twenty-nine MSS, for Acts twenty-eight, for the Epistles twenty-one, for the Apocalypse twenty-four. A few of the more important may be mentioned here, since they are sometimes referred to in connection with the criticism of the Greek New Testament.

A. *Codex Amiatinus*, now in the Laurentian Library at Florence. A magnificent MS of the whole Bible (one of three), written at Wearmouth or Jarrow under the direction of Abbot Ceolfrid, and taken by him as a present to Pope Gregory in 716. Some leaves of a sister MS are in England (one in the British Museum and eleven in private hands). The text arranged colometrically in sense-lines is of the South Italian Cassiodorian type. The Gospels have the Ammonian sections (see p. 84 above), and in Acts the same section-numeration as in F and the Greek MSS ℵ and B. Generally regarded as the best MS of the Vulgate, but this is contested by B. Fischer (see *Biblische Zeitschrift, neue Folge* vi. (1962), pp. 57 ff.), who finds anything but uniformity of text-type between the different books. However, the text of the Gospels and Epistles may still be regarded as good. In Acts there appears to be some influence from the Latin side (**e**) of *Codex Laudianus*, which was in Northumbria when A was written, and used by Bede in his Commentary.

B. *Codex Bigotianus*, at Paris in the Bibliothèque Nationale, formerly at Fécamp, eighth century. Contains the Gospels in a mixed Irish–French type of text.

ᛒF. *Codex Beneventanus*, in the British Museum, formerly at Beneventum; ninth century. Contains the Gospels; according to Berger, the text is of French type, but Wordsworth and White class it with B.

C. *Codex Cavensis*, at La Cava in South Italy, ninth century. Contains the whole Bible, in a small Visigothic hand, and is the leading representative of the Spanish family of MSS, and closely related to T. Frequent Old Latin readings.

D. *Codex Dublinensis*, or *Book of Armagh*, at Trinity College, Dublin, dated 808. Contains the whole Bible, with New Testament in the Irish type of text. The Gospels (in the normal order) are followed by the Pauline Epistles, including the Epistle to the Laodiceans (an early forgery made up of excerpts from the genuine epistles, and coming after Colossians as in F), Catholic Epistles, Apocalypse, and Acts; the Prologues to the Paulines Epistles are attributed to Pelagius. The text of the Paulines is, according to Souter, the same as that used by Pelagius harmonized with the Vulgate. The Gospel text appears to have been corrected from Greek MSS of the Ferrar-group.

E. *Codex Egertoniensis*, in the British Museum, formerly at Tours. Ninth century. Contains the Gospels in Carolingian minuscules with Irish ornamentation. The text is of Irish type, akin to D.

ᛒP. *Codex Epternacensis*, at Paris, ninth century. Contains Gospels, with a note stating that it was corrected in 558 from a MS said to have been written by Jerome himself. The note must obviously have been copied from an ancestor of this MS. The text is mixed, with many marginal readings of a more Irish type.

F. *Codex Fuldensis*, at Fulda, A.D. 541–6. Written to the order of Bishop Victor of Capua. Brought from South Italy to Northumbria by Benedict Biscop or Ceolfrid, it was afterwards given (along with *Codex Laudianus* of Acts) to Boniface, who left it to the Abbey of Fulda, founded by him. Contains New Testament, the Gospels being in the form of a harmony which is believed to reproduce the arrangement of Tatian's *Diatessaron*, though the Old Latin text has been altered to Vulgate, of which it is one of the best representatives, and close to A. Contains the Epistle to the Laodiceans as in D.

G. *Codex Sangermanensis*, at Paris, eighth or ninth century. Contains the whole New Testament; the Old Testament is Spanish in type, Matthew is Old Latin (see g^1 of the Old Latin list), and the rest mixed French and Irish. Especially important for Acts, where Wordsworth and White consider it superior even to A. In the margins of St John's Gospel are a collection of *sortes sanctorum*, used in divination, which are also found in Greek in Codex Bezae.

H. *Codex Hubertianus*, in the British Museum, ninth century. Akin to A and Y, with corrections according to the edition of Theodulf.

I. *Codex Ingolstadiensis*, at Munich, ninth century. Contains the Gospels, Matthew badly mutilated.

J. *Codex Forojuliensis*, divided between Cividale, Venice and Prague. Sixth–seventh centuries. Contains the Gospels in an Italian text of the type found in F and M.

K. *Codex Karolinus*, in the British Museum, ninth century. A huge MS of the whole Bible in the edition of Alcuin, and in Acts the best representative of this edition, which here is almost identical with F.

L. *Codex Lichfeldensis*, or *Gospels of St Chad*, at Lichfield, seventh or eighth century. Contains Matthew, Mark and Luke i. i–iii. 9, with illuminations in Anglo-Celtic style. Text akin to D.

M. *Codex Mediolanensis*, in the Ambrosian Library at Milan. Sixth century. Contains the Gospels in a good Vulgate text of the A F type.

$\overline{\text{M}}$. *Codex Martini-Turonensis*, at Tours. Eighth–ninth century.

Contains the Gospels, written in gold letters. The text is Alcuinian, but according to Wordsworth and White, with a stronger Irish colouring.

O. *Codex Oxoniensis*, in the Bodleian, formerly at St Augustine's, Canterbury, seventh century. Gospels, in a mixed text with some Irish influence, akin to X.

Q. *Codex Kenanensis*, or *Book of Kells*, at Trinity College, Dublin, seventh–eighth century. Contains Gospels in an Irish hand, with the finest existing Celtic decorations. The text also is Irish in character, with a tendency to duplicate renderings.

R. *Codex Rushworthianus*, Bodleian Library, Oxford. Known as the 'Gospels of Mac Regol' after the Irish scribe who died in 820. Irish text, apparently corrected from the Greek, with an interlinear Anglo-Saxon gloss (Matthew in Mercian, the others in Northumbrian as in Y).

S. *Codex Stonyhurstensis*, at Stonyhurst College, seventh century. Said to have belonged to St Cuthbert. A beautiful little copy of John, in a text akin to A Y.

T. *Codex Toletanus*, at Madrid, eighth century. Contains the whole Bible in a Spanish type of text.

V. *Codex Vallicellianus*, at Rome, ninth century. The whole Bible, in the edition of Alcuin, of which it is the best representative in the Gospels.

W. *Codex Willelmi de Hales*, of Salisbury, for whom it was written in 1254, now in the British Museum. Contains the whole Bible in a later Vulgate text of the kind found in early printed editions.

X. *Codex Corporis Christi Cantabrigiensis*, at Corpus Christi College, Cambridge, seventh century. Contains Gospels, in a text akin to O, which, like it, formerly belonged to St Augustine's, Canterbury.

Y. *Codex Lindisfarnensis*, or *Lindisfarne Gospels*, in the British Museum, *c.* 700. Written in honour of St Cuthbert (died 687) and illuminated in the finest style of the Northumbrian Anglo-Celtic school. Contains the Gospels, with interlinear Anglo-Saxon translation added in the ninth century. Akin in text to A; and a table of lections for special festivals shows that it must have been copied from a Bible used at Naples, probably one brought over by the Neapolitan abbot Hadrian, who came to England with Archbishop Theodore in 669. A fragment of Luke attached to a later MS at Durham so closely resembles Y that Prof. C. H. Turner believed it might be the actual exemplar from which Y was copied (see *New Pal. Soc.*, ser. i, pl. 157).

Z. *Codex Harleianus*, in the British Museum, sixth or seventh century. A beautiful little copy of the Gospels with a text differing from that of A Y.

Δ. *Codex Dunelmensis*, at Durham, seventh or eighth century. Traditionally said to have been written by Bede. Gospels, in a Northumbrian text, akin to A Y.

Θ. *Codex Theodulfianus*, at Paris, ninth century. Contains the whole Bible in the edition of Theodulf.

Σ. *Codex Sangallensis*, 1395, at St Gall, sixth century. Consists of leaves used in bindings. About half the Gospels text survives. The Oldest MS of the Vulgate Gospels, but not used by Wordsworth and White. According to C. H. Turner, its text is of the same class as Z, and is closer to the text of Jerome than is the reconstructed text—see his *The Oldest Manuscript of the Vulgate Gospels* (Oxford, 1931). Outside the Gospels the following MSS, cited by Wordsworth and White, are of importance:

B (B$_2$). *Codex Bambergensis*, at Bamberg, but written at Tours; ninth century. Contains the whole Bible, except the Apocalypse, in an Alcuinian type of text.

I. *Codex Iuueniani Vallicellianus*, eighth–ninth century. Contains Acts, Catholic Epistles and Apocalypse. Text akin to A.

L (L$_2$). *Codex Langobardus*, at Paris, eighth century. Contains the Pauline Epistles.

M (M$_2$). *Codex Monacensis*, at Munich, formerly at Freising, where it was written. Eighth century. Contains Pauline Epistles.

O (O$_2$). *Codex Oxoniensis*, in the Bodleian Library, formerly at St Augustine's, Canterbury. Written in the Isle of Thanet in the seventh century. Contains Acts in Anglo-Saxon uncials; known as the Selden Acts. The text is mixed Irish–Northumbrian of the type found in D and A.

R (R$_2$). *Codex Parisinus*, 'Bible de Rosas', at Paris, from Rosas in eastern Spain. Tenth century. The text is late Vulgate apart from Acts, where it belongs to the recension of Alcuin.

R (R$_3$). *Codex Regius*, in the Vatican Library, seventh–eighth century. Contains the Pauline Epistles in a good North-Italian text.

S (S₂). *Codex Sangallensis,* at St Gall, where it was written; eighth century. Contains Acts and Apocalypse. The text is Irish–Gallic, close to F, but with Celtic additions.

U (U₂). *Codex Ulmensis,* now in the British Museum, but written for Hartmut (Abbot of St Gall, 872–3), who added the Epistle to the Laodiceans in his own hand after Hebrews. Contains Acts, Epistles and Apocalypse in a mixed text, in Acts of the same type as S.

Z (Z₂). *Codex Harleianus,* in the British Museum, formerly at Paris. Eighth century. Contains the Pauline and Catholic Epistles (except 3 John and Jude) and Apocalypse. The text has Old Latin readings in Heb. x–xi and the Catholic Epistles, while in 1 John i. 1—iii. 15 it is closely related to the Freising Fragments (**r**).

These MSS fall into several distinguishable groups or families. That which Wordsworth and White (with general acceptance) regard as the best in the Gospels is the Northumbrian group headed by A S Y Δ, written at the time when, under the leadership of Bede and Ceolfrid, Northumbria led the world in Biblical scholarship. It has been argued by Dom Chapman that it descends from the edition known to have been prepared by the scholar-statesman Cassiodorus (died about 580). Closely akin to this group is F, which though not Northumbrian in origin was in those parts in the late seventh and early eighth centuries. A separate and less good group is headed by Z; these are characterized by Turner as non-Cassiodorian texts current in Italy in the sixth century. An Irish group is formed by D L Q R; and O X form a mixed group between this and the Z-group. C T represent the text of Spain, K V the edition of Alcuin, and Θ and the corrections in H that of Theodulf. In Acts several of these MSS drop out, and the editors' preference is for G C A F D, in that order, the agreement of them representing a combination of all the principal lines of text. For the Epistles the principal MSS are the same, but White had not at his death produced an estimate of their respective quality.

The Vulgate is so important for the history of the Bible in the West that it has seemed worth while to describe the authorities for its text at some length; but owing to its very mixed character it is of less value for the recovery of the original Greek than the earlier Syriac, Coptic, and Old Latin versions.

VI. GOTHIC

Only one other version need be briefly mentioned. This is the translation made by Bishop Ulfilas in the fourth century for the Goths in Moesia. It was made from the Greek in both Testaments; in the Old from a Lucianic text of the LXX, and in the New from a text predominantly of the early Byzantine type. But the surviving MSS are all fragmentary (the principal one being the splendid Codex Argenteus at Uppsala of the fifth or sixth century, containing rather more than half the Gospels written in silver letters, with the first line of each section in gold, on purple-stained vellum), and derive from the period after the Goths had settled in Spain and Northern Italy, and their contacts were with the Latin-speaking Church. This provides the most likely explanation for the Western readings of Old Latin type which are found in the extant Gothic MSS, as also for the Gospels being in the Western order—Matthew, John, Luke, Mark. An important part in bringing about this admixture was no doubt played by Latin-Gothic bilingual MSS, such as that which was the ancestor of Codex Brixianus (f of the Old Latin), and of which the fifth-century Latin–Gothic fragments of Luke at Giessen,[1] and of Romans at Wolfenbüttel, are survivals. The version is extremely literal and shows a remarkable uniformity of translation vocabulary, characteristics which are most evident in Matthew and John, and make the reconstruction of underlying Greek tolerably clear. In Luke and Mark the translation-style is less slavish, and the Latin element more marked, which has pointed to the suggestion that Matthew and John are closer to the original Ostro-Gothic version of Ulfilas. In the Epistles the underlying Byzantine text has been more extensively accommodated to the Old Latin (which resembles that of Codex Claromontanus (d) and Ambrosiaster), and the rendering is also less stereotyped than that of the Gospels.

The version has been edited, together with a reconstructed Greek text, by W. Streitberg, *Die gotische Bibel* (Heidelberg, 1919, 1950); see also W. G. S. Friedrichson, *The Gothic Version of the Gospels* (Oxford, 1920), and *The Gothic Version of the Epistles* (Oxford, 1939).

---

[1] This, however, was discovered at Antinoë in Egypt in 1910, and may have had an African origin, though it agrees closely with f.

M

THE FATHERS

One other important source of evidence remains to be mentioned, that of the Scriptural quotations found in the early Christian writers. Most of those that are important in this respect lived at dates earlier than those of most of our oldest MSS, and if we could be sure that we had them as they wrote them, we should have, for the passages quoted, the evidence of older MSS than those which we possess, and we should know that MSS of that particular type were in circulation in a particular part of the Christian world at a known date. Unfortunately we cannot always be sure that the quotations have come down to us intact. At a time when the Bible did not have the modern chapter and verse divisions and quick reference was not easy, writers were apt to quote short passages from memory, with all the attendant possibilities of verbal error, as well as of paraphrase, omission, assimilation and so forth. On the other hand, longer quotations might well be copied direct from a Bible codex, and other things being equal, these would be the more reliable qualitatively as well as quantitatively. But copyists were apt, when they came to a Scriptural passage, to write it down in the form with which they were familiar, more particularly in the case of long quotations or in the headings of a commentary, and so the later MSS of the Fathers not infrequently show a text different from the earlier ones. It is necessary therefore first of all to secure scientifically edited texts of the Fathers themselves; and in this direction considerable progress has been made in the series of Greek Fathers undertaken by the Academy of Berlin, and of the Latin Fathers by that of Vienna. When used with the proper precautions, however, and remembering that some writers are inaccurate quoters, the evidence of the Fathers is of the greatest value in determining the time and place at which the principal types of text came into existence or were current.

A brief summary, therefore, of the Christian writers in the earliest centuries will be useful. In the sub-apostolic age quotations are rare and inexact, and their chief value is to prove that certain books were then in existence. Such are the few passages which appear to show a knowledge of the Gospels and Pauline Epistles in the Epistles of Clement, Barnabas, Ignatius, and Polycarp. From the second half of the second century we have the *Apology* of Justin Martyr, the *Diatessaron* of Tatian (so far as its text is recoverable), and the extensive quotations from Marcion preserved in the writings of those who sought to confute his heresies. Of all of these it can be said that the evidence, so far as it goes, seems to show that they used texts which show a considerable amount of deviation from the Alexandrian type. The same is the case with Irenaeus, whose principal work, a Confutation of Heresies, was produced between 181 and 189, written in Greek but extant mainly only in a Latin translation, the date of which is doubtful. Irenaeus in his youth heard Polycarp in Asia Minor, but lived and worked mainly at Lyons, so that the MSS at his service must have been those current in southern Gaul. In the Gospels and Acts they were of a distinctly Western type such as is found in Codex Bezae.

From Egypt our earliest patristic evidence is that of Clement of Alexandria (*c.* 150–215), a priest of the Alexandrian Church, and from 190 to 202 head of the catechetical school in that city. He was an industrious writer, widely acquainted with pagan as well as Jewish and Christian literature. His quotations are plentiful, and it is a noteworthy fact, in view of his place of residence, that in the Gospels they also are generally not of the ℵ B family, but broadly agree with the Western type found in D, the Old Syriac, and Old Latin. On the other hand in Acts and the Pauline Epistles Clement is closer to the Alexandrian text, though with some old Western readings. All these are overshadowed by Origen, the greatest scholar among the early Greek Fathers. Born about 185, he succeeded Clement, when barely eighteen, as head of the catechetical school at Alexandria, and in that city he worked, save for a visit to Rome in 213 and a four years' residence at Cæsarea in 215–19, until in 231 he was forced to leave Alexandria finally, when he took up his abode at Cæsarea until his death in 254. Origen was essentially a scholar, with some conception of the principles of textual criticism. His labours on the Septuagint have been described in Chapter II. Of the New Testament he made no edition, but he wrote commentaries on nearly every book, in which he not only quoted copiously, but repeatedly refers to varities of readings in different manuscripts. In his earlier writings he used MSS predominantly of the ℵ B type, though readings of a different character are not wanting; but both before and after his final departure to Cæsarea he seems to have used Gospel

MSS of another type, as to which more will be said when we are examining the later history of textual criticism (see p. 190–1 below). In Acts Origen always used a text of the Alexandrian type. In the Pauline Epistles his text is closely related to $\mathfrak{p}^{46}$, B, and **1739** (which, as we have seen, is closely associated with Origen). In Revelation he uses what may be called an Egyptian text, that found in $\mathfrak{p}^{47}$ ℵ and the Coptic versions. At his death his manuscripts remained at Cæsarea, and became the nucleus of a famous library formed by his disciple Pamphilus (d. 309), to which references occur in later literature and in notes in various MSS (e.g. ℵ; see pp. 41–98).

Of the Latin writers after Irenaeus, Tertullian (*c.* 160–225) and Cyprian (*c.* 200–58) have been mentioned above (p. 146) in connection with the Old Latin version. From Rome itself there is only Hippolytus, who flourished about 220, and wrote (in Greek) commentaries on Matthew, John and the Apocalypse in addition to his great *Refutation of All the Heresies*. Of all these works only portions remain, but it appears that outside the Apocalypse (where his text agrees with the best authorities A and C) he used a Western text in the Gospels, and in Acts and Epistles an Alexandrian text with some Western admixture like Clement. For the Syriac Church the most important writers are Aphraates (*fl. c.* 340) and Ephraim (died 373), both of whom are of great value for the reconstitution of the Old Syriac version and (in the Gospels) of the *Diatessaron*. Eusebius of Caesarea (*c.* 270–340), the historian of the early Church, the friend of Pamphilus and bishop of Cæsarea, carried on the tradition of Origen and had access to his library. In the Gospels he used a text of the same Cæsarean type as Origen, though somewhat modified. Athanasius (died 373) and Cyril of Alexandria (died 444), as we should expect, both used a good text of the ℵ B type. In Asia Minor there were during the fourth century Basil and the two Gregories; in Palestine and Syria, Cyril of Jerusalem (bishop 351–86), and especially Chrysostom (*c.* 347–407), who worked at Antioch until 398 and thereafter at Constantinople, and in whose voluminous writings we find, though by no means uniformly so, the first stage of that revised text which eventually became the accepted Bible of the Byzantine Church.

The two great Latin Fathers of the late fourth and early fifth century, Jerome (*c.* 345–420) and Augustine (354–430) have already been mentioned (pp. 156–61). To them may be added Lucifer of Cagliari (died 371) whose text in the Gospels resembles **a,** in Acts is almost identical with **gig,** and in the Epistles with **d.** Ambrose, who made much use of Greek sources and translated directly from them, must be used with caution. 'Ambrosiaster', an anonymous writer of the latter part of the fourth century, perhaps to be identified with Isaac, a Jewish convert to Christianity, wrote a commentary on the Pauline Epistles in which an Old Latin text akin to **d** and g is found, and in Acts he used a text like **gig.** Finally, mention has already been made of the value of Tyconius and Primasius for the Old Latin version of the Apocalypse, and of Priscillian for the Pauline Epistles.

After the first quarter of the fifth century the Fathers lose much of their value for our present purpose. The Byzantine revision was establishing itself in the East, and the Vulgate in the West, and the writings of the Fathers throw less and less light on the subject with which we are concerned, the recovery of the earliest form of the Greek Scriptures.

BIBLIOGRAPHY

The same general works as have been given in the bibliography appended to Chapter III. The principal works relating to each Version have been cited in the descriptions of them. Reference may also be made to the articles on Text and Vulgate in Hastings' *Dictionary of the Bible* (2nd ed., revised by F. C. Grant and H. H. Rowley, 1963), under Bibelübersetzungen in *Die Religion in Geschichte und Gegenwart* (3rd ed., 1957) and *Evangelische Kirchenlexikon* (1956). See also H. W. Robinson (editor), *Ancient and English Versions of the Bible* (1940); A. Baumstark, *Geschichte der Syrischen Literatur* (1922); S. Berger, *Histoire de la Vulgate* (1895); F. C. Burkitt, *Rules of Tyconius* in *Texts and Studies*, iii. 1 (1893), and *The Old Latin and the Itala,* ibid. iv. 3 (1896); H. J. Vogels, *Vulgatastudien* (1928); M. M. Parvis and A. P. Wikgren (editors), *New Testament Manuscript Studies* (1950); A. Vööbus, *Early Versions of the New Testament* (1954). For the Fathers, A. Harnack, *Geschichte der Altchristlichen Literatur bis Eusebius* (1893–1904), and the various Patrologies of B. Altaner (5th ed., 1958), J. Quasten (vol. i, 1950; vol. ii, 1953), etc.

CHAPTER FIVE

The Printed Text, 1516–1881

From their origins until the sixteenth century the books of the Bible circulated solely in manuscript, each copy being to some extent a different unit; and in the preceding chapters the attempt has been made to describe the various forms of manuscripts and the most important individual manuscripts that survive out of the many thousands that must have once existed. With the invention of printing about the year 1450 a radical change was brought about, since thenceforth all copies printed from a single setting of type could be counted on to be identical. From this point we have to deal not with single manuscripts but with editions; and the history of these, which is the history of the Bible text as known to us and as handled by scholars, can be carried somewhat rapidly through the centuries down to our own time.

The earliest printed book that has come down to us[1] is, very appropriately, the Bible; but naturally this was the Latin Vulgate, since that was then the Bible of the Western world. It is the great folio Bible in large type, commonly known as the Gutenberg (from the name of its supposed printer) or Mazarin (from the name of the owner of the copy which first attracted attention in later times) Bible, but now believed to have been printed by Gutenberg in association with Johann Fust and Peter Schoeffer at Mainz and issued early in 1456. The original Greek of the New Testament did not appear until the sixteenth century was well advanced, although the Hebrew Old Testament had already been published in 1488. In 1502 Cardinal Ximenes began to prepare an elaborate edition of the whole Bible, the Old Testament in

---

[1] Fragments remain of the grammatical work of Donatus, much in use in schools, which is believed to have been printed by Gutenberg about 1450.

Hebrew, Greek and Latin (see above, p. 59), the New Testament in Greek and Latin, and by January, 1514, the New Testament, edited mainly by Lopez de Stunica, was finished. Publication was, however, postponed until the Old Testament should also be ready, which it was by July, 1517, so that Ximenes, who died in November of that year, was able to see the completion of his great undertaking. His death perhaps delayed the obtaining of the papal permission to publish, for this was not given until March, 1520; and the five volumes do not seem to have been actually issued until 1522. This great work is known as the **Complutensian Polyglot**, from Complutum, the Latin name of Alcala, where it was printed; and it remains one of the outstanding landmarks in the history of the Bible.

The delay in publication had, however, lost it the honour of primacy. The printer Froben, of Basle, in the autumn of 1515, who had probably heard of Ximenes' undertaking, commissioned the first Biblical scholar of the day, **Erasmus**, to prepare a Greek New Testament for immediate publication. Erasmus had long been studying and commenting on the Bible, and had been anxious to produce an edition of the original Greek; accordingly he readily accepted the invitation. Speed, however, being necessary, he could only use such manuscripts as he had at hand; and on the basis of these the first printed Greek New Testament appeared in March, 1516. Erasmus used only a handful of MSS which happened to be at Basle, but had previously examined MSS in England. For the Gospels he made some use of minusc. 1, which is a good MS, in correcting 2, a very late copy of the ordinary Byzantine text, which was then sent to the printer as copy. For the Acts and Epistles he mainly used 2^{ap}, and for Revelation 1^{r}; and since this MS lacked the last six verses, he retranslated these as best he could from the Latin. In this uncritical form, therefore, the Greek New Testament was given to the world, and its influence endures to the present day.

Erasmus himself produced four more editions of the New Testament (1519, 1522, 1527, 1535), for which he made some use of other MSS. In that of 1522 he introduced the passage in I John v. 7, 8 relating to the Three Witnesses in Heaven (see p. 106), and in that of 1527 he made some use of the Complutensian, but not much. Other editions were produced by other editors, notably by Robert Estienne or **Stephanus** at Paris (1546,

1549, 1550, 1551) and **Beza** (nine editions between 1565 and 1605). The most important, historically, of these is Stephanus' of 1550, because it became the Received Text which was reprinted, with very slight alteration, in all Greek New Testaments (with negligible exceptions) down to the nineteenth century. It is also the first printed edition to be furnished with a critical apparatus, with variant readings from fifteen MSS (including Codex Bezae) placed on the inner margins. It is therefore material to understand what sort of a text it is. In the main it is Erasmus, somewhat revised from the Complutensian and from fifteen MSS then at Paris. One of these was Codex Bezae, but of this little use was made, no doubt because of its marked divergences from the common type. Substantially the *textus receptus*[1] of Stephanus is the common Byzantine text in its latest form. In the edition of 1551 the division into verses (made by Stephanus himself while travelling from Paris to Lyons) appears for the first time.

For English readers it is important to note that the first English-printed New Testament, produced by Tyndale in 1526, was translated from the text of Erasmus; and this, with Latin and German Bibles, was the basis of Coverdale's successive Bibles from 1535 to 1541. For the Geneva Bible (1557 and 1560) and the Authorized Version of 1611 Stephanus' text of 1550 was available. Stephanus' verse-division was adopted in both of these.

By 1550, therefore, scholars in Western Europe possessed the Greek New Testament substantially in the form which had become standardized in the Eastern Church during the later Middle Ages. From this point the history of the text consists of the record of the labours of scholars in collecting material for its revision, and of the attempts from time to time made to revise it—labours and attempts which continue to the present day.

For a century and more after the pioneer work of Ximenes and Erasmus very little was done to test the authenticity of the printed text by comparison with other manuscripts, and no stress was laid on the comparative age of these manuscripts. How many MSS were consulted for the Complutensian is not known. Erasmus, as we have seen, used very few. Neither of them gave

---

[1] The term *textus receptus* first appears in the Elzevir edition of 1633. The Elzevirs of Leyden printed many editions for commercial purposes from 1624 onwards, and that of 1624 became the standard text on the Continent; but it differs little from Stephanus.

any apparatus of various readings. Stephanus in 1550 did give in his margin variants from his fifteen MSS; but this remained a solitary exception for over a hundred years.

The first great impulse towards the collection of materials and the recognition of the value of ancient MSS came in 1627, when the great Codex Alexandrinus (A) reached England as a gift to Charles I from Cyril Lucar, Patriarch of Constantinople. Brian **Walton**, afterwards bishop of Chester, printed readings from it at the foot of the pages of his great Polyglot Bible,[1] the New Testament volume of which was published in 1657; and a supplementary volume contained collations of fifteen other MSS, in addition to those reported by Stephanus. This is the real beginning of the textual criticism of the New Testament. Among the new witnesses adduced by Walton, the most important after A were D and D_2; all the rest were minuscules of no outstanding merit.

The next step forward was made by Dr John **Fell**, Dean of Christ Church, who in 1675 printed the Elzevir text of 1633 with an apparatus drawn, as he claimed, from over 100 MSS (including twelve newly collated in the Bodleian and twenty-two in Rome, as well as 'the Coptic and Gothic versions, with a selection from the Arabic, Persic, Armenian, Aethiopic, Syriac and Anglo-Saxon'). Far more important was the edition which, with the encouragement and pecuniary help of Fell, was produced by John **Mill**,[2] Fellow of Queen's College, in 1707, as the result of thirty years' labour. It consisted of the text of Stephanus, with an apparatus drawn from seventy-eight MSS in addition to those used by Stephanus, from the Old Latin, Vulgate and Peshitta versions, and from patristic quotations. Among the MSS cited are the uncials A, B, D, D_2, E, E_2, E_3, and K, and the minuscules 28, 33, and 69. In addition, in his valuable Prolegomena Mill laid down the principles of the textual criticism of the New Testament for the first time. It was a great work, and remained for a long time the foundation of all subsequent textual study.

It might have been expected that this great collection of evidence would have been followed by an attempt to utilize it for the revision of the printed text; and in fact the foremost classical scholar of the

[1] The example of Ximenes led to a series of Polyglot Bibles in immense volumes. These are the Antwerp Polyglot in eight volumes (1569–72), the Paris Polyglot in ten (1629–45), and Walton's London Polyglot in eight (1655–7); but none of these except the last has any critical importance.

[2] See Adam Fox, *John Mill and Richard Bentley* (Oxford, 1954).

day, Richard **Bentley**, who had corresponded with Mill and defended him against criticism, made preparations for a critical edition of both the Greek and the Vulgate New Testament, by the comparison of which he believed that 'the true exemplar of Origen' might be recovered with almost complete certainty. Proposals for such an edition were issued by him in 1720, and collations were obtained of many manuscripts, including the great uncials B and C; but whether by reason of Bentley's other preoccupations, or because he found the determination of the primitive text less demonstrable than he had hoped, the work never came to birth. Two other English scholars of lesser note, relying almost wholly on the evidence collected by Mill, did however achieve what Bentley failed to achieve. Edward **Wells**, an Anglican clergyman, produced between 1709 and 1719 a New Testament in a revised text, and a Presbyterian minister, Daniel **Mace**, followed his example in 1729. Both of these editors introduced many emendations which have been accepted by modern criticism, but in their own day their work had no effect. General opinion regarded the 'received text' as sacrosanct, and any attempt to alter it as sacrilegious, while even the collection of various readings was deprecated as tending to throw doubt on the authenticity of the Scriptures. The policy of the ostrich held the field.

Up to this point English scholarship had led the way, but it now was silent for over a century, and the primacy passed to the Continent, and especially to Germany.

J. J. **Wetstein**, of Basle, who had worked for Bentley, had been preparing a new edition, the *prolegomena* to which appeared in 1730 and the edition itself in 1751–2. This made no contribution to text-revision, the Elzevir text being printed with little change; but it is noteworthy as having laid the foundations of the numeration of MSS by letters (for uncials) and numbers (for minuscules) described above (p. 63). A new departure, however, was made by J. A. **Bengel**, of Tübingen, who in 1734 produced an edition of the text into which a few emendations were introduced, with an apparatus in which the various readings were classified according to their merit; but more important than this was his proposal to divide the textual witnesses into groups or families, and to establish their inter-relation and characters. He made a division into two families: in one, which he called **African**, he placed the Codex Alexandrinus and such few Greek and Latin MSS as generally agreed with it, together with the Latin, Coptic, and Ethiopic versions; in the other, which he called **Asiatic**, he placed the great mass of later Greek MSS, which he regarded as of altogether lesser value. The principle of discrimination according to age and quality, and of weighing authorities instead of merely numbering them, was thus introduced for the first time. It was developed by J. S. **Semler** of Halle, who, after a first division into two classes, **Oriental**, which he ascribed to Lucian, and **Occidental** or Egypto-Palestinian, which he ascribed to Origen, in 1767 propounded a triple classification: (1) **Alexandrian**, used by Origen and his disciples, and including the Coptic, Syriac and Ethiopic versions, (2) **Oriental**, centred at Antioch and Constantinople, (3) **Occidental**. The mass of later MSS he regarded as having mixed texts, and as possessing little importance.

A pupil of Semler's, J. J. **Griesbach**, elaborated this analysis in a classification which held the field until the days of Westcott and Hort. In an edition of the New Testament, published in 1775–7, he classified the authorities into three classes, substantially the same as Semler's, but in more detail: (1) **Alexandrian**, including the uncials C L K (it will be remembered that B was almost unknown and ℵ undiscovered), the minuscules **1, 13, 33, 69** and a few others, the Bohairic, Harkleian Syriac, Armenian and Ethiopic versions, and the quotations in Clement of Alexandria, Origen, Eusebius and others; (2) **Western**, including D with some support from **1, 13** and **69**, the Latin versions (especially the OL.) and Fathers, and the Peshitta Syriac; (3) **Constantinopolitan**, including A (which he thought Bengel had rated too high) and the mass of later Greek MSS; and this third class he regarded, like Bengel and Semler, as of altogether inferior value. In his text (the final form of which appeared in 1805) he introduced a few corrections, but in his apparatus he indicated many more as more or less probable.

The principle of disregarding the mass of later MSS in comparison with the few earlier authorities, thus laid down by these three scholars, did not commend itself to general opinion. Matthaei, Birch, and Scholz, who continued and amplified the catalogue of MSS begun by Wetstein, adhered to the received Byzantine text and repudiated the doctrine of Griesbach; and that was the attitude of Biblical scholars in general[1]. It was not

---

[1] Thus in 1815 the Rev. F. Nolan wrote an elaborate *Inquiry into the Integrity*

until 1831 that a new departure was made, and the revision of the text from the materials collected by Mill and his successors down to Scholz was seriously taken in hand. This new departure, which marks the beginning of the modern period of textual criticism, stands to the credit of C. **Lachmann**. Lachmann, who was one of the first classical scholars of his day, applied to the text of the New Testament the same critical principles as he applied to the texts of classical authors, ignoring the mass of later MSS, and relying wholly on the more ancient. He did not hope to do more than recover the text current in the Church in the latter part of the fourth century, and for this purpose he relied mainly on the uncials A, B, C, H₃, P, Q, T, Z, and the quotations in Origen; but since of these B was only imperfectly known to him through the collations made for Bentley, C is imperfect, and the others only fragments, sufficient evidence sometimes failed him, and in such cases he had recourse to Western evidence, the bilinguals D D₂ E₂ G₃, the Old Latin **a b c** g, A and F of the Vulgate, and the early Latin Fathers. In order to eliminate the element of personal predilection, he followed always the majority of his authorities; and on these lines he produced a revised text in 1831, and again, with a fuller statement of the principles which he had followed, in 1842–50.

Lachmann's methods were by no means wholly satisfactory, and his materials were not as adequate as could be wished; but in spite of adverse criticism he had given a much-needed impulse towards the treatment of the New Testament text on sound critical principles. Interest in the subject was now aroused, and

of the Greek Vulgate or Received Text of the New Testament, in which he classified the authorities as representing three ancient editions: (1) Egyptian, made by Hesychius under the influence of Origen and of apocryphal works, represented chiefly by the MSS D of Gospels and Acts, D E F G of Epistles, the Codex Vercellensis (a) of the Old Latin, the Bohairic and Sahidic, and the margin of the Harkleian Syriac; (2) Palestinian, made by Eusebius of Cæsarea, influenced by Marcion and Valentinus, and represented by B, A (in Acts and Epistles), 157, the Vulgate (generally), and the Syriac versions; (3) Vulgate or Byzantine, made by Lucian and reproducing the authentic originals with little error, represented by the great mass of Greek MSS headed by G, V, and A (in Gospels), and the Brixianus (f) of the Old Latin. A is regarded as having been written before 367, when the Epistles of Clement were declared uncanonical by the Council of Laodicea; it probably represents the text of Athanasius under whose influence this type of text superseded that supplied by Eusebius to Constantinople, and became the Received Text of the Byzantine Church. B was evidently little known, and not much is said of it. The importance attached to the Brixianus is noteworthy.

the middle of the nineteenth century saw an epoch-making advance, both in the collection of evidence and in the development of textual theory. The former is mainly connected with the names of Tischendorf and Tregelles, the latter with those of Westcott and Hort. From this point English scholarship comes back into the front line, but the first achievements to be recorded are those of a German. Constantin **Tischendorf** (1815–74), immediately after taking his degree, set himself to search for early manuscripts or fragments of manuscripts of both Testaments, to publish them, and to utilize the results in the preparation of revised texts. The list of his achievements, as recorded by his editor, C. R. **Gregory**, is amazing. He discovered 18 uncial MSS (13 being only fragments) and 6 minuscules; he edited for the first time 25 uncials (all fragments) and re-edited 11 more; he transcribed 4 more and collated 13; finally he brought to light the Codex Vaticanus (B) and he discovered the Sinaiticus (א). The story of these two crowning achievements has been told above (pp. 78, 87). Meanwhile, in addition to his publications of these manuscripts, he found time to produce eight editions of the Greek New Testament, four of the Latin, and four of the Greek Old Testament, besides apocryphal gospels and epistles. His texts, though all superior to the Received Text, varied too much under the influence of his latest discoveries to command full confidence, nor had he the necessary equipment in Biblical scholarship other than textual; but his final edition of the Greek New Testament (1869–72), with full critical apparatus, remains, so far as the apparatus is concerned, the standard edition for the use of scholars, and only needs to be brought up to date by the incorporation of the results of later discoveries. This work, as will be recorded later, is now in hand.

Meanwhile an English contemporary, S. P. **Tregelles**, had been working in the same field with equal devotion. He, reacting against Scholz's rejection of the earlier evidence in favour of the numerically preponderant later witnesses, set himself about 1838 (without knowledge of the work of Lachmann, whose exposition of his principles had not yet appeared) to prepare an edition 'on the authority of ancient copies, without allowing the "received text" any prescriptive rights'. He began by publishing an edition of the Apocalypse on those lines in 1844, but thereafter, in pursuit of his larger project, he travelled over Europe, collating all the

MSS he could find. He collated in all 13 uncials and 4 minuscules, together with A of the Vulgate: and by comparison of his collations with Tischendorf's, each scholar was able to improve or confirm his results. Only at the Vatican did he fail, being refused access to B and to other MSS; and he was obliged to content himself with the collations made for Bentley and an earlier one made in 1669 by Bartolocci and preserved at Paris, all of which showed many omissions and divergences. His edition (in which use was also made of the versions and Fathers) was published in parts between 1857 and 1872; it shows a text revised on scholarly principles, but its lasting influence is impaired by the fact that the Gospels were published before Tischendorf's discovery of ℵ and his edition of B.

It was the revelation of these two outstanding authorities, earlier in date than any previously known, and supporting one another in evidence for a text markedly different from the received Byzantine text, that gave the decisive impulse for a revision both of the Greek text in common use and of the English Authorized Version. The latter task was taken in hand by the Convocation of Canterbury in 1870, and resulted in the Revised Version of 1881. With that we are not here concerned; but it largely reflects the influence of two of its members, B. F. **Westcott** and F. J. A. **Hort**, who were simultaneously engaged on an edition of the Greek text. Since their work, which appeared in 1881, consisting of a revised text without *apparatus criticus*, but with elaborate prolegomena and notes on special passages, has formed the basis of all subsequent textual criticism of the New Testament, it is necessary to describe it at some length.

The Prolegomena (written by Hort, but embodying the joint conclusions of the two colleagues) set out a theory which is in the direct line of descent from Bengel and Griesbach, but which deals with a far larger body of material and is argued with greater elaboration. After briefly explaining the origin of various readings, it discusses the methods by which a choice can be made among them. The first is the instinctive preference felt by the critic: but this needs great caution, partly as being too subjective, but still more because the reading which at first sight appears preferable may be due to a correction by a scribe of a reading which presented some difficulty to him. This point was crystallized by Bengel in an aphorism, 'Difficilior lectio potior'. It is necessary to look further, and to see which reading best accounts for the variants that occur, and which can be explained as due to the observed proclivities of scribes, as to which long experience has evolved certain recognized canons. Apparent superiority and latent inferiority are the normal marks of scribes' corrections; and the real superiority of readings is often perceptible only after close study. The next step is to observe which documents most often offer superior readings, and so to obtain a comparative estimate of documents. In cases of doubt a preference may then be given to readings attested by the documents found to be usually superior. Next it will become possible to classify documents in groups, by observing which are commonly found in combination in support of certain readings. This will generally imply descent, more or less remote, from a common ancestor, and so carries back the testimony to a date which may be a century or more earlier than the documents themselves. On this basis Hort proceeds to a classification of the New Testament documents in accordance with the following four main families of text: (α) the later uncials and the great mass of cursives, which contain the type of text he believes to be descended from a revision begun at Antioch towards the end of the fourth century which he calls **Syrian**; (β) the group headed by the great uncials B and ℵ, containing the type of text which, after close scrutiny, he believes to have come down in relative purity free from editorial revision, and so labels **neutral**;[1] (γ) a small group, not embodied wholly in any one MS or group of MSS, comprising readings found in MSS normally akin to the neutral type but differing from the leading representatives of thay type, which, because they show signs of stylistic revision are likels to have arisen in a centre of scholarship, and these he callt **Alexandrian**; (δ) the group headed by D, the Old Latin version and the Latin Fathers, which are characterized by wide divergencies of text from the other families, and which, because of its predominantly Latin attestation, he denominates **Western**.

---

[1] Westcott and Hort in both volumes of their edition, *Text* and *Introduction*, rarely use the word, and then always with a small letter (neutral) and generally in relation to the main types of text, which by contrast are always printed with a capital letter (Western, Syrian, Alexandrian, even Non-Western Pre-Syrian): e.g. 'The third holds a middle or neutral position, sometimes simply opposed to Western or Alexandrian readings, occasionally opposed to Western or Alexandrian readings alike' (Text, p. 547); '*The neutral text and its preservation*' (heading, Introduction, pp. xvi, 126). This usage, clearly deliberate on the part of Hort, will be followed here.

As between these four groups, a basis of choice may be found in the evidence of the Fathers, which shows what type of text was in use at particular times and places; and a cardinal point in Hort's theory is his affirmation that no reading strictly belonging to the α family is found in any Father before Chrysostom. Moreover, this family, on examination, shows all the signs of a revision which aims at smoothing away difficulties by verbal alterations, such as the substitution of conventional phrases for unusual ones, or the modification of readings which might be misunderstood or cause offence, the insertion of names or pronouns in the interests of intelligibility, the harmonization (by amalgamation or substitution) of parallel narratives in the synoptic Gospels, and the like. On these grounds he rules out (as Bengel, Griesbach, Lachmann, Tischendorf and Tregelles had done before him) the great mass of later authorities, and no reading resting on purely Syrian attestation would be accepted by him. The γ group is of minor importance. Its attestation is variable, and it appears to be due to stylistic revision on a small scale, or to represent sporadic readings, early in date but lacking authority.

As between the β and δ groups the choice is more difficult and must be made on other grounds. The Western readings cannot be ruled out on the ground of comparative lateness, for the evidence of the Fathers, which was decisive against the Syrian group, may be adduced rather in favour of the Western. Nearly all the early Fathers, notably Justin Martyr, Tatian, Irenaeus, Tertullian and Cyprian, but including at times even Clement of Alexandria, Origen and Eusebius, who are generally associated with the neutral group, offer readings which are more or less Western in character. The Old Latin and Old Syriac versions are also witnesses of great antiquity, and the former is decidedly Western and the latter shows many Western readings. Here the decision must rest on grounds of intrinsic probability; and in Hort's judgment the comparison is definitely unfavourable to the Westerners. He considers that the characteristic Western readings (of which many examples have been given above in the description of D and the Latin and Syriac versions and more are given in Chapter VII below) are due to a licentious handling of the text by early scribes, when fidelity of transcription was little accounted of, and in comparison with the β family to lack authority and probability. Hort's verdict is therefore emphatically in favour of

the β group, in which he finds none of the marks of deliberate or
licentious alteration, and which he therefore feels justified in
labelling as neutral. Above all he pins his faith to B. Where ℵ
and B agree, as they very frequently do, their evidence is almost
decisive; and where they differ he would give the preference to B.
The only exception he would make is in the case of a few notable
passages, mainly in Luke, which occur in B but are omitted in D
and other Western authorities. These he labels 'Western non-
interpolations'; a simpler designation would be 'neutral interpolations'. Those about which Hort had no doubt in rejecting altogether
are:

Matt. xxvii. 49, *fin* (ἄλλος δὲ . . . αἷμα.)
Luke xxii. 19ᵇ–20 (τὸ ὑπὲρ ὑμῶν . . . ἐκχυννόμενον)
Luke xxiv. 3 (τοῦ κυρίου Ἰησοῦ)
Luke xxiv. 6 (οὐκ ἔστιν ὧδε, ἀλλὰ ἠγέρθη)
Luke xxiv. 12 (ὁ δὲ Πέτρος . . . τὸ γεγονός)
Luke xxiv. 36 (καὶ λέγει αὐτοῖς Εἰρήνη ὑμῖν)
Luke xxiv. 40 (καὶ τοῦτο εἰπὼν . . . πόδας)
Luke xxiv. 51 (καὶ ἀνεφέρετο εἰς τὸν οὐρανόν)
Luke xxiv. 52 (πρυσκυνήσαντες αὐτόν).

Others, with a similar attestation in neutral and Western authorities Hort places in an intermediate class 'open to some doubt'.
These are:

Matt. vi. 15 (τὰ παραπτώματα αὐτῶν)
Matt. vi. 25 (ἢ τί πίητε)
Matt. ix. 34 (οἱ δὲ φαρισαῖοι . . . δαιμόνια)
Matt. xiii. 33 (ἐλάλησεν αὐτοῖς)
Matt. xxi. 44 (καὶ ὁ πεσὼν . . . λικμήσει αὐτόν)
Matt. xxiii. 26 (καὶ τῆς παροψίδος)
Mark ii. 22 (ἀλλὰ οἶνον νέον εἰς ἀσκοὺς καινούς)
Mark x. 2 (προσελθόντες φαρισαῖοι)
Mark xiv. 39 (τὸν αὐτὸν λόγον εἰπών)
Luke v. 39 (οὐδεὶς . . . χρηστός ἐστιν)
Luke x. 41–42 (μεριμνᾷς . . . ἢ ἑνός)
Luke xii. 19 (κείμενα . . . φάγε, πίε)
Luke xii. 39 (ἐγρηγόρησεν ἂν καί)
Luke xxii. 62 (καὶ ἐξελθὼν . . . πικρῶς)
Luke xxiv. 9 (ἀπὸ τοῦ μνημείου)

N

John iii. 31–32 (ἐπάνω πάντων ἐστίν, (32) τοῦτο)
John iv. 9 (οὐ γὰρ . . . Σαμαρίταις).

Such is, in brief outline, the theory of Westcott and Hort, which has been the battle-ground of all subsequent criticism. How far it can be considered to have held its ground must be discussed when the evidence that has come to light since their day and the arguments of later scholars have been put before the reader. Its promulgation closes one period in the history of textual criticism, and begins another.

BIBLIOGRAPHY

Gregory and Scrivener, *opp. citt.*; S. P. Tregelles, *Account of the Printed Text of the Greek New Testament*; Barlow and Moule, *Historical Catalogue of the Printed Editions of Holy Scriptures in the Library of the British and Foreign Bible Society*; B. F. Westcott and F. J. A. Hort, *The New Testament in the original Greek*, Introduction (1882).

CHAPTER SIX

Textual Discoveries and Theories Since 1881

THE publication in 1881 of Westcott and Hort's Greek Text, and of the Revised Version of the New Testament which largely (but not by any means wholly) reflected it, let loose a flood of controversy. The battle was at first between the advocates of the Received Text and its opponents. Dean J. W. Burgon, the protagonist of the former, was a doughty controversialist, and could deal a swashing blow with gusto. He had also behind him the sympathy of those who resented the changes in their beloved Authorized Version and did not understand the reasons for them. Among scholars, however, he found little support, and though his disciple and assistant, E. Miller (who, besides directly controversial books, edited the fourth edition of Scrivener's useful *Introduction*), maintained the fight after his death, this conflict soon died down. The relative lateness of the Byzantine or Received Text was regarded by almost all scholars not only as proved by the evidence of the Fathers, but as in accordance (though on a much larger scale) with the textual history of all ancient literature. Subsequent discoveries have done nothing to disturb this verdict, and this particular issue may be regarded as closed.

It was far otherwise with regard to the question of the comparative claims of the neutral and the Western types of text. Here, if all readings for which there is early evidence, but which were not in the neutral text, were to be reckoned as Western, the evidence of the Fathers, which Westcott and Hort used so decisively against the Syrian text, was rather in favour of the Western, and not a few of the leading scholars were disposed to challenge

Westcott and Hort's almost exclusive reliance on B, if not definitely to prefer the Western text. This, therefore, became the outstanding issue in the criticism of the New Testament, and it is for their bearing upon this problem that the discoveries of the ensuing years were diligently scrutinized. It is with these discoveries, and with the theories to which they give rise, that this chapter is concerned.

The two decades following 1881 saw the appearance, at different times and from different places, of four manuscripts (or rather portions of manuscripts) which are nevertheless closely related in appearance and character. These are the four manuscripts of the Gospels on purple vellum described above as N, O, Σ, and Φ. N and Σ are so closely related in text as to be practically sister manuscripts, and Σ and O are connected by the fact that both contain illustrations. Σ and Φ contain Matthew and Mark, O portions of Matthew, N portions of all Gospels, but chiefly of Luke and John. All are approximately of the same date, probably sixth century, and must have emanated from the same centre.

There is nothing to show what that centre was, but since N appears to have been broken up by Crusaders in the twelfth century, Constantinople or some other large town in the Eastern Empire seems probable. In text, all represent the Byzantine type in an early stage, but O and Φ are not so closely related to the others as N and Σ are to one another. Φ in particular is remarkable for including the long passage after Matt. xx. 28, for which the only other Greek witness is D, but which is found in most MSS of the Old Latin and a few of the Vulgate, and also in the Curetonian Syriac. Before the discovery of W, Σ and Φ (N and O being defective here) were the earliest authorities for the doxology to the Lord's Prayer in Matt. vi. 13. On the whole, however, the discovery of this group of MSS did not materially affect the textual position. The same may be said of the few other uncial MSS that have come to light, though Ψ is noteworthy as falling into the same class as L, like it agreeing in general with B, and containing both the shorter and the longer endings to Mark.

Far more important was the discovery of the Sinaitic palimpsest of the Old Syriac version made by Mrs Lewis and Mrs Gibson in 1892, which has been described above (p. 118). This, with its considerable proportion of non-neutral, and sometimes definitely

Western, readings (markedly greater than in the Curetonian copy of the same version) was a distinct encouragement to the Westerners. It will be clear, however, from the readings quoted in the description of the version, that its adhesion to the Western group is only very partial, and it is possible that its Western readings may be due to the influence of the undoubtedly 'Western' *Diatessaron*. For the moment, however, the extent to which it supported the neutral text was ignored, and it was regarded as a proof that the Western text was prevalent in early times not only in the West but in the East.

In 1906 a fresh discovery of interest was made, that of the Freer or Washington MS of the Gospels (W, see p. 101 above). Here again attention was naturally attracted to the features which differentiate it from either the Syrian or the neutral type; and while in Matthew, Luke and John it belongs to one or other of these families, in Mark it not only has an apocryphal addition after xvi. 14 (quoted above), but is throughout plainly neither Syrian nor neutral, and in the earlier chapters shows strong affinity to the Old Latin. Another Western characteristic is the order of the Gospels, Matthew, John, Luke, Mark. It was natural at first to reckon the whole of this Gospel to the Western side of the account. It was only later research and discovery that threw an altogether fresh light on this estimate.

This research began at a remote and apparently quite unconnected point, in the identification by W. H. Ferrar, of Trinity College, Dublin, of four minuscule manuscripts (those known as **13, 69, 124** and **346**) as forming a single group, closely allied in text and presenting many remarkable readings. The discovery was made by Ferrar as far back as 1868, and after his death the investigation was carried on by T. K. Abbott and published in 1877.

Three of the MSS, **13, 124** and **346** were written in Calabria in the twelfth or thirteenth century; **69**, written in England by Emmanuel of Constantinople in the fifteenth century, must have been copied from an exemplar of the same provenance. Subsequent research[1] has added to this group (known as the Ferrar group or fam. **13**) several other MSS (**174** (except Mark), **230, 543, 788, 826, 828, 983, 1689, 1709**), as descended from the same

---

[1] See especially K. and S. Lake, *Family 13 (The Ferrar Group) Studies and Documents*, xi (London and Philadelphia, 1941).

source and retaining many of its characteristic readings, though
all have been more or less brought into conformity with the
Received Text. The most remarkable variant characteristic of
this group is its transference of the *pericope adulterae* (John
vii. 53—viii. 11) to a position after Luke xxi. 38. Other notable
readings are its agreement with both Old Syriac MSS in omitting
Matt. xvi. 2, 3, and with Sinaitic in omitting Luke xxii. 43, 44;
and in many other passages it separates itself from the Received
Text. In Matt. xiv. 24 it reads σταδίους πολλοὺς ἀπὸ τῆς γῆς
ἀπεῖχεν, with B—the Curetonian has the same words in a
different order; xviii. 11 it omits ἦλθε . . . ἀπολωλός, with
ℵ B Θ and the Sinaitic (but not the Curetonian) OS; Mark vi. 3
ὁ τοῦ τέκτονος υἱός with 𝔓⁴⁵ OL; Luke vi. 1 it supports
δευτεροπρώτῳ of A D Θ; xi. 2 (the Lord's Prayer) it has the
longer Byzantine readings πάτερ ἡμῶν ὁ ἐν τοῖς οὐρανοῖς with
A D W Θ OL and Curetonian (but not Sinaitic) OS, and
γενηθήτω . . . γῆς with ℵ D W Θ OL Bohairic; xv. 16
χορτασθῆναι, with 𝔓⁷⁵ ℵ B D and Curetonian (but not Sinaitic)
OS. At first the significance of this group was far from clear. It
was merely a rather peculiar text, emanating, so far as could be
seen, from Southern Italy at a relatively late date. Subsequent
developments were to add to its importance.

Another group with somewhat similar characteristics was
identified by Professor Kirsopp Lake in his study of *Codex I of the
Gospels and its Allies: Texts and Studies VII*, no. 3 (Cambridge,
1902). This consists of the four minuscules **1, 118, 131, 209**, of
which **1** is the most important. Here, as in W and some other
MSS, it is in Mark that the divergence from the Received Text is
most marked, but the characteristic readings of the group are not
confined to this Gospel. It agrees with ℵ B and OS in the
omissions in Matt. i. 25, v. 44, and xviii. 11, but not in those in
xii. 47, xvi. 2, 3; in xix. 17 it agrees with ℵ B D and OS; in
xix. 29 with ℵ W Θ OL and the Curetonian (not Sinaitic) OS;
xxiv. 36 it omits οὐδὲ ὁ υἱός with the Sinaitic OS; xxvii. 16, 17
it reads Ἰησοῦν Βαραββᾶν with the same (Curetonian is defective);
Mark i. 27 it agrees with ℵ B against almost all others; ix. 44, 46, 49
it has the same omissions as ℵ B W OS and Coptic; it gives
Mark xvi. 9–20 with a note that the passage is omitted in some
copies; Luke i. 28 it omits εὐλογημένη σὺ ἐν γυναιξίν with ℵ B
and Coptic; iv. 44 Ἰουδαίας with ℵ B and OS; vi. 1 it omits

δευτεροπρώτῳ with 𝔭⁷⁵ ℵ B W; ix. 35 ἐκλεκτός with Θ against ἐκλελεγμένος of 𝔭⁷⁵ ℵ B and ἀγαπητός of most authorities; ix. 55, 56 it has καὶ εἶπεν . . . σῶσαι with D and most authorities against ℵ A B W Sinaitic OS and Coptic; xi. 2–4 (the Lord's Prayer) it has the shorter version with 𝔭⁷⁵ B, OS, and generally ℵ; xv. 16 χορτασθῆναι with 𝔭⁷⁵ ℵ B D and the Curetonian; in xxiv it has none of the omissions which characterize D and OL; John i. 28 Βηθαβαρᾷ with both OS and Sahidic; iii. 31 it omits ἐπάνω πάντων ἐστίν with ℵ D and the Curetonian; v. 3, 4 it includes the angel and the stirring of the water; vi. 69 ὁ Χριστὸς ὁ υἱὸς τοῦ Θεοῦ with Θ and the Sinaitic Syriac; at vii. 53 1 omits the *pericope*, but adds it at the end of the Gospel (so also **1582**) while **209**, after writing the first words of viii. 12, deletes them and inserts the *pericope*. The importance of this group, known as fam. **1**, lies not only in its own readings which seem to have an early origin, but still more in the fact, as shown by Lake, that at any rate in Mark it forms part of a family which includes fam. **13** and the minuscules **28, 656,** and **700,** and in which some affinity with the Old Syriac is discernible.[1]

A third stage in a structure which was already assuming some importance was reached when the Koridethi Gospels (Θ) came to light. Attention was first called to it in 1906 by von Soden, who associated it closely with D; but after its publication by Beerman and Gregory in 1913 it was made the subject of a careful study by Lake and R. P. Blake in 1923 (see above, p. 102), who showed that (at any rate in Mark, to which the study is confined), while it had no special association with D, it was closely connected with famm. **1** and **13** and the other minuscules (**28, 565, 700**) which have some relation to them. All these might in fact be linked together into a single family under the title fam. Θ. Moreover through Θ, which Blake believed to have originated in the Georgian colony in Sinai in the ninth century, the Georgian version was brought within the ambit of the group.

The coping stone was placed on this structure, the foundations of which were laid so far back as 1868, by Dr B. H. Streeter in his work, *The Four Gospels*, published in 1924; and it will be convenient to desert chronological sequence in order to complete the

---

[1] Some other minuscules (**22, 282** in Mark, **1278, 1582, 2193**) are included by von Soden in this group; according to Streeter only **1582** is comparable with **1** in importance.

story. In the first place he reinforced Lake's demonstration of the
existence of fam. Θ by showing that it was not confined to Mark
but applied also to the other Gospels. He found also that a
number of other MSS occasionally preserve readings of this type,
which suggests that they descend from an ancestor of this character,
though they have been even more drastically revised into accordance with the Received Text than the more recognizable members
of the group. The most important of these is a group headed by
the minuscule **1424**. The text of fam. Θ stands about midway
between neutral and Western, and has a large number of readings
which do not belong to either. It may therefore, Streeter urged,
claim to be a distinct family, to take its place alongside the three
main families which Hort called neutral, Western and Syrian. It
stands nearer to the Old Syriac than any other Greek MSS, but
not by any means so close as to represent the same text. It is about
equally connected with the Armenian, and more decidedly with
the Georgian. Now on examining the quotations by Origen in his
commentaries on John and Matthew and his *Exhortation to
Martyrdom* (all written between 231 and 240) the surprising result
emerged that while in the first ten books of the Commentary on
John Origen used a copy of Mark of the same type as ℵ B, in the
remaining books of this Commentary and in the subsequent works
he used one of the same type as fam. Θ. Now it is known that
Origen began his Commentary on John at Alexandria and finished
it at Cæsarea; hence Streeter felt justified in arguing that while at
Alexandria he naturally used MSS of the type particularly associated with that city (the ℵ B type), when he came to Cæsarea he
found MSS of a different type there (the Θ type) and thereafter
used it. If this is so, the text of fam. Θ may be rightly named the
Cæsarean text.

This discovery of Streeter's, summing up so much earlier work,
and proving that the texts of Θ, fam. **1**, fam. **13** and their satellites
can be joined together into a single family, and that this family,
in spite of the lateness of its extant members, can be associated
with the great names of Origen and Cæsarea, is an epoch-making
event in the history of Biblical criticism, which deserves the
fullest recognition. In one respect, however, it was speedily shown
to require qualification. Professor Kirsopp Lake, who had already
made such an important contribution to the subject by his study
of Codex **1**, in 1924 published a most valuable article on the

Cæsarean text of Mark,[1] in which, after pointing out that the text of W in the latter part of Mark, which had hitherto been vaguely classed as Western because it was neither neutral nor Syrian, is in fact Cæsarean, he proceeded to examine more closely the connection between this text and Cæsarea. Streeter's argument rested on the fact that in the first ten books of the Commentary on John, Origen quoted from a text differing from that which he used subsequently. But the fact (as quoted by Eusebius from Origen's own statement) is that only the first *five* books were written at Alexandria; and, according to Lake, in these five books the evidence as to the text used is very slight, and is quite as consistent with the use of a Cæsarean text as of an Alexandrian, while in books 6–10 (the first written after his arrival at Cæsarea) he certainly used an Alexandrian text. In the remaining books he seems to have used an Alexandrian text when quoting from the greater part of Mark, but a Cæsarean text after about the middle of chapter xii; and in all his subsequent writings his text is definitely Cæsarean.

It is therefore necessary (if Lake's arguments remain unshaken) so far to modify Streeter's conclusions as to say that Origen may have used the Cæsarean text before he left Alexandria; that he certainly used the Alexandrian text on his first arrival at Cæsarea; and that for the rest of his life at Cæsarea he certainly used the Cæsarean text. From its being thus domiciled in Cæsarea (whence its connection with the Oriental versions would not be difficult) it may rightly retain the name Cæsarean; but the possibility remains open that it existed already in Egypt before Origen's Hejira, and even that it was Origen himself who brought it to Palestine. On this point some further evidence may be adduced when we come to the Chester Beatty papyri.

Meanwhile a fresh classification of the textual evidence had been put forward by H. von Soden in the second part of the prolegomena to his new edition of the New Testament, published in 1906, before the identification of the Cæsarean text. The familiar threefold division is retained, but with some differences, and with some peculiar developments. The division is as follows:

1. K ($Kοινή$): The Textus Receptus, found in the great mass of MSS. This is divided into about seventeen groups, with a somewhat

---

[1] *Harvard Theological Review*, xxi. 207–404.

bewildering nomenclature, which represent a progressive modification of the text in verbal and stylistic details in accordance with
the taste of the times. The three main classes are K^1, the earliest
form of this family, K^r the latest, and K^x which covers all that
lies between them. The earliest complete K^1 MS is ε 61
[Gregory's Ω] of the eighth century and 75 [V], 92 [**0136**], and
95 [**047**] of the ninth; but traces of K readings occur plentifully
in earlier MSS mainly belonging to other families, notably
δ 4 [A], δ 3 [C], δ 2 [ℵ] and δ 6 [Ψ]. K^i and K^{ik} are sub-groups in
which the K^1 text has been influenced by other groups indicated
as J and J^k respectively. K^x is the dominant text of the Middle
Ages, at least from the tenth or eleventh century. Its sub-groups
are distinguished by the different forms in which they have (or
omit) the *pericope adulterae*, K$^{\mu\nu}$, K$^{\mu2}$, K$^{\mu3}$, K$^{\mu4}$, K$^{\mu5}$, K$^{\mu6}$, with
minor varieties in which these have reciprocally influenced one
another. K^r is the final revision made about the twelfth century
with special reference to lectionary requirements, and this from
the thirteenth century onwards became the accepted ecclesiastical
text. The MSS of this class are generally furnished either with
tables of lections or with clearly marked beginnings and endings
of lections in the text. They amount in number to about 200, and
fall into eight divisions according to the fullness of their lectionary
apparatus. Other classes are A^k, consisting of commentaries with
a K text, and K^a, a variant of K^1, to which over 100 MSS are
assigned, notably δ 4 [A], though this has also been influenced by
other groups. This is more fully dealt with below (p. 193) as a
member of the third family. This analysis of the great mass of K
MSS, the result of a vast amount of detailed labour, is a contribution to the history of the New Testament text in the Middle Ages,
but in view of the relative lateness of the K text as a whole and
its secondary character, it has little bearing on the recovery of the
primitive text, which is the prime object of textual criticism.

2. H (Hesychius): roughly equivalent to Hort's neutral text.
This family includes fifty MSS headed by δ 1 [B], δ 2 [ℵ], δ 3 [C],
δ 6 [Ψ], δ 48 [**33**]. δ 1 and δ 2 have a common ancestor, δ$^{1-2}$,
which is by far the best representative of the H text, though not
free from corruption. It has been influenced both by the Coptic
versions and by Origen. δ 1 has been influenced by K^1 (not by K^x)
and by I, and the Sahidic. δ 2 departs more from H, both by
scribal errors and by alterations due to carelessness or intention.

It has a considerable number of readings adopted from parallel passages (which δ 1 has not), also readings from K¹, I, and Sah. It also has some elements in common with δ 5 [D], especially in John. δ 3 is more correctly written than δ 1 or δ 2, but is more influenced by parallel passages and by K, less so by I, and hardly at all by Sah. Other MSS of some importance in the H group are those known in Gregory's list as L, Z, Δ, 579, 892, 1241. There are no subdivisions of the H family, and its readings can in the very large majority of cases be determined with certainty.

3. I (Jerusalem): a family not preserved in substantial integrity in any outstanding MSS, as H is in B and ℵ, and never acquiring a dominating position, as did K, but to be elicited from a number of authorities of mixed characters. This is claimed by von Soden as his special discovery and his main contribution to textual history. It rests upon the observation of the existence of a number of readings common to the Old Latin, the Sinaitic Syriac, famm. 1 and 13, and D, sometimes agreeing with H, sometimes with K, sometimes with neither. It has fourteen sub-groups, the nomenclature of which is bewilderingly arbitrary: (1) H^r = fam. 1; (2) J = fam. 13; (3) Φ^a, headed by δ 30; (4) Φ^b, headed by δ 250 [2191]; (5) Φ^c, headed by ε 1091 [1223]; (6) Φ^r, an offshoot of Φ, of which there are three branches, in none of which is much of Φ left; (7) B, a group much influenced by K, of which there are two branches, the better one headed by ε 1043 [1216], the inferior one by δ 152 [491]; (8) K^a, which has already appeared among the K family, and which is a mixture of K¹ and I, the latter furnishing the basic text, which has been drastically revised from the former, with some slight influence from H; (9) I^r, the weakest member of the I family, being 90 per cent K; (10) A^k, like K^a, a mixture of K and I; and the same may be said of (11) K^i, and indeed of several other branches of the K family and of various individual members of it. More important is (12) Π, composed of the four purple MSS described above as N, O, Σ, Φ which are all fundamentally I texts largely altered to K; and (13) O, a small group headed by ε 90 [U]. Finally (14) I^a is the most important group of all, headed by δ 5 [D], ε 050 [Θ], ε 93 [565], ε 168 [28], etc. This is the best representative of the I family. It was the discovery of ε 050 that first gave it clear definition. δ 5 is a mixture of I and K¹, with many scribal errors, but also with many deliberate alterations, attributable to various ancestors. It is strongly affected

by parallel passages, also by the Old Latin; but this is due not to common descent from the original, but to editorial revision of an ancestor of δ 5.

The constitution of the I family is the most original feature of von Soden's work, but it is to be feared it is also the least sound. It will be observed that it combines, as closely related, the principal representatives of the Western and Cæsarean families, and this does not appear to be valid. At the same time the immense labour devoted to the analysis of all these various groups and the tabulation of their characteristic readings deserves grateful recognition.

Behind these three great families lies the fundamental text I-H-K. It is possible, but not probable, that some readings of this fundamental text have disappeared; but in some cases they may be very slightly supported, so that their identification remains insecure. By far the greater part of the variants are due to the influence (conscious or unconscious) of parallel passages; this is especially strong in K, which originated in Syria, where it was no doubt affected by the *Diatessaron*. Of the three families, K is much the farthest removed from the original. Besides being full of verbal and stylistic alterations, it shows some influence from the Old Syriac. It has also in its turn affected the later Syriac versions, the Peshitta being a revision of the Old Syriac by means of K. The text of Chrysostom is K^1, with some traces of I (derived from Origen), but none of H; in John his text is K^a. The Cappadocian Fathers also exhibit a mixture of I and K, much resembling the group *Π*. The K text originated in Syria, and is perhaps to be attributed to Lucian, the well-known editor of the Septuagint.

H seldom departs from I-H-K except in matters of verbal style, notably the omission of unnecessary words. It is substantially the text of Athanasius, Didymus and Cyril of Alexandria; also of the Sahidic and Bohairic versions. It is obviously Egyptian in origin, and may be assigned to Hesychius, to whom the Alexandrian edition of the Septuagint is due.

I, when recoverable, in general preserves the common original most faithfully. It must have been widely known for a long period, since its influence is far-reaching; but it was eventually submerged by K. It is the text of Cyril of Jerusalem and Eusebius of Cæsarea, and is the basis of the Palestinian Syriac. It is therefore Palestinian in origin, and may presumably be assigned to Eusebius.

The relation of Origen to the I-H-K text would appear to be

that he used it, but did not make it, since he often departs from it. His evidence can be used along with that of I, H, and K for the recovery of I-H-K. The later Egyptian Fathers (Dionysius, Alexander, Methodius) use I-H-K more accurately than Origen; and this was also the text used by Jerome.

Going back behind Origen, we have evidence of the early Fathers and the Old Latin and Old Syriac versions. These show many variations from I-H-K, often palpably inferior, though they may be supported by more than one witness. The cause of this disturbance in the text is to be found, according to von Soden, in Tatian. Such material (as distinct from stylistic) divergences as are found in K are to be attributed to Tatian, and to him is also due the strong influence of parallel passages, in which the preference is generally given to Matthew. Of the versions, the African and European Old Latin are independent translations, almost always differing where difference is possible. When either or both differ from I-H-K, the difference is generally attributable to Tatian. The same is largely the case with the Old Syriac; the translator would appear to have had an I-H-K text before him, but allowed himself to be much influenced by Tatian. Of the Fathers, Origen keeps clear of the influence of Tatian, and there is little of it in Tertullian or Hippolytus. The main text of the two last named is I-H-K, as also is that of Clement of Alexandria, who however has many readings peculiar to himself, in part due to quoting from memory. Irenaeus is mainly I-H-K, with more Tatianic influence. Justin's departures from I-H-K are personal liberties; he sets no store by accuracy in quotation. Among the principal MSS the influence of Tatian is by far most evident in δ 5 [D]; it is noticeable in δ 2 [א], but hardly at all in δ 1 [B] or in δ¹⁻². The very various and sporadic appearances of Tatianic readings is a proof that the *Diatessaron* was the originating influence, not *vice versa*. The appearance of such readings both in East and West thus becomes intelligible. It is by the elimination of Tatianic corruption that the text of I-H-K can be recovered, i.e. the text of about A.D. 140, with the strong probability that it had not been seriously modified before that date.

The above analysis applies only to the Gospels. In Acts and the Catholic Epistles the H and K texts are easily distinguishable, and H is nearer to the original. A third text, which may be identified as I, is a mixture of these two, with some readings of its own. H is to be found best in δ 1 and δ 2, but also in δ 3, δ 4, δ 6, δ 48, and in the Egyptian Fathers and Versions. With regard to the latter, von Soden remarks that since δ 2 contains characteristic Boh. readings which are plainly not original H readings, Boh. must be earlier in origin than δ 2; and the same argument shows that Sah. is earlier than δ 5. The principal representative of I is δ 5; it is also found in the scanty quotations of Eusebius, Cyril of Jerusalem and Epiphanius. The special I readings may perhaps be attributable to Tatian, if, as Eusebius records, he made a revision of the book. Origen, Clement, and Jerome used I-H-K; also Tertullian and Irenaeus, but with more intermixture of Tatian, especially in the latter.

In the Pauline Epistles the three families are all discernible, but the differences are less important. The main representatives of the several families are the same. Marcionite influence is observable, especially on the Latin versions, and to this a great part of the variants in K are probably due. In the Apocalypse, H is represented by δ 2, δ 3, δ 4, and α 3 [א C A P], K by most MSS, with greater uniformity than elsewhere.

Such is, in summary, the textual theory expounded by von Soden. In view of the great amount of labour expended on it, it has seemed right to set it out in some detail; but it must be added that its most original features, the constitution of the I family and the wide-reaching influence ascribed to Tatian, have met with little acceptance, though so far as the Old Syriac is concerned, Burkitt agreed with him.

It will naturally be asked what is the effect of all this research and theory on the text as finally constituted. Here the results may be regarded as disappointing or reassuring according to the view taken. The principles laid down by von Soden are, first, that when the readings of the three main families can be established, the reading supported by two of them is generally adopted; which must mean that where I and H differ, K has the casting vote. Where, however, two families give a text agreeing with a parallel passage, while the third gives a different one, the latter is preferred; which would rule out many K variants. Readings supported by Tatian are generally suspect; so that even if all three families agree with Tatian, an alternative that has the support of early versions or Fathers is preferred. The result is a text not substantially different from that of most other modern editors.

Meanwhile, during all the years from 1881 onwards, a constant stream of fresh evidence was coming from the discoveries of papyri in Egypt. Unfortunately the fragments of New Testament MSS thus discovered were until comparatively recently almost all too small to be individually of much importance. For the most part they played much the same role as Greek and Latin inscriptions do for ancient history, in that from a multitude of small details a general impression may be derived.

But the great papyrus discoveries were still to come. In the winter of 1930–1 Sir A. Chester Beatty, whose remarkable fortune as a collector enabled him to acquire (in addition to his renowned collection of Eastern and Western illuminated MSS) at about the same time a number of valuable ancient Egyptian texts and a group of Coptic versions of lost Manichaean works, obtained from dealers the papyri of the Greek Bible which have been individually described above (pp. 34–7, 69–72). Of these the three New Testament MSS may all be assigned with confidence to the third century: the Pauline MS to the very beginning of it, the Gospels and Acts to the first half of it, the Apocalypse perhaps to the second half. They are very far from perfect, the Gospels and Acts papyrus containing not more than one-seventh (perhaps less) of the text, the Pauline papyrus nearly the whole (excluding the Pastorals and with the loss of the beginning of Romans), and the Revelation papyrus just one-third of the book; but between them they cover nearly the whole New Testament, and provide valuable and substantial evidence of textual conditions in Egypt a century before the Vatican and Sinaitic codices with which our manuscript evidence previously began. The discovery was announced in November, 1931; the Gospels and Acts text was published in July, 1933 (with a complete photographic facsimile of the papyrus in 1934), the ten leaves of the original Pauline acquisition and the Revelation in March, 1934, and the complete Pauline papyrus, with all the leaves subsequently acquired, in June, 1936.[1]

Naturally the greatest amount of interest was taken in the Gospels and Acts MS ($\mathfrak{p}^{45}$), since here the textual problems are most numerous and most important. It was at once apparent that

---

[1] *The Chester Beatty Biblical Papyri: Descriptions and Texts of Twelve Manuscripts on Papyrus of the Greek Bible*, edited by F. G. Kenyon, London, Emery Walker, 1932–6. A facsimile of the Revelation papyrus was published in 1936; that of the Pauline Epistles in 1937.

the new MS could not be assigned wholly to any of the three main
families, whether they be called neutral, Western and Syrian, or
I, H, and K. On the contrary, it appeared that in Mark at any rate
(the book in which textual peculiarities are often most prominent),
if it was to be assigned to any one family, it would be to the newly
discovered Cæsarean. It thus at one stroke appeared to confirm
Streeter's hypothesis of the independent existence of this type of
text, and also Lake's rider that it circulated in Egypt as well as in
Palestine. It may be instructive to repeat from the introduction to
the published text the table which shows its agreements and
disagreements with the principal MSS:

	With papyrus	Against		With papyrus	Against
ℵ	42	108	W	107	52
A	54	94	Θ	65	91
B	44	106	Fam. 1	72	80
C	31	67	Fam. 13	79	73
D	49	100	Cod. 565	68	74
ς (Textus Receptus)	55	94	Cod. 700	57	87

The contrast between the two columns is striking, and is still
more so when it is remembered that many of the differences in
the second column (especially in Θ and the minuscules) may be
attributed to the revision in the direction of the Byzantine text
which all of them have more or less undergone. Even without this,
the preponderance towards the Cæsarean text is unmistakable,
while as between the neutral, Western and Byzantine texts it
stands almost equidistant from all, and that at a considerable
distance.

In Luke and John the position is rather different. Here the
Cæsarean text has not yet been established, so that it is impossible
to say whether the papyrus represents it; but it corresponds with
Streeter's definition of that text as standing midway between
Neutral and Western, while it is nearer to both than it is in Mark.
Thus in Luke, of which more is preserved than of any other
Gospel, it has 158 agreements with B as against 130 disagreements,
while for D the figures are 136 and 137 respectively. In John the
figures are B 40 and 40, D 43 and 37. Of Matthew too little has
been preserved to allow of any conclusion. On the whole, however,
the papyrus adds a conclusive proof that the text of ℵ B was not

exclusively dominant in Egypt in the third century, and also increases the probability that the Cæsarean text did not originate at Cæsarea, but was extant in Egypt before Origen left Alexandria, and may have been taken by him to Cæsarea.

In Acts the papyrus distinctly agrees more with the neutral group, $\aleph$ A B C, than with the Western. It has a number of agreements with D in minor variants, but none of the major variations so characteristic of D and its colleagues in this book. Of 77 readings printed by Clark in heavier type as especially characteristic of the Western text in those portions of the text that are preserved in the papyrus, not one is supported by the papyrus. It is therefore quite definitely not a 'Western' text, and it is a further proof that not by any means all readings which have Western attestation are Western in the sense that the greater variants are.

In the Pauline Epistles the textual variations are less important, but the distinction between the neutral and Western texts is clearly marked, and here the papyrus ($\mathfrak{p}^{46}$) ranges itself definitely on the neutral side. In passages where the two families plainly take different sides, $\mathfrak{p}^{46}$ agrees in Romans with the neutral reading in 89, and with the Western in 51. In the other Epistles the difference is even more strongly marked, the agreements with neutral being 412 and with Western 79.

In Revelation the textual position is rather different. Here, according to J. Schmid's reconstruction of the textual history, there are four main types of text: $\aleph$, the Coptic versions and Origen; A C and the commentary of Oecumenius; the Andreas commentary with the corrector of Sinaiticus $\aleph^a$; and finally the Byzantine. Of these the best is that of A C Oecumenius—$\mathfrak{p}^{47}$, although the oldest authority for the book is closer to $\aleph$ Coptic Origen, but with a good deal of independence.

With the publication of the Bodmer Papyri, which began in 1954, textual scholars have been presented with discoveries which match in importance the Chester Beatty collection of thirty years earlier. Both include what are presumably the remains of Christian libraries which had survived the persecution of Diocletian in 303, though the Chester Beatty collection would seem to have been more fortunate in this respect. On the other hand, the Bodmer Collection contains classical Greek and Coptic Biblical texts, and is richer in non-Biblical Christian writings.

o

$\mathfrak{p}^{66}$ of St John, dated about 200 (or possibly earlier) provided the earliest continuous Gospel text then in existence, comparable with the Chester Beatty $\mathfrak{p}^{46}$ of the Pauline Epistles, and roughly contemporary with it. The question of greatest importance and interest was the extent to which $\mathfrak{p}^{66}$ was related to the text-types, Alexandrian and Western, which had been the subject of so much scholarly debate. In this respect the papyrus was somewhat disappointing, for although it was seen to be mainly of Alexandrian type, and here apparently closest to ℵ, the undeniably Western elements excluded it as a direct ancestor of any of the known uncials. Again, if the papyrus was to be classified as a 'mixed' text, how had the mixture come about? One possibility was that the scribe of $\mathfrak{p}^{66}$ had used two different exemplars, one Alexandrian and the other Western, and followed them indiscriminately. This, however, was to assume that the two families, Alexandrian and Western, were already formed and current in Egypt as separate identities. A further possibility was that the papyrus was not properly a 'mixed' text, but representative of the popular texts which came into being through the multiplication of variants in the second century, and from which, by a process of recension, the later Alexandrian text (of which ℵ is an example) was derived— or alternatively that $\mathfrak{p}^{66}$ was a stage in that process.

The publication of $\mathfrak{p}^{75}$ (*Bodmer XIV–XV*) of Luke and John in 1961 threw a good deal of light on these questions. The very close relationship of the papyrus to B—indeed, $\mathfrak{p}^{75}$ and B stand closer to each other than any other two early witnesses[1]—and the virtual absence of any Western readings, showed that the text-type designated neutral by Westcott and Hort was already in existence at or before the end of the second century, and demolished at one stroke the current widely-held view that the text of Codex Vaticanus in the Gospels was a result of a scholarly process of recension during the third and fourth centuries. Moreover, since their common errors are rare, B is not a direct copy of $\mathfrak{p}^{75}$, nor in turn are both copies of the same archetype: genealogically they appear to be at some distance from each other. The conclusion follows that they both belong to an established textual tradition, conservative in character, which retained a remarkable purity in transmission. The further supposition, namely that the high

---

[1] According to C. L. Porter (*Journal of Biblical Literature* (1962), pp. 363–75), $\mathfrak{p}^{75}$ in John varies from B 205 times, from ℵ 707 times, from $\mathfrak{p}^{66}$ 512 times.

degree of faithfulness in transmission between $\mathfrak{p}^{75}$ and B and their common archetype also holds between the archetype and the original, does not necessarily follow, but it is a possibility that should be borne in mind. It is also the case that from time to time $\mathfrak{p}^{75}$ is found agreeing with $\mathfrak{p}^{66}$ against B, which suggests that behind א also there is an ancestor similar to $\mathfrak{p}^{75}$, but *via* a divergent and (in view of the Western readings of א) a relatively contaminated line of tradition. In passing it is interesting at this point to compare Hort's assessment of B and א with the view more recently held that his 'neutral' text is the result of a deliberate recensional process:

> The ancestors of both MSS [i.e. B and א] having started from a common source not much later than the autographs, they came respectively under different sets of influences, and each in the course of time lost more or less of its original purity. With certain limited exceptions already noticed, the concordance of B and א marks that residual portion of the text of their primitive archetype in which neither of the two ancestries had at any point adopted or originated a wrong reading. Where their readings differ, at least one of the ancestries must have departed from the archetypal text. The possibility that both have gone astray in different ways must remain open. . . . (*The New Testament in the Original Greek*: Introduction, pp. 247–8.)
>
> B must be regarded as having preserved not only a very ancient text, but a very pure line of very ancient text, and that with comparatively small depravation either by scattered ancient corruptions otherwise attested or by individualisms of the scribe himself. On the other hand, to take it as the sole authority except where it contains self-betraying errors, as some have done, is an unwarrantable abandonment of criticism, and in our opinion inevitably leads to erroneous results. A text so formed would be incomparably nearer the truth than a text similarly taken from any other Greek MS or other single document: but it would contain many errors by no means obvious, which could with more or less certainty have been avoided by the free use of all existing evidence (*ibid.*, pp. 250–1).

In the light of $\mathfrak{p}^{75}$ further study of $\mathfrak{p}^{66}$ has yielded some interesting results.[1] Since the neutral text-type of the Gospels was

[1] See especially G. D. Fee, 'The Corrections of Papyrus Bodmer II and early

already in existence when $\mathfrak{p}^{66}$ was written, it is now possible to describe the text of $\mathfrak{p}^{66}$ as 'mixed': basically neutral or Alexandrian with an admixture of Western readings. In an examination of the corrections of $\mathfrak{p}^{66}$, G. D. Fee has shown that when those corrections which are due to the carelessness of the original scribe are set aside—and, as has been remarked, he was exceedingly careless— there remain others which indicate that in going over his first transcript the scribe used for correction a different MS, also of mixed Alexandrian and Western type, but with a somewhat smaller Western element. This can be seen in the following table, where, in relation to the MS or MSS of the first column, the second column gives the number of such readings in $\mathfrak{p}^{66\star}$ *abandoned* by the corrector, and the third column the number of those readings *inserted* by the corrector:

	$\mathfrak{p}^{66\star}$	$\mathfrak{p}^{66c}$
D	39	27
ℵ	32	41
W	28	41
B	31	43
Byzantine	27	46
$\mathfrak{p}^{75}$	20	40

—i.e. in thirty-nine instances the corrector of $\mathfrak{p}^{66}$ changed a D reading of the first hand to another, and in twenty-seven instances altered the first hand into conformity with D. The outcome was to bring the resultant but still mixed text closer to $\mathfrak{p}^{75}$ B ℵ (in that order) and away from D. Moreover, the apparent shift towards the Byzantine text is due to the corrector's preference for a smoother and more intelligible Greek, which in Fee's opinion is to be explained by coincidence of scribal judgement rather than by direct textual relatedness to the Byzantine tradition proper. At the same time these 'Byzantine' readings show that these stylistic tendencies, so characteristic of the later MSS, were already at work in the second century.

The third important Bodmer MS is $\mathfrak{p}^{72}$ containing 1–2 Peter

text transmission', *Novum Testamentum*, vii (1965), pp. 247–57, *Papyrus Bodmer II: Its Textual Relationships and Scribal Characteristics*, Studies and Documents (Salt Lake City, 1966); E. F. Rhodes, 'The corrections of Papyrus Bodmer II', *New Testament Studies*, xiv (1967–8), pp. 271–81; E. C. Colwell, 'Method in evaluating scribal habits: a study of, $\mathfrak{p}^{45}$, $\mathfrak{p}^{66}$, $\mathfrak{p}^{75}$, *Studies in Methodology in Textual Criticism of the New Testament* (Leiden, 1969), pp. 106–24 (reprinted from *The Bible in Modern Scholarship*, ed. J. P. Hyatt (Nashville, 1965)), pp. 370–89.

and Jude.[1] Though somewhat later in date than the two Bodmer Gospel MSS, the overall agreement, as with them, is closest to B. The following table gives an extract from Kubo's list:

Agreements of $\mathfrak{p}^{72}$

B	$246 = 73\%$
1739	$209 = 62\%$
C	$201 = 59\cdot6\%$
33	$198 = 58\cdot7\%$
ℵ	$194 = 57\cdot6\%$
A	$193 = 57\cdot3\%$

This relationship of $\mathfrak{p}^{72}$ to B is especially close in 2 Peter where it can be said to correspond to that of $\mathfrak{p}^{75}$ and B in John, and extends to supporting B readings which otherwise have no attestation in Alexandrian witnesses. At the same time B manifests a tendency to stylistic improvement from the standard of $\mathfrak{p}^{72}$; nevertheless the combination of $\mathfrak{p}^{72}$ B commends itself in nearly every case as superior to other readings.

It is clear that the Bodmer collection of papyri is bound to have a considerable effect on textual theory as it concerns the New Testament. Perhaps the most surprising outcome is the confirmation and apparent vindication of Westcott and Hort's view of the 'neutral' text, and in particular its embodiment in B, as a remarkably pure line of tradition of a very ancient text-form. Certainly it establishes that their neutral text was already in existence in the second century, and that it was not created out of the medley of second-century texts by a later process of editorial recension in which (it might have been supposed) the Cæsarean form was an intermediate stage. There still remains the question of what lies behind the neutral, or Alexandrian, tradition as we now know it, coupled with the fact that in Egypt alone the neutral was only one of a number of texts in use there in the second and third centuries. The detailed history whereby the conventional text-forms (as we have learnt to distinguish them among fourth-century and later MSS) came into existence, as well as their modification in response to stylistic, theological and ecclesiastical influences, is still very far from complete.

[1] See Sakae Kubo, $\mathfrak{p}^{72}$ *and the Codex Vaticanus, Studies and Documents,* xxvii (Salt Lake City, 1965); F. W. Beare, 'The text of 1 Peter in Pap. 72', *Journal of Biblical Literature,* lxxx (1961), pp. 253–60; J. D. Quinn, 'Notes on the text of $\mathfrak{p}^{72}$, *Catholic Biblical Quarterly,* xxvii (1965), pp. 241–9.

Von Soden's edition having proved unsatisfactory, for the reasons given above, and fresh discoveries having accumulated since, the need for a new critical edition, to take the place of that of Tischendorf, was very generally felt; and eventually the task of preparing one was undertaken by an English committee, under the Chairmanship of the late Dr A. C. Headlam, Bishop of Gloucester, with the promise of collaboration from textual scholars in Germany and America. The editorship was entrusted to the Rev. S. C. E. Legg, who had assisted Dr White in the great Oxford edition of the Vulgate. It was decided, after much deliberation, (1) to print the text of Westcott and Hort, rather than the Received Text or a text newly prepared as the basis of the edition, and to adapt the apparatus of variant readings to it, (2) to make a beginning with Mark, as the book on which most textual work had been done, and in which the textual phenomena are of special interest. The fasciculus containing this Gospel appeared in 1935; and Matthew in 1940. The general arrangement follows that of Tischendorf; that is, the various authorities are quoted individually, without attempting (as was done by von Soden) to prejudge results by grouping them in families. Legg's work has been adversely criticised, perhaps unduly, on account of inaccuracies and incompleteness as well as for the arrangement of the evidence. The work is now being continued as an international project, under the title *The International Greek Testament*.

It may be useful to refer also to some smaller critical editions which will answer the purpose of those who do not require the larger work. One is the Oxford Greek Testament edited by Professor A. Souter (Oxford, 2nd edition 1947), in which the text represented by the Revised Version is printed with a select apparatus recording the more important variants of the principal MSS (uncial and minuscule) versions and Fathers—an exceedingly serviceable manual edition. The other is the edition prepared by the late Dr Eberhard Nestle for the Würtembergische Bibelanstalt (25th edition by Dr Erwin Nestle and Kurt Aland, 1963), based upon the texts of Tischendorf, Westcott and Hort, and Weiss (following as a rule the verdict of the majority), with an apparatus containing the readings of these editors when not accepted for the text, with most of the variants of von Soden, and a selection of readings from the principal groups of MSS (von Soden's H and K, famm. 1 and 13), individual MSS (chiefly ℵ B D W Θ, together with the more important papyri), versions and Fathers. When once the rather elaborate system of symbols used in the apparatus has been mastered, this makes a convenient pocket edition. The same text was published in 1904 by the British and Foreign Bible Society, but instead of the usual apparatus gave a conspexus of the differences between Nestle and the Greek Text lying behind the Authorized and Revised Versions. A new edition (1958) has been prepared for the Society by Professor G. D. Kilpatrick of Oxford, with the help of Dr Erwin Nestle. The text is substantially the same as that of 1904, with improvements, but the apparatus, instead of being limited to the variants of the *textus receptus* and the Revised Version, gives 'a selection of the important variant readings, including all readings of moment which may be original, those which are characteristic of the main types of text (such as the Western text) and other readings of special interest', with citations of manuscript and other authorities. Other serviceable editions are by H. J. Vogels (4th edition 1955), A. Merk (8th edition 1957), and J. M. Bover (4th edition 1959). Another edition, constructed on somewhat different lines, should also be mentioned here. This is *The Greek New Testament* published by the United Bible Societies, edited by K. Aland, M. Black, B. M. Metzger and A. Wikgren (Stuttgart 1956), prepared primarily for the use of translators, but of considerable value to students. It contains (1) a critical text produced by the editors, (2) an apparatus of textual variants to readings 'significant for translators or necessary for the establishment of the text', and (3) a second apparatus 'of meaningful differences of punctuation'. The readings under (2) adopted as the text are assigned letters (A, B, C, D) indicating their relative degree of certainty, and they and their variants are supplied with a very full apparatus from Greek MSS, versions and Fathers. Thus, while the apparatus passes over the host of minor variant readings, all those of any importance are set out with a wealth of textual evidence such as could be found only in the largest editions.

The Chester Beatty and the Bodmer papyri described above are the latest of the major discoveries of Greek Biblical MSS, and indeed the greatest since Sinaiticus. But mention may also be made here of two leaves (with a tiny portion apparently of a third) of a papyrus codex[1] containing a hitherto unknown narrative of

---

[1] Now in the British Museum (Egerton pap. 2), edited by H. I. Bell and

our Lord's life. Apocryphal Gospels are by no means uncommon, and many are known to have existed, notably the Gospel of Peter, of which a considerable portion (including the Crucifixion and Resurrection narrative) was recovered (with portions of the Apocalypse of Peter and of the Book of Enoch) from a small vellum book discovered at Akhmim in Egypt in 1886, but not published till 1892. This Gospel, which was found in circulation near Antioch about the end of the second century, has features which at once show that it has no claims to authenticity; and the same is true in greater measure of the other apocryphal Gospels so far as they are known to us—mainly through quotations in patristic writers. But the new narrative differs from all others by reason of its early date and its sober and straightforward character. Palæographers are agreed that the manuscript must be assigned to about the middle of the second century, perhaps a little before, which makes a first century date for the narrative itself at least possible, not to say probable. The fragments contain records of four incidents in our Lord's life. Three of these are incidents which also occur in the canonical Gospels: (1) a controversy with the Jews, with phrases that recur in John v and ix; (2) the healing of a leper (Matt. viii. 2–3, Mark i. 40–42, Luke v. 12–13); (3) the tribute-money (Matt. xxii. 16, Mark xii. 14, Luke xx. 21). The fourth is new, but unfortunately so much mutilated that its exact character cannot be determined. The style is simple and un-exaggerated, very similar to that of the Synoptists; and what is remarkable is that it contains close verbal similarities with all the Gospels. Therefore, either we have here one of the early narra-tives to which Luke refers in his preface, using the materials out of which the canonical Gospels grew, or we have a very early use of the canonical Gospels by a writer engaged on a work of edifica-tion. The opinion of scholars, so far as it has been yet expressed, is in favour of the latter alternative; in which case the papyrus becomes an additional proof of the first century date of all Gospels, including the fourth, which at one time was hotly contested.

An even more decisive proof of the early date of the fourth Gospel, which would have been invaluable for controversial purposes a century ago, came to light when Mr C. H. Roberts,

T. C. Skeat, *Fragments of an unknown Gospel and other early Christian Papyri* (London, 1935), and *The New Gospel Fragments* (London, British Museum, 1955).

working among the papyri in the John Rylands Library at Manchester, found a tiny scrap of a codex containing a few words of John xviii. 31–33, 37, 38, in a hand which can be referred with some confidence to the first half of the second century.[1] Small as the fragment is, and therefore textually unimportant, it is of great value as the earliest extant manuscript of the New Testament, and a conclusive refutation of those who would bring the fourth Gospel far down into the second century.

These recent discoveries of exceptionally early MSS (to which should be added the Tatian fragment described on p. 116) justify the hope of other discoveries which may clear up the many obscurities that still beset the early history of the Bible text, with the present position of which we have now to deal.

BIBLIOGRAPHY

Westcott and Hort, *op. cit.*; G. Salmon, *Introduction to the New Testament* (7th ed., 1894), *Some Thoughts on the Textual Criticism of the New Testament* (1897); H. von Soden, *Die Schriften des Neuen Testaments*, vol. I, pts. 2–4 (1906–10); B. H. Streeter, *The Four Gospels* (1924); F. G. Kenyon, *Recent Developments in the Textual Criticism of the Greek Bible* (1933); *The Chester Beatty Biblical Papyri*, fasc. i–v (1933–6); other literature in the text. See also Bibliography to Chapter III above.

[1] Published in November, 1935: *An Unpublished Fragment of the Fourth Gospel in the John Rylands Library*: edited by C. H. Roberts (Manchester, 1935). See also above, p. 72.

CHAPTER SEVEN

The Present Textual Problem

THE materials for textual criticism have now been described, and the main course of textual theory and practice narrated. It remains to consider what the present position of the subject is and how the theories of critics, from Mill and Bengel to von Soden and Streeter, have been affected by the most recent discoveries. The most convenient method would seem to be to deal in turn with each of the main textual groups, to set out the main authorities composing each of them, and to endeavour to form some estimate of their character, and to consider what progress has been made in elucidating the early history of the New Testament text.

For this purpose it will be best to discard, at any rate at first, the labels that have been attached by critics to the several textual groupings, since such labels tend to prejudge their character. After that character has been established it will be easier to see what title is most appropriate in each case. It is proposed therefore to deal with them under the first letters of the Greek alphabet: (α) the Received Text, of which one of the earliest representatives (in the Gospels) is Codex A; (β) the text which Hort calls neutral, headed by Codex B; (γ) the Cæsarean text; (δ) the Western text headed by Codex D; and such residue as may be found to be left over.

I. THE α TEXT

This is the text found in the great majority of manuscripts, entrenched in print by Erasmus and Stephanus, and known as the Textus Receptus or Received Text, as opposed to the critical editions of modern times. It is Bengel's 'Asiatic', Semler's

'Oriental', Griesbach's 'Constantinopolitan', Hort's 'Syrian', von Soden's 'K', Ropes's 'Antiochian', and it is the text translated in our Authorized Version. Until 1881, in spite of the growing dissatisfaction of scholars, it held the field as the text in practically universal use, and when its position was then decisively challenged, a stiff fight was made in its defence by advocates such as Burgon. It is no longer necessary to argue its claims in detail.

The essence of the case is that this is a text which has suffered progressive revision, not (or only to a slight extent) on doctrinal grounds,[1] but mainly in the interests of intelligibility and by means of verbal and stylistic alterations and by the assimilation (deliberate or unintentional) of parallel narratives. The proof of its secondary character rests partly on internal evidence, which shows by the application of the ordinary principles of textual criticism that its readings, when compared with those of the earlier authorities, can be explained as scribal or editorial modifications of them, while the opposite explanation is less possible or impossible; and partly on the evidence of the early Fathers, from which it appears that readings characteristic of this type first begin to be noticeable in the writings of Chrysostom. This argument is the foundation-stone of Hort's theory, though it should be added that more recent investigation has shown that Chrysostom's text is by no means identical with the later and more or less established form of the ninth and tenth centuries. It may now be taken as an ascertained fact that there is a type of text which begins to make its appearance about the end of the fourth century, that this type in the course of time acquired predominance in the Church of Constantinople, and that it continued to be the text in general use throughout the Middle Ages, and finally was stereotyped in print.

It is not to be understood that this revision was made as a single deliberate act at a single time, or that it assumed its final form at once. It was rather the result of forces and tendencies which continued to operate over a long period. In part it was due to unconscious tendencies, which lead a scribe to substitute familiar phrases for those less familiar; in part to the more deliberate preference for one variant over another, and, in the supposed interests of the reader, the insertion of names or pronouns to make a passage more clear, modifying a passage which

---

[1] For a discussion of this and related questions, see C. S. C. Williams, *Alterations to the Text of the Synoptic Gospels and Acts* (Oxford, 1951).

appeared open to misunderstanding, or objectionable on grammatical, stylistic or doctrinal grounds, removing apparent contradictions between two evangelists, assimilating the narrative of one Synoptist to that of another, the substitution of one word for another, or an alteration in the order of words. All these are changes which might easily be made at a time when accurate reproduction of a writer's words was of less account than that the sacred Scriptures should be readily intelligible.

A few examples will perhaps make it easier to understand the nature of these changes. In Matt. vi. 1 the α text has ἐλεημοσύνην instead of the δικαιοσύνην of the older MSS, substituting a more intelligible word for one which is rather unusual. Similarly in Mark iii. 29 κρίσεως instead of ἁμαρτήματος. In Matt. xv. 8 the words ἐγγίζει μοι ὁ λαὸς οὗτος τῷ στόματι αὐτῶν are added to complete the quotation from the LXX. In Matt. xix. 17 the α text has been assimilated to Mark and Luke, reading τί με λέγεις ἀγαθόν instead of τί με ἐρωτᾷς περὶ τοῦ ἀγαθοῦ of ℵ B D, etc. and in Matt. xx. 22 a similar assimilation to Mark is made by the introduction of the words καὶ τὸ βάπτισμα ὃ ἐγὼ βαπτίζομαι βαπτισθῆναι. In Luke xi. 2–4 the Lord's Prayer is amplified to correspond with the version in Matthew, and the doxology in that version (Matt. vi. 13), which is not in ℵ B D, etc., is probably a liturgical addition. Ecclesiastical usage probably also accounts for τὸ ποτήριον in Mark xiv. 23 instead of the simple ποτήριον. In Mark i. 2 the α text reads ἐν τοῖς προφήταις instead of ἐν τῷ Ἠσαΐᾳ τῷ προφήτῃ, an alteration in the interests of accuracy, since the quotation includes words from Malachi as well as Isaiah. In Mark xv. 28 the words καὶ ἐπληρώθη ἡ γραφὴ . . . ἐλογίσθη, which are not in ℵ A B C D, were probably added with a view to edification; and the omission of οὐδὲ ὁ υἱός in Matt. xxiv. 36 may be due to a fear of doctrinal misunderstanding. In some cases two various readings in earlier authorities are combined or (in Hort's phrase) conflated. Thus in Matt. x. 3 ℵ B read Θαδδαῖος, D k read Λεββαῖος, and the α text has Λεββαῖος ὁ ἐπικληθεὶς Θαδδαῖος and in Luke xxiv. 53, where ℵ B C have εὐλογοῦντες and D has αἰνοῦντες, the α text has αἰνοῦντες καὶ εὐλογοῦντες.

Often, however, the alterations are slighter and more casual. These are to be found in great quantities throughout the Gospels, and may be illustrated by two passages taken quite at random.

Thus in Matt. xxi. 12 we find in the α text ὁ Ἰησοῦς for Ἰησοῦς: ἱερὸν τοῦ Θεοῦ for ἱερόν; 13 ἐποιήσατε for ποιεῖτε; 15 κράζοντας for τοὺς κράζοντας; 18 πρωΐας δὲ ἐπανάγων for πρωΐ δὲ ἐπαναγαγών; 23 ἐλθόντι αὐτῷ for ἐλθόντος αὐτοῦ; 25 παρ' ἑαυτοῖς for ἐν ἑαυτοῖς; 26 ἔχουσι τὸν Ἰωάννην ὡς προφήτην for ὡς προφήτην ἔχουσι τὸν Ἰωάννην; 28 καὶ προσελθὼν for προσελθών; ἀμπελῶνί μου for ἀμπελῶνι; 31 λέγουσιν αὐτῷ for λέγουσιν; 32 πρὸς ὑμᾶς Ἰωάννης for Ἰωάννης πρὸς ὑμᾶς; οὐ for οὐδὲ; 33 ἄνθρωπός τις for ἄνθρωπος; 38 κατασχῶμεν for σχῶμεν; 46 ὡς προφήτην for εἰς προφήτην. Similarly in Luke xiv. 26, οὐ δύναταί μου μαθητὴς εἶναι for οὐ δύναται εἶναί μου μαθητής; 28 τὰ πρὸς ἀπαρτισμόν for εἰς ἀπαρτισμόν; 29 ἐμπαίζειν αὐτῷ for αὐτῷ ἐμπαίζειν; 31 συμβαλεῖν ἑτέρῳ βασιλεῖ for ἑτέρῳ βασιλεῖ συμβαλεῖν; βουλεύεται for βουλεύσεται; ἀπαντῆσαι for ὑπαντῆσαι; 34 καλὸν τὸ ἅλας, ἐὰν δὲ τὸ ἅλας for καλὸν οὖν τὸ ἅλας, ἐὰν δὲ καὶ τὸ ἅλας. Each of these alterations is trifling in itself, but collectively they amount to an extensive modification in the text, and show how freely it was handled by scribes and editors throughout the period when what we now call the Received Text was being developed.

As has already been said, the α text is found in by far the greater number of our extant authorities, but some of the earlier ones show it less fully developed. Thus A and C in the Gospels contain a considerable number of readings of this type. So does W, except in Mark. So do the purple MSS N O Σ Φ. It is fully established in the later uncials E, F, G, H, K, M, S, U, V, Y, Π, Ω, which Legg classes together as representing this type of text. Of the minuscules all may be assumed to have this text until the contrary has been demonstrated; the most important of the exceptional minuscules will be specified later as belonging to other groups; and even these have not wholly escaped its influence. The only large-scale attempt to classify this great mass of materials is that made by von Soden, which has been described above; it will be remembered that his main divisions are K¹, of which the earliest representative (Ω) is of the eighth century; Kˣ, which was dominant from the tenth to the twelfth century; and Kʳ, which prevailed from the thirteenth century onwards; each of these having many subdivisions. One of these sub-groups, included in K¹ and more or less corresponding to Kᵃ (in which von Soden included Codex Alexandrinus) has been studied in detail by Silva Lake (*Family Π and the Codex Alexandrinus, Studies and Documents V*, 1937—see also K. and S. Lake, *The Byzantine Text of the Gospels* in *Memorial Lagrange*, 1940, further extended by J. Geerling's (*Family Π in Luke, Studies and Documents XXII*, 1962, . . . *in John, ibid. XXIII*, 1963) and by Russell Champlin (*Family Π in Matthew, ibid. XXIV*, 1964). This group of twenty-one manuscripts with the ninth-century Codex Petropolitanus (*Π*) at its head is shown to be descended from a MS of the fourth or fifth century, to which A also is related. However, although A and Family *Π* have a common ancestor, they suggest that A should not properly be included in the K^a group, the best representative of which is *Π*. Working on similar lines another group within the K^1 text, approximating more or less to von Soden's K^i, has been distinguished by Russell Champlin (*Family E and its Allies in Matthew, Studies and Documents XXVII*, 1966) and Jacob Geerlings (*Family E and its Allies in Mark, ibid. XXXI*, 1968, . . . in Luke, *ibid. XXXV*, 1968). Besides E (Codex Basiliensis of the eighth century) the family includes the Gospel uncials F G H, and its archetype is dated in the sixth or seventh century—i.e. a somewhat later form of the K text than Family *Π*.

The relatively late date and on the whole secondary character of the α text is generally assumed.[1] But the tendency of scholars like Tischendorf, Westcott and Hort, and their followers to dismiss the α text from further consideration has in recent years been considerably modified. The work of textual scholarship is not now seen as simply the attempt to arrive at the closest possible approximation to the original text, but also to study and as far as possible to clarify the whole process of textual history in relation to time and place. To this extent textual criticism is not without its importance for the study of Church history, of the development of Christian doctrine and liturgical use and so on, just as these disciplines are now recognized as having a bearing on the elucidation of the Biblical text. But it is also becoming increasingly recognized that the later text has preserved here and there ancient readings which have largely disappeared from other branches of

---

[1] One of the last scholars to maintain the superiority of the α text was H. C. Hoskier. He was, however, more concerned to overthrow Hort's claim that the β text had escaped editorial revision; and this, as appears below, may be conceded. It might be truer to say that the extant evidence for the α text is relatively late: its history, no less than that of the other groups, reaches back to early times.

the tradition, and which otherwise have only slight attestation among early witnesses, or even none at all. It does not follow that because a reading is ancient it is necessarily correct, but it is clear that the later text deserves far more attention than so far it has received. For example, it has been remarked that a-type readings are to be found in the oldest papyri—this is noticeably so in the corrections of $\mathfrak{p}^{66}$, with their tendency towards a smoother and more intelligible Greek, but the same phenomenon can be seen in $\mathfrak{p}^{46}$ of the Epistles.[1] Previously these readings had been rejected without further ado as late, and it is of course possible, indeed probable, that some may be due to scribal and editorial concidence. But not all. At any rate, we can now see that readings which were once considered late may be very early indeed, and it follows from this (a) that the early Uncial MSS by no means give a complete picture of textual conditions in the fourth and fifth centuries; and (b) that other readings, as yet known only from late MSS, may be equally ancient and in some cases may be original, though they have disappeared from all other lines of tradition. Indeed, the history of the a-text is not to be told simply in terms of scribal and editorial degeneration; its character, as Hort pointed out long ago, depends to a large extent on a process of selection from already existing readings which it has not created but preserved. The work of von Soden, the Lakes and others needs to be extended by accurate collations which will enable fresh groupings and relations to be discerned in what is still a widely uncharted sea. As to its name, it will be best to discard Hort's title of 'Syrian', both because of the danger of confusion with 'Syriac', and because this type of text, though the process of revision which produced it may have begun in Syria, did not have its main circulation in that part of the Christian world. 'Antiochian' is unsatisfactory for the same reason. The preferable title would appear to be 'Byzantine', which makes no assertion as to its origin, but merely records the unquestioned fact that it is the text which dominated the whole Church of the Byzantine Empire.[2]

[1] See G. Zuntz, *The Text of the Epistles* (London, 1953), pp. 49 ff.

[2] See further, E. C. Colwell, 'The complex character of the Late Byzantine text', *Journal of Biblical Literature*, liv (1935), pp. 211–21; K. W. Clark, 'The effect of recent textual criticism upon New Testament studies', in *The Background of the New Testament and its Eschatology*, edited by W. D. Davies and D. Daube (Cambridge, 1956); G. D. Kilpatrick, 'The Greek New Testament

II. The β Text

This is the text called 'Alexandrian' by Semler and Griesbach, 'neutral' by Hort,[1] and H (Hesychian) by von Soden. It is the most clearly marked of all, and has been the dominating influence in all modern critical editions. It is headed by the two great uncials B and א, to which are now to be added the papyri, $\mathfrak{p}^{75}$ of Luke and John, and $\mathfrak{p}^{46}$ of the Epistles, both dated about 200, B in particular being accepted as the type-specimen of the family. In fact, it may be said that, in the eyes of Hort (its great champion), the β text is the text of B, purged of its scribal errors and amended in a small number of cases (notably in the last chapters of Luke) where some other authority appears, on grounds of textual criticism, to have preserved a superior reading. The uncials which, in addition to א, most often support it (though none of them have escaped other influences) are L R T Z Ξ in the Gospels, Δ in Mark, and in second line P and Q, also Ψ (in Mark), and sometimes A and C when these have escaped revision in the direction of the α text. Among the minuscules, the one which has preserved most β readings is 33, and after that 157. Most other cursives which retain a considerable number of early readings are considered by Hort to owe more to Western than to Alexandrian influences, notable among these being 565. With these Hort also reckons famm. 1 and 13, for which another designation has now been found. Of the versions the most prominent supporters of the β text are the Coptic, Boh. and Sah., the latter more fully so than was known to be the case in Hort's time (see p. 138); while the Ethiopic, though a mixed text, with influences of all kinds, retains many signs of its neighbourhood to Egypt. Jerome in the Vulgate relied largely on MSS of this type; but the fundamental text on which his revision was based, and which he refrained from altering in minor details, was a late form of the Old Latin, i.e. a δ text already modified in the direction of the α type. Of the Fathers, Origen in some of his writings is the most important witness of the β text, though Clement of Alexandria often has readings of this type in Acts and the Epistles. In the Acts and Catholic Epistles A and C join this family, with

text of today and the *textus receptus*', in *The New Testament in Historical and Contemporary Perspective* (Oxford, 1965), pp. 189–208.

[1] See note on p. 181 above.

81, which Hort and Ropes regard as the best of all the cursives in Acts, and the cursives generally retain more readings of this type than in the Gospels. For the Pauline Epistles the authorities are substantially the same, with the addition of **1739,** though it is to be noted that in not a few cases B joins the Western group, as Hort was well aware. Thus in the parts of Romans preserved in $\mathfrak{p}^{46}$, B 16 times joins the D F G group, whereas $\aleph$, A, and C do so only once or twice each; and it is noteworthy that in twelve of these cases it is supported by the papyrus. In the other epistles this distinction is less observable; thus in 1 Corinthians B joins the D F G group again sixteen times (ten times with $\mathfrak{p}^{46}$), but $\aleph$ does so ten times (four times with $\mathfrak{p}^{46}$), C nine times (twice with $\mathfrak{p}^{46}$), and A seven times (once with $\mathfrak{p}^{46}$); in 2 Corinthians the figures are B 10 (7), $\aleph$ 8 (6), C 8 (3), A 2 (0); in Ephesians B 5 (2), $\aleph$ 3 (0), C 0, A 9 (0); in Galatians B 7 (4), $\aleph$ 1 (0), C 1 (1), A 0; in Philippians B 4 (2), $\aleph$ 3 (0), C 1 (0), A 2 (1); in Colossians B 4 (2), $\aleph$ 0, C 1 (0), A 0. In general, the four uncials are nearer to the Western text in Romans than in the other epistles, though even there the differences (where the two texts are definitely distinguishable) exceed the agreements in the proportion of about nine to five. In the Apocalypse, where B is wanting, the older text, according to J. Schmid (see above, p. 199) divides into two streams: $\mathfrak{p}^{47}$ $\aleph$ Origen and the Coptic versions, and A C with the text of Oecumenius' commentary, A being superior to all others.

For the place of origin of this text-type there can as yet be no final certainty, but the witness to it in the earliest papyri and its agreement with the Coptic versions points strongly to Egypt, and this is supported by its use by Origen (at any rate in some of his writings) and to some extent by Clement of Alexandria, and substantially by Athanasius, Didymus and Cyril of Alexandria. Certainly it was established there at a very early date. There is no direct evidence to show where B and $\aleph$ were written, and different views have been held. Hort was inclined to refer both to Rome, but their text is markedly different from that of the Old Latin version and the Latin Fathers, with the exception of Jerome; and his evidence points in the opposite direction, since he avowedly preferred Eastern authorities to Western. Cæsarea has also been suggested, especially by Rendel Harris for $\aleph$. $\aleph$ was certainly at Cæsarea about the sixth or seventh century;

P

but the fact that it was then corrected from MSS at Cæsarea is rather a proof that its own text originated elsewhere. There is some palæographical evidence which points to Egypt, notably the use of the Coptic form of μ in the titles of some of the books in both MSS, and of a peculiar form of ω (with the middle upright excessively prolonged upwards), which is found in ℵ, occasionally in A and B, and also in some Egyptian papyri. Palæographical evidence is somewhat insecure, since we have no contemporary MSS known to have been written elsewhere than in Egypt for comparison; but so far as it goes it supports the ascription to Egypt, which is now generally accepted. And if Egypt is the home of these MSS and this text, one is bound to think especially of Alexandria: for that was the home of scholarship and the centre of the Christian Church, and hardly elsewhere could volumes of such magnificence have been produced. Further confirmation of the Egyptian origin of this family can be derived from the fact that of its principal members after B and ℵ, T is a Graeco-Coptic bilingual, R was found in Egypt, and Z has markedly Egyptian forms of letters.

With regard to its character, the general course of criticism and discovery has not maintained Hort's claim to its full extent. Hort held that the β text, alone among the competing families, bears no mark of editorial revision, and therefore is entitled to the name of 'neutral'. In this he was supported by Bernhard Weiss, who (while rejecting Hort's classification) came to the conclusion that B is the only New Testament MS that has escaped deliberate revision, and that it alone has preserved the true reading in 280 passages in the Gospels, with a similar superiority in the other books. This conclusion was contested by Salmon and Hoskier in this country,[1] and by continental scholars in general, Hoskier describing it as an Egyptian text and arguing that it shows many signs of editorial revision, while Salmon concluded that it was the text which had the highest authority in Alexandria in the third century, and may have reached that city in the previous one. Continental scholars have tended to carry the matter farther, and to identify the β text not only with Alexandria but specifically with the name of Hesychius, who is said by Jerome to have produced an edition of the Septuagint in that city.

[1] G. Salmon, *Some Thoughts on the Textual Criticism of the New Testament* (1897); H. C. Hoskier, *Codex B and its Allies: A Study and an Indictment* (1914).

In reaction to Hort, the view that the β text is the product of recensional activity has gained a great deal of support since his day. In its more extreme form this would take the line that the β text was a 'made' text, and was formed out of the popular texts which had come into existence during the second century. Out of this reservoir of competing readings Alexandrian scholars during the third or early fourth centuries constructed the β type of text, and it would not be inconsistent with the theory to see the 'Cæsarean' text and that of, e.g. $\mathfrak{p}^{66}$ as stages along the way towards the completed recensional form. However, the publication in 1934-6 of the Chester Beatty $\mathfrak{p}^{46}$ of the Epistles showed that the β text, or something very like it, was already in existence in Egypt c. 200—i.e. before the time of Origen's scholarly activity— and the more recently discovered Bodmer $\mathfrak{p}^{75}$ of Luke and John of about the same date, and possibly as early as 180, gave the final blow to any theory of a β recension carried through in the third or fourth centuries. Moreover, it is not just the case that $\mathfrak{p}^{75}$ belongs to the β type as known from the fourth-century uncials B and $\aleph$: the relation of $\mathfrak{p}^{75}$ to B, as we have seen, is closer than that of any other early Greek MSS, in spite of a difference in date of a century and a half or more. For B is not a copy of $\mathfrak{p}^{75}$, nor does it appear that they have a close common archetype— otherwise it might be possible to suppose that B is an example of Alexandrian scholars in the fourth century selecting old copies of high quality as the basis for their own improved form of the text. Indeed it looks now as if there is something to be said for Hort's judgement, formed on the basis of $\aleph$ and B and lacking so much evidence that has since come to light, that the text of these uncials is derived from an ancient common ancestor not very far removed from the apostolic autographs. At the same time it would be too simple to infer that the existence and survival of the text rests on a random choice of exemplars preserved merely by a process of mechanical copying. It may be that the β text is the original text of Egypt, but there is no proof of this: the evidence for the use of the δ text goes back to Clement—i.e. about the time $\mathfrak{p}^{75}$ was written. But some time before the end of the second century ancient and good copies were selected, it must be presumed by scholars who were not unworthy of Alexandrian textual tradi- tions, and that the text thus selected was preserved into the fourth century by a similar scholarly oversight. In the process

not all the corruptions from competing texts were success-
fully resisted, nor those already contained in it rejected, while
Alexandrian preferences in language and style may here and there
have left their mark. It is in this way, to take one example, that
we may regard the sprinkling of readings shared with authorities
of the δ type which occur in different proportions in the various
members of the group. Some of these may be original readings
which have survived in both the β and δ texts (though the attestation can vary on either side); others are δ readings proper which
in spite of editorial vigilance have found their way into some or
all members of the β group. And so the possibility must remain
that some original readings have disappeared from β MSS
altogether, or were not found in its archetype. Nevertheless it
remains that although the β text is not the original text, it contains
more of the original text than any other, or, to put it another way,
the original text is almost always contained in one of its constituent
members, the foremost of which is B itself.

The claim to uncontaminated descent and freedom from
editorial handling cannot be considered quite apart from the
question whether the β text may rightly be described as the text
of Egypt. If it were the case that this text was universally current
in Egypt, it would be easier to maintain that in that province,
dominated by Alexandria with its scholarly traditions, a substantially true text had been preserved, without need of restoration
by the hand of an editor. But the course of discoveries in Egypt
does not confirm the theory of universal dominance. Here the
evidence even of the smaller papyrus fragments is of value, and
it is strongly reinforced by the more substantial Chester Beatty
MSS. Although the papyri often offer readings of the β type,
they are generally mixed with others that are not of this type,
suggesting that the MSS in general circulation were far from
being universally of this class. Some (e.g. $\mathfrak{p}^{38}$, $\mathfrak{p}^{48}$) are quite
definitely of the δ family, while others (e.g. $\mathfrak{p}^{45}$, $\mathfrak{p}^{66}$) have both β
and δ characteristics. But if the β text is not the text of Egypt in
general, its claim to uncontaminated descent becomes more
difficult, since it would have had to descend by a singularly
sheltered channel. This is not impossible, particularly in such a
home of scholarship as Alexandria. The character of B is so
homogeneous throughout the New Testament (though this cannot
be said of the Old Testament) that it would be necessary to

suppose that when its text first assumed codex form a complete set of virtually uncontaminated rolls was available for the purpose. As suggested above, this in itself seems to imply the exercise of editorial selection, and the same editorial activity may well have been extended to the supervision to the text.

The β text, therefore is now generally regarded as a text produced—or perhaps it would be better to say transmitted— in Egypt and probably at Alexandria under editorial care, which was so far accepted in the country that it is found in the Coptic versions and in many manuscripts of Egyptian origin. Whether it can be associated with Hesychius is another matter. This theory was propounded by W. Bousset, and has been accepted by von Soden, who on the strength of it uses the letter H to indicate this type of text. There is, however, singularly little evidence that Hesychius ever extended his labours to the New Testament. It rests on a single passage in Jerome's *Epistula ad Damasum* prefixed to his Vulgate: 'Praetermitto eos codices quos a Luciano et Hesychio nuncupatos paucorum hominum adserit perversa contentio: quibus utique nec in veteri instrumento post septuaginta interpretes emendare quid licuit, nec in novo profuit emendasse, cum multarum gentium linguis scriptura ante translata doceat falsa esse quae addita sunt.' It is clear therefore that Jerome regarded both editions as being marked by additions to the authentic text, and that he held them to be worthless. Of Lucian's edition, if that be identified, as it is by some, with the earliest form of the α text, the first of these criticisms might be true; but it is difficult to see how, on the strength of this quotation, the name of Hesychius is to be attached to a text which is conspiculously not characterized by additions, and which Jerome valued so highly that he used it as his main authority in revising the text of the Gospels. Further, since Hesychius was martyred in 311, he cannot have been the editor of a text which underlies the Sahidic version and was used by Origen. The β text, or something very like it, was, as we have seen, in existence long before Hesychius was born; and even the nearest common ancestor of B and ℵ could hardly be brought within the limits of his activity.

If, then, the extreme claims made by Westcott and Hort on behalf of the β text need to be qualified, it does not follow that the text itself ceases to demand the highest respect. Even though it is an edited text, it may be a well-edited text; and in the case of all ancient literature a well-edited text is the best that we can hope for. The claims of the β text in this respect can best be assessed when the other families, and especially its principal rival, the δ text, have been considered; for there too we may find some diminution of extreme claims.

What name should be assigned to it is not very material. Both Hort's 'neutral' and von Soden's 'Hesychian' have been shown to be unsatisfactory. Nor will 'Egyptian' do, since, as we have seen, it was by no means universally current in Egypt. On the other hand, some indication of its connection with Egypt is desirable; and since its two main representatives are most probably to be assigned to Alexandria, the name 'Alexandrian', which Salmon gave to it, is perhaps the best available. Since, however, the name was used by Hort for later MSS of similar provenance associated with the β text, but influenced to a greater degree by the grammatical and linguistic preferences characteristic of Alexandrian editors, perhaps it would be well to distinguish MSS of the β text proper as 'proto-Alexandrian'.

III. THE γ TEXT

This letter was assigned by Hort to the type of text which he styled 'Alexandrian', represented by no one MS as the β text may be said to be represented by B, or the δ text by D, but comprising a number of readings which are found in MSS usually associated with B, but are not present in that MS and cannot be regarded as properly belonging to the β text. They are found chiefly in such MSS as $\aleph$ A C L T Ψ, where these diverge from B, and in the Coptic versions. They may well retain Hort's designation of 'Alexandrian', which associates them under our grouping with the β text, but with the distinction made above; while the symbol γ is transferred to the so-called 'Cæsarean text', which also has its connections with Egypt.

The identification of the Cæsarean text has been described above (pp. 187–91). It has hitherto been examined for the most part in Mark, in which Gospel its principal representatives are $\mathfrak{p}^{45}$ W Θ famm. 1 and 13, and certain other minuscules, notably 28, 565, and 700. None of these manuscripts is to be regarded as a pure representative of the family, all except $\mathfrak{p}^{45}$ having suffered more or less assimilation to the α type, while $\mathfrak{p}^{45}$, which is anterior to the origin of the α text, has a pedigree which has not yet been established. But by taking the non-Byzantine readings in these MSS it may be possible to go some way towards reconstructing the common text underlying them; and it is to this task that Kirsopp Lake and his colleagues and successors have given much attention. Along with the Greek manuscripts, assistance is to be expected from the Syriac, Armenian, and Georgian versions, and of course from the quotations in Origen (in his later works) and Eusebius, from whose use of texts of this type the title of 'Cæsarean' has been taken for them.

It was expected that Streeter's hypothesis would be subjected to careful and continuing scrutiny, and it has to be admitted that in the opinion of many scholars the claims originally made for it require modification. In the first place, how far can the Cæsarean group be regarded as a 'text' in its own right? Replying to the objection that it was too amorphous an entity, a 'textual process' rather than an independent text, Streeter emphasized that by 'text' he did not mean a 'recension', a careful attempt at revision or standardization of a text from which the various witnesses are genealogically descended, but a local text, the average text in use in Cæsarea, in the sense that we may speak of an 'Alexandrian' text or an 'Antiochian' text. But as we have seen Streeter's theory of local texts breaks down, in so far as the 'Cæsarean' type of text was (as Lake pointed out) probably known to Origen before he left Alexandria, and the discovery of $\mathfrak{p}^{37}$ and $\mathfrak{p}^{45}$ confirms the fact that texts of this type were circulating in Egypt in Origen's day if not before, and may well have originated there—indeed MSS of this type could have been brought to Cæsarea by Origen himself. Again Streeter admitted that the majority of the characteristic 'Cæsarean' readings can be found either in Alexandrian or western witnesses, as for that matter is the case also with characteristic Byzantine readings. But, he maintained, the proportions in which these readings are found and their distribution justify our identifying authorities of this type as a distinct family which may rank alongside those which we know as the α, β and δ texts. Against this, Lake's observation that all that the term 'Cæsarean' means is that the same variants are constantly found in many of the group Θ 565, 700, families 1 and 13, 28, the Georgian version, etc., might seem somewhat negative: the variants do occur, and the pattern is such that the text which can be elicited from these witnesses is distinct from the β text, and is certainly not to be confused (as it was by von Soden) with the text whose leading representative is D. On the other hand Lake's further observation, that the text was too hastily called 'Cæsarean' because of its close relation with the text of Origen and Eusebius, is more serious.

It now seems necessary to distinguish between the Cæsarean group which may be more properly so called, and the earlier pre-Cæsarean stage which has stronger associations with Egypt. The latter comprises W $\mathfrak{p}^{37}$, $\mathfrak{p}^{45}$, which the Spanish scholar T. Ayuso associates not with the main centre of scholarship in Alexandria, but with the Fayyum, where these MSS seem to have their origin. On this side, which was Egyptian before it was Cæsarean, we may also place 28, families 1 and 13. The term Cæsarean, if it is used at all, should then be reserved for the form of the text more particularly associated with Origen and Eusebius, which is found in Θ 565, 700 and the Old Armenian and Georgian versions.

As to the genesis of this type of text, authorities differ. Some, like Lake and Sanders, regard it as formed out of a Western base corrected to the 'neutral' standard, while Lagrange takes the opposite view—a 'neutral' base corrected by means of Western texts. In either case the Cæsarean tradition is not a text in its own right, and cannot command the authority of an independent text-form such as Streeter claimed for it. But there is another possibility—that it is a survival or continuation of the earlier and more fluid stage of the text from which the Alexandrian and Western groups are also descended, the former becoming what it is by a process of scholarly editing, the latter by further degeneration in the West acquiring the form associated with D and its allies. In this way it would be possible to account for the apparent 'mixture' of Western and Alexandrian readings, if by 'mixture' we mean something like the common reservoir from which readings of all these groups were drawn.

In the other Gospels, apart from Mark, the Cæsarean text has not been established in any precise way; and the task will be more difficult because Matthew and Luke always suffered more thorough assimilation to the α text than was the case with Mark. Thus W and Θ fail to be available here, and $\mathfrak{p}^{45}$ is practically non-existent in Matthew. In Luke, of which a substantial portion of $\mathfrak{p}^{45}$ has been preserved, its text is certainly about midway between β and δ

texts, but its relation to them is not the same as in Mark, since it shows a higher proportion of agreement with both. It has, however, a large number of singular readings, which may perhaps prove to be Cæsarean.

Whether there was ever a Cæsarean text of the other books remains to be seen. W, H, fam. 1 and fam. 13 all fail us here. p^{45} in general agrees in Acts with the β text, but has a fair number of minor variants which are found in the representatives of the δ text (whether they are essentially δ text remains to be considered), and also a considerable number of singular readings. For the Epistles we have no authorities that have been identified as Cæsarean.

The Cæsarean text, which is the latest addition to our textual apparatus, requires much more study before its character and extent can be regarded as fully determined.

At present it appears that its chief interest is for the history of textual transmission rather than as an authority which can claim to stand beside the other ancient groupings.

IV. The δ Text

This is Semler's 'Occidental', Griesbach and Hort's 'Western', and forms a part of von Soden's I; but the exact connotation of the term 'Western', which is that commonly in use, varies, and much depends upon it. In general, it denotes a type of text, of which the leading representatives are Codex Bezae and the Old Latin, characterized by very marked and numerous divergences from both the α text and the β text. The term has, however, often been used to cover all readings which are neither α nor β, and to speak of them as if they formed a homogeneous family, the whole weight of which could be thrown into the scale together against the rival families. This was a natural consequence of Hort's division of all authorities into the three classes of Syrian, neutral (with Alexandrian as a satellite) and Western; for any pre-Syrian reading that did not appear in the neutral text fell inevitably into the category of Western. This hard and fast demarcation has been very much shaken by discovery and research since Hort's time, and the whole subject of the pre-Syrian non-neutral texts requires reconsideration.

The definition of the δ or Western text is indeed a prime difficulty. When faced by the question, one is tempted to use Jerome's phrase: 'Respondeant quibus; tot sunt paene quot codices'. In general, the extremer form of divergence is represented by D and the Old Latin; but the Old Latin authorities differ greatly among themselves, and are rarely unanimous in support of any particular reading. As a rule, the older or African form of the version, represented by **k, e** and Cyprian, comes nearest to D, and the Italian or European form (**a, b,** etc.) represents it with varying modifications. The consideration of the problem must, however, begin with the extremer form; for on the determination of its character the whole question depends. It will be convenient to deal with the Gospels first, then with Acts, and finally with the Epistles; for the conditions are different in each case.

In the Gospels there are two phenomena to consider: first a number of whole passages in which the δ text differs from the others, whether by addition or omission, and secondly a large number of verbal variations. Under the first heading, in general the δ text differs from the others on the side of inclusion. There are twenty-four passages in the Gospels where our principal authorities differ in respect of inclusion or omission. They are set out in tabular form on pp. 225–7, with the principal witnesses on either side (ς standing for the Received Text).

It will be seen from this table that, if the passages at the end of Luke (nos. 18, 19) be excluded, D is on the side of inclusion in fifteen cases, and of omission in seven, while B is in favour of inclusion in four and of omission in eighteen. In the passages at the end of Luke the position is reversed, B being for inclusion and D for omission. It is for this reason that Hort here deserts his almost invariable preference for B, labelling these passages 'Western non-interpolations' (i.e. neutral interpolations). Elsewhere the opposite character of the two texts is unmistakable, and the question for critics is whether these passages were in the original text and were struck out by the editor of the β text, or were originally absent and were inserted by the editor or by successive editors of the δ text. For it will be observed that not all these passages are found in all authorities. No. 10 is found only in D, no. 8 only in **k**,[1] and W has a singular insertion in

---

[1] The addition in **k** after μνημεῖον in Mark xvi. 3 is: 'Subito autem ad horam tertiam tenebrae diei [*sc.* diei tenebrae] factae sunt per totum orbem terrae, et descenderunt de caelis angeli, et surgent in claritate uiui di (so MS, *sc.* surgente

	Inclusion	Omission
1. Mt. xvi. 2, 3. The sky at evening.	CDW Θ, fam. 1. O.L., Pesh. ς. Euseb.	אB, fam. 13, O.S., Sah. Orig.
2. Mt. xvii. 21. 'This kind goeth not out save by prayer and fasting.'	CDW, famm. 1, 13, O.L., Pesh. ς.	א*B Θ, 33, e, ff¹, O.S., Sah.
3. Mt. xviii. 11. 'The Son of Man is come to save that which was lost.'	DW, 28, 565, 700, O.L., O.S.ᶜ, Pesh. ς.	אBΘ, famm. 1, 13, 33, e, ff¹, O.S.ˢ, Sah.
4. Mt. xx. 16. 'For many are called but few are chosen' (from xxii. 14).	CDW Θ, famm, 1, 13, O.L., O.S., Pesh. ς.	אBL, Sah.
5. Mt. xx. 28. Precedence at feast (see p. 91).	D, O.L., O.S.ᶜ.	אB, etc. Sah. Pesh. ς.
6. Mt. xxi. 44. The Stone that crushes.	א BC etc., g¹, O.S.ᶜ, Sah. Pesh. ς.	D, 33, O.L., O.S.ˢ.
7. Mt. xxvii. 49. The Piercing of the Side.	א BC	ADWΘ, famm. 1, 13, O.L., O.S.ˢ, Pesh. ς.
8. Mk. xvi. 3. The Resurrection.	Addition in k.	All other authorities.
9. Mk. xvi. 9–20. The supplied ending.	ACDW (with additional passage) Θ famm. 1, 13, O.L., O.S.ᶜ, Sah. (Some MSS), Pesh. ς.	אB, k, O.S.ˢ, Sah. (some MSS), Clem., Ong., Enseb.

	Inclusion	Omission
10. Lk. vi. 4. Man working on Sabbath (see p. 91).	D	All other authorities.
11. Lk. ix. 55. 'Ye know not what spirit ye are of', etc.	D (part) Θ, famm. 1, 13, O.L., O.S.ᶜ, Pesh. ς, Marcion.	𝔓⁴⁵, ⁷⁵ ℵABCW, 28 etc., O.S.ˢ, Sah.
12. Lk. xi. 2–4. Lord's Prayer, additional clauses.	ACDWΘ, fam. 13, O.L., O.S.ᶜ (part), Sah. (part), Pesh. ς.	𝔓⁷⁵ ℵB, fam. 1, O.S.ˢ, Marcion, Orig.
13. Lk. xxii. 19, 20. The Last Supper.	Nearly all authorities.	D, a, e, etc. (O.S.ᶜ).
14. Lk. xxii. 43. The Agony in the Garden.	ℵ*D Θ, fam. 1, O.L., O.S.ᶜ, Pesh. ς, Justin, Iren.	𝔓⁷⁵ ℵᵃABW, fam. 13, f, O.S.ˢ, Sah. Marcion, Clem., Orig.
15. Lk. xxiii. 34. 'Father forgive them', etc.	ℵ*ACDᶜ, famm. 1, 13, O.L., O.S.ᶜ, Pesh. ς, Marcion, Iren., Clem., Orig.	𝔓⁷⁵ ℵᵃBD*WΘ, a, d, O.S.ˢ, Sah.
16. Lk. xxiii. 38. The Writing on the Cross.	ℵ*ADWΘ, famm. 1, 13, O.L., Pesh. ς	𝔓⁷⁵ ℵᵃBC, a, O.S., Sah.
17. Lk. xxiii. 53. The Stone at the Sepulchre (see p. 92).	D, c, Sah.	All other authorities.
18. Lk. xxiv. 6, 12, 36, 40. The Resurrection.	Nearly all authorities.	D, O.L. (some MSS), O.S. (xxiv. 40 only).
19. Lk. xxiv. 51. The Ascension.	Nearly all authorities.	ℵ*D, O.L. (some MSS), O.S.ˢ
20. Jn. v. 3. The Stirring of the Water.	AᶜDWΘ, famm. 1, 13, O.L., Pesh. ς. Tert.	𝔓⁶⁶, ⁷⁵ ℵ A*BC*, O.S.ᶜ, Sah.

	Inclusion	Omission
21. Jn. v. 4. The Angel at the Pool.	AL⊖, famm. 1, 13, O.L., Pesh. ς Tert.	p[66,75] ℵBC*DW, 33, O.S.[c], Sah.
22. Jn. vi. 56. Addition: 'As the Father is in me and I in the Father. Verily, verily I say unto you, if ye receive not the body of the Son of Man as the bread of life, ye have not life in him.'	D and in part a, ff[2].	All other authorities.
23. Jn. vii. 53, etc. The Woman in Adultery.	D, 28 700, O.L. (some MSS) ς.	p[66,75] ℵABCW⊖, O.L. (some MSS), O.S., Sah, Pesh., Iren., Clem., Orig., Tert., Cypr.
24. Jn. xii. 8. 'The Poor ye have always with you.'	Nearly all authorities.	D, O.S.[s].

no. 9. In nos. 22, 23, D has the support of only a portion of the OL authorities, ℵ almost always sides with B, except in Luke xxii, xxiii, where the original text includes, but the corrector marks the passages for omission. Sah. is almost always with ℵ B. As between original inclusion or non-inclusion in general, it must be said that on ordinary critical grounds the presumption is in favour of the latter. It is very difficult to understand the mind of an editor who would strike out such passages as these, while it is easy to see why an editor who had these passages before him from some source should think that they deserved to be incorporated in the record. Also the character of the disputed passages must be considered. It will hardly be maintained that the singular additions in D, **k**, and W and those quoted in the footnote are authentic, and this casts doubt on the other passages where a few other authorities support D.

It is clear in these examples that the main core of the δ text lies in the West, in D (which is semi-Latin), the Old Latin version, and some of the Latin Fathers, such as Cyprian. This again tells against the authenticity of the passages in question; for it is not reasonable to suppose that the original text was preserved in a pure form only in the West and was wholly obliterated in the East, from which it came. The occasional support which the δ text receives from the Old Syriac might be accounted for, as it is by Burkitt, by reference to the influence of Tatian's *Diatessaron*,

... filio dei) simul ascenderunt cum eo, et continuo lux facta est. Tunc illae accesserunt ad monimentum.' Other singular or slenderly supported additions, which illustrate the character of the δ text, are:

Matt. iii. 15, add after ἀφίησιν αὐτόν 'et cum baptizaretur, lumen ingens circumfulsit de aquae, ita ut timerent omnes qui advenerant', **a**, **g**[1]; known to Justin and Ephraem.

Matt. xvii. 26, after υἱοί, ἔφη Σίμων, Ναί. λέγει ὁ Ἰησοῦς, Δός οὖν καί σὺ ὡς ἀλλότριοις, **713**, Ephraem.

Matt. xx. 33, after ὀφθαλμοί, 'Quibus dixit Jesus, Creditis posse me hoc facere? Qui responderunt ei, Ita, Domine', **c**; + 'and we may see thee', OS[c].

Matt. xxvii. 38, after δεξιῶν and εὐωνύμων the names of the thieves are added, 'nomine Zoatham' and 'nomine Camma', **c**.

Mark xii. 22, after ἀπέθανεν, 'sine filiis; cui remanet mulier munda?' **k**, **c**.

Mark xiv. 51, before καὶ κρατοῦσιν αὐτόν, 'and there came many men', OS[s].

Luke xxiii. 5, after ὧδε, 'et filios nostros et uxores avertit a nobis; non enim baptizantur (baptizatur **c**) sicut [+ et **e**] nos' [+ nec se mundant **e**], **c**, **e**.

Luke xxiii. 9, after αὐτῷ, 'quasi non audiens', **c**; 'as if he were not there', OS[c].

Luke xxiii. 48, after ὑπέστραφον, 'Woe to us, what hath befallen us', OS, Aphraates: 'dicentes, vae nobis, quae facta sunt hodie propter peccata nostra; appropinquavit enim desolatio Hierusalem', **g**[1].

John xi. 39, after κύριε, 'Why are they taking away the stone?' OS[s].

if, as is possible, that was produced by him during his residence in Rome, and then taken by him to Syria, where, in its translated form, it first brought the Gospel story to the Church of Edessa in its own tongue, and naturally had some influence on the version of the separate Gospels which was subsequently produced there. Then when the revision which produced the α text took place, many of these alterations were incorporated in it, which accounts for their appearing in the Peshitta and the Received Text.

But besides these major variations, it is necessary to consider the larger number of minor divergences which characterize the δ text. These, just because they are individually small and scattered over the whole text, are difficult to present effectively; but a few specimens may be given as samples of the rest.

β text	δ text
Mt. xviii. 20. οὗ γάρ εἰσι δύο ἢ τρεῖς συνηγμένοι εἰς τὸ ἐμὸν ὄνομα ἐκεῖ εἰμὶ ἐν μέσῳ αὐτῶν.	οὔκ εἰσιν γὰρ δύο ἢ τρεῖς συνηγμένοι εἰς τὸ ἐμὸν ὄνομα παρ' οἷς οὔκ εἰμι ἐν μέσῳ αὐτῶν (D g¹. O.S.ˢ Sah. Clem.).
Mt. xxii. 13. δήσαντες αὐτοῦ πόδας καὶ χεῖρας ἐκβάλετε αὐτόν.	ἄρατε αὐτὸν ποδῶν καὶ χειρῶν καὶ βάλετε αὐτόν (D (W), O.L., O.S. Iren.).
Mt. xxiii. 27. οἴτινες ἔξωθεν μὲν φαίνονται ὡραῖοι, ἔσωθεν δὲ γέμουσιν ὀστέων κ.τ.λ.	ἔξωθεν ὁ τάφος φαίνεται ὡραῖος, ἔσωθεν δὲ γέμει ὀστέων κ.τ.λ. (D, Clem. Iren.).
Mt. xxv. 41. τὸ πῦρ τὸ αἰώνιον τὸ ἡτοιμασμένον τῷ διαβόλῳ.	τὸ πῦρ τὸ αἰώνιον (τὸ σκότος τὸ ἐξώτερον Justin) ὃ ἡτοίμασεν ὁ πατήρ μου τῷ διαβόλῳ (D, fam. 1, O.L. Just. Iren. Clem.).
Mk. viii. 26. μηδὲ εἰς τὴν κώμην εἰσέλθῃς.	ὕπαγε εἰς τὸν οἶκόν σου, καὶ μηδένι εἴπῃς εἰς τὴν κώμην (D, q; other O.L. MSS. otherwise).
Mk. x. 27. παρὰ ἀνθρώποις ἀδύνατον ἀλλ' οὐ παρὰ Θεῷ· πάντα γὰρ δυνατά ἐστιν παρὰ τῷ Θεῷ.	παρὰ ἀνθρώποις ἀδύνατον, παρὰ δὲ τῷ Θεῷ δυνατόν (D, k, a, ff² Clem.).

β text	δ text
Mk. xi. 3. τί ποιεῖτε τοῦτο;	τί λύετε τὸν πῶλον, (D Θ, fam. 13, O.L.).
Mk. xiii. 2. οὐ μὴ ἀφεθῇ ὧδε λίθος ἐπὶ λίθον, ὃς οὐ μὴ καταλύθῃ.	οὐ μὴ . . . καταλύθῃ. καὶ διὰ τριῶν ἡμερῶν ἄλλος ἀναστήσεται ἄνευ χειρῶν (D W, O.L. Cyp.).
Mk. xiv. 4. ἦσαν δέ τινες ἀγανακτοῦντες πρὸς ἑαυτούς.	οἱ δὲ μαθηταὶ αὐτοῦ διεπονοῦντο καὶ ἔλεγον (D Θ, **a, ff², i, r¹**).
Lk. iii. 22. ὁ υἱός μου ὁ ἀγαπητός, ἐν σοὶ εὐδόκησα.	υἱός μου εἶ σύ, ἐγὼ σήμερον γεγέννηκά σε (D, O.L., Just. Clem. Orig.). From Ps. ii. 7.
Lk. v. 10. ὁμοίως δὲ καὶ Ἰάκωβον καὶ Ἰωάννην, υἱοὺς Ζεβεδαίου, οἳ ἦσαν κοινωνοὶ τῷ Σίμωνι. καὶ εἶπεν πρὸς τὸν Σίμωνα ὁ Ἰησοῦς, μὴ φοβοῦ· ἀπὸ τοῦ νῦν ἀνθρώπους ἔσῃ ζωγρῶν· καὶ καταγαγόντες τὰ πλοῖα ἐπὶ τὴν γῆν, ἀφέντες ἅπαντα ἠκολούθησαν αὐτῷ.	ἦσαν δὲ κοινωνοὶ αὐτοῦ Ἰάκωβος καὶ Ἰωάννης, υἱοὶ Ζεβεδαίου· ὁ δὲ εἶπεν αὐτοῖς, δεῦτε καὶ μὴ γίνεσθε ἁλιεῖς ἰχθύων, ποιήσω γὰρ ὑμᾶς ἁλιεῖς ἀνθρώπων. οἱ δὲ ἀκούσαντες πάντα κατέλειψαν ἐπὶ τῆς γῆς, καὶ ἠκολούθησαν αὐτῷ (D, **e**).
Lk. v. 14. εἰς μαρτύριον αὐτοῖς.	D adds ὁ δὲ ἐξελθὼν . . . Καφαρναούμ, Mk. i 45, ii. 1.
Lk. xi. 35, 36. σκόπει οὖν μὴ τὸ φῶς . . . φωτίζῃ σε.	D and O.L. substitute Mt. vi. 23ᵇ; O.S.ᶜ combines Lk. xi. 35 and Mt. vi. 23ᵇ; O.S.ˢ combines Lk. xi. 35 and another phrase (found also in O.L. **f, g**).
Lk. xi. 53, 54. κἀκεῖθεν ἐξελθόντος αὐτοῦ ἤρξαντο οἱ γραμματεῖς καὶ οἱ Φαρισαῖοι δεινῶς ἐνέχειν καὶ ἀποστοματίζειν αὐτὸν περὶ πλειόνων, ἐνεδρεύοντες αὐτόν, θηρεῦσαί τι ἐκ τοῦ στόματος αὐτοῦ.	λέγοντος δὲ αὐτοῦ ταῦτα πρὸς αὐτοὺς ἐνώπιον παντὸς τοῦ λαοῦ, ἤρξαντο οἱ Φαρισαῖοι καὶ οἱ νομικοὶ δεινῶς ἔχειν καὶ συμβάλλειν αὐτῷ περὶ πλειόνων, ζητοῦντες ἀφορμήν τινα λαβεῖν αὐτοῦ, ἵνα εὕρωσιν κατηγορῆσαι αὐτοῦ (D; O.L., O.S., with some differences).

β text	δ text
Lk. xxiii. 42, 43. καὶ ἔλεγεν, 'Ιησοῦ, μνήσθητί μου ὅταν ἔλθῃς εἰς τὴν βασιλείαν σου. καὶ εἶπεν αὐτῷ, ἀμὴν σοι λέγω, σήμερον μετ' ἐμοῦ ἔσῃ ἐν τῷ παραδείσῳ.	καὶ στραφεὶς πρὸς τὸν Κύριον εἶπεν αὐτῷ, μνήσθητί μου ἐν τῇ ἡμέρᾳ τῆς ἐλεύσεώς σου. ἀποκριθεὶς δὲ ὁ 'Ιησοῦς εἶπεν αὐτῷ τῷ ἐπιπλήσσοντι, θάρσει, σήμερον .. παραδείσῳ (D).

These examples, which might be greatly multiplied, may serve to show the character of the discrepancies between the two texts. They are especially numerous in Luke, where, as will be seen from the specimens given, they sometimes amount to paraphrastic versions of considerable passages. This has given rise to the suggestion that Luke himself produced two editions of his Gospel; but this theory will be better dealt with in connection with Acts, where the same suggestion has been made with greater force. It is clear that editorial revision has been at work on a large scale in one text or the other. The decision must be left to the application of the principles of textual criticism, which has to consider which text shows the stronger signs of authenticity; and if in any considerable number of instances the verdict is in favour of one text, a presumption will be established in its favour in other cases where a decision is more difficult. In this connection it is relevant to notice that some of the variations in the δ text appear to be due to the importation of or assimilation to passages from the other Gospels or the Septuagint; it is possible also that some were derived from other narratives of our Lord's life, now lost, or from oral tradition. Also the support of the Old Latin MSS is by no means uniform, and some additions or variations of the same nature appear in some of the Old Latin authorities but not in D. All this seems to suggest a lax handling of the text in the region in which the δ text had its development, and seems, in the eyes of most scholars, to establish a presumption in favour of the β text, which, however, need not be decisive in every case.

The δ text in Acts requires separate consideration, and presents a very difficult problem, which is far from having received a final solution. Here the divergences are both more numerous and more substantial. The most notable of these have been quoted above in the description of D (pp. 92–3); but they are only a few among many. Some other examples may be added here.

Q

β *text*	δ *text*
i. 2. ἄχρι ἧς ἡμέρας ἐντειλάμε-νος τοῖς ἀποστόλοις διὰ Πνεύ-ματος Ἁγίου οὓς ἐξελέξατο ἀνελήμφθη.	ἐν ῃ ἡμέρᾳ τοὺς ἀποστόλους ἐξελέξατο διὰ Πνεύματος Ἁγίου, καὶ ἐκέλευσεν κηρύσσειν τὸ εὐαγ-γέλιον. (reconstructed from African O.L. and D).
i. 5. οὐ μετὰ πολλὰς ταύτας ἡμέρας.	καὶ ὃ μέλλετε λαμβάνειν οὐ μετὰ πολλὰς ταύτας ἡμέρας ἕως τῆς πεντηκοστῆς. (D, Aug. (O.L.)).
ii. 30. ἐκ καρποῦ τῆς ὀσφύος αὐτοῦ καθίσαι ἐπὶ τὸν θρόνον αὐτοῦ.	ἐκ καρποῦ τῆς κοιλίας (καρ-δίας D) αὐτοῦ κατὰ σάρκα ἀναστῆσαι τὸν Χριστόν, καὶ καθίσαι ἐπὶ τὸν θρόνον αὐτοῦ. (D(E), s).
iii. 3. ὃς ἰδὼν Πέτρον καὶ Ἰωάννην.	οὗτος ἀτενίσας τοῖς ὀφθαλμοῖς αὐτοῦ καὶ ἰδὼν Π. καὶ Ἰ. (O, **h**.)
iv. 18. καὶ καλέσαντες αὐτούς.	συγκατατιθεμένων δὲ αὐτῶν τῇ γνώμῃ φωνήσαντες αὐτούς. (D).
v. 18.	Adds καὶ ἐπορεύθη εἷς ἕκαστος εἰς τὰ ἴδια. (D).
vii. 4.	Adds καὶ οἱ πατέρες ἡμῶν οἱ πρὸ ἡμῶν. (D (E Aug.)).
vii. 24.	Adds καὶ ἔκρυψεν αὐτὸν ἐν τῇ ἄμμῳ (from LXX). (D.)
viii. 39. Πνεῦμα Κυρίου ἥρπασε τὸν Φίλιππον.	Πνεῦμα Ἅγιον ἐπέπεσεν ἐπὶ τὸν εὐνοῦχον, ἄγγελος δὲ Κυρίου ἥρπασεν τὸν Φίλιππον ἀπ' αὐτοῦ. (A, **p**, Ephraem. Aug.—D lacking.)

β *text*	δ *text*
ix. 4, 5. τί με διώκεις; εἶπε δέ, τίς εἶ, Κύριε; ὁ δὲ ἐγώ εἰμι Ἰησοῦς ὃν σὺ διώκεις· ἀλλὰ ἀνάστηθι.	τί με διῶκεις; σκληρόν σοι πρὸς κέντρα λακτίζειν (from xxvi. 14). εἶπεν δὲ, τίς εἶ, Κύριε; καὶ ὁ Κύριος πρὸς αὐτόν, ἐγώ εἰμι Ἰησοῦς ὁ Ναζωραῖος (from xxii. 8) ὃν σὺ διώκεις. ὁ δὲ τρέμων καὶ θαμβῶν ἐπὶ τῷ γεγονότι αὐτῷ εἶπεν, Κύριε, τί με θέλεις ποιῆσαι; καὶ ὁ Κύριος πρὸς αὐτόν, ἀνάστηθι. (reconstructed from E, O.L., Vulg.—D lacking).
ix. 7, 8. μηδένα δὲ θεωροῦντες. ἠγέρθη δὲ Σαῦλος ἀπὸ τῆς γῆς.	μηδένα δὲ θεωροῦντες μεθ' οὗ ἐλάλει. ἔφη δὲ πρὸς αὐτούς, ἐγείρατέ με ἀπὸ τῆς γῆς. καὶ ἐγειράντων αὐτόν (reconstructed from O.L.—D lacking).
x. 33. ἐξαυτῆς οὖν ἔπεμψα πρός σε.	ὃς παραγενόμενος λαλήσει σοι. (DE, O.L.). ἐξαυτῆς οὖν ἔπεμψα πρός σε, παρακαλῶν ἐλθεῖν πρὸς ἡμᾶς (D, p).
xi. 17. τίς ἤμην δυνατὸς κωλῦσαι τὸν Θεόν;	τίς . . . Θεὸν τοῦ μὴ δοῦναι αὐτοῖς Πνεῦμα Ἅγιον πιστεύσασιν ἐπ' αὐτῷ; (D, p).
xi. 27, 28. εἰς Ἀντιόχειαν. ἀναστὰς δὲ εἷς ἐξ αὐτῶν, ὀνόματι Ἄγαβος, ἐσήμαινεν.	εἰς Ἀντιόχειαν, ἦν δὲ πολλὴ ἀγαλλίασις. συνεστραμμένων δὲ ἡμῶν ἔφη εἷς ἐξ αὐτῶν, ὀνόματι Ἄγαβος, σημαίνων. (D, p, Aug.)
xii. 3. ἰδὼν δὲ ὅτι ἀρεστόν ἐστιν τοῖς Ἰουδαίοις.	καὶ ἰδὼν ὅτι ἀρεστόν ἐστιν τοῖς Ἰουδαίοις ἡ ἐπιχείρησις αὐτοῦ ἐπὶ τοὺς πιστούς. (D, p).
xiii. 43.	Adds ἐγένετο δὲ καθ' ὅλης τῆς πόλεως διελθεῖν τὸν λόγον τοῦ Θεοῦ. (D—cf. E).

β text	δ text
xv. 5. ἐξανέστησαν δέ τινες τῶν ἀπὸ τῆς αἱρέσεως τῶν Φαρισαίων πεπιστευκότες, λέγοντες κ.τ.λ.	οἱ δὲ παραγγείλαντες αὐτοῖς ἀναβαίνειν πρὸς τοὺς πρεσβυτέρους ἐξανέστησαν, λέγοντές τινες ἀπὸ τῆς αἱρέσεως τῶν Φαρισαίων πεπιστευκότες. (D).
xv. 12. ἐσίγησε δέ.	συγκατατιθεμένων δὲ τῶν πρεσβυτέρων τοῖς ὑπὸ τοῦ Πέτρου εἰρημένοις, ἐσίγησεν. (D, Ephraem).
xv. 41.	Adds παραδιδοὺς τὰς ἐντολὰς τῶν πρεσβυτέρων. (D, c, g).
xvi. 4. ὡς δὲ διεπορεύοντο τὰς πόλεις, παρεδίδοσαν αὐτοῖς φυλάσσειν τὰ δόγματα τὰ κεκριμένα ὑπὸ τῶν ἀποστόλων καὶ πρεσβυτέρων τῶν ἐν Ἱεροσολύμοις.	διερχόμενοι δὲ τὰς πόλεις ἐκήρυσσον αὐτοῖς μετὰ πάσης παρρησίας τὸν Κύριον Ἰησοῦν Χριστόν, ἅμα παραδιδόντες καὶ τὰς ἐντολὰς τῶν ἀποστόλων καὶ πρεσβυτέρων τῶν ἐν Ἱεροσολύμοις. (D, g, Ephraem).
xviii. 21. ἀλλὰ ἀποταξάμενος καὶ εἰπών, πάλιν ἀνακάμψω πρὸς ὑμᾶς τοῦ Θεοῦ θέλοντος, ἀνήχθη ἀπὸ τῆς Ἐφέσου, καὶ κατελθὼν εἰς Καισάρειαν.	ἀλλὰ ἀπετάξατο αὐτοῖς εἰπών, δεῖ με πάντως τὴν ἑορτὴν την ἐρχομένην ποιῆσαι εἰς Ἱεροσόλυμα· [πάλιν δὲ] ἀνακάμψω πρὸς ὑμᾶς τοῦ Θεοῦ θέλοντος κ.τ.λ. (DLP, g). Some add τὸν δὲ Ἀκύλαν εἴασεν ἐν Ἐφέσῳ· αὐτὸς δὲ ἀναχθεὶς ἦλθεν εἰς Καισάρειαν.
xxi. 25. περὶ δὲ τῶν πεπιστευκότων ἐθνῶν ἡμεῖς ἐπεστείλαμεν κρίναντες φυλάσσεσθαι.	περὶ δὲ τῶν πεπιστευκότων ἐθνῶν οὐδὲν ἔχουσιν λέγειν πρός σε, ἡμεῖς γὰρ ἀπεστείλαμεν κρίναντες μηδὲν τοιοῦτον τηρεῖν αὐτοὺς εἰ μὴ φυλάσσεσθαι. (D (E), g).

After xxii. 28 D is deficient

β text	δ text
xxiii. 15. νῦν οὖν ὑμεῖς ἐμφανίσατε τῷ χιλιάρχῳ.	νῦν οὖν παρακαλοῦμεν ὑμᾶς ποιήσατε ἡμῖν τοῦτο· συναγαγόντες τὸ συνέδριον ἐμφανίσατε τῷ χιλιάρχῳ. (p⁴⁸ g h).
xxiii. 23, 24. ἑτοιμάσατε . . . ἀπὸ τρίτης ὥρας τῆς νυκτός, κτήνη τε παραστῆσαι ἵνα ἐπιβιβάσαντες τὸν Παῦλον διασώσωσι πρὸς Φήλικα τὸν ἡγεμόνα.	ἑτοιμάσατε . . . καὶ ἀπὸ τρίτης ὥρας τῆς νυκτὸς κελεύει ἑτοίμους εἶναι πορεύεσθαι. καὶ τοῖς ἑκατοντάρχοις παρήγγειλεν κτήνη παραστῆσαι, ἵνα ἐπιβιβάσαντες τὸν Π. νυκτὸς διασώσωσιν εἰς Καισάρειαν πρὸς Φήλικα τὸν ἡγεμόνα. ἐφοβήθη γὰρ μήποτε ἐξαρπάσαντες αὐτὸν οἱ Ἰουδαῖοι ἀποκτείνωσιν, καὶ αὐτὸς μεταξὺ ἔγκλημα ἔχη ὡς εἰληφὼς ἀργύρια. (reconstructed from p⁴⁸ 614, Harkl. Syr. marg.).
xxiii. 27. ἐξειλάμην, μαθὼν ὅτι Ῥωμαῖός ἐστιν.	ἐρυσάμην κράζοντα καὶ λέγοντα ἑαυτὸν εἶναι Ῥωμαῖον. (p⁴⁸, g).
xxiv. 6.	Adds καὶ κατὰ τὸν ἡμέτερον νόμον ἠθελήσαμεν κρῖναι. παρελθὼν δὲ Λυσίας ὁ χιλίαρχος μετὰ πολλῆς βίας ἐκ τῶν χειρῶν ἡμῶν ἀπήγαγεν, κελεύσας τοὺς κατηγόρους αὐτοῦ ἔρχεσθαι ἐπί σε. (ΕΨ, 33, 614 etc., O.L.).
xxiv. 10. λέγειν.	ἀπολογίαν ἔχειν ὑπὲρ ἑαυτοῦ. ὁ δὲ σχῆμα ἔνθεον ἀναλαβὼν ἔφη. (reconstructed from Harkl. Syr. marg.).
xxiv. 24. οὔσῃ Ἰουδαίᾳ μετεπέμψατο.	οὔσῃ Ἰουδαίᾳ, ἥτις ἠρώτησεν ἰδεῖν τὸν Παῦλον καὶ ἀκοῦσαι τὸν λόγον. θέλων οὖν χαρίζεσθαι αὐτῇ μετεπέμψατο. (reconstructed from Harkl. Syr. marg.).

β text

δ text

xxiv. 27. θέλων τε χάριτα καταθέσθαι τοῖς Ἰουδαίοις ὁ Φῆλιξ κατέλιπε τὸν Παῦλον δεδεμένον.

τὸν δὲ Παῦλον εἴασεν ἐν τηρήσει διὰ Δρούσιλλαν. (614, Harkl. Syr. marg.).

xxv. 24, 25. βοῶντες μὴ δεῖν αὐτὸν ζῆν μηκέτι. ἐγὼ δὲ κατελαβόμην μηδὲν ἄξιον αὐτὸν θανάτου πεπραχέναι. αὐτοῦ δὲ τούτου ἐπικαλεσαμένου τὸν Σεβαστόν, ἔκρινα πέμπειν.

ὅπως παραδῶ αὐτὸν εἰς βάσανον ἀναπολόγητον. οὐκ ἠδυνήθην δὲ παραδοῦναι αὐτὸν διὰ τὰς ἐντολὰς ἃς ἔχομεν παρὰ τοῦ Σεβαστοῦ, ἐὰν δέ τις αὐτοῦ κατηγορεῖν θέλῃ ἔλεγον ἀκολουθεῖν μοι εἰς Καισάρειαν οὗ ἐφυλάσσετο· οἵτινες ἐλθόντες ἐβόων ἵνα ἀρθῇ ἐκ τῆς ζωῆς. ἀκούσας δὲ ἀμφοτέρων κατελαβόμην ἐν μηδενὶ αὐτὸν ἔνοχον εἶναι θανάτου. εἰπόντος δέ μου, θέλεις κρίνεσθαι μετ’ αὐτῶν ἐν Ἱεροσολύμοις, Καίσαρα ἐπεκαλέσατο. (Harkl. Syr. marg.; Vulg. Cod. D (part)).

xxvii. 1. ὡς δὲ ἐκρίθη τοῦ ἀποπλεῖν ἡμᾶς εἰς τὴν Ἰταλίαν, παρεδίδουν τόν τε Παῦλον καί τινας ἑτέρους δεσμώτας ἑκατοντάρχῃ ὀνόματι Ἰουλίῳ, σπείρης Σεβαστῆς. ἐπιβάντες δὲ πλοίῳ. . .

καὶ οὕτως ἔκρινεν αὐτὸν ὁ ἡγεμὼν ἀναπέμπεσθαι Καίσαρι. καὶ τῇ ἐπαύριον προσκαλεσάμενος ἑκατοντάρχην τινὰ ὀνόματι Ἰούλιον, σπείρης Σεβαστῆς, παρεδίδου αὐτῷ τὸν Παῦλον σὺν καὶ ἑτέροις δεσμώταις. ἀρξάμενοι δὲ τοῦ ἀποπλεῖν εἰς τὴν Ἰταλίαν ἐπέβημεν πλοίῳ. (reconstructed from 97, 421, h, Harkl. Syr. marg.).

xxviii. 16. ἐπετράπη τῷ Παύλῳ μένειν καθ’ ἑαυτόν.

ὁ ἑκατόνταρχος παρέδωκεν τοὺς δεσμίους τῷ στρατοπεδάρχῃ, τῷ δὲ Παύλῳ ἐπετράπη μένειν καθ’ ἑαυτὸν ἔξω τῆς παρεμβολῆς. (614, Byzantine MSS, g).

β text	δ text
xxviii. 19.	Add ἀλλ' ἵνα λυτρώσωμαι τὴν ψυχήν μου ἐκ θανάτου. (614, c, g, p).
xxviii. 29. Verse omitted by β text.	καὶ ταῦτα αὐτοῦ εἰπόντος ἀπῆλθον οἱ Ἰουδαῖοι πολλὴν ἔχοντες ἐν ἑαυτοῖς συζήτησιν. (614, c, g, p).
xxviii. 31.	Adds ὅτι οὗτός ἐστιν Ἰησοῦς ὁ υἱὸς τοῦ Θεοῦ, δι' οὗ μέλλει ὅλος ὁ κόσμος κρίνεσθαι. (reconstructed from m, p, Vulg. codd., Harkl. Syr.).

A study of these variants (a few of which found their way into the Received Text) will show how marked in this book is the difference between the β and δ texts. It will be plain also that they are not the result of casual scribal errors, but must be due to deliberate alteration on one side or the other, the δ text being habitually the longer and fuller of the two. In his earlier work (*The Primitive Text of the Gospels and Acts*, Oxford, 1914) A. C. Clark laid stress mainly on his theory that the ancestors of our uncials were written in columns with very short lines, and that the shorter text was produced by frequent scribal omissions of one or more of such lines. Against this it could be argued (1) that since the number of letters in a line is never constant, the method of counting letters becomes quite unreliable except for short passages, since any moderately high number can be accounted for by some combination of multiples of a variable base,[1] (2) that such narrow columns are extremely rare in the early papyri, (3) that accidental scribal omissions would not account for the habitual correspondence of the omissions with breaks in the sense, (4) that most of the variants are not due to simple omissions, but to differences in the wording. Even if the text were written in στίχοι, or sense-lines, as it is in D, the last-named class of

---

[1] E.g. if the archetype be supposed to have lines of 10–13 letters, any number from 30 upwards can be accounted for as a combination of lines of such length, so that the argument loses all cogency.

variants would remain to be explained; and there is no evidence for the early use of stichometrical arrangement. None of the early papyri yet known shows it,[1] and it is probable that it first came into use in bilingual manuscripts, where it was desired to show the correspondence between clauses in the two languages.

In his later work (*The Acts of the Apostles*, Oxford, 1933) Clark practically abandoned this explanation in favour of the much more plausible one of deliberate editorial alteration. Such an explanation was first put forward at the end of the seventeenth century by Jean Leclerc, who suggested that Luke had himself produced two editions of Acts. This hypothesis found no support at the time, and though it was mentioned with approval by no less a scholar than Bishop Lightfoot, it was not seriously considered until it was revived by the great German classical scholar, Friedrich Blass, in 1895. Blass' theory was that Luke originally wrote his Gospel in Palestine, and that when he came to Rome with St Paul and was asked by the Christians there for a copy of his work, he wrote it out again with such alterations as an author naturally feels free to make in dealing with his own work. Similarly with regard to Acts, one copy was made for Theophilus, to whom it was addressed, and another for the Church at large. These two editions Blass would identify with the β and δ texts respectively; and, on the rather doubtful assumption that revision implies abbreviation by the removal of the superfluous, he concludes that the δ text represents the later edition of the Gospel and the earlier of Acts, while the B text represents the earlier edition of the Gospel and the later of Acts.

There is an undeniable plausibility in this theory, which would account satisfactorily for many of the variations. An author is at liberty to alter his own work, and when every copy had to be made by hand, there was frequent opportunity for it. This would account not only for alterations in substance, but also for verbal variations which are in themselves indifferent. It is not surprising, therefore, that the theory was received with favour, even by scholars of the standing of Salmon and Nestle. There are, however, serious difficulties. D substitutes the genealogy of Matthew for that which appears in the ordinary text of Luke; is it conceivable that Luke made this alteration in his second edition,

[1] The Chester Beatty papyrus of Ecclesiasticus (probably late fourth century) is written stichometrically; but this is poetry.

or if, as Blass admits, this cannot be due to Luke himself, may not the editor who made this alteration be responsible also for others? Further, it is hard to believe that Luke, in revising his Gospel, struck out the Word from the Cross and the clauses relating to the Resurrection and Ascension; what could be his motive? In Acts also, if the δ text is to be regarded as the earlier, it is difficult to understand an author omitting some of the details found in it. The gain in space is small, and the loss in descriptiveness is sometimes such as, in Clark's words, to reduce the narrative to 'a colourless abstract', or even to contradict the original narrative. Having correctly described the break of the journey from Cæsarea to Jerusalem at the house of Mnason (xxi. 16), he would not be likely to alter it so as to make it incorrect. He would hardly have omitted a clause from the decisions of the Jerusalem Council (xv. 20, 29), or have altered the language of the letter of Claudius Lysias (xxiii. 26–30) or Paul's speech to Agrippa (xxv. 24, 25). A further difficulty arises from the variations of the δ text in the other Gospels, which, though less numerous, are of the same character, such as the additions at Matt. xx. 28 and John vi. 56. For these Blass finds other explanations which increase in complication and decline in probability.

For reasons such as these Clark does not accept the theory of a double Lucan authorship, but substitutes that of an editor who by alterations and omissions reduced the δ text to the form of the β text. This is far more possible, and if Acts stood alone it would be undeniably attractive, though there would still be some difficulty in understanding the mentality of the editor who would cut out the often picturesque details contained in the δ text. Ultimately we come up against the question whether these passages are best explained as omissions by one editor or additions by another. Here different scholars have taken different views. Ropes, the other scholar who in recent times has made a detailed study of the text of Acts, takes the opposite side to Clark, preferring the authenticity of the β text. For the δ text it might be said that its characteristic passages seem to show personal knowledge of the incidents in question; e.g. the fuller account of Peter's mission to Cornelius, the seven steps in the story of Peter's deliverance from prison, the narrative of Paul and Silas in the prison at Philippi, the explanation of Apollo's journey from Ephesus to Corinth, the hours of Paul's teaching in the school of Tyrannus, the touching at Trogyllium on the voyage to Jerusalem, the residence of Mnason in a village between Cæsarea and Jerusalem, the mention of the στρατοπεδάρχης at Rome.[1] It is also quite admissible that the original text of Acts should have been produced at Rome, and therefore should have been preserved in the geographically Western authorities; though it has to be remembered that the 'Western' text as a whole cannot be localized in this way.

On the other hand it is difficult to understand the motive for the abridgement of the text by the β editor. It is true that the β text in the Gospels also is marked by omissions rather than by additions; but there the contrast between the two texts is of a very different character, and the balance of probability seems on internal grounds to be decidedly against the insertions of the δ text; and in view of the general homogeneity of character of the β text in the New Testament it is hard to understand why he should in Acts have broken out into a passion for the pruning away of detail and even the alteration of statements of fact. But perhaps the greatest difficulty (which is not faced by Clark) is the existence of the δ text in the Gospels. There is no reason to ascribe a Western origin to the Gospels, and there are signs of a free handling which, as an evidence to character, tells against the authenticity of the δ text. It is *a priori* more probable that the details in the δ text of Acts were added by an editor who was concerned to 'improve' the text, among other things by giving a more circumstantial turn to the narrative by expansion and periphrasis, than that they were originally present and were excised, without apparent reason, by a subsequent editor. Attractive as Clark's theory is at first sight, and admirable as is the learning and industry with which it is set out, it leaves many difficulties un-

---

[1] A conspicuous instance where the δ text may well be right is in xx. 4, where all MSS except D and g read Γαῖος Δερβαῖος. D has Δουβ[.]ριος, d has douerius, and g doberius. Since Gaius is described in xix. 29 as a Macedonian, he cannot have been a native of Derbe; and Clark was the first to point out that a town named Doberus in Paeonia is mentioned by Thucydides (ii. 98–100), and a tribe of Doberes near Mt Pangaeus by Herodotus (vii. 113). The mutilated word in D should therefore be Δουβηριος for which Δερβαιος is a mistake by a scribe who knew nothing of Doberus but remembered Derbe. The error is scribal rather than editorial, since a deliberate editor would hardly have forgotten that Gaius was a Macedonian 16 verses before; but as Ropes remarks, 'it must never be forgotten that the basis of the "Western" revision was a text far more ancient than any MS now extant'.

removed; and unless future discoveries should supply a solution, the problem must be solved according to the intrinsic probabilities of the methods of insertion or excision.

In the Pauline Epistles there is a quite distinguishable δ text, represented by the Graeco-Latin bilinguals D_2 E_3 F_2 G_3 with the Old Latin MSS mentioned above (p. 155). It is however, of much less importance than in the Gospels and Acts. There are few variations in substance; probably the writings of Paul had too much individuality to admit of the free handling which was admissible in the anonymous narratives of the lives of our Lord and the apostles. Most of the variants are purely verbal, or affect only the order of the words. Sometimes there are slight expansions, either because the expanded form was usual, or for the sake of slightly greater definition; e.g. Rom. x. 15, the completion of the quotation by the addition of the words τῶν εὐαγγελιζομένων εἰρήνην, xii. 17 the addition of οὐ μόνον ἐνώπιον τοῦ Θεοῦ, ἀλλὰ καί, 1 Cor. xvi. 22 the addition of Ἰησοῦν Χριστόν to Κύριον, Gal. vi. 17 the expansion of Ἰησοῦ to Κυρίου ἡμῶν Ἰησοῦ Χριστοῦ, Heb. ix. 18 the addition of διαθήκη after πρώτη. In such cases the presumption is always against the addition, as being more in accordance with the practice of scribes influenced by familiar phrases or anxious to make the text clear. In some cases, though the same motives are discernible, the addition is rather unintelligent; e.g. Heb. x. 28 the addition of καὶ δακρύων after οἰκτιρμῶν, 1 Cor. ix. 7 the addition of καὶ πίνει after ἐσθίει, x. 17 the addition of καὶ τοῦ ἑνὸς ποτηρίου after ἄρτου (though the previous words are concerned with ἄρτος only), xvi. 15 the addition of καὶ Φορτουνάτου or Φ. καὶ Ἀχαϊκοῦ because those names are mentioned below, Phil. iii. 16 the insertion of τὸ αὐτὸ φρονεῖν before τῷ αὐτῷ στοιχεῖν. Some of the variants are, however, quite possible, and a minority of them are supported by our earliest authority, 𝔭[46]—e.g. 1 Cor. xii. 10 ἐνεργήματα δυνάμεως, which is probably correct. Again it is noticeable also that (as mentioned above, p. 215) B in several instances joins the δ group, and in some of these is supported by 𝔭[46]—cf. 1 Cor. ix. 9 κημώσεις B* D* G 1739, which is probably the correct reading against 𝔭[46] ℵ A etc. φιμώσεις, Heb. ix. 11 τῶν γενομένων ἀγαθῶν 𝔭[46] B D* 1739 against ℵ A etc. τ.μελλόντων ἀγ. In such examples as these the question arises whether indeed they are at all properly described as 'Western' variants, but are rather elements in the ancient tradition on which both the β and δ texts drew. On the whole, however, the δ variants in the Epistles belong to the category of minor verbal variants, and are not of the same class as those which command attention in the Gospels and Acts.

For the Apocalypse there is no Greek MS representative of the δ text, which has to be sought in the few Old Latin MSS that contain this book, **g** and **h,** and in the quotations in Primasius (covering practically the whole book), Cyprian and Tyconius.

The general tendency of modern discoveries and criticism has been to break up the unity of the δ text as at one time envisaged. It has been made clear that not all early non-neutral readings are to be classed as Western. The range of such readings, as attested by manuscripts, versions, and Fathers, is spread all over the Christian world, but they are far from forming a homogeneous text. The Old Latin MSS differ widely among themselves, and the use by the early Fathers is sporadic and inconsistent. The difficulty of forming a 'Western' text is illustrated by Blass' attempt to form such a text of Luke, which practically consists of an arbitrary selection of readings from authorities regarded as Western. Some of the authorities formerly so classed have now been more accurately placed in other groups. Famm. 1 and 13 have gone into the Cæsarean group, together with parts of W and Θ and some of the quotations in Origen and Eusebius, and the Armenian and Georgian versions. Others will be dealt with in the material which has still to be considered. For the most part, then, it appears that the δ-text finds its main attestation in authorities which are geographically Western—the Graeco-Latin uncials and a few kindred minuscules, the Old Latin version (especially the African form of it), and the Latin Fathers. But that it can be called 'Western' in the sense of being a local text is clearly misleading and far from the truth. Besides this must be set the papyrus fragments $\mathfrak{p}^{38}$ and $\mathfrak{p}^{48}$, which show that a Greek text of this type was known in Egypt in the later third century, and effectively dispose of the question raised at one time as to whether this type of text ever existed in Greek, except as a Greek text revised from Latin sources. To these should be added the 'Western' element in the Old Syriac and the Cæsarean group. When we turn to the quotations of the early Fathers and others— e.g. Justin Martyr, Marcion, Irenaeus, Clement of Alexandria—

it is clear that it existed at a very early date as well as being widely disseminated. Moreover from the fact that, apart from the more obviously characteristic δ-readings (of which the additions in the Gospels and Acts are the most prominent examples), so-called 'Western' variants frequently find sporadic support in the other groups, including the Alexandrian, it would be a fair inference that these belong to the uncontrolled popular text which flourished in the second century, the common 'reservoir', as it has been called, of variant readings, taking on local colour in the various Christian centres. Many would take the further step in suggesting that it was out of this reservoir that the later textual groupings (Eastern, Western, Cæsarean, Alexandrian) were alike derived by a process of reduction and recension. Whether this is altogether true of the β text we have seen reason to doubt, but that the β text was altogether unaffected by the popular text is even more unlikely. As to the δ text itself, it would seem that this ancient base has been worked over, more noticeably in the Gospels and Acts (possibly in some centre or centres where oral traditions still survived), and thus took on the particular forms characteristic of the δ text as we know it in Codex Bezae, the Old Latin, etc. When and where this revision took place it is not possible to say—Ropes suggests before 150, perhaps in Syria or Palestine, and at a time when the Canon of the New Testament was taking shape. Unfortunately the documentary evidence available to us for the δ text, when compared with that of the β text, is relatively small and largely confined to geographically western authorities, so that these and related problems are as yet far from solution.[1]

In previous editions of this book the text of Syria was given separate representation as the ε text, but whether it can be said to constitute a text in its own right is doubtful. Formerly the tendency was to bring this group into the orbit of the δ text which, as we have seen, was at one time very widely spread. There is no doubt that the Old Syriac version in many cases has δ read-

[1] See further A. F. J. Klijn, *A Survey of the Researches into the Western Text of the Gospels and Acts* (Utrecht, 1949), Part Two 1949–69 (Leiden, 1969); G. D. Kilpatrick, 'Western text and original text in the Gospels and Acts . . . Epistles', *Journal of Theological Studies*, xliv (1943), pp. 24–36, xlv (1944), pp. 60–5.

ings, but whether, as Burkitt believed, this 'Western' colour was not original, but was due to the importation of a text of this kind in the form of Tatian's *Diatessaron* would seem now to be at best only partially true. In the twenty-four 'major' variants quoted on pp. 225-7 the Old Syriac in one or other of its forms supports the δ text in thirteen of them; but Sin. and Cur. together oppose δ's additions six times (exx. 1, 2, 16, 17, 22, 23), and three out of four of the δ omissions in Luke xxiv. 6-40 (ex. 18). In the eight instances where the witness of Sin. and Cur. is divided it is noticeable that support for the δ text is much more pronounced on the Curetonian side—seven out of eight (exx. 3, 9, 11, 12, 13, 14, 15—all δ additions except 13) against only one on the Sinaitic (ex. 6). On the other hand, Sin. supports δ's omissions four times (exx. 6, 7, 19, 24—but in all except two of these Cur. is defective). In the fifteen 'minor' variants on pp. 229-31 the Curetonian is defective in ten of them, and in the remaining five together with the Sinaitic supports the δ text three times (in two instances with some differences), the β text once, and divides once where Sin. supports the δ text and Cur. β. In the other ten instances where Sin. is alone it reads with the β text except once (Mark xi. 3) where it supports W fam. 1. Other figures more favourable to the δ text are given on p. 127. The quotations from Acts in the Armenian translation of Ephraem also indicate a much closer approach to the δ text. It may be said, then, that in the Gospels the Syriac New Testament has affinities both with the β text and the δ text, but also preserves a proportion of readings which are neither β nor δ, but belong to the unassorted readings which we believe to have been very numerous in the early centuries. Subsequently this mixed text was further revised, perhaps by Rabbula, under the influences which produced the α text, and in this form, as the Peshitta, it became the accepted Bible of the Syrian Church. The Philoxenian version appears to have been of the α type but never obtained much authority; and the Harkleian revision of it was due to the use of Greek MSS of the δ type, and, though useful for the reconstruction of the δ text, tells us nothing of the text native to Syria. The Palestianian Syriac contains elements of all kinds.

V. THE RESIDUE

If the foregoing classification be accepted, there will remain a considerable residue of unclassified readings. They do not form a coherent text; their essence is that they are a congeries of unassorted early readings, left behind by the restriction of the β group to the text mainly represented by B, and of the δ group to the text mainly represented by D and the Old Latin. They include the readings of which Hort formed his γ group or 'Alexandrian' text; they include also a number of readings found in the papyri; they probably include also an unascertained number of readings which have found a home in other groups, especially the Western, but which are essentially of a different character. Although no coherent whole can be formed out of them, they are not therefore unimportant. On the contrary, they throw a considerable amount of light on the early history of the New Testament text.

Hort's 'Alexandrian' text was avowedly not to be found in any extant manuscript. It consisted of residual readings, found in manuscripts which on the whole are associated with the β text, though many of them also have a proportion of δ readings. They are not very closely defined, or perhaps definable, but are rather what is left after α, β, and δ readings have been identified and segregated. It is no long step to the suspicion that there never was an 'Alexandrian' text in this sense; and this suspicion is strengthened by the papyri, which often, and indeed generally, offer texts which cannot be classified as wholly either β or δ, while they are certainly earlier than α. It is important to recognize the existence of this category, and not to sweep all early non-β readings into the δ class. When, for example, the Chester Beatty fragments of Acts show eighty-nine agreements with D, but not a single one of the more characteristic δ readings, it would be absurd to rank it among the δ family, or to regard it as giving even a qualified support to it as against its rivals. What it does is to add its confirmation to the view that the textual history of the second and third centuries cannot be arranged in an orderly genealogical *stemma*, but presents rather a welter of unassorted variants, out of which the families that we have come to recognize are composed.[1]

[1] See E. C. Colwell, 'The significance of grouping of New Testament manuscripts', *New Testament Studies*, IV (1958), pp. 73–92, 'Method in locating a newly-discovered manuscript . . .', *Texte und Untersuchunzen*, lxxiii (1959), pp. 757–77, 'The origin of text types of New Testament manuscripts', *Early Christian Origins*, ed. A. Wickgren (Chicago, 1961), pp. 128–38, 'Genealogical method: its limitations and achievements', *Journal of Biblical Literature*, lxvi

It is not to be understood from this that the New Testament text was at first a chaos of Democritean atoms, from which in course of time an ordered form emerged. At the first each book had its single original text, which it is now the object of criticism to recover; but in the first two centuries this original text became submerged under a mass of variants, created by errors, by conscious alterations, and by attempts to remedy the uncertainties thus created. Then, as further attempts to bring order out of chaos were made, the families of text that we now know took shape. They were, however, nuclei rather than completed forms of text, and did not at once absorb all the atoms that the period of disorder had brought into existence. There was a residue of various readings, which attached themselves more or less fortuitously to the one centre or another, and which now confuse our conception of the several families. If it is true that none of the families which modern criticism has distinguished preserved uncontaminated the original text of the New Testament books, we may imagine for each of them an editor or editors who at some point in the period of obscurity gave each of them its characteristic form. But he (or they) drew on, and chose out of, a mass of material, much of which consisted of relatively minor details; and while we may, and indeed must, if we are to arrive at any conclusion, believe that one or other of the main lines of tradition is less contaminated than the rest, it does not follow that it is right in all details. We may believe Alexandrian or Western or Cæsarean to be on the whole preferable, without binding ourselves to accept it in all respects. There remains this floating residue, to be found in the representatives of each and all of them, which at once reminds us of the conditions out of which they came into being, and presents the material out of which we must choose in completing the details of the best text at which it is possible, in the present state of our knowledge, to arrive.

If the present state of opinion with regard to the several textual groups be compared with that formulated by Westcott and Hort nearly a century ago, it will be seen that there have been several modifications. It does not now seem possible to regard the β text (Hort's neutral) as having descended without editorial intervention

(1947), pp. 109–33, reprinted as Chapters I, II, III, IV of E. C. Colwell, *Studies in Methodology in Textual Criticism of the New Testament* (Leiden, 1969.)

and substantially unaltered from the original, but rather that it owes its present form to competent editorial treatment in accordance with the principles of trained textual scholarship, such as we know to have existed at Alexandria. We can now see from the Chester Beatty papyrus of the Epistles ($\mathfrak{p}^{46}$) and the Bodmer Luke–John ($\mathfrak{p}^{75}$) that a text of this type was in existence in Egypt by or before 200, and that it had close affinities with B, written 150 years later. Even so, the β text is no fixed entity, and although the overwhelming superiority which Westcott and Hort assigned to the group has been substantially borne out, the truth is not *always* to be found in B or $\mathfrak{p}^{46}$ or $\mathfrak{p}^{75}$ or in any other member of the group, whether singly or in combination. The early process of corruption, from which the Alexandrian editors have striven to purify their text and to keep it pure, has left its mark even here, and more often than Hort would have allowed the best reading is to be found elsewhere.[1] On the other hand, its principal rival, the δ text (Western), which at one time was regarded as a text pervading the whole Christian world and with earlier attestation than any other, has been broken up and reduced to a group geographically mainly Western in its surviving witnesses, the extreme form of which offers wide variations from all other groups. Out of the agglomeration formerly classed as Western have been carved two other groups, the Cæsarean, with attestation from the time of Origen, and the text of the Church of Syria. These two last-named groups have affinities both with Egypt and the West, and all take their rise from a period of much confusion of texts, which has left a residue of readings which may appear now in one and now in another of the main groups. Finally the α text remains much as Hort left it, an essentially secondary text,

---

[1] At the same time it is only fair to say that Westcott and Hort were not obsessed by B to the extent that is often alleged or implied, as a reading of Section II of the *Introduction to the New Testament in Greek*, and even more their practice, will show. Not infrequently singular and sub-singular B readings which they rejected on internal grounds are now seen, in the light of supporting evidence which has come to light since their day, to be probably correct; e.g. Luke ix. 62, where $\mathfrak{p}^{45,75}$ now support B in omitting πρὸς αὐτόν; x. 38 *om.* εἰς τὴν οἰκίαν $\mathfrak{p}^{45,75}$ B Sah.; John vii. 39, where W. H. accepted οἱ πιστεύσαντες B L T, now confirmed by $\mathfrak{p}^{66,75}$ W, but rejected Πνεῦμα Ἅγιον δεδομένον B e q. This is even more the case in the Pauline Epistles, as a careful study of the many examples cited by G. Zuntz in Chapter II of *The Text of the Epistles* (London, 1953), will amply demonstrate—though it would have added to the usefulness of this important examination of textual evidence and theory if the author had indicated Westcott and Hort's preferences along with his own.

R

based upon a process of eclectic revision which began about the end of the fourth century and continued for several centuries, affecting the descendants of all the earlier groups to varying extents, and finally dominating the Byzantine Church until the invention of printing, when it became the Received Text of the whole Church until the rise of modern criticism under the influence of the discoveries and research of the last century. Its progressive development has been to some extent elucidated by the labours of von Soden, but much more still needs to be done.

In addition, recent discoveries have materially increased our knowledge of the condition of the text during the earliest Christian centuries. We now have texts, substantial in the case of the Gospels, Acts, and Apocalypse and almost complete in the case of the Pauline Epistles, which go back to the end of the second and early part of the third century. The interval between the composition of the books of the New Tesament and the earliest extant manuscripts of them has been reduced by a hundred and fifty years, and we actually have evidence (small but decisive) of the circulation of the Fourth Gospel in the first half of the second century—that is, within about a generation of the date usually assigned to its composition. The general effect of this new evidence is to confirm the substantial integrity of our texts of the New Testament Scriptures, but also to show that in the third century, and therefore presumably for some time back into the second, the text was in detail very far from being settled. Instead of a state of orderly descent, though with an ever-widening genealogical pedigree, from the original autographs to the extant copies of the fourth century, we seem to see a period of increasing disorder, from which a state of comparative order was ultimately produced when the Church reached more settled conditions.

To understand the state of the New Testament text, it is necessary to form as clear a picture as the evidence permits of the circumstances of the early centuries. It is in this respect that the textual history of the New Testament differs materially from that of other ancient books. The works of classical literature were produced in peaceful conditions. They were copied by professional scribes. They were the work of recognized authors, whose individuality was respected, so that a scribe, though he might try to correct what seemed to him to be errors of transmission, did not feel at liberty to revise his author. They were not exposed to deliberate destruction, at any rate until, after many centuries, the Christian Church made war on pagan literature. The textual tradition which has come down to us is probably that of the great libraries, where good copies were preserved under the eyes of men of letters. In all respects they have had a respected and protected course until they suffered in the decline of civilization in the Middle Ages.

In all these respects the fortunes of the Christian Scriptures were different. In the earliest days the Christians were a poor community, who would seldom have been able to command the services of professional scribes. There were no recognized centres for the promulgation of authorized copies of the Scriptures. The New Testament books were not indeed Scriptures with a capital S. The sacred books of the earliest Christians were those of the Old Testament; the writings of Mark and Luke and Paul were just memoirs and letters for present needs. Nor were there the usual literary standards to protect the integrity of their texts. The letters of Paul were, indeed, individual expressions of opinion which would not lightly be altered; but the anonymous Gospels and Acts were not regarded as the literary compositions of their authors, but as narratives of the life of our Lord and the work of His apostles, compiled with the purely practical object of disseminating the knowledge of their lives and teachings among the Christian community, and with no eye to a future which in any case would soon be curtailed by the Second Coming. There was no need to be meticulous in verbal accuracy. The substance was what mattered, and if additions, believed to be authentic, could be made to it, why should they not? Then there were little means, even if it had been thought needful, to secure uniformity of transmission. Each book circulated originally as a separate roll, and there was no fixed Canon of Christian Scriptures. Not every Christian community would possess a complete set of Gospels or of Paul's epistles, but each would supply itself as best it could from its neighbours. Many copies would be made by untrained provincial copyists, and there would be no opportunity of correcting them by comparison with other copies, except such as might be in the immediate neighbourhood. Such revision as there might be would be local and unmethodical. Then there was always the danger of destruction. Christianity was often a tolerated religion, when books could be multiplied and distributed without hindrance; but there were also periods of persecution, sometimes local and occasionally general, when the Christian books were exposed to danger. There was much destruction of Christian property, and in the general persecutions the sacred books were special objects of search, when those which belonged to churches, which would be likely to be of superior quality, were the least likely to escape. So long as Christianity was at best tolerated and at worst persecuted, the transcription and circulation of the Scriptures were exposed to difficulties from which the pagan literature was free.

In circumstances such as these it was natural that varieties of readings should multiply. Apart from the growth of errors through untrained scribes, there was no restriction on casual alterations, made with the best intentions with a view to greater lucidity and the avoidance of possible misunderstandings. Such revision as there was would be local and casual, due to the initiative of individual bishops or scholars, and its influence would be confined to the immediate neighbourhood. This would tend to the creation of local types of text, extending at most to a province or to part of a province. At times copies would be brought from one part of the Empire to another, from Rome to Antioch or Alexandria or *vice versa*, and certain copies would be corrected from them, leading to the intermingling of local texts. Only when times were peaceful, and only decisively after the recognition of Christianity by Constantine, could revision be seriously taken in hand, and by that time the confusion had been created, the original autographs had long ago disappeared, and absolute verbal accuracy was no longer obtainable.

It is at this point, however, that we should ask how far evidence allows us to speak of revisions (in the larger sense) and of recensions in regard to the families of text now known to us, and if so, when, where and by whom they were made. A few names are known. In the second century Marcion produced editions of Luke and Paul for his own unorthodox purposes, and Tatian compiled the *Diatessaron*. Later on, as we have seen, Origen revised the text of the Septuagint, and Lucian and Hesychius are reported to have done the same, but there is no real evidence that any of them touched the New Testament. At a later date we know of the labours of Jerome on the Latin Bible and, probably, of Rabbula on the Syriac. On the other hand, any scribe who in copying tried to elucidate the text before him by making deliberate alterations, or by selecting one out of two or more variants, was in a sense acting in an editorial capacity. When this kind of thing operated over a long period considerable development might take place, but it is better thought of as a process rather than as a revision, while it would be proper to speak of a 'recension' only if at some point a deliberate attempt was made to fix a particular form of the text and take steps for its adoption in a certain area. And in fact all that we can really say is that by the fourth century certain main varieties of tradition had been developed, and we can judge of the character of the editors or processes only from the results. If, however, we think of the anonymous individuals concerned in the process of transmission of the text along its different lines, who in one sense or another may be termed editors, we can see that they had to do with a great welter of various readings which had come into existence in the early period of disorder, and that they would deal with the varied material which they found before them in a variety of ways. To some (and this was the commonest type) the governing idea was to make the text plain and easy. To this end the order of words was altered, names and pronouns were introduced, normal phrases were substituted for less usual ones, words which might be misunderstood or misinterpreted in an unorthodox manner were omitted or changed, narratives in one Gospel were assimilated to those in another, inexact quotations from the Old Testament were made exact, alternative readings in different manuscripts were combined, and so on. The result was an easy, intelligible text, at some sacrifice of character, and ultimately differing considerably in detail, though not in essential teaching, from the original. In this way such a text as the α text was produced.

Another editor, of more independent frame of mind, might treat the text more freely, varying phrases to suit his own taste, importing short passages from other sources, drawing on oral tradition, amplifying the narrative for the sake of effect, including rather than omitting, and attaching little importance to accuracy of transmission, though with no doctrinal motives. This would be the genesis of the δ text. At the opposite extreme to him would be the trained scholar, whose guiding principle would be accuracy, not edification, who would be thinking of the author rather than of the reader. He would be careful to consult the oldest manuscripts accessible to him, and would compare their variant readings in the light of critical science, considering which was most likely to give the author's original words. He would tend to omit superfluities or insufficiently attested words or passages, and to prefer the more difficult reading to the easier, as more likely to have been altered. These are the lines on which the closest approximation to the original would be arrived at. They are the established principles of textual science, which are applied to the editing of classical texts; and it is because the β text appears to have been transmitted on these lines that most modern scholars, even if they are not satisfied that it has preserved the authentic original in uncontaminated integrity, nevertheless hold that on the whole it offers us the purest text.

Of the other families, the γ text would now appear to be not so much a local text as a process of textual transmission associated with a number of closely related MSS, and at certain points in its history with the names of Origen and Eusebius. How far the affinities which these families have with other groups is due to direct influence is a matter of opinion. But the possibility of such interchange of influence has indeed to be recognized as a constant factor in textual history. Hardly any manuscript is free from influences from authorities of a different complexion from itself. The readings characteristic of each family have for the most part to be extracted from manuscripts which in greater or less degree have been revised into conformity with the prevalent text—generally and increasingly the Received Text, which ultimately submerged all others, leaving only here and there a few relics, like the wandering blocks of geology, of a more primeval form.

But to whichever family a critic may give his general preference, it by no means follows that he should regard it as always right. So long as the β text was regarded as practically free from editorial revision it was natural to give it the preference except when it is obviously wrong—as every manuscript must sometimes be. But if once editorial treatment is admitted, then it stands to reason that the editor cannot always have been right. He had to make a number of choices where the balance of probability was quite undetermined, and, being human, he cannot always have chosen correctly. Therefore a modern editor must be free to consider readings with an open mind, whether he finds them in a manuscript predominantly of α or β or γ or δ character. He may not be any more exempt from error than the ancient editor, but he has far more material to choose from, and centuries of experience to guide him, and he must make his decision to the best of his ability, though without dogmatism.

We may put the matter in another way by saying that the genealogical method has proved to be of much more limited application in tracing the early history of the New Testament text[1] than would appear from Westcott and Hort's theory. The method assumes the prior existence of a limited number of archetypes at no great distance from the original text, from which the main lines of tradition are descended, and that these archetypes can be reconstructed. But the extreme paucity of the surviving early witnesses (which themselves cannot be arranged on any precise genealogical map) makes such a reconstruction impossible. Moreover, when we have traced the various lines of tradition as far back as they can be taken, we are confronted not with less variety but with more, the 'barrier of the second century' as it has been called, the 'common reservoir' out of which the various groups have emerged. A consequence of this is that in recent years there has been a marked emphasis on other criteria than those chiefly relying on the evaluation of textual groups and of particular manuscripts within those groups: in other words there has been a reaction away from what Westcott and Hort called 'documentary attestation' in favour of the 'internal evidence of readings', and to fresh scrutiny of variant readings in relation to scribal habits and failings, the known stylistic and grammatical usage and vocabulary of the different New Testament writers and (equally important) of those who transmitted them,[2] the development of Christian doctrine and worship, the vicissitudes of the Church's history against the wider background of the ancient world, and so on. Now, as we have seen, it is not the case that

[1] In the case of certain later groups of MSS—e.g. families 1 and 13, the 'purple' MSS etc.—which can be placed relatively to each other in terms of genealogical descent, the method is extremely useful.

[2] See, e.g. C. H. Turner, 'Marcan usage', *Journal of Theological Studies*, xxv (1924), pp. 377–86, xxvi (1925), pp. 12–20, 145–56, 225–40, 337–46, xxvii (1926), pp. 58–62, xxviii (1927), pp. 9–30, 349–62, xxix (1928), pp. 275–89, 346–61; G. D. Kilpatrick, 'Some notes on Marcan usage', *Bible Translator*, vii (1952), pp. 2–9, 51–8, 146, 'Some notes on Johannine usage', *ibid.* v (1960), pp. 175–7, 'Atticism and the Text of the Greek New Testament', *Neutestamentliche Aufsätze: Festschrift für Prof. Josef Schmid* (Regensburg, 1963).

Westcott and Hort ignored these considerations: on the contrary, the selection of readings on grounds of 'Intrinsic Probability' (i.e. as to what the author probably wrote) and of 'Transcriptional Probability' (i.e. the known proclivities of copyists) was basic to their evaluation of the New Testament documents, and to their selection of the β text and of B in particular as closest to the original; and clearly their rule *knowledge of documents should precede final judgement upon readings* did not prevent their setting aside on occasion the readings of B (and of the β text as a whole) in favour of others intrinsically better. Nevertheless it is also the case that the new manuscript evidence, especially of the papyri, and increasing knowledge in the various fields associated with textual studies, linguistic historical and so forth, would have made fresh scrutiny, and fresh evaluations, both of readings and documents, necessary. Since, as we have seen, no manuscript or group is infallible, it follows that the original reading may have survived in any part of the tradition, and consequently all variants must be considered on their merits, and not, e.g. set aside at the outset as 'late' (which may mean no more than that the manuscript attestation is late), or as occurring only in the versions, nor on the other hand given undue consideration because they appear in certain authorities or combinations of them. That reading will be chosen which, after consideration of all relevant factors, best explains the emergence of the other variants. This method of criticism, described by its proponents as 'rational' or 'eclectic',[1] is also sometimes referred to as the 'subjective' method, and in dealing with such matters as style and vocabulary much might seem to depend on the critic's own intuitions. In practice, however, the appeal is generally to a statistical analysis of the particular author's usage—though the questions remain whether that author's usage can be said to be known until the text is certain,

---

[1] E.g. M.-J. Lagrange, *Critique Textuelle. II. La critique rationelle* (Paris, 1935); G. D. Kilpatrick, 'An eclectic study of the text of Acts', *Biblical and Patristic Studies in Memory of Robert Pierce Casey* (Freiburg, 1963), pp. 64–77. See also J. N. Birdsall, 'The New Testament Text', *The Cambridge History of the Bible*, vol. i (Cambridge, 1970), pp. 308–77; G. D. Kilpatrick, 'Western text and original text in the Gospels and Acts', *Journal of Theological Studies*, xliv (1943), pp. 24–36, xlv (1944), pp. 60–5, 'The Greek New Testament text of today and the *textus receptus*', *The New Testament in Historical and Contemporary Perspective* (Oxford, 1965), pp. 189–208. See also E. C. Colwell, 'Hort Redivivus: a plea and a progam', *Studies in Methodology in Textual Criticism of the New Testament* (Leiden, 1969), pp. 148–71.

whether it can be assumed that an author is always consistent, and whether apparent consistency may sometimes be due to the preferences of copyists. Similarly with regard to Atticism: there is no doubt that the cultivation of the archaic style became prevalent in literary circles in the first and second centuries A.D., and may be expected to have influenced the transmission of the New Testament text in some degree, but whether it inevitably follows that scribal change was always in one direction—i.e., towards the Atticising form—is another matter: scribes may equally well in some instances have preferred what they regarded as Biblical idiom. And indeed it would be expecting too much to suppose that internal criteria will settle every instance of conflicting readings. Where there is doubt (many will think) documentary evidence still has its part to play, the more so as the eclectic method confirms the overall superiority, in comparison to other authorities, of the β text.

The natural conclusion, then, is that while one family may in the overwhelming majority of cases be found to preserve the original text, it is probable that readings found in other families will sometimes be right. This is the conclusion to which all the evidence derivable from the early papyri points, and notably that of the Chester Beatty and Bodmer papyri. For the present purpose it matters not whether the text of these papyri be regarded as good or bad. What is significant is that they prove that in Egypt in the early part of the third century readings were in circulation which were derived from, or which eventually became attached to, all the principal families, together with a not inconsiderable number of which no other witness has survived. We must therefore be prepared to find that the best manuscript or family is not always right.

This conclusion is strongly reinforced by what we have learnt from the papyri with regard to the texts of classical authors. Here again they have greatly enlarged our knowledge of the early history of these texts. There was a time when it was supposed that they were handed down in substantial purity through the Hellenic and Hellenistic periods, and that the corruptions which we find in the texts as they have reached us are due to unintelligent Byzantine scribes. We now have hundreds of papyri and fragments of papyri from periods earlier than the Byzantine (from the third century B.C. to the third century A.D.), and we know that this picture is a false one. Most of the corruptions found in our modern texts were already in existence in the earlier period. More than this, we find that this early evidence not infrequently supports readings hitherto known only from late and inferior manuscripts. It is true that, as a whole, the papyri confirm the general superiority of the manuscript or manuscripts which modern scholarship regards as the best for the several Greek authors, and to which it has often pinned its faith almost exclusively; but in a minority of cases it supports the 'inferior' manuscripts against them. Indeed, it may be said as a general rule that the papyri support the better manuscript in two cases out of three, and the inferior manuscripts in the third. The evidence with regard to the classical texts therefore entirely supports the conclusion at which we have arrived in respect of the Biblical texts, that exclusive trust must not be placed in any one authority.

Although this conclusion suggests that absolute certainty in details is unobtainable, it is entirely justifiable to end on a note of hopefulness. In the first place, those who are attached to the Bible will be glad to find that all the discoveries which have been so plentiful of late years have tended to confirm the authenticity and general integrity of our texts, and to establish them on a firmer basis than ever. The fears of those who, since the days of Mill, have been led by lack of faith to dread and doubt the free investigations of scholarship have been shown to be groundless. Truth has flourished in an atmosphere of free research. And secondly, if so many discoveries have been made in this century, there is every reason to hope that more discoveries may still be awaiting us in the sands of Egypt. A mid-second-century Gospel is by no means an impossibility; we already have a tiny fragment of one, and more extensive remains of two books of the Septuagint. But if such a treasure should appear, it will be well not to expect too much. It will probably show that errors already pervaded the sacred texts as they circulated in provincial Egypt; and in any case it would have to be remembered that it was originally only one copy among many, and that its evidence as to the best text may not be decisive. Another find even more to be desired is a substantial portion of the *Diatessaron*: for this might determine the vexed question of the disturbing influence of Tatian's work, both on the Syriac Gospels and the whole textual tradition, and might bring us appreciably nearer to a comprehension of the history of the New Testament text, which is the final goal of textual criticism.

ἅπανθ᾽ ὁ μακρὸς κἀναρίθμητος χρόνος
φύει τ᾽ἄδηλα·
κοὐκ ἔστ᾽ ἄελπτον οὐδέν.

1. INDEX OF NAMES AND SUBJECTS

S

INDEX OF MANUSCRIPTS

3. INDEX OF PASSAGES OF WHICH VARIOUS READINGS ARE QUOTED